Ten Fifteenth-Century Comic Poems

Garland Medieval Texts
Number 13

Garland Medieval Texts
A.S.G. Edwards
General Editor

Ten Fifteenth-Century Comic Poems

edited by
Melissa M. Furrow

GARLAND PUBLISHING INC.
NEW YORK & LONDON
1985

Library of Congress Cataloging-in-Publication Data

Main entry under title:

Ten fifteenth-century comic poems.

(Garland medieval texts ; no. 13)
Bibliography: p.
Includes index.
1. English poetry—Middle English, 1100–1500.
2. Humorous poetry, English. I. Furrow, Melissa M.,
1954–   . II. Title: 10 fifteenth-century comic
poems. III. Series.
PR1195.H8T38 1985 821'.07'08 83-48231
ISBN 0-8240-9428-X (alk. paper)

Printed on acid-free, 250-year-life paper
Manufactured in the United States of America

Mum

CONTENTS

Contents

PREFACE

This book has grown out of earlier research I had done on comic responses to Middle English romances. From that research I discovered that there is a body of fifteenth-century comic material that is of great interest but has never been readily available in an adequate critical edition. It is the intent of this book to provide such a critical edition for ten of these comic poems. I have tried with each poem to capture the closest possible reading to that written by the poet. Often it is not possible to come close, but I have emended the text wherever violation of the sense, stanzaic pattern, rhyme scheme, or rhythm have suggested a need to do so, if a plausible alternative reading was available. Textual notes below the poems indicate where such emendations have been made.

Each poem is preceded by an introduction of its story, its textual transmission, its metre, its language and provenience, and its scribal spelling and language (if these are early enough to be of interest), together with an explication of the editorial principles followed in presenting it.

After the group of poems there are explanatory notes to clear up difficulties in the language or to address particular points that seem interesting or that need clarification. Then there are a glossary of difficult words and an index of proper names.

The bibliography falls into three parts: a list of previous editions of the poems, a list of lexical and proverb dictionaries cited, and a select list of other works cited. This latter is select in the sense that it does not include the large number of works described in the introductions as having been bound with or grouped in a manuscript with one of the ten poems edited here, but otherwise it aims for completeness.

A table of abbreviations and abbreviated references on p. xvii explains the short forms often used in the text to identify languages, grammatical works, dictionaries, indices, series, and collections of analogous poems.

ACKNOWLEDGEMENTS

It is a pleasant task to acknowledge the generosity of the
Killam Trust, which supported me for a full year as a Killam
post-doctoral fellow to work on these poems, of the Social
Sciences and Humanities Research Council of Canada, which
funded my research, and of the Dalhousie University Research and
Development Fund, which granted money for the acquisition of
microfilms and for the productions of the final text.

Warm thanks are due to those who typed the manuscript: to
Anne Kverme, who helped in the early stages; to Leslie Adamson,
who typed the final copy swiftly, accurately, and under budget;
and to Barbara Goodman, Tina Jones, and Gretchen Mosher, who
have triumphed with their good humor, skill, and persistence
over what must have seemed a potentially endless and certainly
tedious chore.

I am grateful to the librarians and staff of the Henry Hun-
tington Library, who provided me with information and a photo-
graphic reproduction of *The Friars of Berwick*, and to the li-
brarians and staff of the British Library, the National Library
of Scotland, the National Library of Wales, the Bodleian Li-
brary, the Cambridge University Library, the Pepysian Library
at Magdalene College, Cambridge, and the Balliol College Li-
brary at Oxford, who provided me with reproductions of the
various manuscripts and texts, and answered my questions about
them. I also thank the Master and Fellows of Magdalene College,
Cambridge, for their permission to make use of the Maitland
Folio manuscript, and the Master and Fellows of Balliol
College, Oxford, for their permission to make use of Balliol
MS 354.

I thank Katherine Pantzer, editor of the *Short Title Cata-
logue*, for taking the time to answer my questions about *The
Friars of Berwick*. And thanks to Thomas Cooke of the Univer-
sity of Missouri-Columbia, with whom I have exchanged a great
deal of information about these poems, and whose forthcoming
section on comic tales in *A Manual of the Writings in Middle
English 1050-1500* will undoubtedly fill in gaps in my own work.

Finally I must thank those whose help and encouragement
have in one way or another served to begin or bring to an end

this project. My colleagues in the English Department at Dal-
housie University have been warmly supportive, and I thank
Ron Huebert, Bob Dawson, Hubert Morgan, and Patricia Monk for
answering questions about drama, woodcuts, manuscripts and Old
Norse, and word processors. I owe special thanks to two women:
Anne Higgins, who has very kindly proofread the text and
prevented many errors (and who would have been an invaluable
resource if only she had joined the department earlier), and
Elizabeth Edwards, who worked conscientiously and shrewdly
as my assistant for several months, with particular responsi-
bility for the glossary. Thanks to Tony Edwards of Victoria,
who encouraged me to do this edition and has shepherded it to
its completion. And last, thanks to Fred Robinson of Yale,
the mentor who helped me to develop this project and whose
support has been invaluable to me.

INTRODUCTION

I make no extravagant claims for the poems presented in this edition, as the very cautious title *Ten Fifteenth-Century Comic Poems* should make clear. For instance, I do not claim that they are "selected" poems of the fifteenth-century, because the term might suggest they were chosen for their quality, and they were not. Some (I think of *The Friars of Berwick*) are rather good; others (such as *Sir Corneus*) are rather bad. The main criteria for inclusion were whether a poem (of medium length, of the fifteenth-century, and ostensibly comic) was well edited and readily available elsewhere: if not, it may be included here. I cannot call this an anthology, for ten poems do not make an anthology, especially when four of them belong to closely related pairs of poems (*John the Reeve* and *The King and the Hermit*; *Sir Corneus* and *The Boy and the Mantle*). I do not make the claim that these are fabliaux (though several of them must be, by any definition of the term), because the label is a controversial one and the pages of an edition are not a proper place to enter into the controversy.

On the other hand, exception could be taken to almost all of the limited claims I do make in the title. I speak of ten poems, but there are at most nine and a half, for *The King and the Hermit* is a fragment. I assign all the poems to the fifteenth-century, at least in their original forms, and I will not be surprised to see that claim debated, for some have, in the past, been dated in the sixteenth or even seventeenth century. I call them "comic" poems, but tastes vary, and some readers may find *The Boy and the Mantle* too acrid or too arid, and the jokes in *The Feast of Tottenham* unpalatable. But at least these are inarguably poems.

Much of the material that follows is of necessity technical and directed towards specialists, but I hope that other readers will be able to enjoy the poems with the help of the glossary and explanatory notes at the back, and a judicious selection of information from the introductions.

ABBREVIATIONS AND ABBREVIATED REFERENCES

Full bibliographic references will be found in the bibliography, pp. 485-499.

Arber: Edward Arber, ed. *A Transcript of the Registers of the Company of Stationers of London 1554-1640 A.D.*
B-P,   Johannes Bolte and Georg Polivka. *Anmerkun-*
Bolte-Polivka: *gen zu den Kinder- und Hausmärchen der Brüder Grimm.*
BR: Carleton Brown and Rossell Hope Robbins. *The Index of Middle English Verse.* Rossell Hope Robbins and John L. Cutler. *Supplement to the Index of Middle English Verse.*
Brunner: Karl Brunner. *Die Englische Sprache.*
Child: F.J. Child, ed. *The English and Scottish Popular Ballads.*
DNB: *Dictionary of National Biography.*
Dobson: E.J. Dobson. *English Pronunciation 1500-1700.*
DOST: *Dictionary of the Older Scottish Tongue.*
EETS: Early English Text Society.
Jordan: Richard Jordan. *Handbook of Middle English Grammar.*
Kristensson: Gillis Kristensson. *A Survey of Middle English Dialects 1290-1350: The Six Northern Counties and Lincolnshire.*
L: Latin.
Luick: Karl Luick. *Historische Grammatik der englischen Sprache.*
ME: Middle English.
MED: *Middle English Dictionary.*
MMW: Samuel Moore, Sanford Brown Meech and Harold Whitehall. "Middle English Dialect Characteristics and Dialect Boundaries."
Mossé: Fernand Mossé. *A Handbook of Middle English.*
MR: Anatole de Montaiglon and Gaston Raynaud, eds. *Recueil général et complet des fabliaux des xiiie et xive siècles.*

Oakden:	J.P. Oakden. *Alliterative Poetry in Middle English*.
OE:	Old English.
OED:	*Oxford English Dictionary*.
OF:	Old French.
ON:	Old Norse.
SND:	*Scottish National Dictionary*.
Stationers' Register:	See Arber.
STC:	A.W. Pollard and G.R. Redgrave. *A Short Title Catalogue*.
Thompson:	Stith Thompson. *Motif-Index of Folk-literature*.
Whiting:	B.J. Whiting and Helen W. Whiting. *Proverbs, Sentences and Proverbial Phrases from English Writings Mainly before 1500*.

The Lady Prioress

The Lady Prioress

The Story

The Lady Prioress is similar to the story of Francesca,
Rinuccio, and Alessandro, the first tale of the ninth day in
Boccaccio's Decameron. Pestered by two suitors, the lady
Francesca sends word to the first, Rinuccio, to take the
place of a corpse which she says is to be carried to her
house that night. She sends word to the second, Alessandro,
to go fetch the corpse. As Alessandro is carrying Rinuccio
in his graveclothes through the dark streets to her house,
they are surprised by the watch, and both flee, thus for-
feiting any claim to Francesca's love by failing to accom-
plish her orders.

Benjamin Thorpe recounts an analogous Netherlandish
tale, an oral tradition of the Long Wapper of Antwerp, in his
Northern Mythology (London: Lumley, 1852), vol. 3, pp. 217-8.
The Long Wapper (a malicious spirit) takes the form of a
promiscuous lady of Antwerp. The first of her lovers is
promised her hand if he will go to the churchyard and sit on
the transverse of the great cross. The second is sent, with
the same promise, to lie in a coffin under the cross. The
third is sent to knock three times on the coffin lid, and the
fourth must run three times around the cross, rattling an
iron chain. The first three wooers drop dead from fright,
and the fourth returns to the lady with the news of the
three corpses. But she knows nothing of the Long Wapper's
scheme, and kills herself in remorse. It is the fear of
ghosts and demons that affects the wooers in this tale, not
the fear of the officers of the watch that makes Rinuccio
and Alessandro run.

Other early versions of the story, like The Lady
Prioress, have three wooers at the gravesite frightening each
other away: Johannes Pauli's tale number 220 in his Schimpf
und Ernst (1522; ed. Johannes Bolte, Berlin: Stubenrauch,
1924); Nicolas de Troyes' second tale, Les Trois galants au

cimetière, in his Grand parangon des nouvelles nouvelles
(1536; ed. Krystyna Kasprzyk, Paris: M. Didier, 1970); the
anonymous Farce de trois amoureux de la croix (first ed.
c. 1540?; ed. Gustave Cohen, Recueil de farces françaises
inédites du quinzième siècle [Cambridge, Mass.: Mediaeval
Academy of America, 1949]). In none of the other stories is
the lady a nun: in Pauli's she is an ugly but rich widow
who knows the suitors to be after her money, in Nicolas's she
is unmarried, in the farce she is a married woman. The roles
played by the suitors vary from version to version: in
Pauli's tale a corpse, angel, and devil; in Nicolas's a
corpse, gendarme, and devil; and only in the farce, as in
The Lady Prioress, a priest, corpse, and devil. The denoue-
ments in Pauli's tale and Nicolas's are similar to that in
The Lady Prioress; but in the farce, the suitors eventually
recognize each other, and give up their folly out of a sense
that the lady is not worth having.

No clear lines of relationship emerge out of the simi-
larities and differences in these stories. Although the
Decameron tale is the earliest, its difference from the
others suggests that it is not an ancestor, but only an
analogue. Descendants of the Decameron tale such as Hans
Sachs' Schwank Die jung erbar witfraw Francisca and his
Fastnachtspiele of October 31, 1560 (Hans Sachs, ed. Adelbert
von Keller, Bibliothek des literarischen Vereins, Band 125
[Stuttgart: Anton Hiersemann, 1875], vol. 9, pp. 424-9 and
193 [1892], vol. 20, pp. 47-63) follow Boccaccio's story-line
and borrow his characters, using even the same names.

The anonymous poet has taken cues from other literature,
the most obvious being from Chaucer for the suggestion of
the prioress as an out-of-place romance heroine. Another
influence may account for the tale the prioress tells of a
man whose corpse has been forbidden burial because of his
debts. The corpse denied burial and then treated reverently
by a pious hero is a folklore motif (Thompson E341.1), a
motif made well known by the Book of Tobit. But it is also
a very prominent feature of Sir Amadace, a late fourteenth-
century romance of the Northwest Midlands, the very area from
which The Lady Prioress originates. In The Lady Prioress, as
in Sir Amadace, the corpse lies on a bier in the chapel, with
two candles burning beside it; in both poems the corpse is
refused burial because of debts. It seems likely that the
poet had this particular romance in mind as he wrote. In
making his knight vow to stay in the chapel all night, the
poet may have remembered The Avowynge of King Arthur, an
early fifteenth-century romance in which the three principal

characters make vows, Gawain's being to watch all night at
Tarn Wadling. The Avowynge, Sir Amadace, and The Awntyrs
off Arthure (a late fourteenth-century alliterative romance
with a ghost, and a stanzaic form somewhat like that of The
Lady Prioress) all appear in the first section of MS Ireland
Blackburn, probably originating in Hale, southern Lancashire,
and dated in the third quarter of the fifteenth century (see
Ralph Hanna's introduction to his edition The Awntyrs off
Arthure at the Terne Wathelyn [Manchester: Manchester
University Press, 1974], pp. 6-7). Since the first section
of the Ireland Blackburn manuscript, containing the romances,
is bound with a second section containing manorial records
of Hale from 1403 to 1472, and since the manuscript as a
whole was in the hands of the Ireland family well into the
modern era, it was probably kept at Hale from the time of
its writing. It is thus entirely possible that the poet of
The Lady Prioress, whose dialect associates him or her with
southern Lancashire, could have read that actual manuscript
at Hale. MS Ireland Blackburn is now in the Taylor collec-
tion at Princeton. The last potential influence is the
literature of questing knights in general, and the Grail
legend in particular, for the place to which the lady sends
her knight. Though the poet was probably writing before
Malory, he may have read the scene that Malory uses from the
thirteenth-century Queste del saint Graal (pp. 57-61 in the
edition by Albert Pauphilet, Paris: Champion, 1923), in
which Lancelot is unable because of his lechery to enter an
enchanted chapel in the woods and achieve the Grail quest.

The Manuscript

The Lady Prioress appears in a single manuscript,
British Library MS. Harley 78. Harley 78 is a collection of
miscellaneous papers--some of political and historical
interest and some poetical--mounted on stubs, and in modern
binding. The poem belongs to a booklet of only six leaves,
judging by the watermarks collated A-C^2, and judging by its
appearance creased across the middle, presumably to hold the
leaves together before they were bound. The leaves are
paper, about 21 cm. wide by 30 tall, with a writing block
around 14 cm. by 25. The booklet has only the modern folio
numbers of the MS. as a whole (running from 74 to 79), and
no signatures or catchwords.

The Lady Prioress takes up six and a half pages of the twelve in the booklet; after it appears the short poem by Lydgate known as "A Ditty Against Haste" ("All hast ys odyus where as dyscrecyon"), and below that, the name "lydgatt". Presumably Lydgate's name at the end of the booklet caused a later reader to understand both poems to have been his, and to have written "Lydgate" over The Lady Prioress, which is otherwise untitled.

Two scribes are responsible for the booklet, the main one having written both poems, and the second having corrected only The Lady Prioress. The principal hand is an informal Anglicana book-hand of the last quarter of the fifteenth century. The corrector's hand is similar and contemporary. Only if the corrector had access to the exemplar as he wrote are his corrections of much value. At least two of his alterations are poor guesses: one discussed below, and one at v. 64, where he sets lett beside MS. hyght (for original hete) to provide an "improved" rhyme for gett, shett, and swett. Yet at vv. 24-6, both scribes seem to be struggling to make sense of a damaged exemplar, and the second is responsible for the (probably correct) reading brow₃th in v. 24, a reading he is unlikely to have invented, since he could not find adequate emended rhymes for it in the other two lines. Then, too, the second scribe corrects only The Lady Prioress and not the following poem, as he might well have done if he had been emending purely conjecturally. (It seems likely that the first scribe wrote out the two poems one right after the other, since the three sheets of the booklet are identical.) Probably he emended not only from the exemplar, but sometimes from his own imagination.

The form in which the first scribe wrote out the poem sometimes conceals its stanzaic shape: he often divides long lines into two short lines or runs two short lines together. At vv. 200-201, where the lines are particularly confused, the second scribe adds a short line (his second obviously faulty emendation) to provide a rhyme for a word that ought to be embedded in the middle of v. 201.

According to Andrew G. Watson, Harley 78 has in it on various items the hands of three book collectors: John Stow, Ralph Starkey, and Sir Simonds D'Ewes (The Library of Sir Simonds D'Ewes [London: The Trustees of the British Museum, 1966], List X, p. 318). D'Ewes bought Starkey's manuscripts on the latter's death in 1628. Presumably Starkey had acquired all or part of the Harley 78 group of papers at

Stow's death in 1605. So at least some of the papers went
from Stow to Starkey, from Starkey to D'Ewes; D'Ewes died and
left his collection to his son Willoughby in 1650; Willoughby
D'Ewes in turn left it to his son, another Simonds, in 1685;
he sold it to Robert Harley, first Earl of Oxford, in 1705;
and after the death of his son and heir, Edward, in 1741, the
latter's widow, Lady Oxford, sold the vast Harleian manu-
script collection to the nation. There is nothing to suggest
that The Lady Prioress was bound with any of the other pieces
in the Harley 78 miscellany (other than the Lydgate poem)
until the time when Stow or Starkey or even D'Ewes or Harley
himself assembled the volume. A list of the other contents
of Harley 78 can be found in the Catalogue of the Harleian
Manuscripts in the British Museum (London: British Museum,
1808), vol. 1, pp. 20-21.

Metre

        The poet begins ambitiously, attempting the alliterative
long line rhymed, in stanzas with a rhyming wheel of five
short lines, and an effort at stanza-linking by repetition.
The nine-line stanzas rhyme aaaabcccb, as do those in The
Tale of the Basin in the present volume, The Tournament of
Tottenham, and the Towneley Secunda Pastorum. The Awntyrs
off Arthure, though it rhymes abababcddddc and has only four
short lines rather than The Lady Prioress's five, has not
only rhyme, alliteration, and a short-line wheel, but also
stanza-linking through the iteration of a part of the last
line of one stanza in the first of the next; thus it could
have served as a model for our poet. But in The Lady
Prioress the stanza-linking does not last long, appearing
only in vv. 9-10, 18-20 (one word only, and skipping a line)
and 45-6 (again one word only). And the alliteration is a
secondary consideration for the poet: there are many lines
which do not alliterate at all, or in which the alliteration
does not cross the cæsura between the half-lines; and the
poet recognizes no restrictions on which lifts may alliter-
ate. Even the rhyme scheme occasionally breaks down as well,
and the poet resorts to an aaAAbcccb variant, as in vv. 55-63,
127-35, 163-171.

        The metre of the poem is based on rhythms of late
Middle English alliterative verse, the long lines having two
stressed syllables or lifts in each half-line (but very often
with three lifts in the first half-line) and the short lines
having two or three lifts. There can be a clash between

lifts (that is, they can be next to one another), or there
can be one, two, or several unstressed syllables making up
the dip preceding or following a lift. The commonest rhythms
in The Lady Prioress are rising in both half-lines, and
rising-falling in the first:

	/ /	
rising	There was no hegge for me to hey	v. 229a
	/ /	
	hys matters to amend	v. 39b
	/ /	
rising-falling	The lady that was lovely	v. 19a.

Less frequent are second half-lines with a single dip,

$$\text{/} \qquad \text{/}$$
               clen he had forgett   v. 154b

falling half lines
                 /   /   /
                 "Do thy deuer," the lady sayd   v. 100a

and half-lines with a clash,
                      / /   /
                 The pryst demyd them devyllys both   v. 156a.

There are, as well, over-heavy lines:

four lift short line

                 /   /   /   /
                 Hys hartte hoppyd, hys wyll [towoke] v. 96

three lift second half-line
                 /   /   /
                 busche, gryne, nor grett   v. 157b.

     The poem sounds unlike more traditional alliterative
verse for a number of reasons. It does not use the special
vocabulary, the hosts of synonyms beginning with different
phonemes (like burn, lede, freke, and gome for man) that sur-
vive only to serve the alliterative poet's needs; nor does it
use the convenient alliterative tags like hardy under helm or
stiff in stalle. More traditional verse would have a greater

incidence of falling rhythm in both half-lines. In the second half-line, unrhymed alliterative verse would have more rising-falling and fewer rising rhythms: The Lady Prioress tends toward masculine rhymes, final -e no longer being pronounced.

The poet rhymes original open long e with close, and open long o with close:

go(inf.)/doo (pa.pple.)/doo (inf.)/goo (pa.pple.)
(vv.136-9)
[hett]/gett (inf.)/shett/swett (vv. 64-7).

The rhymes suggest that the open vowels were narrowed in the poet's speech, as they often were in the North and East, in final position or before a dental (see Dobson II, 121 and 148).

Language and Provenience

That the poem is Southumbrian is shown by the combined evidence of a number of rhymes:

1) styll/hell (vv. 122, 126)
   egged/deggyd/be[gg]yd/leggyd (vv. 145-8)
   venter/wyntter (vv. 55-6)

The rhymes show short i to have neutralized to short e in a closed syllable (Jordan 36 and 271). The spelling elsewhere in the manuscript reflects the same neutralization (see Spelling, below).

2) lyght/quyt (vv. 167, 171)

The fricative in light must have silenced for it to rhyme with quite (Jordan 295).

3) Of the strong and anomalous verb past participles in rhyme--do (vv. 59 and 137), goo (v. 139), forgett (v. 154), boren (v. 183), ibore (v. 218), forlore (v. 220)--all but one (boren) have southerly forms.

On the other hand, the poem must belong to a northern area of the Midlands.

1) was/plase/chase/hase   (vv. 19-22)

The form <u>has</u> places the poem north of MMW line G, the southern limit for -es in the third person singular present of verbs. (The -eth form demonstrated by g[e]th/deth/ me[t]he/breth at vv. 208-11 is, of course, possible north of the line.)

2) bl[yffe]/on lyffe/wyff   (vv. 231-3)

Devoicing of the /v/ brought into final position by the early northerly silencing of final -e must be present in <u>blive</u> and the petrified dative <u>on live</u> for a rhyme with <u>wife</u>. According to Jordan (217), such devoiced forms "reach south-wards to the mouth of the Humber, to southwest Yorkshire ... and to Lancashire."

That the poem belongs to the West Midlands is suggested by the following rhymes:

1) fayer/pyre/here/dere   (vv. 28-31)

According to Jordan (94, remark 1) there is a "late ME Western development of *ai" to long open <u>e</u>. An open <u>e</u> in <u>fair</u> would form a sufficient rhyme to the close <u>e</u> of <u>peer</u>, <u>hear</u>, and <u>dear</u>, while the diphthong normal to the rest of England would fit less well.

2) went/sent/amend/[rent]   (vv. 37-40)

Jordan (200): "In accented syllables loss of the voicing [of <u>d</u>] is limited to position after <u>n</u>, <u>r</u>, <u>l</u> and is found only in WML."

The area circumscribed--non-northern, yet north of the devoicing line, West Midlands--is a small one and covers only southern Lancashire.

1) styre/bere/[quyer]   (vv. 123-5)

Lengthening of the vowel in <u>stir</u> (short <u>i</u> from Old English short <u>y</u>) to long close <u>e</u> is necessary for a rhyme with the long close <u>e</u> of <u>bier</u> and that of <u>quire</u> (modern <u>choir</u>). Such lengthening (in this case presumably a level-ling of lengthening in an open syllable in the inflected forms of the verb) "is found in all dialects of the North and encroaches westward into South Lancashire" (Jordan 36).

Although by the fifteenth century such levelling would have spread to parts of Southumbria, there it moved from the East Midlands to the south, not through the West Midlands.

It should, however, be noted that the silencing of the fricative in lyght and the preponderance of southern forms of the past participle are not consonant with an area as far north as southern Lancashire, and that these forms can at best be explained as borrowings licensed by the need for a rhyme.

As for dating, the rhymes at vv. 141-3 suggest a time after the vowel shift:

slowe/howe/wyndow

A rhyme on the diphthong in slow (from OE slāw) and window (from ONorse vindauga) is possible only after the /uː/ of how (from OE hū) has passed through the Southumbrian diphthongizing of the vowel shift. And the silencing of the fricative in lyght can hardly be earlier than the end of the fourteenth century. The vocabulary of the poem is of some help here: the only citation of the verbal substantive gesttyng (v. 1) in MED and OED is c. 1460, and the verb undernim in the sense in which it is used in the poem (vndernom, v. 3: "reproved, rebuked") is cited in OED no later than c. 1449. Probably the poem was written not much later than the mid-fifteenth century.

The peculiar sets of rhymes on corse invite investigation:

corse/rose/grose   vv. 204-6

bost/corse/purpos   vv. 213-5

They imply an assimilation of r to following s that is predominantly Southumbrian (Jordan 166). The apparent loss of final t after another consonant in bost is elsewhere attested in the spelling of MS Cotton Nero Ax (see Jordan 199), a northwest midlands manuscript.

Spelling and Scribal Language

The principal scribe's spelling has no features that
conflict with the dialect of the poem. He frequently uses
-f(e) or -ff(e) for final -v(e), but also uses -u(e): louff
(v. 34), loffe (v. 108) as well as loue (vv. 127, 133, 202
etc.), alyffe (v. 207), gyfe (v. 2). He spells ill and till
as ell (v. 159) and tell (v. 131, but elsewhere tyll), and
did as ded (vv. 227, 240), his spelling reflecting his or the
poet's neutralizing of short i in a closed syllable. Lowyth
(v. 25), with -w- for medial v, is an inverse of the northern
substitution of v for w (Jordan 163), attested as far south
as Lancashire. The scribe prefers the inflexional endings
-ys, -yth, and -yd to -es, -eth, and -ed. He sometimes drops
initial h in his (e.g. ys, v. 164). Sherwly (v. 145) for
shrewly shows northerly metathesis of r (Jordan 165).

This scribe shows intrusive -e- in mid-word (e.g. ower,
consayet, voyedes) and in particular in many words in which
-n follows a vowel or -r-:

awen; twayen; begyen, ryen, skyen; wyen; soen; nooen;
dowen, gowen, (growend, sowend); boren, scoren, thoren.

What his practice represents in pronunciation I cannot say.

He doubles final -t after long stressed e (close or
open); this practice probably indicates a shortening of the
vowel in a closed syllable (see Jordan 27). The poet's fett
is meant to rhyme with pett and hyt at vv. 105-7; so poet and
scribe are in agreement as to the shortness of the vowel.
But presumably the scribe's shett and swett (vv. 104, 108)
would have been long vowels for the poet, meant to contrast
with the three short-vowel rhyme words they envelop.

The corrector's orthography is more conservative than
that of the first scribe, as he uses þ and ȝ, and sch- where
the first scribe writes sh-. His use of the form hur(e) for
her is western.

Editorial Treatment

In the following text, I have reproduced the spelling of
the manuscript, except that I have silently normalized the
spelling of the second scribe to that of the first, regular-

ized word divisions and capitals to modern usage, and
expanded abbreviations, using -ys rather than -es as the
scribe's preferred form. I have ignored such otiose strokes
as the scribe's frequent line over final -n (e.g., meñ) and
have left initial ff- as it stands in the manuscript, in
which it does not seem to be used as a capital. I have added
punctuation.

The Lady Prioress

O gloryus God oure gouerner, glad in all thys gesttyng,

And gyfe them ioye that wyll here whatt I shall saye or
syng.

Me were loth to be vndernom of them that byn not connyng:

Many maner of men there be that wyll meddyll of euery
thyng,

5 Of resons [ten] or [twelfe].

Dyuerse men fawttys wyll fele

That knowyth no more then doyth my hele,

Y[e]t they thynke no thyng ys well

But yt do meve of themselfe.

10 But yt move of themselfe forsoth they thynke yt ryght
nowght.

Many men ys so vsyd; ther terme ys soen tought.

Sympyll ys there consayet when yt ys forth brought.

To meve you of a matter forsoth I am bethought,

Declare you of a case:

15 Make you mery all and som,

And I shall tell you of a noone,

The fayryst creator vnder the son,

Was pryorys of a plase.

Textual notes: The Lady Prioress begins f. 74a. No title
in MS. v. 5 ten or twelfe: MS x or xii; v. 8 Yet: MS Yt;

The lady that was lovely, a lorddys dowter she was,
20 Ffull pewer and full precyous provyd in every plase.
Lordys and laymen and spryttuall her gan chase.
For her fayer beawte grett temtacyon she hase,
Her love for to wynne.
Grett gyftys to here they [brought].
25 Many men lowyth here out of [thought].
How hereselfe myght [kepe from shame she sought];
She wyst not how to begyen.

There wooyd a young knyght, a fresse lord and a fayer,
And a person of a paryche, a prelet wythouttyn pyre,
30 And a burges of a borrow. Lyst and ye shall here
How they had layed ther loue apan the lady dere,
And nooen of other wyst.
[Ever more they went and com,]
Desyryd of here louff soon;
35 They sware by son and mone
Of here to haue there lyste.

v. 24 they brought: MS they put [*Corrector strikes out*
put *and adds* brow3t]; v. 25 here out of thought: MS here
out of mynd [*Corrector strikes out* out of mynd *and changes*
to there þei hur soste]; v. 26 myght kepe from shame she
sought: MS myght from shame shytt [*Corrector adds* them
wrowthe]; v. 28 *begins f. 74b*; v. 33 MS They goo and com
[*Corrector strikes out the line and adds the one given*
above];

The young knyght for the ladys loue narrow tornyd and
went;
Many bokkys and dooys to the lady he sent.

The person present her preuely (hys matters to amend)
40 [With] beddys, brochys, and botellys of wyen. [Of his
gold and rent]
The burges to her broght.

Thus they troblylyd [her] thorow tene.

She wyst not how hereselfe to mene

For to kepe here soule clene,

45 Tell she her bethought.

The young knyght bethought hym mervelously wyth [the]
lady for to mell.

He flatteryd her wyth many a fabyll; fast hys toung gan
tell.

Lessyngys lepyd out amonge as sowend of a bell:

["Madam, but I haue my lyst of yow I shall myself quell:]

50 Youre lovfe vnto me graunt.

In batyll bolde [I] th[a]re abyde,

To make the Jues there heddys hyde,

[Wyth grett strokys and bloddy syde,]

And sle many a grette gyaunt.

v. 38 lady he: MS lady þat he [*corrector's addition*];
v. 40 With beddys: MS Beddys; wyen of his gold and rent:
MS wyen he to the lady sent; v. 42 troblylyd her thorow:
MS troblylyd thorow; v. 46 wyth the lady: MS wyth lady;
v. 49 [*corrector's addition*]; v. 51 bolde I thare abyde:
MS bolde there abyde; v. 52 the Iues: MS the <Iude>
Iues; v. 53 [*corrector's addition*];

55 "All ys for your loue, madame; my lyfe wold I venter,
   So that ye wyll graunt me I haue desyryd many a wyntter,
   Vnderneth your comly cowle to haue myn intent."
   "Syr," she sayd, "ye be ower lord, ower patron, and ower
                                                     precedent:
   Your wyll must nedys be do,
60 So that ye wyll goo thys tyde
   Dowen to the chapyll vnder the woodsyde
   And be rewlyd as I wyll ye gyde."
   "All redy," sayde he thoo.

   Dowen in the wode there ys a chapell: ryght as I you
                                                     [hett]
65 Therein must ye ly all nyght, my loue and ye wyll gett.
   Ly there lyke a ded body sowyd in a shett--
   Than shall ye haue my loue, myn awen hony swett--
   Vnto morow that yt be lyght.
   "Madame," he sayed, "for your loue
70 Yt shall be don, be God aboue!
   Ho sayeth 'naye,' here ys me gloue
   In that quarrell [for] to fyght."

v. 58 *begins f. 75a*; v. 64 you hett: MS you hyght
[*Corrector adds* <u>lett</u> *at the end of the verse*]; v. 67 myn
awen: MS my nawen; v. 72 quarrell for to: MS quarrell
to [*Corrector adds* <u>for</u>];

That knyght kyssyd the lady gent; the bargen was made.

Of no bargen [syth] he was borne was he neuer halfe so
glade.

75 He went to the chapell as the lady hym bad,

He sowyd hymselfe in a shett, he was nothyng adr[a]d,

He thought apon no sorrow.

When he com there he layed vpryght

Wyth [two] tapers bornynge bryght:

80 There he thought to ly all nyght,

To kys the lady on the morrow.

As soon as the knyght was go she sent for Syr John.

Well I wott he was not long: he cam to her anon.

"Madam," he sayd, "what shall I do?"   She answered to hym
than:

85 ["Syr," she sayd, "I shall tell you my conssell sone,]

Blowen yt ys so brode.

I haue a cosyn of my blode

Lyeth ded in the chapyll wood;

Ffor owyng of a som of good

90 Hys bery[i]ng ys forbode.

v. 74 syth: MS syght; v. 76 adrad: MS adred; v. 79 two:
MS ii; v. 83 *begins f. 75b*; v. 85 sayd I shall: MS sayd
hyt schall [*v. 85 is the corrector's addition*]; vv. 82-5
have inexact rhymes, and the passage may be corrupt; v.
90 berying: MS beryng;

"We be not abyll to pay the good that men do crave;
Therfore we send for you ouer worshype [for] to save.
Say hys dorge and masse and laye hym in hys grave--
Wythin a whyle after my loue shall you haue--
95 And truly kepe consell."
Hys hartte hoppyd, hys wyll to[w]oke,
To do all thys he vndertoke.
To say hys seruys apon a boke
He sware be heuyn and hell.

100 "Do thy deuer," the lady sayd, "as farforth as thou may.
Then shalt thou haue thy wyll of me." And serten [to the
                                                    I] saye,
Syr John was as glad of this as euer was fowle of daye.
Wyth a m[a]ttake and a showyll to the chapyll he takyth
                                                    the waye,
Where he lay in his shett.
105 When he cam ther he made hys pett
And sayed hys dorge at hys fett.
The knyght lyeth styll and dremyd yt,
That "my loffe" whas hys swett.

v. 92 worshype for to: MS worshype to [*Corrector adds
for*]; v. 96 wyll towoke: MS wyll to oke [*Corrector alters
to* toworke *and writes* worke *in margin*]; v. 101 serten to
the I saye: MS serten to I the [to *added above line by
main scribe*]; v. 103 mattake: MS mttake; v. 107 yt
[*Corrector changes to* hyt];

As soen as the pryst was gon the yong knyght for to bery,
110 She sent after the marchaunt.   To her he cam full mery.

"Dowen in the wode ther ys a chapell, ys fayer under a
pere;
Therin lyeth a ded corse; the[r]fore must ye stere ye
To helpe vs in ower ryght.

He owyth vs a som of golde;
115 To forbyd hys bery[i]ng I am bolde.

A pryst ys theder, as yt ys me tolde,
To bery hym thys nyght.

"Yf the corse beryd he and ower mony not payed
Yt were a fowlle sham for vs so for to be bytrayed.
120 And yf ye wyll do after me the pryst shall be afrayed:
In a devellys garment ye shall be arayed
And stalke ye theder styll.

When ye se the pryst styre
To bery hym that lyeth on bere,
125 Lepe in at the [dore of the quyer]
Lyke a fend of hell."

v. 109 *begins f. 76a;* v. 112 therfore: MS thefore;
v. 115 berying: MS beryng; v. 119 be bytrayed [by
squeezed in slightly above the line by main scribe];
v. 122 theder styll: theder full styll [*corrector's
addition*]; v. 125 the dore of the quyer: MS the quyer
dore;

"Madam, for your loue soen [I] shall be [tyred],
So that ye wyll graunt me that I haue ofte desyryd."
"Syr," she sayd, "ye shall yt haue, but first I will be
                                                    sewryd
130 That ower cownsell ye wyll kepe, that they be not
                                                    dyscuryd.
    Tell tomorow that yt be day
    Yf thou voyedys or ellys flee
    For euer thow lesyst the loue of me."
    "I graunt, madame," sythe [sayth he],
135 And on wyth ys araye.

    He dyght hym in a dyvellys garment. Ffurth gan he goo;
    He cam in at the chyrch dore as the dyrge was doo,
    Rynnyng, r[o]ryng wyth hys rakyls as devyllys semyd to
                                                    doo.
    The pryst brayed vp as a boke, hys hart was all[most]
                                                    goo.
140 He demyd hymselfe but ded.
    He was aferd he was to slowe;
    He rose vp he wyst not howe
    And brake out [at] a wyndow,
    And brake fowle ys heed.

    v. 127 soen I shall be tyred: MS soen yt shall be
    tryed [*corrector's alterations*]; v. 134 sythe sayth he:
    MS sythe/[*Corrector adds* sade he *above the line*];
    v. 138 roryng: MS r<a>ryng [o *added above the line*];
    v. 139 allmost goo: MS all<a>goo [*corrector's altera-*
    tions]; v. 143 out at a: MS out a [*Corrector adds* at];

145 But he that bod all the brunt, how sherwly he was egged,

For to here hys dyrge do and se hys pet deggyd.

"I trow I had my damys curse: I might haue byn better
                                                    be[gg]yd,

For now I am but lost, the lyghtter but I be leggyd."

And up rose he then.

150 The devyll se the body r[i]se;

Then his hart began to gryse--

I trow we be not all wyse--

And he began to ryen.

Hys ragys and hys ra[kyl]s clen he had forgett;

155 So had the yong knyght that sowyed was in the shett.

The pryst demyd them devyllys both, wyth them he wolde
                                                    not mett.

He sparyd nother hyll nor holt, busche, gryne, nor grett.

Lord, he was fowle scrapyd!

The other twayen was ell aferd;

160 They sparyd nethe[r] styll ne sherd.

They had leuer then mydyll erd

Ayther from other have scapyd.

v. 145 *begins f. 76b;* v. 147 beggyd: MS beddyd;
v. 150 the body rise: MS the <rose> body rose; v. 154
rakyls: MS rattel_ys_; v. 160 nether: MS nethe;

The pryst toke a bypathe; wyth them he wolde not mett.

Ys hed was fowle brokyn, the blod ran dowen to ys fett.

165 He ran in a fyrred gowen: all hys body gan reke.

He cast of all hys clothys to the bare breke

Because he wolde goo lyght.

He thought he harde the devyll lovshe;

He start into a bryer boushe

170 That all hys skyen gan rowsshe

Of hys body quyt.

The knyth he ran into a wood as fast as he myght weend.

He fell apon a stake and fowle hys lege gan rentt.

Therefore he took no care; he was aferd of the fend.

175 He thought yt was a longe waye to the pathes end,

But then cam all hys care:

In at a gape as he glent,

By the medyll he was hent;

Into a tretope he went

180 In a bokys snarre.

v. 164 Ys: Ms Yt ys; vv. 165-7 MS he ran in a fyrred
gowen he cast of all hys clothys all hys body gan reke/
to the bare breke because he wolde goo lyght;

The marchaunt ran apon a laund, there where growyth no
thoren.

He fell apon a bollys bake: he causte hym apon hys
[horen].

"Out, alas!" he sayd, "that euer I was boren,

For now I goo to the devyll bycause I dyd hym scoren,

185 Vnto the pytt of hell."

The boll ran into a myre.

There he layed ower fayer syer.

Ffor all the world he durst not stere

Tyll that he herde a bell.

190 On the morrow he was glad that he was so scapyd.

So was the pryst also, thoo he was body nakyd.

The knyght was in the tretope: for dred sore he quaked.

The best iowell that he had, fayn he wolde forsake [yt]

For to come dowen.

195 He caught the tre by the tope;

Y[s] and [br]eke the calltrape.

He fell and brake hys foretope

Apon the bare growend.

v. 182 horen: MS hornys; v. 184 <u>bycause</u> *begins f. 77a;*
v. 193 forsake yt: MS forsake/; v. 196 <u>Ys and breke the:</u>
MS Ye and eke the;

Thus they went from the game begylyd and beglued.
200 Nether on other wyst; hom they went beshrewyd.

The person tolde the lady on the morrow what myschyf ther
                                             was shewed,
How that he had ronne for her loue; hys merthys wer but
                                                    lewed,
He was so sore dred of deth.

"When I shuld have beryd the corse,
205 The devyll cam in, the body rose:
To se all thys my hart gr[o]se;
Alyffe I scapyd vnneth."

"Remember," the lady sayth, "what mysschyfe heron g[e]th:
Had I never louer yet that euer dyed good deth."
210 "Be that lord," sayd the pryst, "that shope both ale and
                                                    met[h]e,
Thow shaltte neuer be wooed for me whylyst I haue spech
                                                 or breth,
Whyle I may se or here."
Thus they to mad ther bost:
Ffurthe he went wythout the corse.
215 Then com the knyght for hys purpos
And told her of hys fare.

vv. 200-201 MS nether on other wyst the person tolde the
lady on the morrow/ hom they went be shrewyd what myschyf
ther was shewed [*Corrector has added words above v. 199,
with a line and a caret to show that they should be
inserted between* shrewyd *and* what. *These words are: by*
feldys *and* by felldys *and* by forrow]; v. 206 grose:
MS grese; v. 208 geth: MS goyth; v. 210 methe: MS mette;

"Now I hope to haue your loue that I have seruyd yore,

For bought I neuer loue soo dere syth I was man ibore."

"Hold they pese," the lady sayd. "Therof speke thou no
more,

220 For by the newe bargen my loue thou hast forlore

All thys hundryth wynter."

She answered hym; he went hys way.

The marchaunt cam the same day;

He told her of hys grett afray

225 And of hys hygh aventure.

"Tyll the corse shulde beryd be the bargen I abod.

When the body ded rise, a grymly gost agl[oo]d,

Then was tyme me to stere; many a style I bestrood.

There was no hegge for me to hey, nor no watter to brod

230 Of you to haue my wyll."

The lady said "Pese" full bl[yffe].

"Neer," she said, "whylle thou art man on lyffe,

For I shall shew yt to they wyff

And all the contre yt tyll,

v. 217 yore: MS youre; v. 225 hygh: MS hyght; v. 226
begins f. 77b; v. 227 aglood: MS a gleed; v. 231 blyffe:
MS bleth;

235 "And proclaym yt in the markyt towen they care to
                                                  encrese."
      Therwyth he gaue her [twenty] marke that she shold hold
                                                  her pese.
      Thus the burges of the borrowe, after hys dyses,
      He endewed into the place wyth dedys of good relese
      In fee foreuer more.
240 Thus the lady ded fre:
      She kepyth hyr vyrgenyte,
      And indewed the place with ffee,
      And salvyd them of ther soore.
                Explycyt.

      v. 235 proclaym yt: MS proclaymytte; v. 236 twenty:
      MS xx.

The Feast of Tottenham.

The Feast of Tottenham

The Story

The editor Thomas Wright first gave the poem its title,
The Feest of Tottenham, in his Early English Poetry: The
Turnament of Totenham and the Feest (London: W. Pickering,
1836). Although Tottenham is never mentioned in The Feast,
Wright had observed the poem's connection with the better
known Tournament of Tottenham, a poem in which the hero and
heroine, Perkyn and Tyb, bear the same names as the hero and
heroine of The Feast. The Feast appears in only one manu-
script, Cambridge FF. 5. 48, and that is one of the two manu-
scripts in which The Tournament survives.

The Tournament, which is readily accessible in several
collections, including that of W.H. French and C.B. Hale,
Middle English Metrical Romances (New York: Prentice-Hall,
1930), pp. 987-98, is a burlesque of romance tournaments, a
skirmish among countrymen for the hand of Tyb, the reeve's
daughter. The poem ends with the wedding feast, of which the
poet tells us simply

> At that fest were þei seruyd in a rich aray,
> Every fyve and fyve had a cokeney.
> (Ff. 5. 48, vv. 226-7)

That is, instead of the rich abundance of dishes set before
every two lords and ladies at a celebration such as the first
New Year's feast in Sir Gawain and the Green Knight, each
group of five dines off an egg, and perhaps an unusually
small egg at that (see OED, cockney). But the poet of The
Feast is not content with that ending, and concocts his own
burlesque of a romance meal:

Certes, of alle þe festis
þat euer I saw in gestis
þis may ber þe prise.
                                   (Feast, vv. 46-8)

Though it has no direct source, the poem is related to
another burlesque, which survives in two versions, both
printed in Thomas Wright and J.O. Halliwell's Reliquiæ
Antiquæ, Vol. 1 (London: W. Pickering, 1841). One, incipit
"Herkyn to my tale that I shall to yow schew," appears in MS
Advocates 19. 3. 1; the other, incipit "Herkons to my tale
that I schalle here schow," appears in MS Porkington 10. In
both versions, the burlesque tells of marvels said to be seen
by its author: various kinds of fish performing parts of a
church service, elements of a feast like that in our poem,
animals performing on musical instruments, and inanimate
objects and living creatures doing unlikely things.

The two versions of the burlesque are much closer to
each other than they are to The Feast of Tottenham, but each
shares lines with The Feast that the other does not have.
Probably, then, the three poems have a common original, from
which burlesques P (Porkington) and A (Advocates) descend,
and from which the author of The Feast has borrowed ideas and
lines. The Explanatory Notes give lines from P and A that
resemble those in The Feast.

The poem is full of specialized terms from medieval
cookery. Many medieval dishes have the same basic ingredi-
ents: almond milk (apparently made by steeping ground almonds
in sugar water), broth, eggs, flesh, fowl, or fish, sugar,
and a good deal of spices. A sew (v. 15) is usually a broth.
A pottage (v. 21, potage) can be a much thicker dish, from a
thick soup to a solid that can be sliced. Porray, cullis,
browet, mortress, jussell, charlet, dariole, lorey, malmeny,
and blaundsore are all pottages. Porray (v. 19, porra) is a
thick, strained soup, like a pea soup. Cullis (v. 50,
cullys) is another soup, based on a meat or poultry broth,
sometimes thickened with bread crumbs; it may have boiled
flesh added. Brute of Almayne (v. 56) is a browet, a meat or
poultry soup, with almond milk, minced lard, minced onions,
cloves, raisins, saffron, sugar, vinegar, ginger, and cinna-
mon. Mortess (v. 23, mortrewys) is based on almond milk, or
broth and ale, thickened with bread crumbs or flour, with
eggs, finely chopped meat, and spices, mostly ginger. Jussell
(v. 37, iussall) is a thick mixture, as is charlet (v. 43,
charlett). Charlet is essentially flesh with milk, whole

eggs, and ale, curdled, and served with broth; jussell is a
composition of grated bread, blended with flesh or fish in a
mortar, or with eggs, and boiled in broth until the whole
mixture solidifies. Dariole (v. 58, doralle) is like a
quiche or custard pie, often with pieces of marrow or other
meat in it, sometimes with pieces of fruit, and often sweet-
ened. Lorey (v. 20, lorra) is a simple blend of milk or
broth and eggs, with some addition, like plums. It can be
squeezed dry in a piece of linen and sliced. Malmeny (v. 29,
mawmany) is a more complex dish, based on equal quantities of
strong wine and white sugar, pine nuts, sandalwood (for
coloring), quince, ale, and the flesh of pheasant, partridge,
or capon. It is seasoned with ginger, saffron, salt, cloves,
and cinnamon. Again the texture is thick; it is to be served
flattened with a saucer. Blaundsore (v. 34, blawndisare and
v. 40, white sorre) is based on broth, sweet wine, and almond
milk. It contains cut up capon flesh and sugar, and is
served in a bowl, garnished with red anise or blanched
almonds.

The fritter (fruture) of v. 61 is our modern fritter,
made of batter coating apple or meat slices and fried. But
the gravy of v. 28 is not modern gravy, based on pan juices
and fat; it is based on broth, almond milk, and wine or ale.
Comfit (v. 49, comfyt) is a sugar glaze preparation, used not
only on fruits and spices, but also on meat.

Readers interested in the actual recipes for these
dishes should consult the Early English Text Society volumes,
Two Fifteenth-Century Cookery Books, ed. Thomas Austin, EETS
91 (London, 1888) and The Babees Boke [etc.] (Manners and
Meals in Olden Time), ed. F.J. Furnivall, EETS 32 (London,
1868), as well as M.S. Serjeantson, "The Vocabulary of Cook-
ing in the Fifteenth Century," English Association Essays
and Studies 23 (1937), 25-37.

The Manuscript

The Feast of Tottenham appears on ff. 115a-116a of MS
Cambridge Ff. 5. 48. See the introduction to The Tale of the
Basin for a description of the manuscript. Cambridge
University Library describes the writing of The Feast as "a
late fifteenth-century current hand resembling an ordinary
business hand, in which anglicana and secretary features are
both found." It is written twenty-four lines to the page,

not counting the b verses (which appear to the right of the
couplets) as separate lines. The writing block is approxi-
mately 11.5 cm. by 11.5 cm.

    Ff. 5. 48 falls into five booklets, or groups of
gatherings in which the end of a poem coincides with the end
of the last gathering. The gatherings are grouped into
booklets as follows: abcd, e, f, g, hi. The Tournament of
Tottenham (ff. 62a-66a) comes at the end of gathering d,
except for the short filler item 13, prognostications from
the days of the week on which Christmas falls, which occupies
f. 66b. The Feast of Tottenham begins gathering h; so it is
likely that gathering h was originally intended to follow
abcd immediately, particularly since the beginning of The
Feast ("Now of þis feest telle I can") makes little sense
unless coupled with The Tournament.

Metre

    The Feast, with its aabccb rhyme scheme and short lines,
is markedly different from The Tournament of Tottenham,
which has a rhyme scheme (aaaabcccb) and line lengths like
those of The Lady Prioress and The Tale of the Basin. Like
The Lady Prioress, The Tournament also begins with an ambi-
tious attempt at alliteration which it is unable to keep up.
On the other hand, The Feast, like burlesques P and A, seems
to imitate alliterative verse throughout, but to imitate it
poorly. P and A are one step closer to alliterative verse,
being in alliterative long line:

        x   x   /   x   x / x   x / x   x   / x
        Ther was pestels in porres,   and ladulls in lorres;
                                                (A, v. 39)

whereas a whole line of The Feast corresponds to an allitera-
tive half line:

        x   x   /   x   x / x
        Ther was pestels in porra

        x   / x   x   / x
        And laduls in lorra.
                      (Feast, vv. 19-20)

But alliteration on a given letter rarely continues into a
second line, just as in the burlesque it rarely crosses the
cæsura. The poet seems not to have been familiar with the
rhythms of alliterative poetry; his lines are irregular, and
those at the beginning and end, where he is not dependent on
a source, are better read as accentual syllabic verse:

$$\text{For } \overset{\smallsmile}{\text{ouer}} \overset{/}{\text{ }} \overset{/}{\text{alle}} \overset{\smallsmile}{\text{ in }} \overset{/}{\text{ilke}} \overset{\smallsmile}{\text{ a }} \overset{/}{\text{schire.}}$$

(v. 4)

Language and Provenience

There is scanty evidence for the place of origin of the
poem. The frequent and consistent use of ilke and ilke a
instead of southerly eche, eche a is probably not merely
scribal, and suggests an origin in the North or North
Midlands. This evidence is given slight support by OED's
observation (top sb. 24d) that the phrase top over tail is
"Chiefly north-dial."; The Feast uses "Toppor (for top?)
ouer tayle" in v. 90. Other poems in the present collection
use the same phrase: John the Reeve at v. 539 and The Friars
of Berwick at v. 579 (Bannatyne MS only). The former is
northern, the latter Scottish in its origin. Whiting lists
the phrase as T425, Top (Tail) over tail (top). However, the
rhyme sight/knytt at vv. 85-6 implies the loss of the frica-
tive in sight, a loss which is Southumbrian, so that North
Midlands is the best guess for the poem's place of origin.
Sich in vv. 8 and 12 and hem in v. 98 are both Southumbrian
but may be only scribal.

Interestingly, Oakden says of burlesque A, "The dialect
is undoubtedly N.W. Midl. of a late period, which we may
guess to have been c. 1400, judging from the style, metre,
and language" (p. 109).

Three rhyming pairs suggest that the poem was written
before the completion of the dominance of the vowel shift.
The three rhymes on adjacent long and short vowels are
tolerable, whereas their post-vowel shift pronunciation would
not be. At vv. 3 and 6, west rhymes with fest (from OE west
with short e, OF feste with long open e); at vv. 73-4,
kydde/syde (from ON kið? with short i, OE side, with long i);
and at vv. 85-6 sight/knytt (from OE sihþ, with i lengthened
as the fricative is lost, OE cnytt with short i). The poet

habitually uses "Ther <u>was</u>" to introduce plural nouns.

Spelling and Scribal Language

The spellings <u>stid</u> rather than <u>sted</u> (vv. 68, 78) and
<u>Inglond</u> (v. 9) suggest a raising of short <u>e</u> in a closed syl-
lable (assuming a short rather than long vowel in <u>stid</u>), a
raising that is more common in the northern parts of England
than the southern (Jordan 34). But the -<u>lond</u> in <u>Inglond</u> is
Southumbrian. The appearance of a back vowel before liquids
in unstressed syllables of <u>saduls</u> (v. 22), <u>gryndulstones</u>
(v. 28), <u>clapurs</u> (v. 34), <u>nobull</u> (vv. 35, 41), <u>nedur</u> (v. 52),
and <u>feturlokis</u> (v. 63) indicates an area centered in the
West Midlands, but extending into the western parts of the
East Midlands and the northwestern parts of the South
(Jordan 135). The spelling <u>send</u> rather than <u>sent</u> in v. 5 is
a reverse spelling showing the habitual unvoicing of -<u>d</u>
after -<u>n</u>- in a stressed syllable, an unvoicing that is west
midland. And the spelling <u>con</u> rather than <u>can</u> in v. 18 shows
west midland short open <u>o</u> from OE <u>a</u> before a nasal. Since
none of these forms conflicts with the evidence we have for
the provenience of the poem itself, we cannot be sure they
are the scribe's and not the poet's spellings, but the abun-
dance of west midland forms suggests that the scribe who
produced the copy we have did belong to the West Midlands.

The scribe is conservative in his orthography, using the
symbols <u>þ</u>, <u>ȝ</u>, and <u>sch-</u>. He frequently uses abbreviations.
His habitual ending for plural nouns is -<u>ys</u> or -<u>is</u>.

Editorial Treatment

In the following text, I have reproduced the spelling of
the manuscript, silently expanding the frequent abbrevia-
tions, and regularizing word divisions and capitals to modern
usage. I have added punctuation.

The Feast of Tottenham

Now of þis feest telle I can,

I trow, as wel as any man,

    Be est or be west,

For ouer alle in ilke a schire

5 I am send for as a sire

    To ilke a gret fest.

For in feith þer was on!

Sich on saw I neuer non

    In Inglond ne in Fraunc[e],

10 For þer hade I þe maistry

Off alle maner of cucry,

    Si[c]h þen was my [c]haun[ce].

Thar was meytis wel diȝt,
Well sesoned to þe right,
15   Off rost and of sew.
Ther was meytis, be heuen,
þat were a maistre al to neuen,
But sum I con yow sh[ew].

Ther was pestels in porra
20 And laduls in [l]orra
      For potage,
And som saduls in sewys
And mashefattis in mortrewys
      For þe leest page.

25 Ther was plente of alle
To theym þat were in halle,
      To lesse and to more.
Ther was gryndulstones in gravy
And mylstones in mawmany,
30   And al þis was þ[ore].

v. 18 shew: MS ew *illegible*; v. 20 lorra: MS rorra;
v. 30 þore: MS ore *illegible*;

But ȝet lett þei for no costis,

For in cum mylne postis,

 Three in a disshe,

And bell clapurs in blawndisare

35 With a nobull cury

 For þ[o] þat ete no f[isshe].

Þer come in iordans in iussall,

Als red as any russall

 Come þer among,

40 And [h]o[r]st[o]rdis in white sorre,

Was of a nobull curry

 With spicery strong.

Þer come chese crustis in charlett,

As red as any scarlette,

45 With ruban in rise.

Certes, of alle þe festis

Þat euer I saw in gestis

 Þis may ber þe prise.

v. 36 þo: MS o *illegible*; fisshe: MS isshe *illegible*;
v. 37 *begins* f. 115b; v. 40 horstordis: MS blobsterdis
[*See Explanatory Note*];

Þer was costrell in c[o]m[f]y[t]
50 And capuls in cullys
    With blandament indorde.
Þe nedur lippe of a larke
Was broght in a muk cart
    And set befor þe lorde.

55 Þen came in stedis of Spayn
And þe brute of Almayne,
    With palfrayes in paste,
And dongestekis in doralle,
War forsed wele with charcoll--
60   But certis þat was waste.

Þen com þer þe fruture
With a nobull sauour,
    With feturlokis fried,
And alle þe cart whelis of Kent,
65 With stones of þe payment,
    Ful wel wer þei tried.

v. 49 comfyt: MS cambys [*See Explanatory Note*]. *From
v. 56 on, some of the leftmost words on the page are
discernible only under ultra-violet light.* v. 58
dongestekis: MS dongesterkis;

Þen come in a horse hed
In þe stid of French brede,
    With alle þe riche hide.
70 Now hade I not þis seen
Sum of ʒow wold wene
    Ful lowde þat I lyed.

Þer come in þe kydde
Dressyd in a horse syde
75   Þat abyl was to lese,
[Three] yron harows
And many whele barowes
    In þe stid of new chese.

When they had drawen þe borde
80 Þen seid Perkyn a worde
    Hymselfe to avownce:
"Syn we haue made gode chere
I red ilke man in fere
    Goo dresse hym to a downce."

v. 73 *begins* f. *116a*; v. 76 Three: MS iij. *From v. 81 on, the right-hand lines again become difficult to read.*

85 þer ȝe myght se a mery sight
    When þei were sammen knytt
            Without any fayle.
    þei did but ran ersward
    And ilke a man went bakward,
90   Toppor ouer tayle.

    Tybbe we[x]e full [c]harr[y] of hert;
    As sche dawnsid she late a fart
            For stumbulyng at [a stole].
    Now, syrs, for your curtesy,
95 Take this for no vilany,
            But ilke man crye "ȝole!"

    Off þis fest can I no more,
    But certes þei made hem mery þore
            Whil þe day wold last.
100 ȝet myght þei not alle in fere
    Haue eton þe meytis I reckond here
            But þeyr bodys had br[ast].

            Explicit ffabula.

    v. 91 wexe: MS were; charry: MS tharre; v. 93 a stole:
    MS *altogether illegible*; v. 98 hem mery þore: MS hem
    þore [*Scribe adds* mery *above the line*]; v. 102 brast:
    MS ast *illegible*.

The Tale of the Basin

The Tale of the Basin

The Story

Magic objects to which a number of people become affixed
are a popular motif in European folk-literature: see Johannes
Bolte and Georg Polívka's Anmerkungen zu der Kinder- und
Hausmärchen der Brüder Grimm, 2nd ed. (1914; rpt. Hildesheim:
Georg Olms, 1963), II, article 64, on the Grimm brothers'
story Die goldene Gans. The Tale of the Basin seems to be
the earliest of the stories in which the sticky situation
arises as a punishment for adultery. The closest analogues
(and perhaps descendants) of the tale are in English: The
Lancashire Cuckold (London: J. Blare, [1690?]), Wing L309,
and part of The History of Jack Horner (Newcastle, 1760).

The Manuscript

Cambridge MS Ff. 5. 48 is a folio manuscript belonging
to the University Library at Cambridge. It is bound in brown
leather, labelled "English Poems/Ff. 5. 48" on its spine. A
fragment of an earlier spine in red leather, also labelled
"English Poetry," is affixed to the inside of the front
cover. The first full leaf bears the notation "Repaired by
Gray, Cambridge, July 1969." The first leaf of the manu-
script proper is now missing: the folio numbers, which are
modern, run from 2 to 135. There are no ff. 93 and 94. The
collation is as follows: A^{15} (16 - 1 at the beginning),
$B-C^{16}$, D^{18}, E^{12}, F^{14} (16 - 2 at the end), G^{20}, H^{16}, I^{5}
(10 - 5 at the end). There are no catchwords, and only
modern signatures. The leaves measure about 14.5 cm. by 22,
with a writing block about 11 cm. by 18 in The Tale of the
Basin, where there are about 34 lines to the page. The end-
papers are fragments of an early printed text, headed "Pauli
burgensis contra perfidia iudcorum. Ca. iii fo. lxv."
Paulus Burgensis, or Pablo de Sancta Maria (1362-1435), was

the author of additions to the Postilla of Nicolas of Lyra,
and of the Scrutinium Scripturarum. Descriptions of the
manuscript are to be found in Manfred Görlach, The Textual
Tradition of the South English Legendary, Leeds Texts and
Monographs New Series 6 (Leeds: The University of Leeds,
1974), pp. 126-7 and in J.Y. Downing, A Critical Edition of
Cambridge University Library MS Ff. 5. 48 (Univ. of
Washington Ph.D. thesis, 1969).

There are a number of different hands, at least five.
Jayne Cook of the Cambridge University Library describes
that in which The Tale of the Basin is written as "a late
fifteenth-century hand betraying much secretary influence,
but with some anglicana forms."

The principal contents of the manuscript are as follows:

1. Mirk's Instructions for Parish Priests (Lacks 65
lines at beginning: incipit "Womans seruyce þou muste
forsake." Ff. 2a-8b; BR 961).
2. The ABC of Aristotle (Ff. 8b-9a; BR 4155). Fol-
lowed by a drawing of a horned billy goat looking over his
shoulder at a sorry-looking dog.
3. "Here sueth a tabull of diuerse moneth[es] in the
ȝere,/If thonder be herd in theym, what it betokeneth"
("When thonder comeþ in Janeuere." Ff. 9b-10b; BR 4053.)
4. "Contra fures et latrones." A charm in Latin,
scribbled over. (F. 10b.) Followed by a picture of a beast
consuming a bird.
5. The Northern Passion. ("Herkyns now if ye wille
here." Ff. 11a-43a; BR 1907. "Explicit passio Domini nostri
Ihesu Christi quod Dominus Gilbertus Pylkyngton Amen.")
6. Seven signs of death in macaronic verse ("When þi
hed whaketh." F. 43a.)
7. The Wounds of Christ as Remedies against the Seven
Deadly Sins ("With a garlonde of thornes kene." Ff. 43b-44a;
BR 4185.)
8. Poem on incest and repentance. ("Herkyns now bothe
more and lasse." Ff. 44a-48b; BR 1107.)
9. The King and the Shepherd ("God þat sittis in
trinite." Incomplete. Ff. 48b-56b; BR 988.)
10. Dialogue on love between a nightingale and a clerk
("In a mornyng of May as I lay on slepyng." Incomplete.
F. 57a-57b; BR 1452.)
11. The Tale of the Basin ("Off talys and trifulles
many men tellys." Ff. 58a-61b; BR 2658.)

12. The Tournament of Tottenham ("Of alle þese kene conqueroures to carpe is oure kynde." Ff. 62a-66a; BR 2615).

13. Prognostications from the day of the week on which Christmas falls, in Latin. (F. 66b).

14. The Adulterous Falmouth Squire ("Man for thy myschif þou the amende." Ff. 67a-70a; BR 2052.) F. 70b is a blank.

15. A lament of the Virgin on the death of Christ ("Listyns lordyngs to my tale." Ff. 71a-72b; BR 1899.)

16. Another ("Off all women þat euer wer borne." Ff. 73a-74b; BR 2619.)

17. A prayer to Mary from the Speculum Christiani ("Mary moder wel þou be." Ff. 74b-75b; BR 2119.)

18. Prognostications from the day of the week on which the year begins ("A man þat will of wisdam lere." Ff. 75b-78b; BR 73.)

19. Legend of St. Michael from The South English Legendary ("Sant michaell þe archangell and his fellagh also." Ff. 79a-84a; BR 3029.)

20. The Feast of the Annunciation from The South English Legendary ("Sauynt Mary day in lenton among hir dayes gude." Ff. 84a-84b; BR 2989.)

21. Septuagesima from The South English Legendary ("Festis þat fallis in þe ʒer þat we call styrande." F. 84b; version of BR 791.)

22. Quadragesima from The South English Legendary ("Lentyn comes sone afterward þat sex wokes lastes." Ff. 84b-87b; variant of BR 1859.)

23. The Southern Passion from The South English Legendary ("Before sex dayes of paske at palme sonnday it is." Incomplete. Ff. 87b-92b; BR 483.) Most of f. 92b is blank. Ff. 93 and 94 are missing.

24. "Principium Anglie" ("Herkenet hiderward lordynges." Ff. 95a-112a; BR 1105.)

25. The Mourning of the Hare ("Ffer in frithe as I can fare." Ff. 112b-113b; BR 559.)

26. On the weather and crops, in prose ("An hote wynter a drye somer a wyndy hervest." F. 114a-114b.

27. "I haue forsworne hit whil I life to wake the well" ("The last tyme I the wel woke." F. 114b; BR 3409.)

28. The Feast of Tottenham ("Now of þis feest telle I can." Ff. 115a-116a; BR 2354.)

29. The Lady who Buried the Host ("God þat on þe rode was rent." Ff. 116b-118b; BR 622.)

30. Thomas of Erceldoune ("As I me went þis anders day." Ff. 119a-128b; BR 365.)

31. A Little Jest of Robin Hood and the Monk ("In somer when þe shawes be sheyn." Ff. 128b-135b; BR 1534.)

The contents of the manuscript fall into a number of independent booklets, as follows:

Booklets	Gatherings	Folios	Principal Hands	Paper
1	abcd	2-66	1	a and b
2	e	67-78	2	c and d
3	f	79-92	3	e
4	g	95-114	4	c
5	hi	115-135	5	f

It is evident that f is an entirely independent booklet, in a distinctive hand (with more anglicana features than the others) and on different paper from the others. Angus McIntosh tentatively attributes it to West Yorkshire, according to Görlach (p. 127). Its content all derives from The South English Legendary. Probably it was not originally intended for this particular collection. The rest of the manuscript is an assemblage of didactic, historical, religious, prophetic, and comic pieces. It is unusual only in having four such comic poems as The Tournament of Tottenham, The Feast of Tottenham, The Tale of the Basin, and The King and the Shepherd.

The name Gilbert Pylkyngton is associated with one poem, The Northern Passion (item 5): "Explicit passio Domini nostri Ihesu Christi quod Dominus Gilbertus Pylkyngton Amen." Pylkyngton was more likely the scribe than the poet. A distinguished family by that name lived in the town of Pilkington, Lancashire, in the fifteenth century, and a Lancashire scribe is in keeping with the west midland spellings in The Tale of the Basin, also in booklet 1 and probably by the same scribe.

On f. 32b is a little list of accounts that must have been written on the page before the Passion was:

Smith	i	d
Godleff	i	d
Vicar	i	d
West	i	d
Osmund	v	d

Other interesting marginalia include the scrawls "Buley of stake Wyllmo sunt" on f. 57b; "wytnes that I haue Reseued of Rychard" on f. 112a; and "bryan hys my name etc." on f. 114b.

The manuscript belonged to Richard Holdsworth (1590-1649), the theologian and master of Emmanuel College. In his life, Holdsworth was associated with other book collectors: among his pupils was Sir Simonds D'Ewes, and he was called to the deathbed of Robert Cotton in 1631. After Holdsworth's death in 1649, there was a period of dispute over his library between Cambridge University and Emmanuel College. The university paid the college two hundred pounds, and in 1664 acquired possession of the books, ten thousand printed volumes and nearly two hundred manuscripts.

Before Holdsworth, the manuscript was in the possession of George Wither, the poet, at least from the period 1624-31. His friend William Bedwell printed an edition of The Tournament of Tottenham in 1631 from Wither's manuscript. In an epistle to the reader Bedwell writes, "It is now seauen or eight yeares since I came first to the sight of the copy, and that by the meanes of the worthy, and my much honoured good friend, M. Ge. Withers: Of whom also, now at length, I haue obtained the use of the same." The word pope is scribbled over in the manuscript wherever it appears, and Wither was an ardent puritan: perhaps the obliteration is his handiwork. DNB records that Wither sold his estate in 1642 to raise money for the parliamentary troops. It might have been then that his manuscript passed into the hands of Holdsworth.

Metre

The stanza of The Tale of the Basin is the same as that of The Lady Prioress, rhyming aaaabcccb. The four-stressed a lines have the rhythm of alliterative long line, with a cæsura between the two half-lines. The c lines, while they too might have as many as four stressed syllables, sound markedly different because there is no cæsura and there are fewer unstressed syllables, or dips. The b lines are short, usually with two stressed syllables. The overall effect of the bcccb part of the stanza is like that of the bob and wheel in stanzaic alliterative poetry, although the a lines are rhymed rather than alliterative. The poem shows its indebtedness to alliterative poetry in the first line:

$$ / \qquad / \qquad / \qquad / $$
Off talys and trifulles   many man tellys.

But it shows little other than decorative alliteration elsewhere.

Language and Provenience

This short poem provides few rhymes that are dialectally
criterial. The third person singular ending -ys (-is) at
vv. 1 and 3 (in "many man tellys" and "þat ... dwellis"),
fixed in rhyme with ellis and spellis (vv. 2 and 4) suggests
an origin in the North or North Midlands, though the -es
ending in verbs spread rapidly southward throughout the
fifteenth century. The rhyme ende/fynde (vv. 201, 205) is
probably on short i. Short e could go to short i under the
influence of covered n (Jordan 34); the shortening of the
/i:/ in fynde before nd is most likely to have occurred in
the North (Jordan 36). The form of the second person verb
in v. 149--þou may--is a northern one (Mossé 104). This evi-
dence favors the North as the area of origin of the poem.

A sequence of rhymes at vv. 188-91 is compatible with
this ascription:

       throw/trowe/row/saw

The rhyme must be on /aU/, since that is the only possible
pronunciation of the diphthong in the noun saw, from OE saȝu.
Both row (from OE raw) and throw (from OE þrāwan) would have
this diphthong in the North, and could have it in other areas
of the country as well (Jordan 105). And trowe (from OE
trēowian) would have /aU/ only as a widening of the open o
diphthong, a widening which took place in many areas of
Southumbria (Jordan 109), but also in the North. The pos-
sible areas for this set of rhymes are the North, the West
Midlands, Essex and London, Kent, and the Southwest.

The most probable area for the composition of the poem,
then, is the North, though it is surprising that there are no
signs of the descendants of OE long a remaining as a, and in
fact such descendants are frequently rhymed on descendants of
OE long close o:

       euermoo/þertoo/also/goo   (vv. 80-4)
   from a: o: a: a:

       anone/sone   (vv. 93, 97)
   from a: o:

       John/ston/done/gon   (vv. 125-8)
   from   a: o: a:
       John usually has an open o.

froo/doo   (vv. 183, 187)
from a: o:

As far as the dating of the poem is concerned, a rough
terminus ad quem is given by the handwriting and paper of the
manuscript, which belong to the late fifteenth century. The
vocabulary gives a little help. Ryve (v. 20) is last cited
by OED in the sense "promptly" (rife adv. 4) c. 1450, then in
The Tale of the Basin itself, there dated c. 1525. The rare
verb slech (v. 46) is attested in OED in its transitive
sense (see sletch v. 1) only a. 1400 and in this poem. The
phrase "draw a draught" (v. 60: "A draw3t þer is drawen
amysse") is last cited in MED (under draught n. 3e) a. 1470.
Raste (v. 166) is a part of MED's rasen v.3, cited by MED no
later than a. 1470, OED's rase v.4, cited by OED no later
than 1390. And towte (v. 199; OED toute) is last cited c.
1460. This evidence from the vocabulary suggests a date not
much later than the third quarter of the fifteenth century.
It is contradicted only by smache (v. 25), first attested in
OED (smatch sb.1) in the metaphoric sense "A slight indica-
tion ... of some quality" from c. 1525 in The Tale of the
Basin itself, then 1548; but it should be noted that the term
had existed in the literal sense "taste" since a. 1200, and
the metaphoric extension of meaning is an easy one.

Spelling and Scribal Language

The spelling of The Tale of the Basin indicates the West
Midlands as the scribe's place of origin. Con (v. 36 etc.)
is the usual spelling of can, with OE a before a nasal
changed to o (Jordan 30). Furst (v. 186) is a west midland
spelling, with u representing an older rounded vowel from OE
y (see Jordan 42). The past participle spende (v. 42), with
the inverse spelling -nd for -nt, can belong only to the West
Midlands (Jordan 200). The devoicing of the weak past tense
and past participle ending -ed to -et indicated in the spell-
ings hengett (v. 201) and lewtnesse (v. 218) is also consis-
tent with the West Midlands (Jordan 200). The a of baly
(vv. 39 and 162) represents older æ from OE a before l +
consonant and belongs to the West Midlands as well, outside
the AB area (Jordan 62). Other spellings suggest an area to
the north of the AB region. White (v. 49) is an inverse
spelling for quite, indicating an area where OE hw- is highly
aspirated, the area north of Oakden line B. The spelling
hamwarde (v. 94), with a representing OE long a, also

suggests a region inside the northern dialect area. Spell-
ings such as dryfe (v. 3) and to liffe (v. 73) with devoicing
of /v/ brought into final position, are also northern, but
such devoicing extends into southern Lancashire (Jordan 217).
The verbs are inflected according to the northern system
(þou was, v. 68; þou shalle, v. 209), or northern and north
midland (þou lyves, v. 70; þou takis, v. 65; it faris,
v. 72). Surprisingly, summe byn (v. 2) belongs to the East
Midlands. The northern features may, of course, be retained
from the poet's language. But that so many northerly fea-
tures are retained, particularly in the verb inflexions,
suggests that the scribe came from a northern area of the
West Midlands.

       The spelling sheuell (vv. 189, 199) for shovel is idio-
syncratic. Gif (v. 149) is normally a Scottish spelling:
elsewhere this scribe uses 3if.

Editorial Treatment

       Scribal abbreviations have been silently expanded. I
have regularized word divisions and capitals, and added
punctuation. Initial Ff- in this scribe's usage stands con-
sistently for F, and I have treated it as such.

The Tale of the Basin

Off talys and trifulles many man tellys;
Summe byn trew and sum byn ellis.
A man may dryfe forth þe day þat long tyme dwellis
With harpyng and pipyng and oþer mery spellis,
5 With gle and with gamme.
Off a person ȝe mowe here
(In case þat hit soth were),
And of his broþer þat was hym dere
And louyd well samme.

10 The ton was his fadirs eyre of hows and of lande,
The toþer was a person as I vnderstande.
A riche man wex he and a gode husbande,
And knowen for a gode clerke þoro Goddis sande,
And wyse was holde.
15 The toþer hade littul thoȝt;
Off husbandry cowth he noȝt,
But alle his wyves will he wroȝt,
[And did as she hym tolde.]

Textual notes; The Tale of the Basin *begins f. 58a.* No *title in MS.* v. 18 *missing, no gap in MS.*

A febull husbande was he on as many ar on lyve:
20 Alle his wyves biddyng he did it full ryve.
   Hit is an olde seid saw, I swere by Seint Tyve,
   Hit shal be at þe wyves will if þe husbond thryve,
   Bothe within and withowte.
   A wyfe þat has an yvell tach,
25 þerof þe husbond shalle haue a smache,
   But ȝif he loke well abowte.

   Off þat ȝong gentil man was a gret disese:
   After a ȝere or two his wyfe he myȝt not pleese;
   Mycull of his lande lay to þe preestys ese.
30 Sche tauȝt hym euer among how þe katte did snese,
   Riȝt at hir owne wille.
   He þat hade bene a lorde
   Was nouþ at bedde ne at borde,
   Ne durst onys speke a worde
35 When she bade be stille.

vv. 24-5 *The stanza is short a line here, no gap in MS.*
v. 30 þe katte did: MS þe did [*Scribe adds* katte *above*
line]; v. 32 *begins* f. 58b;

Litull of husbondry þe godeman con thynke,
And his wyfe louyd well gode mete and gode drynke.
She wolde nouþer þerfore swete ne swynke,
But when þe baly was full, lye down and wynke,
40 And rest hir neder ende.
Soo long þis life þei ladde
þat spende was þat þei hadde.
Þe wife hir husbonde badde
Belyfe forth to wende,

45 "To the person þi broder þat is so rich a wrech,
And pray hym of þi sorow sumdel he wolde slech.
Fourty pounde or fyfty loke of hym þou fech.
So þat þou hit bryng litull will I rech,
Neuer for to white."
50 To his broþer forth he went,
And mycull money to hym he lent,
And also sone hit was spent:
Thereof they hade but lyte.

Micull money of his broþer he fette;
55 For alle þat he broȝt he ferd neuer þe bette.
Þe person wex wery and thouȝt he wolde hym lette:
"And he fare long thus he fallis in my dette,
And ȝet he may not the.
Betwene hym and his wife, iwysse,
60 A drawȝt þer is drawen amysse.
I will wete, soo haue I blisse,
How þat hit myȝt be."

ȝet on a day afterwarde to þe person he ȝede
To borow mone, and he ne myȝt spede.
65 "Broþer," quoth þe person, "þou takis litull hede
How þou fallis in my dett--þerof is all my drede--
And ȝet þou may not the.
Perdy, þou was my faders eyre
Off howse and lande þat was so feyre,
70 And euer þou lyves in dispayre.
What deuell! How may þis be?"

"I ne wot how it faris, but euer I am behynde.
For to liffe manly hit come me be kynde.
I shall truly sey what I thynke in my mynde."
75 The person seyde, "þou me telle."
"Broþer," he seid, "be Saynt Albon,
Hit is a preest men callis Sir John.
Sich a felow know I non:
Off felawes he berys þe bell.

v. 65 *begins f. 59a;* v. 73 come me be: MS come be
[*Scribe adds* me *above line*]; vv. 72-4 *The stanza is short
a line here, no gap in MS;* v. 75 *in large letters,
extending into the left margin;*

80 "Hym gode and curtesse I fynde euermoo.
   He harpys and gytryns, and syngs wel þertoo;
   He wrestels and lepis, and castys þe ston also."
   "Broþer," quoth þe person, "belife home þou goo,
   So as I þe say.
85 ȝif þou myȝt with any gynne
   þe vessell owt of þe chamber wynne,
   þe same þat þei make water in,
   And bryng hit me, I þe pray."

   "Broþer," he seid blithly, "þi will shal be wroȝt,
90 It is a rownde basyn, I haue hit in my thoȝt."
   "As priuely as þou may, þat hit be hider brouȝt,
   Hye þe fast on þi way. Loke þou tary noȝt,
   And come agayne anone."
   Hamwarde con he ride;
95 þer no longer wolde he byde.
   And then his wife began to chyde
   Because he come so sone.

v. 96 *begins f. 59b;*

He hent vp þe basyn and forth can he fare.
Till he came to his broþer wolde he not spare.
100 þe person toke þe basyn and to his chaumber it bare,
And a priue experiment sone he wroght thare,
And to his broþer he seyde ful blithe,
"Loke þou where [þou] þe basyn fette,
And in þat place þou hit sett,
105 And þan," he seid, "withowytyn lette,
Come agayne right swythe."

He toke þe basyn and forth went.
When his wife hym saw hir browes she vphent.
"Why hase þi broþer so sone þe home sent?
110 Hit my3t neuer be for gode, I know it verament,
þat þou comes home so swythe."
"Nay," he seid, "my swetyng,
I moste take a litull thyng,
And to my broþer I mot hit bryng,
115 For sum it shall make blithe."

v. 103 where þou þe: MS where þe;

Into his chaumber priuely went he þat tyde

And sett downe þe basyn be þe bedde side;

He toke his leve at his wyfe and forth can he ride.

She was glad þat he went and bade hym not abyde.

120 Hir hert began to glade.

She anon riȝt thoo

Slew a capon or twoo,

And oþer gode mete þertoo

Hastely she made.

125 When alle thyng was redy, she sent after Sir John

Priuely at a posterne ȝate as stille as any ston.

They eten and dronken as þei were wonte to done

Till þat thaym list to bedde for to gon,

Softly and stille.

130 Within a litull while Sir John con wake,

And nedis water he most make.

He wist wher he shulde þe basyn take

Riȝt at his owne wille.

v. 127 *begins f. 60a;*

He toke þe basyn to make water in.
135 He myȝt not get his hondis awey all þis worde to wyn.
His handis fro þe basyn myȝt he not twyn.
"Alas," seid Sir John, "how shall I now begynne?
Here is sum wych crafte."
Faste þe basyn con he holde,
140 And alle his body tremeld for colde.
Leuer þen a [hundred] pounde he wolde
þat hit were fro hym rafte.

Riȝt as a chapmon shulde sell his ware
þe basyn in þe chaumber betwix his hondis he bare.
145 þe wife was agrevyd he stode so long thare
And askid why so; hit was a nyce fare
So stille ther to stande.
"What, woman!" he said, "In gode fay,
þou must helpe, gif þou may,
150 þat þis basyn were awey:
Hit will not fro my honde."

v. 141 hundred: MS ¢;

Vpstert þe godewyfe--for nothyng wolde she lette--
And boþe hir hondis on þe basyn she sette.
Thus sone were þai boþe fast, and he neuer þe bette.
155 Hit was a myssefelisshyppe a man to haue imette,
Be day or be ny3t.
They began clepe and crye
To a wenche þat lay þam bye,
That she shulde come on hye
160 To helpe 3if she my3t.

Vpstert þe wench er she was halfe waked
And ran to hir maistrys all baly-naked.
"Alas," seid hir maistrys, "who hase þis sorow maked?
Helpe this basyn wer away þat oure sorow were slakyd.
165 Here is a sory chaunce."
To þe basyn þe wench she raste.
For to helpe hade she caste.
Thus were they sone alle thre fast.
Hyt was a nyce daunce.

v. 168 they sone alle: MS they alle [*Scribe adds* sone
above line];

170 Ther þei daunsyd al þe nyȝt till þe son con ryse.

The clerke rang þe daybell as hit was his guise.

He knew his maisters councell and his vprise.

He thoȝt he was to long to sey his seruyse,

His matyns be þe morow.

175 Softly and stille thider he ȝede.

When he come thider he toke gode hede

How þat his mayster was in grett drede

And browght in gret sorow.

Anon as [he] Sir John can se he began to call.

180 Be þat worde þei come down into þe hall.

"Why goo ȝe soo?" quote þe clerke.   "Hit is shame for
                                                        you alle.

Why goo ȝe so nakyd? Foule mot yow falle.

The basyn shalle yow froo."

To þe basyn he made a brayde,

185 And boþe his hondis þeron he leyde.

Þe furst worde þat þe clerke seyde

[Was], "Alas, what shall I doo?"

v. 179 as he sir: MS as sir; v. 187 Was alas: MS /Alas;

The carter fro þe halle dor erth can he throw,

With a sheuell in his hande, to make it cle[n], I trowe.

190 When he saw thaym go rounde upon a row

He wende hit hade bene folys of þe fayr (he told hit in
his saw).

He seid he wolde assay, iwysse.

Vnneth he durst go in for fere.

Alle saue þe clerke nakyd were.

195 When he saw þe wench go there

Hym thoȝt hit went amysse.

þe wench was his speciall þat hoppid on þe rowte.

"Lette go þe basyn er þou shalle haue a clowte!"

He hit þe wench with a shevell a b[l]o[w]e on þe towte.

200 The shevyll sticked þen fast withowte any dowte,

And he hengett on þe ende.

Þe carter, with a sory chaunce,

Among þam alle he led þe daunce.

In Englonde, Scotland, ne in Fraunce

205 A man shulde non sich fynde.

v. 188 *begins f. 61a;* v. 189 clene: MS cleue; v. 199 a
blowe: MS aboue;

The godeman and þe person came in þat stounde.

Alle þat fayre feliship dawnsyng þei founde.

Þe godeman seid to Sir John, "Be cockys swete wounde,

Þou shalle lese þine harnesse or a hundred pounde.

210 Truly þou shalle not chese."

Sir John seid, "In gode fay,

Helpe this basyn were awey

And þat mone will I pay

Er I this harnes lese."

215 The person charmyd þe basyn þat it fell þaim fro;

Euery man þen hastely on þaire wey can goo.

The preest went out of contre for shame he hade thoo,

And then þai leuyd þaire lewtnesse and did no more soo,

But wex wyse and ware.

220 Thus þe godeman and his wyfe

Leuyd togeder withowt stryfe.

Mary for hir ioyes fyfe

Shelde vs alle fro care.

Finitur

v. 216 *begins f. 61b*; v. 222 for hir: MS for y hir.

Jack and his Stepdame

Jack and his Stepdame

The Story

There are no known sources for the story of <u>Jack and his
Stepdame</u>, though the motifs of wishes, magic objects, and
wicked stepmothers are old and widespread.

There are two main versions of the tale, that attested
by manuscripts RQP, and a longer one represented in varying
forms by ECMDAFB, called <u>The Friar and the Boy</u>. In both ver-
sions, the boy is granted three magical gifts, and uses them
in three conflicts of increasing seriousness: the first, in
which the boy is threatened by his stepmother's malevolence,
ends in her humiliation; the second, in which he is threatened
by a friar's violence, ends in violence inflicted on the
friar; the third, in which he is threatened with his father's
condemnation, ends with his father's approbation. In the
shorter version, that victory is the end of any threat from
the boy's enemies. The longer version adds an episode in
which the friar and stepmother take the boy to court, where
he defeats them again: it is both redundant and repetitive.

All versions of the story run together to line 414. The
next two stanzas in RQP give an abrupt conclusion to the poem,
finishing with a sentdntious moral:

> He þat hath not all hes will,
> Be it good or be it ylle,
> He holdyth hym not apayde.

Although a quick moralizing conclusion is not unusual in
fabliaux (cf. Chaucer's <u>Summoner's Tale</u>), various scribes seem
to have found the ending inadequate and to have provided their
own. P gives more moralizing, RQ more tying up of the plot,
and the others delete the stanzas past v. 414 and add the
court episode. But then ECMDAFB coincide for only 57 lines;

apparently their parent manuscript was damaged at that point,
for the conclusion of E shows signs of inept attempts to
invent (see especially vv. E97-100), and the CMD conclusion is
written in four-line stanzas, not the regular six-line
stanzas of the rest of the poem. The AFB conclusion is in the
regular stanza, but follows the content of CMD closely: the
reviser who modernized the CMD version of The Friar and the
Boy for the later printed editions also recast the concluding
stanzas in six lines.

The printed version of the poem, The Friar and the Boy,
was very popular. Robert Burton mentions it in his Anatomy
of Melancholy, and owned A, the 1617 Allde edition of the
poem now in the Bodleian library. The sixteenth- and
seventeenth-century editions exist in only one extant copy
each: it is likely that there were further editions which did
not survive. Indeed, the poem is entered in the Stationers'
Register to J. Wally in 1557-58, to John Alde in 1568-9,
though the earliest surviving edition from the Allde family
is dated 1584-9, and conditionally to Edward White on August
16, 1586. Besides the editions used in this text, there are
four known later seventeenth-century ones: one printed by
Jane Bell in London around 1655 cited by Hazlitt, the present
location of which is unknown; one from Glasgow, 1668, now in
the British Library; one from London, 1690?, now in Magdalene
College Library, Cambridge; and the last dated 1698, probably
also from Glasgow, now in the Harvard University Library.
Throughout the eighteenth century the poem continued to be
reprinted, and The Second Part of the Fryer and Boy is often
found bound together in chapbook collections with the first.
This second book of Jack's adventures is more bawdy and scato-
logical than the first, and has a much less well-developed
plot. The eighteenth-century editions of The Friar and the
Boy come from a variety of places: London, Glasgow, Birmingham,
Hull, Newcastle, Doncaster, Stirling. Its popularity was
obviously widespread as well as long-lasting.

The tale had a parallel popularity in Flemish. In 1528
in Antwerp Michael Hillien published Vanden Jongen ge/heeten
Jacke: die sijns/Vaders beesten wachte int velt ende vanden/
brueder dye daer quam on Jacke te castien, a translation
apparently of the edition published ca. 1510-13 by de Worde,
Hillien's former apprentice. (The woodcut of Jack piping to
the friar in the thornbush that Hillien used appears to be
the same as that later used in the English editions D, A, and
F.) Hillien's edition was the ancestor of a long line of
editions in Flemish.

Readers interested in the later history of the story in various European languages should consult "Der Jud im Dorn" in Bolte-Polívka II, 490-503.

The Texts

The art of editing by recension may be at the moment under suspicion, but it is of great use in dealing with a poem like Jack and his Stepdame, with its five manuscripts and five early editions. For Chaucer's work or Langland's, an editor might well best rely on his familiarity with the poet's thought and his style to choose between alternative readings or emend to an unattested one, but this poem's author is anonymous, and his style and thought known through only about four hundred lines of verse. Langland's alliteration and accentual patterns or Chaucer's metre may allow an editor to distinguish right readings from wrong, but this poem's loose metrical requirements are not of much help. Recension can provide very useful information to the editor of such a poem, and without the complications apt to be introduced by contamination in other, more famous works. We know that many manuscripts of The Canterbury Tales and Piers Plowman circu-lated in medieval England, and the works were considered important enough for a scribe to take the time to check troubling readings against other manuscripts. But in the case of a slight poem like Jack and his Stepdame, there would have been fewer manuscripts and so less likelihood of finding an accessible second version of a line; and there would have been less motivation for any but an extremely conscientious scribe or printer to search out alternative readings. (The second scribe of the Rawlinson manuscript version did seek out another examplar to complete his damaged gathering, but pre-sumably his original examplar was then beyond his reach.) Editing by recension can often produce, if not the original line, at least the reading of the parent manuscript.

The family-tree of this poem's manuscripts happens to have only two main branches, and as Donaldson points out, a bifid stemma never decides between readings for the editor,[1]

---

[1]The failure of most stemmata to comprise three main branches, so that the evidence of any two can outweigh the disagreement of one, is for Donaldson the "final flaw in the beautiful machine" of editing by recension. E.T. Donaldson,

but (<u>pace</u> Donaldson) such a stemma does help in the case of
those substantive differences which seem unlikely to have been
caused by the types of copying error and scribal correction
Kane discusses.[2]   Among the manuscripts and printed texts of
<u>Jack</u> <u>and</u> <u>his</u> <u>Stepdame</u>, R and Q agreeing against a variety of
readings in the other texts are more likely to represent the
parent manuscript than ECMDAFB agreeing against a variety of
readings in the other texts; and if only R, Q, and P agree
against all the others, their reading is nevertheless that of
the parent manuscript.

     With the foregoing for apology, here is the stemma for
the texts of <u>Jack</u> <u>and</u> <u>his</u> <u>Stepdame</u> or <u>The</u> <u>Friar</u> <u>and</u> <u>the</u> <u>Boy</u>,
up to about 1650:

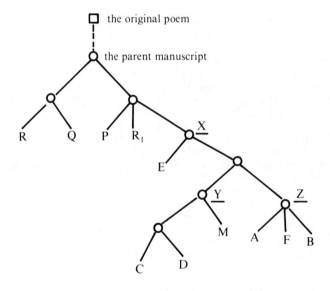

"The Psychology of Editors of Middle English Texts," in his
<u>Speaking</u> <u>of</u> <u>Chaucer</u> (London: Athlone Press, 1970), p. 111.

     [2]George Kane, "Editorial Resources and Methods" in the
introduction to his edition, <u>Piers</u> <u>Plowman</u>: <u>The</u> <u>A</u> <u>Version</u>
(London: Athlone Press, 1960), pp. 115–165.

R

Manuscript Rawlinson C. 86 (Bodley 11951) is a miscella-
neous compilation: much religious verse, some secular verse
including Higden's Polichronicon, The Wedding of Gawain and
Dame Ragnell, and pieces by Lydgate and Chaucer, and a number
of prescriptions. It is a folio manuscript in paper and
vellum, in ii & 190 & ii folios. The manuscript, its colla-
tion, and its contents are fully described by J.J. Griffiths,
"A Re-examination of Oxford, Bodleian Library, MS Rawlinson
C. 86," Archiv für das Studium der neueren Sprachen und
Literaturen 219 (1982), 381-8.

The manuscript is 28 cm. by 40, with a writing block
roughly 21 by 8 in the main part of Jack and his Stepdame.
The first folio of the poem, on the outermost full leaf of the
manuscript's fourth gathering, must have been lost very
early. It is supplied by another hand, apparently from a
different exemplar. On the stemma, that replaced segment is
represented as R1. The two hands evident in Jack and his
Stepdame are both mixed cursive hands, basically anglicana
but containing secretary elements, and belonging to the
second half of the fifteenth century, according to the opin-
ion (in June of 1981) of Albinia de la Mare of the Department
of Western Manuscripts at the Bodleian. However, Griffiths'
1982 article in Archiv adduces evidence to place the manu-
script's origin early in the sixteenth century.

The history of the manuscript is not entirely clear.
Early in the sixteenth century at least its first booklet,
containing The Northern Passion (ff. 1-30), was in the posses-
sion of a Benedictine monk named William of Aylesbury at the
abbey of Saint Saviour of Bermondsey, just southeast of
London, though he was not its first owner. The original name
in the formula "iste liber constat" on f. 30b has been black-
ened out so thoroughly that the paper has ruptured. On f. 1a
appear two names: Randal Dreames (the surname discernible
only under ultraviolet light, only the R and final al of the
Christian name clear) and William Howarde; the latter has
been identified as William, Lord Howard of Naworth (1563-
1640). On f. ia is written "MS Knox Ward Clarencieux."
Apparently, then, the manuscript was owned by William Howard
during the early part of the seventeenth century; it may have
been owned at some point by one Randal Dreames; and before
Richard Rawlinson acquired it and left it to Oxford at his
death in 1755, it was in the possession of Knox Ward,·
Clarence King of Arms from 1726 to 1741. Other names appear-
ing elsewhere in the manuscript are less likely to have been

owners. They are discussed by Griffiths, pp. 384-7.

Q

Manuscript Balliol College 354 is a folio manuscript,
folded the long way, of 248 paper folios with eight addition-
al short leaves following f. 143. It is in a vellum wrapper.
The leaves are 29 cm. tall by 11 wide, with a writing block
about 24 by 7. The writing is small and very neat, a mixed
cursive hand, with fifty or sixty lines to the page, dry-
ruled. Many pages have a line of red chalk drawn down the
left-hand margin, so that the effect is a rough rubrication
of initial letters. The same red is used to rubricate other
headings, and the outer edges of the pages, top, bottom, and
side, are reddened as well. A description of the manuscript
and its complicated collation is given by R.A.B. Mynors,
Catalogue of the Manuscripts of Balliol College Oxford
(Oxford: Clarendon, 1963).

The work titled "Jak & his stepdame & of the ffrere"
begins on the recto of the first of two consecutive folios
numbered lxxxxviii and runs to f. Cb.

A full description of the contents would take too much
room here, but interested readers should consult Roman
Dyboski, Songs, Carols, and Other Miscellaneous Pieces from
the Balliol MS. 354, Richard Hill's Commonplace-Book, EETS
101 (1908 for 1907), pp. xxxiv-lix for a table of contents,
and the rest of the volume for an edition of much of the
manuscript. The book contains recipes, remedies, information
on the values of goods and exchanges of money, samples of
business correspondence in English and French, lists of
English fairs, of Lord Mayors of London and of feast days in
that city, rules for movable feasts, and notes on the neces-
sary qualities of a priest and the functions of popes and
bishops. There are no romances, but many lyrics, and a large
collection of short and mostly moral tales, including a number
from Gower's Confessio Amantis, The Seven Sages of Rome, The
Siege of Rouen, How the Wise Man Taught his Son, Stans Puer,
Little John, The Churl and the Bird, and The Nutbrown Maid.
The volume is titled A Boke of dyueris tales and balettes and
dyueris Reconynges.

The book was largely compiled and written by Richard
Hill, a citizen and grocer of London, who was born shortly

before 1490. Readers interested in Richard Hill should consult W.P. Hills, "Richard Hill of Hillend," Notes and Queries 177 (1939), 452-6. Hill records on f. xvii that he was "borne at Hillend in Langley in the parishe of Hinchyn in the shire of Hartfford." The book passed to his son John (b. Nov. 17, 1518) on Richard's death. After that its history is unknown, but it does contain farming memoranda, including a note on horses dated 1791 on f. xvib and one on oats on f. xviib, notes which may be in the same hand as the name Robert Tombs, which appears twice on f. xviiia. The other name not connected with the Hill family which appears in the manuscript is that of John Stokes: on the top of f. clxxviii appears the early (perhaps sixteenth-century) notation "Iste liber partinet John Stokes," with a line drawn through it. When the manuscript was acquired by Balliol is unknown. Mynors reports, "It was at Balliol before 1852 (the date of Coxe's catalogue); W. Chappell, Popular Music of the Olden Time i (1855) 50 says it 'has been recently found in the library of Balliol College, Oxford, where it had been accidentally concealed, behind a book-case, during a great number of years'" (p. 354).

P

Manuscript Porkington 10 of the National Library of Wales is a quarto manuscript of iii & 211 & ii, in vellum and paper, made up of a number of independent booklets but apparently all compiled by a group of persons, probably a family. Folios 1-20, 23, 24, and 211 are vellum, the rest paper. The gatherings are as follows: i conjugate with pastedown; ii-iii with iii on a stub bifoliate to ii; A^{10}; B^{10} (Ff. 11/20 must have been originally an outer leaf for A, and then turned to be an outer leaf for B. F. 19b has a scroll with catchwords at the bottom. Ff. 14-15 are signed iii-iiii, f. 20 signed Ev.); C^6 (F. 25 is marked 1.); D^8 (Ff. 28-30 are signed ii-iiii. F. 34b has scroll and catchwords.); E^8 (6 & ff. 35, 36. F. 35 is signed Gvii, ff. 36-38 signed ii-iiii.); F^8 (F. 43 is signed, but trimmed so that the signature is illegible; ff. 45-46 signed iii-iiii. F. 50b has scroll and catchwords.); G^8 (6 & ff. 57, 58. Ff. 45-46 are signed iii, iiii. F. 58b has scroll and catchwords. F. 52b has a scroll with the name H. Hattun.), H^6, I^{10} (Ff. 66b and 74b both have scroll and catchwords.); J^8 (6 & ff. 81, 82. F. 82 has scroll and catchwords.); K^8 (6 & ff. 89, 90. F. 83 is signed Nxiii, ff. 84-85 signed ii-iii, signature of f. 86 partly trimmed.);

L^8 (F. 91 is signed Oxiiii. Ff. 91b-94b are signed 1-4 in
contemporary Arabic numerals. F. 98 has scroll and catch-
words.); M^8 (F. 99 is signed Pxv. Ff. 99b-102b are signed
1-4. F. 106 has scroll and catchwords.); N^8 (F. 107 is signed
Qxvi. Ff. 107b-110b are signed 1-4. F. 114 has scroll and
catchwords.); O^8 (F. 115 is signed Rxvii. Ff. 115b-118b are
signed 1-4. F. 122 has scroll and catchwords.); P^8 (F. 123
is signed Sxviii. Ff. 123b-126b are signed 1-4. F. 130 has
scroll and catchwords.); Q^8 (F. 130 is signed Txix.); R^8 (F.
139 is signed Vxx. Ff. 139b-142b are signed 1-4. F. 146 has
scroll and catchwords.); S^8 (F. 147 is signed Xxxi. Ff.
147b-149b are signed 1-3. F. 154 has scroll and catchwords.);
T^8 (F. 155 is signed Yxxii. F. 162 has scroll and catch-
words.); U^8 (F. 170 has scroll and catchwords.); V^8 (F. 171 is
signed 4xxiii, but the signature is cut off by the edge of the
page. F. 178 has scroll and catchwords.); W^8 (F. 179 is
signed 9xxv. F. 186 has scroll and catchwords.); X^8 (F. 187
has the lower right-hand corner missing.); $Y-Z^8$ (Ff. 195 and
203 both signed, but the signatures trimmed off. F. 120 has
scroll and catchwords.); AA^1 (ending incomplete), iv, v con-
jugate with pastedown.

The manuscript falls into a number of booklets with con-
tents independent of the others:

Booklets	Quires	Folios	Hands
1	A-C	1-26	a,b
2	D-K	27-90	c,a
3	L-Q	91-138	d,a
4	R-X	139-194	d,a
5	Y	195-202	d,a
6	Z,AA	203-211	a

(However, Auvo Kurvinen, in "MS. Porkington 10, Description
with Abstracts," Neuphilologische Mitteilungen 54 (1953), 33-
67, discerns nineteen different hands.)

Various watermarks appear, the two most frequent being a
bull's head and a fragment of a cross and crescent which
appear in booklets 2, 3, 5, and 6; the repetition of water-
marks, as well as hands, from one booklet to another reinfor-
ces the impression that the manuscript was compiled at one
place and time by a group of connected people.

The contents of the manuscript are listed by Kurvinen in
the article mentioned above and by Madden in Syr Gawayne.

P includes some scientific tables and tracts, practical
instruction on planting trees and making ink, some saints'
lives, The Siege of Jerusalem, Timor mortis conturbat me,
several carols, one of the burlesques described in this volume
in connection with The Feast of Tottenham, and Syre Gawene
and the Carle of Carelyle. Jack and his Stepdame appears on
ff. 139a-149b.

The manuscript is in modern binding, and has modern
folio numbers throughout. It is about 13.7 by 11.5 cm. The
size of the writing block varies, as does the number of lines
to a page. The manuscript is pricked, and ruled in ink. The
hands are current hands of the fifteenth century.

Many marginal notes and names appear in the manuscript,
and most of these are clearly connected with Wales. But the
manuscript itself is in English. Of the names in P, the most
interesting are William Marice (f. 4b) and John Owen (f. 26a).
William Maurice (1542-1622) of Clenennau estate in Carnarvon-
shire married Margaret Wyn Lacon, the heiress to Porkington
in Shropshire. If the manuscript passed into the hands of
the Welsh family by this marriage, it would have descended
from William to his granddaughter Elin (1578-1626), who mar-
ried John Owen of Bodsilin, Anglesey. Their descendants
include the Ormsby-Gores, who eventually deposited this manu-
script, among others, in the National Library of Wales at
Aberystwyth.

E

Cambridge University Library Manuscript Ee. 4. 35 is a
folio manuscript in two parts. The first 24 leaves, of thick
paper with no watermarks, are bound as a single gathering,
with the stitches visible between 12b and 13a. But since the
first item is a fragment, there was clearly at one time more
than one gathering. The second part comprises 89 leaves of
parchment, containing only The Prick of Conscience; it is
apparently earlier than the first part. It is the first part
of Ee. 4. 35 that is of interest here. Jack and his Stepdame,
here called The Cheylde and hes Stepdame, appears on ff. 6b-
13b. Other contents of the manuscript are:

1. A fragment of The Adulterous Falmouth Squire (Ff.
1a-2b; BR 2052).

2. <u>The Lady who Buried the Host</u> (Imperfect at begin-
ning. Ff. 3a-5a; BR 622).
3. A Calculation of Easter (F. 5a).
4. A short moralizing piece ("Kepe well x." F. 5a;
BR 1817).
5. Another ("I had mey gode <u>and</u> mey ffrende." F. 5a;
BR 1297).
6. "The vii vertwys agyn the vii dedly synys" (Ff. 5b-
6b; BR 469).
7. "The x comandements" (F. 6b; BR 3685).
8. "The Cheylde <u>and</u> hes stepdame" (Ff. 6b-13b; BR 977).
9. "The Expenses of flesche at the Mariage of mey
ladey Marget <u>b</u>at sche had owt off Eynglande" (F. 14a; Margaret
Tudor, m. Edinburgh 1503?   Or Margaret, sister to Edward IV,
m. Bruges 1468?).
10. <u>Robin Hood and the Potter</u> (Ff. 14b-19a; BR 1533).
11. <u>The King and the Barker</u> (Ff. 19b-21a; BR 4168).
12. An arithmetical puzzle: "In yngland ther ys a
shepcote" (F. 21a).
13. <u>On Light, Right, and Might</u> (F. 21a; BR 3532),
followed by two blank leaves.
14. "The Boke of Cortesey" (Ff. 22b-23b; BR 1920).
15. <u>Reasons for Hearing Mass</u> (F. 24a; in Latin).
16. <u>Nine Steps of Dying and Repentance</u> (F. 24a; in
English and Latin).

On f. 24b appears the notation "Iste liber constat
Ricardo Calle," followed by a device made up of the letters
of his name.

All the contents are in a single hand, with very peculiar
spelling, probably that of "Ricardo Calle."   Mrs. Jayne Cook
of the Cambridge University Library has sent me the following
description of the writing of Ee. 4. 35 part 1: "Apparently
written for the most part in a variable current hand of the
early sixteenth century, with many secretary forms, very close
to the normal business handwriting of the period.   This
dating assumes that the Lady Margaret referred to [in item 9]
is Margaret Tudor, the sister of Henry VIII, as in the old
printed catalogue.   Otherwise, the hand could be late
fifteenth-century."

This Calle could not have been the Richard Calle who was
steward to the Pastons and married Margery Paston, although
the identification is tempting, since Margery's two brothers
John were both in Bruges for the marriage of a prominent Lady
Margaret, the sister of Edward IV, who married Charles Duke of

Burgundy in 1468. See Letter 330, ed. Norman Davis, <u>Paston</u>
<u>Letters</u> <u>and</u> <u>Papers</u> <u>of</u> <u>the</u> <u>Fifteenth</u> <u>Century</u>, I (Oxford:
Clarendon Press, 1971), 539-40. The spelling of MS E is
markedly different from the steward Calle's. See for example
his letter to Margery Paston, Letter 861, Davis, II (1976),
498-500.

There was a Richard Caly, a Benedictine monk of Durham
Cathedral Priory, who was admitted to Oxford as a candidate
for the degree of Bachelor of Theology in 1495, became Almoner
of Durham Priory, and was still alive as prior of Finchale
(in Durham) in 1527, according to A.B. Emden, <u>A</u> <u>Biographical</u>
<u>Register</u> <u>of</u> <u>the</u> <u>University</u> <u>of</u> <u>Oxford</u> <u>to</u> <u>A.D.</u> <u>1500</u>, 3 vols.
(Oxford: Clarendon, 1957). If we accept 1503, the date of
the marriage of Lady Margaret Tudor, as the <u>terminus</u> <u>a</u> <u>quo</u>
for the manuscript, Richard Caly could well be the "Ricardo
Calle" to whom the manuscript belonged, and who undoubtedly
compiled it. He could hardly have been from Durham original-
ly, however, given his numerous Southumbrian spellings.

It was probably within decades of its compilation that
the manuscript passed into the hands of the book collector
Thomas Knyvett of Ashwellthorpe in Norfolk (c. 1539-1618),
though it is conceivable that it was actually acquired not by
the elder Knyvett, but by his grandson and heir to the collec-
tion, the younger Thomas Knyvett, before the collection was
catalogued in 1630. At this time the outer folios were
apparently in reverse order. F. 2b is marked "Sed 40" (from
the younger Knyvett's note for location: sedes 40) and f. 2a
is marked Ee. 4. 35, with its fragment of poetry marked 1.
Apparently the manuscript was not much read.

The younger Thomas Knyvett died in 1658, leaving his
books to his son, John. When John's son Thomas died in 1693,
the library was probably dispersed, and much of it went to
John Moore, bishop of Ely, though the circumstances are
unknown. George I bought the library upon Moore's death in
1714 and gave it to Cambridge in 1715. Readers interested in
the collection should consult D.J. McKitterick, <u>The</u> <u>Library</u>
<u>of</u> <u>Sir</u> <u>Thomas</u> <u>Knyvett</u> <u>of</u> <u>Ashwellthorpe,</u> <u>c.</u> <u>1539-1618</u>
(Cambridge: University Press, 1978).

The manuscript was most recently bound in 1875. Its
leaves are 27 cm. by 16.5, with a writing block of 21.5 by
13. It has no signatures, catchwords, or pagination; the
foliation is modern. There are about thirty lines to the
page. Many leaves are now on stubs.

B

British Library Additional Manuscript 27879 is the famous
Percy Folio, a paper manuscript dating from the mid-seventeenth
century. The antiquarian Thomas Percy, later Bishop of
Dromore, gives its history in a note dated 1769 on f. 1b of
the manuscript: it was made by one Thomas Blount and inherited
by his descendant, an apothecary also named Blount, of
Shiffnal, Shropshire. It was bought by Humphrey Pitt, whose
maids were using the tattered manuscript to kindle the fire
when Percy saw it and begged it of him. The bookbinder who
subsequently bound it damaged the manuscript still farther by
paring it. The manuscript is very late, but an important wit-
ness to otherwise lost pieces, including The Boy and the
Mantle and John the Reeve in the present volume. The version
of Jack and his Stepdame preserved in it is relatively unim-
portant, being simply a transcription of a printed text very
closely related to A and F. The manuscript remained in the
hands of the Isted family, descendants of Percy's daughter
Barbara, from 1798, when Percy entrusted it to her for safe-
keeping, until the mid-1860's, when it was sold to the
British Museum.

The full leaves of the manuscript are 13.5 cm. wide by
39 long. The writing now fills the page from top to bottom,
but is only 8 cm. wide. Originally the manuscript was folded
across the middle, and many leaves have split on the fold. A
number of the halves are missing from the beginning; the
remaining fragments are window-mounted on long sheets. Of the
original manuscript, there remain 29 short leaves, 4 scraps,
and 228 long leaves. Every page has been numbered as a folio
in the upper right-hand corner: for example, "fol. 195" is
given its own number, but is really just the verso of the page
numbered "fol. 194." A modern hand has renumbered each leaf,
starting with the blank f. 1[a]. Catchwords appear irregular-
ly, as often on the recto as on the verso of a folio. The
paper has a pot watermark, very common to English paper of the
seventeenth century; a clear example can be seen on ff. 121-2.

The poems of the manuscript are too numerous to be listed
here. They are printed by J.W. Hales and F.J. Furnivall,
eds., Bishop Percy's Folio Manuscript: Ballads and Romances,
3 vols. (London; Trübner and Co., 1968), with an extra volume
printed by the editor, F.J. Furnivall, Bishop Percy's Folio
Manuscript: Loose and Humorous Songs (London, 1868). The
Friar and the Boy is in the latter.

The Printed Texts

C: Wynkyn de Worde

The de Worde edition is article Sel. 5. 21 in the
Cambridge University Library, STC 14522. It was formerly
AB. 4. 58[22], one of twenty-six chapbooks (those that are
dated run from 1496-1511) bound together in a single volume.
The poem is headed "Here begynneth a mery geste of the frere/
and the boye" and bears the colophon, "Thus endeth the frere
and y[e] boye. Enpryn/ted at London in Fletestrete at the sygne
of/the sonne by Wynkyn de Worde." The edition is tentatively
dated 1510-13 by the condition of the de Worde device, which
appears below the colophon. The book is in quarto gathered
in eight, Ai-iii, [iv-viii]. There is no pagination or
catchwords. The paper has no visible watermarks. The leaves
are 17.5 cm. by 12.5, with a print block of 15.5 by 7.5,
including the signature line; there are thirty-two lines of
poetry per page, and the lines are not grouped by stanza. A
woodcut of the friar in the bush and the boy piping to him
appears below the heading of f. Aia (number 876 and fig. 96
in Edward Hodnett, English Woodcuts 1480-1535, 2nd ed.
[Oxford: Oxford University Press, 1973]). It is about 8.5 cm.
by 5.5.

C was acquired by the Cambridge University Library in
1715, as part of the collection of John Moore, Bishop of Ely
(see E above). The twenty-six chapbooks in the group were
probably bound together while in the bishop's possession.
Several owners' names appear on more than one chapbook in the
collection; so it is probable that Moore acquired at least
part of the group as a group. The following are the twenty-
six items: Nychodemus gospell (de Worde, 1509) STC 18566;
The Castell of Laboure [Pierre Gringoire] (London: de Worde,
1506) STC 12381; The remors of conscyence [W. Lichfield's
Complaint of God (de Worde, c. 1510)] STC 20881.3; The abbaye
of the Holy Ghost (Westmestre: de Worde [c. 1496?]) STC 13609;
The lamentacyon of our Lady (London: de Worde [1509-10?])
STC 17537; A ryght profytable treatyse ... to dyspose men to
be vertuously occupyed (n.p., n.d.); Ars moryendi (London: de
Worde, 1506) STC 788; The meditacyons of saynt Barnard
(Westmester: de Worde, Mar. IX, 1496) STC 1917; The bowge of
courte [John Skelton] (London: de Worde [c. 1510]) STC
22597.5; The Parlyament of devylles (de Worde, 1509) STC
19305; A treatyse agaynst pestelence, by the Bishop of
Arunensis, Denmark (de Worde [c. 1510?]) STC 4592 and 24235;
Stans puer ad mensam (London: de Worde [c. 1510?]) STC

17030.5; A treatise of husbondry by "Bishop Groshede"
[actually by Walter of Henley] ([London: de Worde, c. 1510])
STC 25007; Robert the devyll (de Worde [1500?]) STC 21070;
Jacob and his twelve sons (London: de Worde [1510?]) STC
14323.3; The proverbes of Lydgate (London: de Worde, [1510?])
STC 17026; Dystruccyon of Iherusalem by Vaspazyan and Tytus
(London, Richarde Pynson [1513?]) STC 14517; Geste of Robyn
hode (London: de Worde [before 1519]) STC 13689; The assemble
of gooddes, [John Lydgate (de Worde, c. 1500?)] STC 17006;
The boke of kervynge and sewynge (London: de Worde, 1508) STC
3289; The demandes Joyous (London: de Worde, 1511) STC 6573;
The frere and the boye (London: de Worde [1510-13?]) STC
14522; How the plowman lerned his pater noster [de Worde,
1510?] STC 20034; The chorle and the byrde [John Lydgate]
(London: de Worde [1510?]) STC 17012; Treatyse of the horse
the sheep and the ghoos [John Lydgate (de Worde, c. 1495?)]
STC 17020; The governall of helthe (London: de Worde [1510?])
STC 12139 and 24219.5.

The notation "by me John Cony" appears in The frere and
the boye on f. Aviib; it appears again, cancelled, in The
assemble of gooddes (f. Dv); and in Robyn hode (f. Av)
appears "By me John." Other recurrent names are those of
Edward and George Powell (Nychodemus gospel, f. Aii: "By me
Edward Powell"; Robert the Devyll, f. Avii: "Be i[t] known
vnto al men by this presente that I Edwar[d] powell"; Robyn
hode f. Evii: "George poll is my name/briche and buttocks/
kysse the same/Amen so be it/dico wobis"), and of Audery
Holman (Stans puer, f. Biv: "This is aud··· holman· booke";
Robert the Devyll, f. Cviii: "This is auderie holmans booke
till Edwarde Powell come a gaine"; Robyn hode, f. Bviiib:
Avdary Holmans booke"; and f. Evii: "By me avdery holman of
titsey." There is a Titsey in Surrey.) So a group, largely
of the more secular books in the collection, passed from John
Cony to the Powells, and then to Audrey Holman, before being
acquired by John Moore. That group included The frere and the
boye.

M: Middleton

This fragment is article C.125.dd.15(7) in the British
Library, STC 14522.5. There are four loose leaves, 13.5 cm.
by 19, with a print block 8.5 cm. by 15.5, including the sig-
natures and catchwords. The ink has bled through, and there
are worm holes in the paper, made while all four sheets were

on top of one another. The sheets are signed B.i., B.ii., and B.iii., with B4 marked in pencil in a modern hand. There are thirty-two lines of poetry per page, not grouped by stanza. Catchwords appear on all but the last page. The text runs from v. 251 ("His cope and his scapulary") to the end. Part of a watermark is visible on the ragged inner margin of Bii.

The Friends of the National Library donated these leaves to the British Museum in 1950 in a group of eight sixteenth-century fragments taken from the binding of Sir Anthony Cope's Historie of two the noble capitaines of the worlde, Anniball and Scipio (Thomas Berthelet, 1548). Of the other fragments, only one is dated, and it, like Cope's Historie, was published in 1548. The Friar and the Boy was entered in the Stationers' Register to J. Waley in 1557-8, but Middleton's edition must have been published not long before. STC dates it c. 1545. The fragment of Middleton's edition bears the following colophon (damaged by worm holes): Imprynted at/ Lon[d]on in Fletestrete at the/sygne of the George next to saint/[J]ones Churche by me/[Wy]llyam Myddylton.

D: Edward Allde

Edition D is article S. Seld. d. 45 (17) in the Bodleian Library, STC 14522.7. Like C, it was originally bound with other chapbooks; in this case too there were twenty-six together. A full description of the collection and its history is given in the introduction to Dane Hew in the present volume. The poem is headed "Heer beginneth a mery Iest of/of [sic] the Frier and the Boy"; below the heading appears the same woodcut as that in C. The pages are 17.5 cm. by 12.5, with a print block of 15.5 cm. by 7.5, including the signature line, just as in C; the poetry is set thirty-two lines to a page in D as well as in C. The two editions are so closely related textually that they likely come from the same source. The leaves are signed A, Aii-iii, [Aiiii], B, Bii-iiii; and catchwords appear at the bottom of all pages except the last.

The colophon reads "Imprinted at/London at the long shop/ adioyning vnto Saint Mil/dreds Church in the/Pultrie by Edward/Alde." The Freer and the boye had been entered in the Stationers' Register to J. Allde (Edward's father John) in 1568-9. STC dates D 1584-9.

A: Edward Allde

Edition A is article Arch. A.F. 83 (7) in the Bodleian
Library, STC 14523. Like C and D, A was originally bound
with other chapbooks; there are twelve in this group. Both
D and A were printed by Edward Allde, but A is revised
throughout.

The pages are 13 cm. by 8, with a print block of 12.5
cm. by 6. The book is twelve leaves, quarto, gathered in
eight and four, signed A [1-2], 3, [4-8], B1-2, [3-4]. On
f. A1a is the woodcut from C and D of the boy piping and the
friar dancing in the bush, printed sideways on the page. The
title page is f. A2a, cropped on the right, bearing the title
"The Fryer, an[d]/the Boy" and the same woodcut (also cropped
on the right), followed by the information "London/Printed by
E.A. dwelli[ng]/neere Christ-Church/1617." F. A3a is headed
"A Mery Iest: of the/Frier and the Boy" and has a round wood-
cut, 5 cm. in diameter, of an archer shooting at another man,
while a boy behind the archer looks on and points. Below the
woodcut the poem begins. The lines are grouped by stanza on
this page only. There are twenty-eight lines of poetry to
the page. Catchwords appear throughout. There are no vis-
ible watermarks.

The books in the collection are Loues Garland, or Posies
for Rings etc. (London: Iohn Spencer, 1624) STC 16856; A New
Booke of new Conceits, Thomas Iohnson (London: E[lizabeth]
A[llde], 1630); A Description of the King and Queene of
Fayrie (London: Richard Harper, 1635); Pancharis: The first
Booke, [Hugh Holland] (London: Clement Knight, [1603]); A
True Tale of Robbin, Martine Parker ([T. Cotes, 1632?]) STC
19274.5; The Figvre of Fovre, The Second Part (London: John
Wright, 1636); The Fryer an[d] the Boy (E[dward] A[llde],
1617) STC 14523; Harry White his humour, M[artin] P[arker]
(London: Thomas Lambert, [1637]) STC 19242; Doctour Doubble
Ale (n.p., n.d.); Robin Conscience, or Conscionable Robin,
M[artin] P[arker] (London: F. Coles, 1635) STC 19266; A Booke
of Merrie Riddles (London: Robert Bird, 1631); A Banquet of
Ieasts, or Change of Cheare (London: Richard Royston, 1630).
All of these except A New Booke of new Conceits, The Figvre
of Fovre, The Fryer and the Boy, Harry White, and Robin
Conscience have the initials R.B. in them. The books were
part of a larger collection bequeathed to the Bodleian by
Robert Burton (author of the Anatomy of Melancholy) at his
death in January of 1639/40.

F: [Elizabeth] Allde, 1626

Edition F is article C.57aa.13 in the British Library, STC 14524.3. It is currently bound in deep green leather stamped in gold together with eleven leaves that have been used as a memorandum book. The memorandum pages are full of names and dates (John Sherwood his book 1651; September the :29: 1653 Receved at the hand of Richard Sherwood; Joseph Tovey ... [of] Purton ... March 27, 1757; John Tovey; Mistress Hopkins; T. Limey), but it does not seem likely that the memorandum book and The Fryer and the boy were bound together while these markings were being made. The memorandum book has many leaves with rounded corners; the printed book has none. The current binding is new-looking; perhaps the memorandum book and printed book were bound together shortly before the volume was sold to Maggs Brothers, the London book dealers. The British Museum acquired the volume in 1903 from Maggs Brothers; the dealers have no record of its origin.

The printed text has been remounted on stubs. The signatures run A[2], 3-4, [5-8], B1-2, [3-4]. F. A1 is missing, and f. B4 has been reversed: the page that is now f. B4a is a dirty blank, while the one that is now f. B4b has a woodcut. The leaves are 14 cm. by 8.5, with a print block of 12.5 cm. by 6.5. There are thirty lines of poetry to the page. Catchwords appear throughout. F. A2a bears the heading "Here beginneth/a merry Iest, of the Fryer/and the boy," followed by the old woodcut of the friar in the bush and the boy piping, and "LONDON./Printed by Edw: Allde./1626." Edward Allde's death has been dated 1624 or 1625. Presumably his widow Elizabeth printed the book, continuing to use her husband's name.

The book contains five woodcuts. The first is mentioned above. The second, on the verso of f. A2, is an 8 cm. by 7 cm. woodcut, printed sideways on the page, of a man and woman conversing within arches; it is blank in the lower middle as if something clearly unsuited to this story has been omitted. On f. A3a is the round woodcut which appears in edition A, f. A3a. F. A4a has an unframed woodcut of a young man with a stick making ripples in the water beneath him and a bull. The last page has a very worn printing of the woodcut of the friar in the bush, sideways.

Metre

Jack and his Stepdame is written in a rough accentual
metre. In each six-line stanza, the first, second, fourth,
and fifth lines usually have four stresses, the third and
sixth lines three, with varying numbers of unstressed syl-
lables. The early printed editions are somewhat revised
towards greater accentual-syllabic regularity, and the later
printed editions much more so.

The aabccb rhyme scheme is not a demanding one, but the
poet allows himself frequent licences of inexact rhyme (eg.
grete/lepe vv. 244-5). Rhymes between close and originally
open vowels are discussed under Language and Provenience,
below.

Language and Provenience

The most striking phonological peculiarity of the poem
is the rhyming of boy on words in -ay: day/boye (vv. 46-47)
and faye/boye (vv. 202-203). The debate on the phonological
history of the word boy has never satisfactorily been
resolved. Arguments by E.J. Dobson ("The Etymology and
Meaning of Boy," Medium Ævum 9 [1940], 121-54, and "Middle
English and Middle Dutch Boye," Medium Ævum 12 [1943],
71-76) have been largely over-turned by A.J. Bliss ("Three
Etymological Notes: II Boy and Toy," English and Germanic
Studies 4 [1951-52], 22-29); Bliss's arguments are in turn
denied by G.V. Smithers (in his introduction, under
"Language and Provenance," to Kyng Alisaunder, EETS 237
[1957 for 1953], 52-55). In particular, Bliss's support of
Dobson's theory that the forms bey and bay may be developed
from the normal boy, by means of a development of ME oi to
ai by unrounding of the first element of the diphthong conse-
quent on the unrounding of ME ŏ to ă exemplified in strap for
strop (Dobson, 1943, p. 76, quoted by Bliss p. 27), is under-
mined by Smithers on various grounds, including that of
chronology (what evidence there is for the unrounding of ŏ to
ă is later than the earliest occurrences of bay).

But Smithers' own observation on oi/ai rhymes that
"[t]he rhymes in question may not be phonetically exact"
(p. 54) does not give a satisfactory explanation of what is
going on in the case of boy, which is sometimes spelled bay
or bey, as well as being rhymed on words in -ay. Sixteenth-

and seventeenth-century evidence collected by Dobson (see
English Pronunciation 1500-1700, II, paragraph 256, note 1)
suggests that the minority pronunciation rhyming on day
(whether bay has a long open e, as Dobson contends, or
whether it has a diphthong) was geographically widespread.
But a combination of MED and OED citations yields only four
different medieval works using the bay or bey forms: The
Seven Sages of Rome from Essex or Middlesex, Kyng Alisaunder
from London, Promptorium Parvulorum from Norfolk, and Ludus
Coventriæ from Lincolnshire (instances from the first two
mentioned occur in rhyme). Place names in the article by
Klaus Dietz, "Mittelenglisch oi in heimischen Ortsnamen and
Personennamen: II. Das Namenelement Boi(e) und die Etymologie
von boy," Beiträge zur Namenforschung 16 (1981), 361-405,
include Bayford in Kent and Bayford in Somerset, but it is
not clear that these are related to the word boy. The unequi-
vocal Middle English instances of bay or bey for boy belong
to the East Midlands, and Jack and his Stepdame can be tenta-
tively assigned to the same region.

Other phonological features of the poem fit with this
ascription. The poem is Southumbrian, as shown by a number
of rhymes.

1) lost/durst (vv. 21, 24)

The r in durst must have assimilated to the following
s (see Jordan 166).

2) Of the past participles of strong and anomalous verbs
in rhyme--agon (v. 165), forgete (v. 200), go (v. 267), be
(v. 289), bore (v. 402)--all but the first lack northern
-(e)n, and it has the southern prefix. Mossé identifies the
past participle be as belonging to the East Midlands (p. 84).

That the poem is more southerly still is shown by the
following rhyme:

3) bowe/blowe (vv. 238-329)

South of Oakden line F bowe (from OE boȝa) and blowe (from
OE blāwan) would in most places rhyme on the diphthong /ɔU/.
In some areas--in Kent, Essex, London, the West Midlands, the
South West (see Jordan 105)--the diphthong in both words could
widen to /aU/. But north of line F the false rhyme /ɔU/au/
would result.

In an appendix to his 1940 <u>Medium Ævum</u> article, Dobson
discusses the localization of certain texts, among them <u>The
Frere and the Boy</u> (pp. 153-54). He ascribes the poem to the
Southeast Midlands, on the basis of the following features:

> a) e < OE y: <u>chere</u>/<u>fyre</u>, <u>went</u>/<u>stynte</u>,
>   <u>rente</u> pp./<u>stynte</u>
> b) The 'northern' inflexion in <u>gose</u> 'goes':
>   <u>close</u> and <u>gose</u>: <u>arose</u> and contrariwise
>   the southern plural in <u>fone</u> 'foes':
>   <u>anon</u>.

But the "southern plural" <u>fone</u> appears in the printed
texts CMD (Y80) and AFB (Z105), and not in the original ver-
sion.

The rhyme <u>chere</u> (v. 369; with /e:/, from OF <u>chiere</u>) and
<u>fyre</u> (v. 372; with /e:/ from OE $\bar{y}$ in a closed syllable) ought
to indicate origin in Kent, Sussex, Surrey, or the Southeast ·
Midlands (see Jordan 40), but it is an unreliable criterion:
" $\breve{y} > \breve{e}$ forms were often borrowed on account of the rhyme
possibility, particularly before <u>nd</u>, <u>nt</u> as in <u>kende</u>, <u>dent</u> and
<u>fēr</u> 'fire,' in the romances up into the North" (Jordan 40,
remark 1). The same unreliability is present in the -<u>nt</u>
rhymes <u>wente</u> (v. 355; with short open <u>e</u> from OE <u>wende</u>)/<u>stent</u>
(v. 356; with apparent short open <u>e</u> from OE <u>styntan</u>) and
<u>torente</u> (v. 171; with short open <u>e</u> from OE <u>rend</u>)/<u>stent</u>
(v. 174). Dobson does not mention it because it does not
occur in the printed version of the poem from which he is
working, but there is also the rhyme on <u>shet</u> (v. 153; past
participle of <u>shut</u>, from OE <u>scyttan</u>)/<u>bet</u> (v. 156; comparative
of <u>well</u>); however it cannot be taken as evidence of southeast
midland origin either. Rather than the short open <u>e</u> of <u>shet</u>
coming from OE /y/, it may simply be a case of the transition
of /I/ (in this case, from OE /y/) to a short open <u>e</u> in a
closed syllable in the vicinity of /š̆/ (see Jordan 36).
There is thus no compelling reason to place the poem as far
south as the Southeast Midlands.

A southern limit for the poem's place of origin is set
by the rhymes on the third person singular present tense forms
of verbs.

> close/goes (vv. 141, 144)
> arose/goos (vv. 205-6)

Though the -es forms do move southward during the fifteenth
century, MMW line G can be taken as a rough southern boun-
dary.

    The poem's place of origin is therefore probably within
the area of southern Lincolnshire, Central Nottinghamshire,
or West Central Derbyshire.

    The rhymes on wilt/it (vv. 88-9) and wylte/fytte (vv.
351, 354 and 412-3) are probably not of dialectal signifi-
cance. They are comparable to the later "colloquial"
(according to Helge Kökeritz, *Shakespeare's Pronunciation*,
[New Haven: Yale University Press, 1953], p. 215) pronuncia-
tion of wilt without l presumably indicated in *Hamlet* V, i:
"Woo't weep? Woo't fight? Woo't fast? Woo't teare thy
self?/Woo't drink up Esill ...?" (Second Quarto). But the
instances here have apparently not the same centralization
of the vowel.

    There are rhymes on originally long open and long close
o, originally long open and long close e: eg., tho/do (from
OE þā, dōn; vv. 154-5), mete/cheke (from OE mete, *ceōcian;
vv. 187-8), wons/nons (wons, from OE wunian, having long
close o with northern lengthening of /U/ to /o:/ in an open
syllable, a lengthening which extends into the Midlands
[Jordan 38], and nons having long open o from /a:/ of OE
þan ānes). But the /o:/ of do could be shortened and arti-
ficially relengthened to rhyme with tho after the vowel shift:
see E.J. Dobson, *English Pronunciation* II, 4. Such rhymes
as the other two pairs may be dependent on raising of the
open vowels in Middle English: see Dobson, II, 121, 148.

    The poet is careful with the vowels of his rhymes, so
the rhyming pair myld/ffeld (vv. 40-1) is particularly inter-
esting. The rhyme may have been true only within a geogra-
phically restricted area: all sources but R and Q amend the
rhyme, though P retains a -y- spelling for field. The rhyme
is probably on short i. See Dobson I, 109-10, who suggests
that the sixteenth-century spelling reformer William Bullokar
(a Sussex man) rhymed child/field on short i. See also
Dobson II, 9 note 2 and paragraph 11.

    The poem's date is difficult to establish. Final e has
obviously fallen away (witness rhymes such as freke/nete at
vv. 37-8 from OE freca/neat, and wyte/ly3t at vv. 58-9, from
OE witan/lȳt), but in the Northern Midlands the process of
silencing, even after long syllables, was complete by the end
of the fourteenth century.

A <u>terminus a quo</u> of the middle of the fourteenth century
is determined by the following rhyme:

wete (inf.)/shete (inf.)   (vv. 223-4)

Original short <u>i</u> from OE <u>witan</u> has lengthened to long close
<u>e</u> in an open syllable, providing a rhyme with the long close
<u>e</u> of <u>shete</u> from OE <u>sceōtan</u>. In the Midlands, this lengthen-
ing takes place in the second half of the fourteenth century
(Jordan 26).

But a somewhat later date seems to be more likely.
Dating from vocabulary is always risky, but the rare and
obsolescent words in the poem combine to support the impres-
sion that the poem belongs to the earlier part of the fif-
teenth century. Here follows a list of some of these words
with MED citation dates for the word itself or the particular
sense used in the poem. The OED citation dates are given
where the MED ones are not yet available:

v. 167 gonne	MED gonne (3)	?c.1425
v. 272 to-rag	OED	this poem and c.1430
v. 276 harnes	MED harneis (4)	a.1328-a.1450
v. 301 benedicite	MED (1b)	c.1300-a.1475
v. 303 (without) stryff	OED strife (2c)	1297-c.1407
v. 327 lettinge	MED letting(e (5b)	c.1330-a.1450
v. 330 sprynge	OED sb^2(1)	c.1384 and c.1460

Spelling <u>and</u> Scribal <u>Language</u>

Only the language of the four early manuscripts, R, Q,
P, and E will be discussed.

R

Manuscript R, as the copy-text, is the first to be con-
sidered here. Two scribes are responsible for <u>Jack and his
Stepdame</u> in this manuscript, presumably with the main scribe
having written out the whole poem and the other having
replaced the first leaf, up to line 58, after it became lost
from the gathering.

The most striking spelling characteristic of the scribe
of the first leaf is his tendency to double final consonants

after a short vowel (eg., Nott, v. 19; yett, v. 21; evill,
v. 22) and to double f after even a long vowel (eg., liff,
v. 4; wyff, v. 10 and elsewhere). He uses þ rarely (þe,
v. 17) and ʒ not at all.

   The main scribe on the whole uses Southumbrian forms:
the dropping of h- in oste (v. 283; see Jordan 293); the
silencing of the palatal fricative before final t indicated
by the inverse spelling in lyʒt(e) (from OE lȳt, vv. 59 and
226; see Jordan 295); such spellings as londe (v. 211), hond
(v. 343), bond (v. 344) for which Oakden's line D is a nor-
thern limit; and the use of the grapheme e to represent
etymological short i in a closed syllable in such words as
hes (v. 424), yeftis (v. 104), and yef (v. 122) (Jordan 36,
271). An origin still farther south is indicated by the con-
sistent use of hem for the third person plural accusative
pronoun (vv. 101, 125, 150, 152) and even once of her for the
third person plural possessive (v. 371). The one use of
theym (v. 4) comes early in the poem, in the other scribe's
section; it may represent the form in the exemplar used by
that scribe, who later (v. 42) uses hem too. MMW line E sets
a northern limit for the use of hem.

   The scribe's habitual form for the third person indica-
tive present tense of verbs is -yth (-ith) or sometimes -eth,
eg., gewyth (v. 115), lokyth (v. 118), aylith (v. 220), and
stareth (v. 117). These forms merely confirm that the
scribe's spelling is rather southerly than northerly.

   The replacement of v by w (and inversely, of w by v) in
syllable initial position in gewyth (v. 115), sewyn (v. 414),
and vent (v. 208) helps to locate the scribe in the east.
According to Jordan (300), "[t]he phenomenon includes chiefly
the SEML northwards to Norfolk, however, according to the
evidence of the present dialects it spread also through Kent
and east Sussex ('the land of wee') and the older vulgar
speech." The principal scribe, then, apparently came from an
area somewhat to the south of the poem's place of origin; the
scribe responsible for filling in the first leaf would likely
have been working in the same area as the other scribe.

   The scribe's use of her for the third person plural pos-
sessive dates the manuscript as no later than the end of the
fifteenth century: the last citations in OED are there dated
in the 1480's, those in MED, ante 1500.

Q

As for manuscript Q, with its late date and certain ascription to Richard Hill, born in Hertfordshire and resident of London in the early sixteenth century, the spelling is of no interest in localizing the manuscript. However, it is of interest to note the instances in which even an early sixteenth-century manuscript retains some of the fifteenth-century London forms mapped out by M.L. Samuels in "Some Applications of Middle English Dialectology," English Studies 44 (1963), 81-94, notably myche (vv. 23, 189, 198; see Samuels map 5) and sigh (v. 55; cf. Samuels' si3 or sih as opposed to saw, sey and other forms of the past tense of to see, map 10).

Hill uses the initial ff- consistently, with no attempt to reserve it for capitals, and he also uses it frequently in final position, even after long vowels: lyff (v. 4), wyffes (v. 8), wyff (v. 10). He does not necessarily use final e to mark long vowels: eg., wyne (for win, v. 36). He uses neither 3 nor þ, but makes frequent use of y in abbreviations.

Hill's usual spellings of field--ffylde (v. 41), ffild (v. 48), and ffilde (v. 206)--suggest that the poem's rhyme on mild/field at vv. 40-1 is for him a true rhyme, probably on short i.

P

The spellings and forms in manuscript P of Jack and his Stepdame are mixed in character. The frequent presence of the third person plural pronouns hem (eg., vv. 150, 152, 161) and her (eg., vv. 371, 425, P10) clearly indicate an origin south and west of MMW line E. If we could put equal faith in the scribal origin of three -ys forms in the third person singular of verbs (v. 220 aylys, v. 222 menys, v. 290 thenkys), the language would be established as north of MMW line G, and thus restricted to the Northwest Midlands. However, the more usual verb form is -yth (eg., v. 39 slepyth, v. 122 lokyþe, v. 221 faryþe), and it is entirely possible that the -ys forms are remnants of the north midland origin of the poem itself, or some previous exemplar. There is a great deal of evidence that the writing is Southumbrian: the non-northern form alyche (v. 87); past participles such as be

(vv. 165, 168, 292) and <u>bore</u> (v. 366); deletion of initial <u>h</u>
in <u>arnes</u> (v. 276) and <u>oste</u> (v. 283), as well as <u>wych</u> and <u>wer</u>
(for <u>which</u> and <u>where</u>; vv. 86 and 289), with inverse <u>whent</u>
(for <u>went</u>; v. 385)--see Jordan 293. On the other hand, there
are northern forms such as <u>ar</u> (v. 149, for the third person
plural present tense of <u>to be</u>), and <u>gyfe</u> (v. 79; the past
participle of <u>to give</u>, with apparent northerly devoicing of
/v/ brought into final position [see Jordan 217]. But /v/
could be brought into final position only in the non-
northern form of the past participle without final -<u>en</u>;
perhaps <u>gyfe</u> is north midland.) <u>Sete</u> for <u>shet</u> (v. 143; the
past participle of <u>to shut</u>) is more likely a slip than rela-
ted to the phenomenon of development of /š/ to /s/ in
unstressed syllables north of MMW line C. The scribe is
probably simply retaining enough of the language of an
already mixed exemplar to obscure his own dialect. It is
worth noting, however, that like the Lancashire scribes of
<u>The Lady Prioress</u> and manuscript E of this poem, the scribe
of P sometimes doubles final <u>t</u> after long stressed <u>e</u>, perhaps
indicating shortening in a closed syllable (Jordan 27):
<u>mette</u> (v. 18; for <u>meat</u>), <u>ette</u> (vv. 59, 74; for <u>eat</u>).

The scribe prefers the grapheme <u>y</u> to <u>i</u>. He uses both
<u>þ</u> and <u>ȝ</u>, as well as the combination <u>sch-</u>.

The scribe's use of <u>her</u> for the third person plural
possessive gives a <u>terminus ad quem</u> of the end of the fif-
teenth century, as in the case of manuscript R.

E

Manuscript E has a great number of distinctive spellings.
In a number of features the writing is akin to the language
of <u>The Lady Prioress</u>. Most prominent of these is the neutral-
izing of short <u>i</u> to short <u>e</u> in a closed syllable, a feature
which is doubtless exaggerated by this scribe's refusal to
use the grapheme <u>i</u>: eg. <u>lesten</u> v. 5, <u>fferst</u> v. 10, <u>hes</u> vv. 13,
14 and <u>passim</u>, and many others. This feature is Southumbrian
(Jordan 36 and 271). The presence of intrusive <u>h-</u> in such
words as <u>hewyll</u> (for <u>evil</u>, v. 22) and <u>het</u> (for <u>it</u>, twice in
v. 55) points to a Southumbrian silencing of initial <u>h</u>
(Jordan 293) also present in the writing of <u>The Lady Prioress</u>.
Another dialectally criterial similarity is the substitution
of <u>w</u> for <u>v</u>--for example, in <u>hewyll</u> (v. 22) and <u>lowys</u> (v. 58)--
which is an inverse of the northerly substitution of <u>v</u> for
<u>w</u> (Jordan 163). Jordan gives examples as far south as

Lancashire. Like The Lady Prioress, the E transcription also
uses the -ys ending for the third person singular present
tense form of verbs, eg., kepys (v. 38), sclepys (v. 39),
lowys (v. 58). The rough southern boundary for this form is
MMW line G. But the scribe's origin must be more northerly
still, as shown by his use of the spellings f and ff to rep-
resent devoiced /v/ brought into final position by the early
northerly silencing of final -e: to gyffe (v. 69), [to] gefe
(v. 80), we haffe (v. 38). Such devoicing reaches as far as
Lancashire, according to Jordan (217). The scribe also shows
the west midland devoicing of /d/ after /n/ in a stressed
syllable in tent (for to tend, v. 6). All of these are fea-
tures which pointed to the south Lancashire origin of scribe
and poet of The Lady Prioress, and they point to the same
origin for the scribe of E.

   Another striking feature of this scribe's writing, which
serves to confirm his western and Southumbrian origin, is his
indication of a rising diphthong at the beginning of words
with initial open or close long e or o: eg., wolde (vv. 62,
67, 73, etc.), yet (for ate, v. 77), wother (vv. 248, 252),
wost (for host, v. 283), yeuer (vv. 351, 355), yether
(v. 389), yeke (v. 399), and inverse spellings such as eyr
(for year, v. 414). Jordan (283) gives examples as far north
as southern Lancashire.

   The scribe's use of intrusive -e- (or -y-) in fforet
(for forth, vv. 52, 54, etc.) and particularly in words end-
ing in -n or -nd such as towyn (v. 139), toren (v. 273),
sclayen (v. 308) and sowend (v. 140) is comparable to the
similar phenomenon in the writing of the principal scribe of
The Lady Prioress. The doubled -t in the spelling mett (for
meat, v. 68) probably indicates a shortening of the vowel in
a closed syllable (Jordan 27) as it does for the scribe of
The Lady Prioress.

   The E scribe often uses final t instead of th--soyt
(vv. 32, 64, 66 etc.), fforet (v. 54), thenkyt (v. 290)--and
inversely, -th for -t--reythe (v. 96), awth (v. 115), meythe
(vv. 120, 130), neythe (v. 131), etc. Perhaps these spell-
ings indicate a late very highly aspirated pronunciation of
final t.

   Surprisingly, the velar and palatal fricatives have
clearly silenced in bowth (v. 59), awth (v. 115), thowt
(v. 237), reythe (v. 96), meythe (vv. 120, 130), neythe
(v. 131). Such a silencing is not to be expected so far

north in the West Midlands, if we are to believe Jordan (294, 295), but cf. The Lady Prioress lyght/quyt (vv. 167, 171).

Probably the most idiosyncratic of the scribe's spellings are bow (vv. 26, 82 etc.) and bowy (vv. 91, 112), and once even woy (v. 172) for boy. He also uses the spelling boy, particularly towards the end of the poem.

The scribe simply does not use the grapheme i (except in the single dubious case of the past participle isatte (v. 145), and so his spelling appears odder than it might. He uses the combination ey consistently to represent a usual long i (eg., leyffe, v. 4, and keynde, v. 12a), but also sometimes in the place of short i (eg., dreynke, v. 18, leytell, v. 47), though short i usually yields e in his writing, and probably in his speech. The ey for historical long i perhaps is a means of representing the diphthongizing of the vowel. But it is interesting to note that Gillis Kristennson (A Survey of Middle English Dialects, 1290-1350: The Six Northern Counties and Lincolnshire, Lund Studies in English 35 [Lund: Gleerup, 1967]) reports the spelling Feynkhale for Finchale, Durham in 1313, Finchale being the very place where Richard Caly, the owner (and probably scribe) of the manuscript was prior in 1527. Kristennson suggests that the spelling is a "compromise" (p. 75), presumably meaning by his remark that since one usual representation of i lengthened to long e in an open syllable was the spelling -ey-, the same spelling might well be extended to i that remained short. The 1313 spelling with -ey- is of course far too early to represent diphthongization.

Very rare more northerly spellings (deys for does, v. 189, sare for sore v. 157) suggest an origin north of Oakden's line B (the boundary for the fronting of /o:/ was probably the same as the /a:/ɔ:/boundary; see Jordan 54). Perhaps these spellings represent the influence of Caly's Durham dwelling place, or perhaps that of a northern exemplar.

As mentioned above, Caly never uses i, and often he neglects the obvious alternative, y. Only rarely does he use ȝ. He uses þ as well as th, sch- for /š/, and often sc- for /s/. Once he even uses -sc- for usual /š/--bescrow (v. E69)-- and once sch- for usual /s/--schorow (v. 177). He sometimes uses the unstressed form a for he (vv. 255, 260) and also for have (v. 308).

The manuscript and therefore its language can be dated as belonging to the early sixteenth century on external grounds (see Section E, under Texts, above).

Editorial Treatment

     R is the copytext: its spelling is easy and it requires
less emendation than the others. But there are only two lines
in the entire poem on which all of the versions agree (vv. 15
and 301). I have not indicated deviations from R with square
brackets in the text, in part because to do so would imply
that R has more authority where it is not emended than it
does have. Readers should assume that no reading is attested
by R until they have checked the textual notes.

     In the textual notes, an entry begins and ends with words
agreeing with those in the text, whenever the disagreement is
less than a full line. Thus v. 55, "When he saw it was bad"
has the note, "was so bad RAFB": in v. 55, RAFB read "When he
saw it was so bad." Often slight variations are indicated in
parentheses. At v. 60, the text reads "Tyl ny3t þat I come
home." The note "that he (came home C), (home came D) CD"
indicates that C and D have the slightly differing readings
"Till night that he came home" and "Till night that he home
came." But at v. 83, the note "It is best (that) I have a
bowe (C)D" shows that C reads "It is best that I have a bowe,"
while D has only "It is best I have a bowe." Occasionally
where there is danger of ambiguity, a slash mark is used to
indicate the beginning or ending of a line in the note.
Whereas v. 130 reads "Allmy3ty God þat best may," the note
"/God that moost best may CD" shows that in CD the first word
of the line is "God" and not "Almighty," despite the upper
case G. A notation such as "E blank" at v. 108 indicates
that E does not have a version of v. 108.

     The spelling of the text is that of R; the spelling of
the notes is that of the first manuscript or text listed after
the variant reading. Punctuation is not given in the notes,
and upper case letters are retained only when they correspond
with modern usage. In the text itself, punctuation, word
division, and capitalization are editorial. Expanded con-
tractions are underlined in the notes, but not in the text.
Abbreviations for and have not been expanded in the notes to
this poem.

The Tale of Jack and his Stepdame

God that died for vs all

And drank both eysell and gall

Bring vs oute of bale,

And graunt theym good liff and long

5 That woll listyn to my song

And tend to my tale.

Textual notes: Title: Expleycet [sic] the cheylde & hes stepdame E; Jak & his stepdame & of the ffrere Q; Here begynneth a mery geste of (of) the frere and the boye C(D[sic]) F; A Mery Iest of the Frier & the Boy A; Ffryar and Boye B; no title RP; 1 That God AFB, [R: beginning of f. 52a; Q: beginning of f. 98a; P: beginning of f. 139a; E: beginning of f. 6b; C: f. Aia; D: f. Aia; A: f. A3a; F: f. A3a; B: beginning of p. 97]; 2 both vineger and AFB, drank aysell QE; 3 Bring theym ovte R, He bryng vs all oute off bale P, Kepe yow owt of blame E; 4 liffe long R, And gyve hym P, And gyue them CD, And giue them bothe good AFB; 5 lystyn vnto my Q, woll attend to P, That lysteneth CD, Which listen doe vnto my AFB, to song [sic] E; 6 tende vnto my Q, And herkyn on to P, Or tendeth to CD, Or tend vnto my AFB;

Ther dwelt a man in my contre

The which had wyves thre

In processe of tyme.

10 By the ffyrst wyff a child he had

The which was a propre lad

And an happy hyne.

Hys ffader loved hym well;

So did his stepdame neuer a dele--

15 I tell you as I think.

All she thought lost, by the rode,

That did þe boy any good

Of mete oþer of drynk.

7 Ther was a RQE, man of my Q, dwelled an husbonde CD, in
thes contre E; 8 Which had R, which weddid wyffes Q, That had
ECD, Which in his life had AFB; 9 of certyn tyme P, By pro-
cess ECD, A blessing full of ioy AFB; 10 By hys P, a son he
ECDAF, a sonne he AFB; 11 Which R, That was a hapey ladde E,
That was a good sturdy ladde CD, Which was a pretty sturdy
lad AFB; 12 happy iuvyn Q, a hasty hyne R, And ryght an P, a
partey heynde E, A good vnhappy boy AFB; 12a Corteyse he was
& keynde E *only*; 13 & his P, Ffor soth his Q, hym ryght well
P, him passing well F, [A: *beginning of f. A3b*]; 14 And his
moder neuer R, his stepmoder never Q, Hys steppe dame lovyd
hym neuer a dell P, Bot hes E, his moder neuer CD, But his
stepmother neuer AFB; 15 [F: *beginning of f. A3b*]; 16 thought
by R, Sche thowth E, She thoght hyt lost P, thought was lost
CD, All things she AFB; 17 (Of) all that euer did hym good
(R)P, the lytell boye CD, Which to the boy did any AFB; 18
mete or of R, mete or elles of Q, Ayder met or ED, Other
mete or C, As either meat or drink AFB;

Nott half inough therof he had

20 And forsoth it was right bad,

And yett she thought it lost.

Therfor evill mott she fare,

Ffor ofte she did hym much care

As farforth as she durst.

20 And yett forsoth R, And ȝyt in faybe hit was full bad P,
[P: *beginning of f. 139b*]; ECDABF *reverse lines 19-20*:

And yet forsoyt yt was badde

Not halffe ynowh ber of he hadde

19 yet ywys it was but badde CDAFB, [CD: *beginning of f. Aib*];
20 Nor halfe AFB, And therof not halfe ynough he had CD; Q
has the same order as PR, *but within a reversal of the two
halves of the stanza*:

Therefore evill mote she fare

Ffor ofte she dide hym myche care

As fferre forth as she durste

Not half ynowgh yerof he had

& ffor soth it was right bade

& yet she thowght it loste

21 Yett she R, And all hyr thoght yt lost P, Oft he was a
fforst E, But euermore (of) the worste (CD)AFB; 22 Y pray god
evyll P, Hes dame hewyll E, And therefore euill might she
AFB; 23 Ofte sche ded the boy car E, For euer she dyde the
lytell boye care CD, (That AB), (Which F) did the little boy
such care AFB; 24 As ffer as E, So farre forth AF, Soo forth
B;

25   The goodwiff to her husband gan say,

     "Sir, ye moste putt this boye away,

     I rede you in haste.

     In fayth it is a shrewed lad;

     I wold some other man hym had

30   That wold hym better chaste."

     The goodman answered agayn

     And said, "Dame, I shall thee sayn,

     He is butt yong of age.

     He shall abide with me þis yere

35   Till he be more strenger

     To wynne better wage.

25 To her husbond gan sche say E, Unto the man the wife gan
say AFB; 26 Ffor to putt RP, a way þys boy P, Poot thes bow
a wey E, I wolde ye wolde put CD, I would (you'd AF), (you
wold B) put AFB; 27 And that ryght soone in haste CDAFB,
That thow hast her E, Y hold yt for þe beste P; 28 Ffor in
R, fayth he hys a leþer lade P, Y wes het ys a corsed lade E,
Truly he is a cursed ladde CDAFB; 29 som man E; 30 better
chaystyse E, That could him D, þat beter myȝt hym chaste P;
31 answered her agayn Q; Than anon spake þe good man P, Than
be spake the god man E, Than sayd the good man agayne CD,
Then said the good-man dame not so AFB, [R: *beginning of f.*
52b]; 32 And to hys wyff sayd he than P, Ffor soyt he seyde
dam E, Dame I shall to thee sayne CD, I will not let the
young boy goe AFB; 33 ys to yong E, but tender of CDAFB; 34
me a yere R, schall beyde with me thes they [*sic*] yer E,
shall be with vs lenger P, shall with me this yeare abide AF,
shall this yeere with me abyde B, [E: *beginning of f. 7a*];
35 Tyll þat he P, be strenger RP, be of mor powyr E, be growne
more strong and tride AFB; 36 wyne hym better Q, wages E,
For to CDAFB;

"We haue a man, a strong freke,

Which kepyth in the feld our nete,

And slepith half the day.

40 He shall com home, by Mary myld;

The boy shall into the ffeld

And kepe hem if he may."

The goodwiff was glad verament

And thereto sone she assent

45 And said, "It is best."

Vpon the morowe when it was day

Fforth went the litell boye:

To the ffeld he was ffull preste.

37 a gret freke E, a stoute freke CD, a sturdy lout AFB;
38 kepyth on the R, þe wyche on fyld kypyþe owr nette P,
That ys yn ffelde kepys howr net E, That in the felde kepeth
our nete CD, keepeth our neat the fields about AFB; 39 He
sclepys all the E, Slepynge all the CD, sleepeth all the
AFB, [P: *beginning of f. 140a*]; 40 hom sa god me schelde EC,
home as God mee sheeld DAFB; 41 And the ECDAFB, shall go yn
to E, shall forth in to Q, And to þe fylde schall go þe
chyld P, [A: *beginning of f. A4a*]; 42 them yf I may Q, To
kepe AFB, To kepe the bestes ther E, To kepe our beestes yf
CD; 43 glad & well ament Q, þe wyff was not glad varamente P,
The <y> weyffe seyde verement E, Than sayd the wyfe (in)
verament CD(AFB); therto she gaff sone her assent Q, Nere þe
les þer to sche a sente P, Ser ther to y a sent E, Therto
soone I assent CD, Husband thereto I giue concent AFB; 45
said so it Q, sir þat ys P, Y halde het be the best E, For
that me thynketh moost nedy CD, For that I thinke it neede
AFB, [F: *beginning of f. A4a*]; 46 Erly yn þe P, On the ECDAFB;
47 Ffurþe than went P, The leytell boy toke the wey E, The
lytell boye wente on his waye CDAFB; 48 was preste R, ffeld
foll E, felde full redy CD, Vnto the field with speed AFB;

Vpon his bak he bare his staff.

50 Of no man he ne gaff:

He was mery inowgh.

He went forth, the soth to sayn,

Till he com to þe playn.

His dynner fforth he drewe.

55 When he sawe it was bad

Ffull lytill lust therto he had

And putt it vp anon.

Be Cryst, he was nott to wyte.

He seyde, "I will ete but ly3te

60 Tyl ny3t þat I come home."

49 hes scholder he cast hes E, Of no man ryght no3t he gaffe
P, Of no man he had (no) care (C)D, Of no man he tooke any
care AFB; 50 man no force he gaff Q, Vppon hys schulder he
bare his stafe P, But sange hey howe away the mare CDAFB; 51
þe boy was P, All glad he was y now E, And made ioy inough
CD, Much mirth he did pursue AFB, [CD: *beginning of f. Aiia*];
52 Ffurth he went (as y 3ow sayn P), (þe soyt to say E),
(truly to sayne CD), (with might and maine AFB) PECDAFB; 53
com on··playn R [*blotted*], com in to þe P, cam on a playne E,
Untill he came vnto the plaine AFB; 54 dynner·······drewe R
[*blotted*], fforet he bar E, Where he his dinner drew AFB; 55
was so bad RAFB, sawe þat yt P, he het saw E, was but bad CD,
But when AFB; 56 Lytill RP, Leytell gey ther of he hade E,
little list thereto AFB, [Q: *beginning of f. 98b*]; 57 He put
P, But put it (vp agayne CD), (vp from sight A), (from sight
B), (vp from light F) CDAFB; 58 Therfore he CD, I wysse he P,
In feyth he Q, nott for to R, not wite Q, not moche to wyte P,
He seyde mey dame lowys me not E, Saying he had no list to
tast AFB, [P: *beginning of f. 140b*]; 59 but a lyte R, And sayd
P, sayd he wold ette PCD, Be god that me der bowth E, But that
his hunger still should last AFB, [R: *beginning of f. 53a*]; 60
Tyll evyn þat he com hom P, that he (came home C), (home came
D) CD, Till he came home at night AFB, Thes ys a bar bonne E;

Vppon an hill he hym set.

An olde man þerwith he met,

Cam walkyng be the wey.

He seide, "God spede, good son."

65 The boye said, "Sir, ye be welcome,

The sothe you for to saye."

The olde man was anhungrid sore

And sayde, "Hast þou any mete in store

That þou mayst geve me?"

70 The boye seide, "So God me save,

Thow shalt se suche as I haue,

And welcome shalt þou be."

61 Vpon the hyll he down satt Q, And as the boye sate on a
hyll CDAFB; 62 & an old man yer he Q, man sone after he P,
man with hem met E, man came hym tyll CD, There came an old
man him vntill AFB; 63 Com walkyng Q, Com oyer [sic]
walkyng E, Walkynge CD, Was walking AFB, [F: beginning of
f. A4b]; 64 good sir R, God sped he sayd good sone P, Good
spede god son the soyt to say E, Sone he sayd god the se
CDAFB; 65 He seide sir welcome R, said sir welcome Q, Sir he
sayd 3e be ry3te welcom· [hole in MS] P, Sir he sayde welcom
<þe mey ffey> E, Syr welcome mote ye be CD, Now welcome
Father may (ye AF), (you B) be AFB; 66 sothe for RQ, <the
soyt to say> E, The lytell boye gan saye CDAFB; 67 was
hungrid R, olde <v> was [sic] Q, man seyde y hongar sor EDAFB,
man sayd I am anhongred sore C; 68 sayde son hast R, He sayde
son hast Q, mete astore R,/Hast thou ECD, Then hast thow AFB,
[E: beginning of f. 7b]; 69 geve to me QD, Ffor to gyffe me
E, Which thou mightst giue to me AFB, [A: beginning of f.
A4b]; 70 boy sware so god hym save Q, The cheylde seyde ECD,
The childe repli'de so AFB, Sir he sayd so P; 71 schalt haffe
seche E, To soche (vytayllys as PD), (vytayle as C), (poore
victuals as AFB) PCDAFB; 72 (Right AFB) well com (schalt E),
(shall CDAFB) ye be ECDAFB, Þou art wolcom to me P;

He toke hym suche as he had
And bad him ete and be glad
75   And seide, "Welcome trewly."
The olde man was full good to pleise:
He ete and made him well at eise,
And sayde, "Sonne, gramarcy.

"Ffor þis mete þow hast geve me
80   I shall gyffe þe gyftes thre
That shall not be forgete."
The boye sayde, "As I trowe,
It were best I hadde a bowe
Byrdys for to shete."

73 The lytill boye gaffe hym R, The boye gaff hym Q, (Therof)
the wolde man was gladde E(CD), Of this the olde man was full
glad AFB, [B: *beginning of p. 98*]; 74 & mak hym glad Q, And
than toke seche as he hadde P, The boye drewe forth suche as
he had CDAFB; 75 welcom ȝe be P, And made hem ryght merey E,
sayd do gladly CD, said goe to gladly AFB, 76 man for to
[*sic*] R, was glad to Q, was yeffte to [*sic*] E, was easy to
CD, man easie was to AFB; 77 & yade hem [*sic*] E, him at R,
made himselfe at AFB, [P: *beginning of f. 141a*]; 78 sayde sir
gramarcy RQ, Garamersy sone sayd he P, He seyde son god
amarsey E, Saying sonne (gramercy AF), (god amercye B) AFB;
79 Ffor þe mete R, this thow Q, Ffor they mete þat þou E,
Sone (he said) thou hast gyuen mete to me CD(AFB); 80 gyffe
ye R, shall þe gyve P, shall the gyue thynges thre C, thee
things three D, And I will giue three things to thee AFB; 81
Thow schalt hem (not E), (neuer CD) fforgett ECD, What ere
thou wilt intreat AFB; 82 seyde het ys best y trow E, Than
sayd the boye (as I trowe CD), (tis best I trowe AFB) CDAFB;
83 best þat I R, Ffor me to haffe a bowe E, It is best (that)
I haue a bowe (C)D, That you bestowe on me a bowe AFB, [CD:
beginning of f. Aiib]; 84 to shote RQCD, At berdes E, With
which I birds may get AFB;

85   "Bowe and boltes þou shalt haue blyve

That shall laste þe all þi lyve

And euer alyke mete.

Shete whersoeuer þou wilt,

Thow shalt neuer fayle of it:

90   The markys þou shalte kepe."

85 and bolte R, haue ryve R, Þou schalt have a bowe &
boltes blyth P, A bowe sone I shall the gyue CD, A bowe my
sonne I will thee giue AFB, E *blank*; 86 shall serue thee Q,
þe wych schall dure þe P, (Such as AF), (The which B) shall
last while thou doe liue AFB, E *blank*; 87 And euery while
mete Q, euer to þe a lyche P, At any keyte þat þou mete R,
Was neuer bowe more fit AFB, E *blank*; 88 Loke þou kepe þi
pylt R, Shote therin whan thou (good) thynke (C)D, For if
thou shoot therin all day AFB, E *blank*; 89 fayll þou schalt
it kyll P, And shote where at þou wylt R, For yf thou shote
and wynke CD, Waking or winking or any way AFB, E *blank*; 90
markes shalt thow kepe Q, Þe pryke rydy þou P, The prycke
thou shalte hytte CD, The marke thou still shalt hit AFB, E
blank, [R: *beginning of f. 53b*];

The bowe in hand anon he felt

And put þe boltys vnder his belt.

Lowde than he lough.

He saide, "Had I now a pipe,

95   Thouh it were neuer so lite

Than were I mery inowe."

"A pipe þou shalte haue also:

Trve of mesure shall it goo,

I put þe owte of dowte.

100 All þat euer þis pipe dothe here,

They shall not hemself astere

But lepe and daunce abowte.

91 bowe anon in hand he R, hand sone he P, When the bowy the
bowe bent E, Whan he the bowe in honde felte C, (Now) when
the bowe in hande he felt D(AFB); 92 And his boltys R, ye
shaftes vnder Q, þe boltes he pot vndyr P, And the arow onder
the belt E, And the boltes CD, And arrowes had vnder A, And
had the arrowes vnder FB; 93 Ly3tely þan he drewe RQ, Ryght
meryly þan he lowe P, Ther of he lowe lowde E, (Hartily AB),
(Boldly F) he laught I wis AFB, [F: *beginning of f. A5a*]; 94
Be my troth had y a pype P, sayd now had I a CD, And said had
I a pipe withall AFB; 95 And het E, Though nere (so) little
or so small (AF)B [*sic*]; 96 I reythe merey E, I gladde ynough
CD, I then had all my wish AFB, [P: *beginning of f. 141b*];
97 pype boy þou P, peype schall thow haffe E, pype (my) sone
thou CDA(F)B, [A: *beginning of f. A5a*]; 98 Trve mesure (it
shall R), (shall it Q) goo RQ, Off trow not schall E, In
true musyke it shal go CD, (That AF), (Which B) in true
musike so shall goe AFB; 99 I do þe QE, I do the well to
wyte C; 100 euer þat pipe R, euer may it here Q, What man
þat thys P, that schall the peype her E, that may (the C),
(thy D) pype here CD, As who that liues and shall it heare
AFB; 101 hemself aftre astere R, He schall not hem selfe
stere P, Schall not (them E), (themselfe CD) ster ECD, Shall
haue no power to forbeare AFB; 102 But hope and P, But laugh
and lepe aboute CDAFB;

"Let se, what shall þat other be?

Ffor þou shalt haue yeftis thre

105 As I þe hy3t before."

The litell boye than lowde lowgh

And sayde, "Be my trowth I haue inowe;

I will desire no more."

The olde man saide, "Y þe ply3t:

110 Thow shalt haue as I þe hy3te.

Therfore sey on, let se."

The lytill boye seyde, "Be Saynt Jame,

I haue at home a steppedame;

She is a shrowe to me.

103 Say on boy what schalt [*sic*] þe oþer be P, What schall
the (thothe [*sic*] E), (thyrde CD) be ECD, Now tell me what
the third shall be AFB; 104 Gyfftys y schall gefe the iij E,
For I wyll gyue the (gyftes C), (things D) thre CD, For
three things I will giue to thee AFB; 105 As I hote þe P, y
seyde before E, As I haue sayd (to the) before (C)DAFB; 106
The boye R, boy stode & low3e P, The bow lowhe lowde E, boye
on hym lough CD, The boy then smiling answer made AB, The boy
with smiling answer saide F; 107 sayd in fayþ y P, seyde <u>sir</u>
y ECD, I haue ynough for my poore trade AFB; 108 E *blank*;
109 said to hym aply3t RQ, sayd my trouth (I CD), (is AFB)
plyght CDAFB; 110 haue þat I ECD, haue all I thee behight
AFB; 111 Sey on a non let se E, Saye on now (and) let me se
(CD)AFB; 112 seyde full sone RQ, þe boy P, The bowye seyde
<atha·> than E, Than sayd the boye anone CD, At home I haue
the boy replide AFB; 113 haue a steppemoder at home RQ, In
ffeythe y haffe a E, I haue a stepdame at home CD, A cruell
step-dame full of pride AFB, [E: *beginning of f. 8a*; Q:
beginning of f. 98 bis a]; 114 Sche ffares ffull with me E,
Who is most curst to me AFB;

115   "When my fadir gewyth me mete
      She wold þe devill wold me cheke,
      She stareth so in my face.
      When she lokyth on me so
      I wold she myght lette a rappe goo
120   That myght rynge all þe place."

      The olde man sayde to him þo,
      "Yef she loke on þe so
      She shall begynne to blow.
      All þat euer maye her heere,
125   They shall not hemself astere
      But lauȝh vpon a rowe."

115 Ffor whan P, me awth E, When meat my father giues to me
AFB, [CD: *beginning of f. Aiiia*]; 116 devill had me R, devill
schuld me P, wolde theron that I were cheke C, would therwith
that I were cheat D, Be god that me der bowth E, She wishes
poyson it might be AFB, [P: *beginning of f. 142a*]; 117 She
stare so R, stareth fast in Q, stares yn E, And stareth me in
the face CB, And stareth in DAF; 118 Now when she gazeth on
AFB, What theym sche lokys so E, 119 Yef she RQ, sche lete a
crake or too P, sche scholde let a blast go E, she sholde
(let a rappe go C), (a rap let goe DAF) CDAF, might a rapp
let goe B; 120 & rynge in all Q, (That DB), (That it C),
(Which AF) myght rynge (ouer all C), (through DAFB) the place
CDAFB; 121 sayd þe boy on too P, man answered then anon AFB,
Than sayd the olde man tho CD; 122 & yf Q, Whan sche lokyþe
on PECD, When ere she lookes thy face vpon AFB; 123 Her tayle
shall wind the horne AFB, [F: *beginning of f. A5b*]; 124 þat
maye RE, euer it may here CD, And as many as her doþe here P,
So loudly that who (shall AF), (shold B) it heare AFB; 125
shall hem not astere R, Schell not hem selffe sterre ECD,
Ffor lawyng schall they not stere P, Shall not be able to
forbeare AFB, [R: *beginning of f. 54a*; A: *beginning of
f. A5b*]; 126 Bot dans on a E, laugh on a C, laugh all on a D,
laugh her vnto scorne AFB, Whyll sche ys þere y trowe P;

"Ffarewele," saide þe olde man,

And "Ffarewele, sir," þe boye saide than,

"I take my leve of the.

130   Allmyȝty God þat best may

Spede þe both nyȝte and daye."

"Gramarcy, sone," sayde he.

Than aftyrward whan it was nyȝte

Home went þe boy full ryght

135   As was his ordinaunce.

He toke his pipe and began to blow.

Than all his bestis on a row

Abowte him gan to daunce.

127 Nowe farwell P, Fare well quod the C, So farewell sonne
the old man cride AFB; 128 /Ffare sir Q, farwell sayd þe boy
than P, Ffarwell seyde the cheylde a geyn E, God kepe (the C),
(you D) sayd the chylde than CD, God keepe you sir the boy
replide AFB, No more þan I ne can R; 129 But take R, My leve
I take of P, Y thanke mey leyffe of good & of the E, leue at
the C; 130 /God that moost best may CD, /God that (best AF),
(blest [sic] B) of all thinges may AFB, /God that ys most of
meythe E; 131 Spede yow both R, Kepe the CD, Keepe thee safe
both AFB, Saffe the bowe be the day & neythe E; 132 Gramarcy
syr sayde RQ, God amarsey seyde the bowe E; 133 Afterward P,
Then (het drow ED), (drewe it C) towarde the neythe ECD, When
it (grew AB), (drew F) neare (vpon AB), (vnto F) the night
AFB; 134 went this boye right Q, Homard he wentt reythe E,
Jacke hym hyed home ful ryght CD, Jack well prepar'd hide hom
ful right AFB; 135 This was RQ, It was CDAFB, [P: *beginning
of f. 142b*]; 136 and gan QP, And as he went his pipe did blow
AFB; 137 And all E, All CD, Hys bestes com rakyng on a rawe
P, The whilst his cattle on a row AFB; 138 him begun to R, A
bowt gan they dawnce Q, hym þey gan to daunce P, gan dance E,
hym they (can) daunce C(D);

The boye went pypyng þorow þe towne.

140   The bestes folowid him be þe sowne

Vnto his fadirs close.

Whan he had beshet hem euerychone

He went homeward anon

And into þe halle he goes.

145   His fader at sooper sat.

The litill boye spyed wele þat

And spake to him anoon.

He seyde, "Jak, welcome.

Where be my bestes, good son?

150   Hast þou brouȝte hem home?"

139 boy pypyd throwȝ P, Thos went he pypyng (thorow EC), (to
D) the towne ECD, Thus to the towne he pipt full trim AFB,
[B: *beginning of p. 99*]; 140 folowed by Q, bestes hym foloyd
all & some P, Hes bestes ECD, beestes hym folowed by C, His
skipping beastes did follow him AFB; 141 Hom to his P, In to
his CDAFB, E *blank*; 142 had them ther echone Q, had pot hem
vp yeuerychone E, He wente and put them (vp) echone (CDAF)B
[*sic*], Whan he was come home R, Anone as euer he com home P;
143 went hom sone anon E, Homewarde he wente anone CD, Which
done he homeward went anon AFB, He beshet hem euerychone R,
He shete them fast in a non Q, He sete vp hys bestes a none
P; 144 In to the QE, he dyd goe E, (In to his CD), (To's AF),
(Vnto his B) faders hall CDAFB; 145 at his souper CAFB; 146
The boye R, boy a spyed þat P, (And) lytell Jacke espyed well
CD(AFB); 147 spake to hys fader a none P, And seyed to ECDAFB,
to hem non E, [CD: *beginning of f. Aiiib*]; 148 seyde welcome
R, said siker you art welcome Q, said ffather god ye spede E,
Fader I haue kepte your nete CD, Father all day I kept your
neat AFB; 149 bestyes R, Wher ar þy bestes P, All yowr bestes
y haffe hom browte E, (At night AFB) I praye you gyue me
(some CDB) mete CDAFB; 150 þou hem broȝt hom P, (I am CDB),
(I'me AF) (an hongred CD), (hungry AFB) by saynt Jhone CDAFB,
E *blank*;

"Ye, fadir, in good faye,

I haue kepte hem all þis daye,

And now þey are vp shet."

A capons legge he toke him tho

155   And sayde, "Jak, þat is wele do.

Boy, þou shalte fare þe bet."

That grevid his dame herte sore:

Euer she was tenid more and more.

Than she starid in his face.

160   And anon she let go a blaste

That she made hem all agaste

That wer within þat place.

151 Ffader he sayd yn P, I haue sytten metelesse CD, Meatless
I haue lïen all (the AB), (this F) day ABF, E *blank*; 152 haue
hem kept all P, All this daye kepynge your beestes CD, And
kept your beasts they did not stray AFB, E *blank*; 153 are
shet R, And they be now vp P, & I haue them in ye close shett
Q, My dyner feble it was CD, My dinner was but ill AFB, E
blank, [AF: *beginning of f. A6a*]; 154 he cast to hym Q, hem
then E, His fader toke a (capons CDAF), (capon B) winge CDAFB,
[P: *beginning of f. 143a*]; 155 sayde sone þat P, that was
well Q, And at the boye he (gan CD), (did AFB) it flynge
CDAFB, E *blank*; 156 þou schalt P, And badde hym ete a pace
CD, Bidding him eat his fill AFB, E *blank*; 157 hart full sore
P, his stepmoders herte CD, This griev'd his stepdames hart
full sore AFB, Q *blank*, [E: *beginning of f. 8b*]; 158 As y
(have) told ʒow be fore (P)CD, Who loath'd the lad still more
and more AFB, QE *blank*; 159 Sche P, And stared E, She stared
hym in the face CDAFB, The goodwyff stared fast on Iak Q, [R:
beginning of f. 54b]; 160 And she R, Anone sche P, a gret
blaste R, lete a gret crake Q, let a E, With that she CDAFB,
goe such a AFB; 161 That euery man þerof was a gaste R, That
all the compeney wer agast E, That (they in the C), (all the
D) hall were agaste CD, (As AF), (That B) made the people all
agast AFB, Q *blank*; 162 That was in þat R, wer in that E, It
range ouer (all) the place (C)D, It sounded through the place
AFB, Q *blank*;

    All they lowgh and had good game.

    The wyffe wex red for shame;

165 She wolde ffayne be agon.

    Jak seide, "I wol ʒe wytte

    This gonne was wele smytte

    As it had be a stone."

163 Euer they R, Each one (did laugh AF), (laught B) and
(make A̅), (made FB) good game AFB, Q *blank*; 164 wyffe sche
wex P, weyff weppyd for E, But the curst wife grew red AFB,
red through shame F, Q *blank*; 165 wold a be agon P, And
welde be awey gone E, wold (that) she had ben gone (C)D, And
wished she had beene gone AFB, Hit range lyke a gonne Q;
166 seide wele I wote R, said well ye may witt Q, sayd wyll
ʒe wytte P, The boy seyde wyll yow wyt E, Quod the boye well
I wote CD, Pardy the boy said well I wot AFB; 167 I hope this
Q, þat gonne P, I trow þis game were wele smote R, That gonne
was well shote CD, (That A), (This F) gun was both well
chargd & shot AFB, Thes game was well <yset> schot E; 168
þough it had be a gon stone R, be of a Q, Thoʒ it had be
with a P, And het E, And might haue broke a stone AFB;

        Angerly lokid she on him þo.
170 Anoþer rappe she let goo;
        Her ars was ny torente.
        Jak seid, "Will ye se?
        My dame can let a pelet fle
        Or euer she will stent."

175 Euer þey lough and had good game.
        The wyffe went awaye for shame:
        She was in moche sorow.
        The goodman seide, "Go þi weye,
        Ffor it is tyme, be my faye:
180 Thyn arce is not to borowe."

169 Fful angerly Q, Fful egerly lokid R, Angerly sche lokyd
on P, corsedley sche lokyd on ECD(AFB); 170 An oyer ffarte
lete she goo Q, Another blast sche ECD, That looke on other
crack let goe AFB; 171 And <she> euer she a vey went R, &
ffowle she was shent Q, Sche was not well nortored E, She was
almoost rente CD, Which did a thunder raise AFB; 172 The woy
[*sic*] seyde E, Quod the boye wyll CD, Quoth the boy did you
euer see AFB, Q *blank*; 173 My moder can R, Anoþer pelat sche
wyll lete fley P, How mey E, How my dame letteth pellettes
fle CD, A woman let her pellets flee AFB, Q *blank*, [P:
beginning of f. 149b]; 174 she astent R, euer þat sche P, In
fayth or euer she stynte CD, More thick (and AB), (or F) more
at ease AFB, QE *blank*; 175 and good [*sic*] R, Euery man low3
P, All they E, The boye sayd vnto his dame CD, Fie said the
boy vnto his dame AFB, Q *blank*; 176 went hyr way P, Tempre
(thy CDAF), (your B) (tel-tale AFB) (bum DAFB), (bombe he
sayd C) for shame CDAFB, Q *blank*; 177 in mykyll sorowe P, was
ffoll of schorow ECD, Which made her full of sorrow AFB, Q
blank; 178 <Afterwar> The R, said by my lyff Q, seyde dam go
E, Dame said the goodman go CDAFB; 179 Ffor y sey be E, For I
swere to the by CD, For why I sweare by night nor day AFB, I
know not what eileth my wiff Q, [CD: *beginning of f. Aiva*];
180 not thy borowe P, They ger ys ECDAFB, not all to E, I
trowe her arse be rent Q;

Afterward þan will ye here,

To þe howse þer cam a frere

That lay þer al ny3te.

Owre dame thou3th him a saynte.

185   Anon to him she made her pleynte

And tolde hym anon ryght:

"We haue a boy þat in þis howse wons:

He is a shrew for þe nons.

He doth me moche care.

190   I dare not ons loke hym vpon.

I am ashamed, be Seynt Jhon,

To telle yow how I fare.

181 Aftir þat will R, Than after ye shall here Q, (Now AFB)
afterwerde as (ye EC), (you DAFB) (may E), (shall CDAFB) her
ECDAFB, [A: *beginning of f. A6b*; Q: *beginning of f. 98 bis b*];
182 yat hows Q, Tho in to þat howse cam R, howse cam E, Vnto
the AFB; 183 Evyn that same nyght Q, And loggyd þer P, To ley
ther ther [*sic*] all neythe E, To lye there C, all the night
D, And lay there all the night AFB, [F: *beginning of f. A6b*];
184 þe wyff lovyd hym as a seynt PECD, The wife this frier
lou'de as a saint AFB, With hym full sone she was a quaynt Q;
185 made a pleynte R,/& vnto hym Q, hym mad sche hyr P, made
complaynt E, And to hym made (her CD), (a great AFB) complaynt
CDAFB; 186 tolde to hym R, hym full ryght P, hem all a reythe
ED, hym aryght C, Of Jackes most vile despite AFB; 187 I haue
RQ, haue boye yat with vs wonnys Q, þat with vs wonnys P,
bowe yn thes howse E, boye within ywys CD, haue quoth she
within iwis AFB; 188 ys shrewed for Q, A corsed cnaffe ffor
E, A shrewe for the nones he is CD, A wicked boy none shrewder
is AFB; 189 And doþ P, Which doth me mighty care AFB, [R:
beginning of f. 55a]; 190 I may not RQ, not loke ons hym R,
hym on Q, note loke PECD, not looke vpon hys face AFB; 191 be
swet seynt P, But I haue a shame by R, But I am shamed by Q,
Or hardly tell my shamful case AFB; 192 I telle (þe R), (you
Q) how RQ, So filthily I fare AFB, [P: *beginning of f. 144a*];

"Mete hym in þe fylde tomorow.

Loke ye bete hym and do hym sorowe

195   And make þe boye lame.

Iwis it is a cursed byche.

I trow þe boye be some wycche:

He dothe me moche shame."

The frere seid, "I will wete."

200   "Y pray þe lete it not be forgete,

Ffor þat wold greve me sore."

The frere seide, "In good faye,

But I belasshe wele þat boye

Truste me neuer more."

193 And ȝyff ȝe mete þat boy to morow P, I praye you mete
the boye to morowe CD, For Gods loue meet (the AF), (this B)
boy tomorowe AFB; 194 Loke þou bete R, Bet hem E, Bete hym
well & gyve hym sorow PCDAFB; 195 make þat lad lame P, (And
AB), (Or F) make him blinde or lame AFB; 196 Be god he ys a
schrewd byche P, Quod the ffreyr y schall hem (methe E),
(bete CD) ECD, The frier swore he wold him beat AFB; 197 In
fayth y trow he be a wyche P, Sche preyed hem not forgeyt E,
Quod the wyfe do not forgete CD, The wife prayd him not to
forget AFB; 198 me mykyll grame P, Do the boy schame E, dooth
to me D, The boy did her (much AB), (such F) shame AFB;
199 Y ffeythe he ys a corsed beche E, I trowe the boye be
some wytche CD, Some witch (quoth she he is AF), (he is quoth
shee B) I smell AFB, Q blank; 200 þe sir lete P, She prayde
him not for gete R, Y holde the boy a weche E, Quod the
frere I shall hym teche CD, But quoth the frier Ile beat him
well AFB, Q blank; 201 þat will greve R, He greues me so
sore E, Haue thou (therof) no care C(D), Of that take you no
care AFB, Q blank, [E: *beginning of f. 9a*]; 202 Quod the
ffreyr & y may the boy methe [methe *raised above the line*]
bethe E, I shall hym teche yf I may CD, Ile teach him witc-
craft if I may AFB; 203 I lasshe R, y chastys well P, Y well
hem bethe bake & seyde E, Quod the wyfe I (the C), (you D)
praye CD, O quoth the wife doe so I pray AFB; 204 Do hym not
spare CD, Lay on and doe not spare AFB;

205 Vpon þe morow þe boye arose

     And forth into þe felde he goos.

     His bestis gan he dryve.

     The frere vent ovte at þe gate;

     He went he had come to late

210 And ran aftyr full ryve.

     Whan he cam into þat londe

     The lytill boye þer he founde

     Kepyng his bestis echon.

     He seide, "Boye, God gif þe shame.

215 What haste þou do to þy dame?

     Loke þou tel me anon."

205 boye rose Q, Erly in þe morow þe boy he ros P, The
cheylde on the morow roys E, On the CD, Early next (morne AF),
(morow B) the AFB; 206 Fforth Q, And into R, And ly3tly to þe
P, And to the ffelde (full) sone he goys E(AFB), Into the
felde soone he gose CD; 207 bestes he gan dryve P, bestys for
to dreyffe ECD, His cattell for to driue AFB; 208 ffrere
ffolowed after at Q, frere leppyd owt E, frere ranne out C,
frere ran out of the [sic] D, The frier (then AB) vp (as AF)
early gate AFB [B: severely cropped at top: beginning of
p. 100]; 209 wend he schuld have com P, wende to com E, He
was aferde (leest he came C), (he came D), (to come AFB) to
late CDAFB, [A: beginning of f. A7a]; 210 ran fforthe bleythe
E, (He PAB), (But F) ran (full AFB) fast & blyth PAFB, He
ranne fast and blyue Q; 211 into the lond Q, com on hye þe
lond P, cam apon (the EDA), (a C) londe ECDA, But when AFB,
came (into F), (unto B) the land FB, [CD: beginning of f.
Aivb; P: beginning of f. 144b]; 212 Sone þe boy P, Leytell
geynkyn ther E, Lytell Jacke there CD, He found where little
Jacke did stand AFB; 213 And his RQ, beasts alone AFB,
Dryuynge his beestes (all) alone (C)D, [F: beginning of f.
A7a]; 214 said you boy Q, Boy he sayd god PECD, Now boy he
said God AFB; 215 doon vnto thy D, thy step-dame AFB; 216
Haue do and tel me/R, I rede the tell Q, Tell thow me ECD,
Tell me forthwith anon AFB;

"But yf þou can escuse þe bet

Thou shalt abye: thyn ars shall be bete.

I will no lenger abyde."

220 The boye seide, "Frere, what aylith þe?

My dame farith as wele as ye.

What menys þou thus to chyde?"

217 þe þe bet R, But you Q, þe better P, Bot thow can
askowse the/E, thou (canst) excuse the well (C)D, And if
thou canst not quit thee well AFB; 218 Be my trouth þi
maroe shall R, In feyth thyn ars shall be hett Q, a bye be
þou seker P, a bey y tell the E, By my trouth (bete I the
[sic] C), (beat thee I D) wyll CD, Ile beat thee till thy
body swell AFB, [R: *beginning of f. 55b*]; 219 will not
longer B, longer bide AB, No leyngger well y a beyde E;
220 seide what R, The said [sic] Q, Yake he seyde ffreyr
withheylde the E, Sir he sayd what aylys þe nowe P, Quod the
boye what CD, The boy reply'd what AFB; 221 as thowe PE, My
stepdame is as well as (yee AF), (thee B) AFB; 221a And that
ys gret pethe E *only*; 222 Wat heyldes the to E, What nedeth
the to CD, What need you thus AFB, to clyde [sic] B, Thow
haste no cause to chyde RQ;

The boye sayde, "Will þou wete

How fele byrdis I can shete

225   And oþer thynges withall?

I trowe þough I be but ly3t

Yonder birde shall I smyte

And geve it þe I shall."

Ther sat a byrde on a brere.

230   "Shete on," quod the frere,

"That lystyth me to se."

The boye smote it on þe hede

That it felle dovne dede:

It my3te no lenger flee.

223 þou wite R, said frere wilt Q, well yow wet E, Sir he
sayd & 3e wyll wytt P, Quod the boye wyll (ye C), (you D)
wete CD, Come will you see (mine A), (my FB) arrowe fly AFB;
224 How feld byrdes Q, How well byrdes þat y P, How y can
(the berdys E), (a byrde CD) schete ECD, And hit yon small
bird in the eye AFB; 225 thynges all RQ, thynges all sco E,
other thynge withall C, And do hem down to fall P; 226 Syr he
sayd though I be lyte CD, Sir frier though I haue little wit
AFB, 3ondyr is on þat ys but lytte P, 3endyr leytyll berde
þat þou seyst set E; 227 byrde wyll I CD, As y trow y schall
hym smytt P, Y schall her schett & geff her the E, Yet yonder
bird I meane to hit AFB; 228 it to the Q, gyve hym þe P,
gyue her (to) the C(D), giue (her AF), (B a hole) you I AFB,
E blank; 229 byrd vpon a CD, a small bird (on AF), (in B) a
AFB, Þe byrd sat (vpon þe P), (on a E) breyr PE; 230 on þat
quod R, on boy sayd þe P, on boye quod CD, Shoot shoot you
wag then said the frier AFB, [P: *beginning of f. 145a*]; 231
That me luste to Q, Ffor that me (leste P), (lysteth C),
(longeth D) to se PCD, For that I long to see AFB, That wolde
y ffayne se E; 232 boy hyt þe byrd vpon þe P, He het the
berde on the ECD, Jacke hit the bird vpon the AFB; 233 dovne
þer dede R, That sche fell ECD, Yn þe hegge he fell down dede
P, So right that she fell downe (for AB), (starke F) dead
AFB; 234 no forther fley P, No fforther meythe sche ffle ECD,
No further could she (flee AB), (flye F) AFB;

235 The ffrere into þe hegge went
    And þe birde vp he hente
    As it was for to don.
    The boye leyde aside his bowe
    And tooke hys pype and began to blowe
240 Fful ly3tly and full sone.

    Whan þe frere þe pipe herde,
    As a wodman he ferde
    And began to lepe abowte.
    Amonge þe bowis smale and grete
245 Ffast abowte he gan to lepe,
    But he cowde nowhere owte.

235 hegge he went P, the bosches went E, frere to the busshe wente CD, Fast to the bush the frier went AFB; 236 And ly3tly he it vp hent P, Vp the berde ffor to hent ECD, And vp the bird in hand he hent FB; 237 Hem thowt het was well doyn E, He thought it best for to (done C), (be doon D) CD, Much wondring at the chance AFB, [B: *beginning of p. 101*; A: *beginning of f. 7b*]; 238 boy cast down hys P, boy cast a wey hes E, Ye boy to his pipe & began to blowe Q, Jacke toke his pype and began to blowe CD, Meane while Jack tooke his pipe & plaid AFB; 239 Fful hastly as I trowe RQ, Wheytley a non E, Than the frere as I trowe CD, So loud the frier grew mad apaid AFB; 240 And tooke his pype sone R, & sone he pyped thoo Q, pype a non E, Began to daunce (ful) soone C(D), And fell to skip and dance AFB; 241 But whan Q, As sone as the E, As soone as he the pype CD, (No AF), (Now B) sooner was the pipes sound heard, [E: *beginning of f. 9b*; Q: *beginning of f. 99a*]; 242 wood man than he P, a mad man he E, Lyke as a made man he Q, Lyke a CD, But Bedlamlike he (bounst AF), (boucet [*sic*] B) and far'd AFB; 243 to stertyll a bowt P, He began to lepe & dans a bowth E, He lepte and daunced aboute CD, And leapt the bush about AFB, [C: *beginning of f. Ava*; D: *beginning of f. Bia*; F: *beginning of f. A7b*]; 244 the boyschys small PE, CDAFB blank; 245 A bovte (ly3tly R), (hastely Q) gan he lepe RQ, The ffrere ffast gan leppe E, CDAFB *blank*; 246 cowde not com owte P, ECDAFB *blank*;

Bremblis cracched hym in þe face,

And eke in many anoþer place,

That his sydes began to blede.

250   He rent his clothis by and by,

His kirtill and his chapelery

And all his oþer weede.

247 Brambild [*sic*] Q, þe bramblys P, The bryres (scrat E),
(scratched CD) hem ECD, The sharpe briers (scracht AF),
(cacth [*sic*] B) him by the face AFB, [R: *beginning of f. 56a*];
248 And i̲n̲ PECD, a wother plays E, And by the breech and
other place AFB; 249 His body be gan RQ, That ffast he gan E,
That the blode brast out CD, That fast the bloud ran out
AFB, [P: *beginning of f. 145b*]; 250 And rent P, And tare his
CD, It tare his cloathes downe to the skirt AFB; 251 [*The
Middleton fragment begins here with f. Bia*], His girdill and
RQ, Hes kope & (hes) skapularey (ECM)D, His cope his coole
(and AF), (his B) linnen shirt AFB; 252 And euery other AFB;
CMDAFB *add three lines here*:

He daunced amonge thornes thycke

In many places they dyde hym prycke

That fast gan he blede

252a among the thornes CD, amonge the thorne thycke M, The
thornes this while (were AB), (was F) rough and thick AFB;
252b many a place they M, And did his priuy members prick
AFB; 252c fast he gan to bleed D, fast began to blede M,
fast they gan to bleede AFB;

The boye blewe and lewh amonge.

How þe frere lepe and wronge!

255 He hopped wonder hye.

Than sayed þe boye and sware withall,

"Be my trowth, here is a sporte ryall

Ffor a lord to se with yee."

Euer þe frere hyld up his hande

260 And cryed unto þe boye amonge

And prayed hym to be stylle:

"And here my trowth I ply3te to þe,

Þou shalte haue no harme for me:

I will do þe non ylle."

253 Euer þe R, boy lowhe & blew a monge E, Jacke pyped and
CMD, Jack as he piped laught AFB, P *blank*; 245 & wownd Q,
The ffreyr lepyd yn the bosches þuys E, The frere (amonge the
CM), (in the D) thornes was (thronge CD), (brought M) CMD,
The frier with bryers was vildly stung AFB, P *blank*; 255 &
hoppid Q, He leped wonder R, A hoppyd wonderley hey E, hopped
(wonders CD), (wonderous MAFB) hye CMDAFB, P *blank*; 256 The
boy seyde & lowhe withall E, PCMDAFB *blank*; 257 In fayth this
is Q, Thes ys E, PCMDAFB *blank*; 258 Ffor any man to RQ, to
se/E, PCMDAFB *blank*; 259 þe freyr often held P, At the last
the ffreyr leffyd op hys honde E, At the last he helde CMD,
At last the frier AFB; 260 And callid to hym amonge R, A
seyde y haffe dansed her all to longe E, And sayd I haue
daunced (to C), (so MD) longe CMD, And said I can no longer
stand AFB; 261 hym be RQ, Y prey the holde the stell E, That
I am lyke to dye CMD, Oh I shall dauncing dye AFB; 262 Her P,
here I plight my trowth to Q, Her mey trowt y pleyt the E,
Gentyll Jacke (holde thy pype CMD), (thy pipe holde AFB)
styll CMDAFB; 263 haue non harme of me Q, shalte neuer haue
harme of me R, schalt not haffe no E, And my trouth I plyght
the tyll CMD, And heere I vow for good (nor AB), (or F) ill
AFB; 264 Ffor I Q, Nor neuer wyll do þe yll P, the no woo
CMD, To do thee any woe AFB, E *blank*;

265   The boye seide yn þat tyde,

       "Crepe owte on þat oþer syde,

       And hye þe þat þou were go.

       My dame made her pleynte to þe

       And now I can non oþer se:

270   Thow must go pleyne to her also."

       The frere ovte of þe hegge wente,

       All toraged and torente

       And torne on euery syde.

       Vnneth he had any clowte

275   Ffor to wynde hys body abowte

       His harnes for to hyde.

265 seide to hym þat RQ, Jacke sayd CMD, Then seyde the boy
a non E, Jacke laughing to him thus replide AFB; 266 Than
crepe Q, on þe toþer P, owte at þe fferther seyde E, Frere
skyppe out on the (ferder C), (other MDAFB) syde CMDAFB;
267 þe þou R, hye þat þou ware a goo P, Weyt ley that E,
Lyghtly that CMD, Thou hast free leaue to go AFB; 268 made a
pleynte R, dam haþe mad hyr complaynt to P, ECMDAFB *blank*;
269 In fayth þe best þat y kan se P, ECMDAFB *blank*; 270 must
compleyne R, But you must Q, Goo P, ECMDAFB *blank*; 271 the
bossches went E, the busshe went CMD, Out of the bush the
frier then went AFB, [A: *beginning of f. A8a*]; 272 & all to
rent E, All martyrd ragged scratcht and rent AFB; 273 To
torne on P, Toren & rent on E; 274 He had not left an holl
clowte P, On neyt had he a cloyt E, (Unnethes CD), (Scantly
M) on hym (had one [*sic*] C), (he had a MD) cloute CMD,
Hardly on him was left a clout AFB, [P: *beginning of f. 146a*];
275 Fforto wende hys R, Wherwith to hyde hys body abowte P,
Ffor to wrap hes preveyte E, His bely for to wrappe aboute
CMD, To wrap his belly round about AFB; 276 His arsse for R,
His armes ffor Q, arnes heng full syde P, Nor his armes for
M, His harlotry to AFB;

Boþe his ffyngers and his face

Were becrached in many a place

And bebled all with bloode.

280 Euery man þat myght hym se

Was hym fayne for to fle:

They went he had bene woode.

Whan he cam to his oste

Of his jorney he made no boste.

285 He was both tame and talle.

Moche sorow in hert he had,

Ffor euery man of him was drad

Whan he came into þe hall.

277 The breres (had hym scratched so in C), (hath scratched
him on M), (scratched him in D) the face CMD, The thornes
had scratcht him by the face AFB, PE *blank*, [R: *beginning of
f. 56b*]; 278 Were cracهed R, And (in) many an other place
C(MD), (On AF), (The B) hands (on A), (and F), (the B) thighes
and euery place AFB, PE *blank*; 279 And berayed all R, And
bebrewed all in blode Q, He was all (to bledde with CD),
(bebled with M), (bath'd in AFB) blode CMDAFB, PE *blank*, [F:
beginning of f. A8a]; 280 þat hym gan se R, All that (dyd E),
(myght CMD) the freyr se ECMD, So much that who the frier did
see AFB, P *blank*; 281 They were hym R, Was full glad hym to
Q, War ffayne (ffor to E), (awaye to CM), (to D) ffle ECMD,
For feare (of him AB), (from him F) (were faine AF), (was
faine B) to flee AFB, P *blank*, [C: *beginning of f. Avb*; D:
beginning of f. Bib]; 282 he went þe frere had RQ, They
thought he M, Thinking he AFB, P *blank*; 283 cam in to Q, came
hom to E, When to the good wife home he came AFB, [B:
beginning of p. 101]; 284 jorney made he no RP, He made no
bragges for very shame AFB, [E: *beginning of f. 10a*]; 285 &
tale R, To gret nother to smale E, His clothes were rente all
CMD, To see his cloathes rent all AFB; 286 in his hart
QCMDAFB, [M: *beginning of f. Bib*]; 287 man was a drad R, man
hym dradde Q, Ffull sore of hym they war adrad P, Euery E,
And euery man (hym dradde CMD), (did gesse him mad AFB)
CMDAFB, 288 he was in the AFB;

      The goodwyf sayed, "Where has þou be?
290 In shrewde place as semyth me,
      Me thynke be þyn araye."
      He seid, "Dame, I haue be with þy son;
      The devill of helle hym ouercom,
      Ffor certes I ne may."

295 With that cam in þe goodman.
      "Lo, sir," seid þe goodwyf þan,
      "Here is a shrewid araye.
      They son þat is þe so leef and dere
      Hath almoste slayne þis holy frere,
300 Alas, alas, and weleaweye."

289 The wyfe CMD, thou bene CMDAFB, The weyffe seyde ffreyr/
Wher has thow beyn E; 290 In evill places as Q, as thynkys
me P, In corsed plas so thenkyt me E, (In an CD), (In some
M), (Sure in some AFB) euyll place I wene CMDAFB; 291 Hyt
semyth be P, Lekely be E, It semeth by M, By sight of thine
AFB; 292 seid I R, Dame he said I Q, þe freyr sayd y P,/Dam
y cam ffrom they son E,/Dame I CMD,/Dame said he I came from
thy AB, The frier said to her right soone F; 293 dewyll hem
selffe owyrcom E, deuill and he hath me vndone AFB; 294 For
no man (elles CMD), (hem E) may ECMD, No man him conquer may
AFB; 295 Than cam R, Soon af<u>te</u>r com hom þe P, that the good-
man he came in AFB; 296 Be god sayd þe wyffe than P, The
weyffe seyde (to ECM), (vnto D) hem than ECMD, The wife set
on her madding pin AFB; 297 an evill arraye Q, ys (a) ffolle
a raye (ECM)D[*sic*], Cride heer's a foule array AFB, [Q:
beginning of f. 99b]; 298 is to þe R, is to the dere Q, þe
lyffe PC, is so leffe E, is to the M, is thy life and DAFB;
299 Had all most slayn þ<u>i</u>s swet freyr P, slayn owr holy E,
slayn the holy CDAFB, [A: *beginning of f. A8b*; P: *beginning
of f. 146b*]; 300 Alas and RCMAFB, Alas alas a well a way P,
Alas sche seyde & E, Alas now well away D;

The goodman seide, "Benedicite!

What hath þe boye don to þe?

Tell me without stryff."

"Sir," seyde þe frere, "Be Seynt Jame,

305   I haue dauncid in þe devilles name

Tyll I had ny loste my lyff."

The goodman seyde to hym tho,

"And þou haddist lorne þi lyf so

þou haddist be in grete synne."

310   "Nay," seide þe frere, "I shall tell why:

Me thou3te his pipe went so merely

That I cowde neuer blynne."

302 hath my boye R, hath yat boye Q, done frere to CM, the
vilde boy AFB; 303 me anon blyve R, (Now) tell me withowt let
ECMD(AFB); 304 The frere seyde be RQ, Sir he sayd be P,
ffreyr þer euyll mot he spede E, The frere sayd the deuyll
hym spede CMD, The deuill him take the frier (then AF), (he
B) said AFB; 305 He (made me EAFB), (hath made me C), (caused
me to MD) dans (magre ECDM), (despite AB), (in spight of F)
my (hedd ECMDAF), (bead B) ECMDAFB, [R: *beginning of f. 57a*];
306 The goodman seyde to hym belyve R, Thes wordes said he
blyff Q, Yn the breyres & bysches with hay a bowte E, Amonge
the thornes (the AFB) hey (go bette CMDAF), (to bee B)
CMDAFB; 307 These woordes seyde (he tho R), (ye goodman than
Q) RQ, saide vnto him DAFB; 308 Yff þou had lost thy P,
Haddest thou lost thy CMD, Father hadst thou been murdred so
AFB, Thow meytys a be sclayen so E, Thow hast ben a wild yong
man Q; 309 & you hast bene Q, (That E), (It CMD) had byn
grete ECMD, It had bene deadly sinne AFB, [F: *beginning of
f. A8b*]; 310 The frere seide I R, Sir sayd þe freyr (sekerly
P), (be howr ladey E) PE, The frere sayd by our lady CMD, The
frier to him made this reply AFB; 311 thou3te þe pipe RQ,
thou3te he pyped so P, /Hes E, The pype CMD, The pipe did
sound so AFB; 312 cowde not blynne RM;

þe goodman seide, "So mot I thee,

Than is þat a mery gle,

315 Or ellys þou art to blame.

That pipe," seide he, "will I here."

"So will not I," quod þe frere,

"Be God and be Seynte Jame."

Afterward whan it was ny3te,

320 Home came þe boy full ryght

As it was for to done.

Whan he came into þe hall

Anon his fader gan hym call

And seide, "Come heder soone."

313 Be my trowth þan seide he R, That pipe will I here
trewly Q, ECMDAFB _missing the entire stanza_; 314 The ffrere
said so will not I Q; 315 And ellys þou war to P, by god &
by seynt Ihame Q; 316 That pipe will I here trvly R, pipe
sertise will Q, pype he sayd woll P; 317 Nay for god quod Q,
The frere saide so will not I R; 318 Sure it is no game Q,
[P: _beginning of f. 147a_]; 319 Than after whan Q, Whan het
drow toward (the CD) neythe ECMD, Now when it grew to almost
night AFB, [C: _beginning of f. Avia_; D: _beginning of f. Bia_];
320 come this boye Q, Homeward went þe boy ryght R, The boy
gan hom hem dyth, (Jack) the boye came home full ryght
CMD(AFB), [E: _beginning of f. 10b_; M: _partly illegible_]; 321
As he was wont to (done P), (do CMDAFB) PCMDAFB, As het was
hes wone E; 322 As soon as he RQ, But when AFB; 323 fader did
hym RAF,/Hes E, His fader dyde hym soone call C, (Full AFB)
soone his father (dyd MB), (gan DAF) hym MDAFB; 324 seide
(boye) come heder a non (R)Q, sayd hydyr com þou sone P,
hether son E, And badde hym (to) come hym to (C)MDAFB;

325 "Herke þou boy, now þou arte here,

What hast þou don to þis frere?

Telle me withowte lettynge."

"Ffader," he seide, "in good faye,

I did ry3t nou3t to hym þis day

330 But piped him a sprynge."

"That pipe," he seide, "will I here."

"Nay, for God," quod þe frere,

"Þat were an evill thynge."

The goodman sayde, "Ys, be Goddes grace."

335 The frere cried "Owt" and seide "Alas";

His handes he gan wrynge.

325 Herke boy R, Boy he sayd now P, Boye he sayd (come) tell
me here CMD(AFB), E *blank*, [M: *beginning of f. Biia*]; 326 to
the freyr ECM, done vnto the frere D, don vnto this AFB;
327 without lessyng PECD, me no leasynge M, Lye not in any
thing AFB; 328 sayd by my faye CMD, said now by my birth AFB,
He said fader in Q; 329 ry3t not nou3t R, dide no thyng to
QE, hym to day PE, I dyde nought elles as I you saye CMD, I
playd him but a fit of mirth AFB; 330 But pipe him R, pypyd
to hem E, And pipte him vp a spring AFB; 331 pipe truly will
Q, Boy þat pype wyll P, pype quod the god man wolde y E, That
(pype MDAFB) sayd his fader wolde I (faine F) here CMDAFB;
332 for godes sak quod Q, So wyll not y quod P, God ffor
ffend qod E, Mary god forbede sayd the CMD, Now God forbid
(cride AB), (cryes F) out the frier AFB; 333 Ffor þat wer
hevy tydyng P, That ys an euyll tythyng E, His handes (he
dyde C), (dyd he MD), (he then did AFB) wrynge CMDAFB, [A:
beginning of f. Bia]; 334 Eys qod the god man by E, Yes said
ye good wiff by Q, Yes sayd the goodman (by CD), (for M)
goddes grace CMD, You shall the boy (said AB), (laid [*sic*] F)
by Gods grace AFB, [R: *beginning of f. 57b*]; 335 frere seide
alas alas RP, owt & alas E, Than sayd the frere (out) alas
(CD)M, fryer replide woe and alas AFB; 336 Has [*sic*] handes R,
hondes gan he wryng Q, And handes began to wryng P, And hes
handys ded wreyng E, And made grete mournynge CMD, Making his
sorrowes ring AFB;

"Ffor Goddes love," quod þe frere,

"And yf ye will þe pipe here,

Bynde me to a poste.

340   Iwis I can no better rede:

Well I wote I shall be dede.

My lyffe is ny hand loste."

Ropys anon þey toke in hond

And to þe poste þey hym bond

345   That stode in midward of þe hall.

All they þat at souper satte

Had good game and lough þerat

And seid, "Þe frere shall not fall."

337 love sayd þe P, For the loue of god (quod C), (sayde MD)
the frere CMD, loue said the (wretched AF), (werched [*sic*] B)
frier AFB, [P: *beginning of f. 147b*]; 338 And ye RE, Yff ȝe
wyll thys pype P, If ye wyll that (he) pype here (C)D, Yf ye
M, will that strange pipe AFB; 339 to þe poste R, me fast to
QAFB, me on to P; 340 Ffor now y can no nother redde E, For
I knowe none other rede CMD, For sure my fortune thus I read
AFB; 341 I wote R, Ffor well Q, (Bot) & y dans y am bot dede
(E)CMD, If dance I doe I am but dead AFB; 342 lyffe wyll
sone be loste R, ys nygh loste Q, leyffe y schall lesse E,
Well I wote my lyfe is lost CD, And my lyfe then were lost M,
My wofull life is lost AFB; 343 þey had in RQ, Strong ropes
they (hent E), (toke CMD) yn hande ECMD, Strong ropes they
tooke both sharpe and round AFB; 344 To a post Q, Þe freyr
(to þe post PCMD), (on tell a post E) they bond PECMD, poast
the frier (they) bound (AF)B; 345 in þe RQ, in þe mydes of
P, Yn E, In the myddle of CDAF, In the myddest of MB, [F:
beginning of f. Bla]; 346 Tho þat RQ, at þe soper P, All that
at the soper EC, All that M, at the table sat D, they which
at the table sat AFB; 347 They had RQ, had game Q, Lowȝ &
had good gam (þer ate PCMD), (all E) PECMD, Laughed and made
good sport thereat AFB; 348 seid now þe R, freyr myȝt not P,
frere wolde not CMD, Saying frier thou canst not fall AFB;

Than bespake þe goodman.

350   To his son he seyde þan,

"Pipe on whan þou wylte."

"All redy, fader," seide he,

"I shall yow showe of my gle:

Ye shall haue a fytte."

349 Than spake R, Than sayd the CMDAFB, goodman to the boy
AFB, E *blank*; 350 And to hys sone sayd he than P, (And
seyde) pype on god son (E)C, Pype sonne as thou can MD,
Jacke pipe me vp (some AF), (a B) merry toy AFB; 351 on what
þou RQ, When that yeuer thow welt E, Hardely whan thou
(wylte C), (will D) CD, Begyn whan thou wyle M, Pipe freely
when thou will AFB, [C: *beginning of f. Avib*; D: *beginning
of f. Biib*]; 352 Ffather he seyde so mot y the ECMD, Father
the boy said verily AFB, [Q: *beginning of f. 100a*]; 353
shewe a mery glee Q, 3e schall her of P, Ye schall hafe gret
plente E, Haue ye schall ynough of gle CMD, You shall haue
mirth enough and glee AFB; 354 & ye Q, Y wyll geve 3owe a P,
Tyll ye bydde me be styll CMDAFB, E *blank*;

355   As soon as euer þe pype wente

      Ther my3te no man himselfe stent

      But began to daunce and lepe.

      All þat gan þe pype here,

      They my3t not hemself stere,

360   But hurled on an hepe.

      Tho þat at souper satte,

      Ouer þe table anon þey lepte

      And sterid in þat stounde.

      They þat sat on þe forme

365   Had no tyme hem to turne,

      But they were borne to þe grounde.

355 soon as þe RQ, Anon as yeuer E, soone as Jacke the pype
hent CMD, With that his pipe he quickly (hent AF), (sent B)
AFB; 356 They my3t not hemselfe stent R, Ther was on that
stell stode E, All that there were verament CMD, And pipte
the whilst in verament AFB, [P: *beginning of f. 148a*;
M *partly illegible*]; 357 Began CMD, Bot then a bowt they
lepyd E, Each creature gan to dance AFB, [M: *beginning of
f. Biib*; E: *beginning of f. 11a*]; 358 yat euer myght it here
Q, They þat P, All that dyd the E, Whan they gan the pype
(to) here CM(D), Lightly they (skipt AF), (scikipt [*sic*] B)
and leapt about AFB, R *blank*; 359 them self asstere Q, Myght
not P, Cowd not E, Yerking (in) their legs now in now out
AF(B [*sic*]), R *blank*; 360 But worled on Q, hurled vpon an P,
But hurcled on D, Striuing aloft to prance AFB, RE *blank*;
361 They that Q, Than they þat P, ECMDAFB *lack the entire
stanza*; 362 tabull 3ede som vnder crape P; 363 And sterte vp
in P; 364 sat vpon þe P; 365 They had no leyser them Q, tym
for to P; 366 They R, to grownd Q, But war bore down to P,
[R: *beginning of f. 58a*];

The goodman was in dispeyre:

Streyte he sterte owte of þe cheyre

With an hevy chere.

370 Som lepe ouer þe stoke

And brake her shynnes ageyn þe bloke,

And som felle in þe fyre.

367 good man wex in P, god man (stod E), (was CMD) in no
despyr ECMD, goodman as in (sad AB), (mad F) dispaire AFB,
[B: *beginning of p. 102, line partly pared off*; A: *beginning
of f. B1b*]; 368 Bot weytheley ros ffro hes soper E, (And P),
(But CMD) (ly3tly PCM) (he P) lept out of his chare PCMD,
Leapt out (and AF) through & ore his chaire AFB; 369 And
with a full good chere P, With ryght a god cher E, With a
good chere C, As a man that had no feare M, All with a
goodly cheer D, No man could caper hier AFB; 370 Som sterte
ouer RQ, the blokk Q, Som in fayth lepe P, Some others leapt
(quite) ore the stocks (A)F(B); 371 a geyn bloke R, ye stokk
Q, (And E) (som ECDM) stombellyd at (the ECM), (a D) bloke
ECMD, Some start at strawes and fell (ore AF), (att B)
blocks AFB; 372 som in þe fyre felle R, som stombelled yn E,
fell flatte in CMD, Some wallowed in the fier AFB;

The goodwyfe cam all behynde.

She began to lepe and wynde

375   And sharpely for to shake.

But when she lokid on litill Jak,

Anon her arsse to her spake

And lowde began to crake.

373 cam in be hynde R, þan com in þe good wyff be hynd P,
The goodman had (grete CM), (good D) game CMD, The good-man
made himselfe good sport AFB; 374 & to wynd P, How they
daunced all in same CD, To daunce and lepe he thought no
shame M, To see them dance in this mad sort AFB, E *blank*;
375 And fast be gan to P, scharpeley gan sche loke E, The
(good D) wyfe after (him M) (gan CD), (dyd M) steppe CMD,
The good-wife sate not still AFB, [P: *beginning of f. 148b*];
376 Whan sche PE, on her son Jake E, Euermore she kest her
eye at Jacke CD, And euer she cast her eye to Jacke M, But
as she danst she look't on Jack AFB; 376a And hyr neybors to
hyr spake P *only*; 377 Her arsse to hym spake R, Hyr ars be gan
to crake P, Weyteley her tayle spake E, (And) fast her tayle
began to cracke (C)M(D), And fast her taile did double each
crack AFB; 378 And the weynd began to crake E, (Lowde [*sic*]
C), (Louder MD) than they coude speke CMD, Loud as a water-
mill AFB; P *blank*;

      The frere was allmoste loste:

380   He beete his hede ageyne þe poste.

      He had non oþer grace.

      The rope rubbid of þe skynne

      That þe blode ranne doune be hym

      In many a dyuers place.

385   The boye went pypyng in þe strete

      And after hym hurled all þe hepe:

      Þey myȝte neuer stente.

      They went owte at þe dore so thyke

      That eche man fell in oþers neke,

390   So wiȝtly ovte þey wente.

379 all most dede E, frere hymselfe was CMD, frier this while
was almost AFB; 380 He knokyd hys (hed PE), (pate AFB) aȝen
þe post PEAFB, For knockynge his heed ayenst the post CMD;
381 had no better grace QP, ('Twas then AF), (It was B) his
dancing grace AFB, [F: *beginning of f. B1b*]; 382 Ropes rubbed
Q, robyd away þe P, ropys wrong hem by the E, rubbed hym
vnder the chynne CMDAFB; 383 I woote þe R, ran to hys chyne
P, blod downe (het ran E), (dyde rynne CMD) ECMD, ran from
his tatterd skin AFB; 384 many dyuers R, a naked place AFB;
385 Þan whent þe boy pypyng in P, The bow pypyd yn to the E,
Jacke (piping) ranne in to the CMD(AFB); 386 After worled all
Q, hym hoole all R, They lepyd after all E, After (hym CD)
fast (dyde CD) they lepe CMD, They followed him with nimble
feet AFB; 387 neuer astente R, never stynt Q, Þey cowd not
hem selfe stynt P, Ther nas nat on cowed stent E, Truly they
coude not stynte CMD, Hauing no power to stay AFB; 388 owt of
ye QD, They ran owte of the E, And in their haste the doore
did cracke AFB; 389 eche leped in other neke Q, That yether
ffell E, fell on others C, Each tumbling over his fellowes
backe AFB [C: *beginning of f. Aviia*; D: *beginning of f. Biiia*];
390 So myȝtely ovte R, weyteley they trepyd E, So pretely
(out C), (ouer D) they CD, So properly out M, Vnmindfull of
their way AFB;

Tho þat dwellyd þerby

That harde þe pype sekyrly

In places þer they sette,

Anon þey lepte ouer þe hacche;

395 They had no tome to vndo þe lacche,

They were so lothe to lette.

391 They þat R, Than þe men þat P, Ther neybers þat E, (The
AFB) neyghbours that were (fast CMD), (dwelling AFB) by
CMDAFB; 392 Harde R, They herd P, (Herde CMD), (Hearing AFB)
the pype (go CM) so meryly CMDAFB, E *blank*; 393 In place þer
they sat R, they were sett [were *added above the line*] Q,
In setes wher they sette P, they sat E, (They ranne CMD),
(Came dancing AFB) (in to CM), (to DAB), (in at F) the gate
CMDAFB; 394 Som in fayth lepe P, They lepyd weyteley ouer E,
Some lepte CMD, Some leapt ore doores some ore the hatch
AFB: 395 no tyme to QPCMD, to seche þe P, to drawe the CMD,
Some had M, No man would stay to draw the AFB, E *blank*, [R:
beginning of f. 58b; P: *beginning of f. 149a*; M: *beginning of
f. Biiia*; A: *beginning of f. B2a*]; 396 to be lette Q, Ffor
they wer loth P, So weyteley they wer to lepe E, (But AFB),
(They CMD) (wende C), (thought MDAFB) (they CMDB), (he AF)
(had come C) (came MDAFB) to late CMDAFB;

      They þat laye in þer bedde,

      Anon þey hyld vp þer hede,

      Bothe þe lesse and eke þe more.

400   Into þe strete, as I hard saye,

      Anon þey toke þe ryght waye

      As nakyd as þey were bore.

397 And þo þat R, ther beddys Q, Than they þat in here bedys
lay P, Some laye (in CM), (on D) theyr bedde CMD, Some sicke
or sleeping in their bed AFB, E *blank*; 398 they lyfte vp
ther hedes Q, Stert vp ly3tly as y 3ow say P, Vp they start
that het harde E, And helde CMD, As they by chance lift vp
their head AFB, [E: *beginning of f. 11b*]; 399 & the more Q,
Both las & (yeke) more P(E), Anone they were (waked C),
(awaked MD) CMD, Were with the pipe awaked AFB; 400 In þe R,
I here saye Q, strete to þe play P, They can weytley the soyt
to say E, Some sterte in the waye CMD, Straight foorth they
start through doores & locks AFB; 401 In (good) feyth þey
R(Q), ye way Q, Yn to the strete they toke the wey E, Truly
as (I) you say (CM)D [*sic*], Some in their shirts some in
their smockes AFB; 402 were borne R, as ever they Q, Som as
nakyd E, (And some) starke bely naked CMD(AFB);

Whan þay wer gaderid all abowte,

Than was þer a grete rovte

405   In þe myddes of þe strete.

Some were lame and myȝte not goo,

Yet þey hoppid abovte also

On handes and on fete.

403 But whan Q, By that they were gadred aboute CMD, When
all were gathered round about AFB; 404 Than ther were a Q,
a full grete P, Ther was a gret schowte E, Iwys there was a
CMD, There was a vild vnruly rout AFB; 405 þe medyll of R,
Yn medward of E, Dauncynge in the CMD, That (danced AF),
(dancing [*sic*] B) in the AFB; 406 þey þat wer P, Of which
some lame that could not AFB; 407 ꝑt [*sic*] þey R, But they
hopped all a bowt tho Q, And yet they began to dans all so
E, But yet ywys they daunced (to C), (so MD) CMD, Striuing
to leape did tumble so AFB, [Q: *beginning of f. 100b*]; 408 On
her hondys & fete P, On hande and on fote M, They dancst on
hands and feet AFB, And some began to crepe R;

The boye sayde, "Fader, wyll ye reste?"

410 "In feyth," he seide, "I holde it beste,"

With a full good chere.

"Make an ende when þou wilte

In feyth þis is þe meryest fytte

That I hard þis sewyn yere."

415 Whan þe pype went no more

Than wer þey all amerveylid sore

Of þer gouernaunce.

"A, Seynt Mary," sayde some,

"Wher is all þis myrth become

420 That made vs for to daunce?"

409 Þe boys fader sayd it is tym to reste P, seyde het ys
best to rest E, (They [*sic*] C), (The MD) boye sayd now (wyll
CM) I rest CMD, Jack tyred with (the sport) said now I'le
rest AF(B); 410 For in feith I Q, All redy fader y hold þat
for þe beste P, Hes ffather seyde E, Quod the goodman I CD,
Then seyde the good man I M, Doe quoth his father I AFB;
411 With ryght a good R, a glad cher E, a mery chere CMD,
Thou cloyst me with (this AB), (thy F) cheare AFB, That ye
reste here Q, [F: *beginning of f. B2a*; ch[eer] *partly
illegible*]; 412 His ffader said whan Q, Seys (on) son when
thow welt (E)CD, Sease my sonne I lowe thy wytte M, I pray
thee boy now quiet sit AFB; 413 þis was þe RAFB, feyth it is
ye (merrieste Q), (beste P) fytt QP, Ffor thes ys the meryst
ffest E; 414 /I AFB, That I had þis QE, [P: *beginning of
f. 149b*]; 415 *From here on, only RQP have this ending.* But
whan Q; 416 Than þey amerveylid R, Than all they marveled
sore Q; 417 of þe gouernaunce RQ; 418 /Seynt RQ; 419 all ye
mirth Q; 420 vs thus to P;

Euery man was of good chere
Save þe goodwyfe and þe frere:
They were all dysmayde.
He þat hath not all hes will,
425   Be it good or be it ylle,
He holdyth hym not apayde.

421 was good of chere Q, Thus eue̲r̲y man mad good P; 422
Thank þe; 424 hes witt R, Wheþe̲r̲ it be good or yll P; 425
They þat have not her wyll P, [R̲: *beginning of f. 59a*]; 426
not we̲l̲l a payd Q, They wyll not hold þem payd P;

P *adds the following two stanzas:*

Hyt ys euery good wyffys wone
Ffor to love hyr husbondes sone
Yn well and eke yn woo.
In olde termys it is fownd
P5 He þat lovyþe me lovyþe my hound
And my servaunt also.

So schuld euery good chyld
Be to hys moder meke and myld.
Be good yn euery degre.
P10 All women þat love her husbondes sone,
Yn hevyn blys schall be her wone.
Amen, amen, for charyte.

P7: *beginning of f. 150a.*

RQ *add the following two stanzas:*

Now haue ye herd all insame
How Jak pleyde with his dame
And pypid before þe frere.
Hym lykyd noþyng þe boyes lay;
RQ5 Therfor he toke his leve and went his wey
Somedele with hevy chere.

The goodman norysshyd forth his chylde,
His stepmoder was to hym full myld,
And fared wele all in fere.
RQ10 That Lorde yow kepe, frendes all,
That dranke both eysill and gall,
Holy God in His empere. Amen.

Here endyth þe tale of Jak and his stepdame

RQ1 haue he ye [*sic*] R; RQ4 The frere liked not ye Q; Ther
fore shortly he went a way Q; RQ8 The stepmoder R, hym mylde
R; RQ9 And fare wele R; RQ10 That lordes yow R; RQ11 drank
aysell Q; RQ12 empere/Q.

ECMDAFB *add the following stanzas, following v. 414*
(ending X):

When they had daunced all insame,
Some laughed and had good game
And some had many a fall.
"Thou cursed boye," said the frere,
X5   Here I somon the that thou appere
Before the offycyal.

"Loke thou be there on Frydaye.
I wyll the mete and I may,
For to ordeyne the sorowe."
X10   The boye sayd, "By God I auowe,
Frere, I am as redy as thou
And Frydaye were tomorowe."

C *is the copytext.* X1 Thus whan they had dansed all/E, They
daunced CMD, all the same M, All those that dancing thither
came AFB; X2 Laught heartily and made good AFB; X3 Yet some
got many AFB; X4 Thow ffals boy E, boye quod the C, boy
cry'd out (the AF), (thy [*sic*] B) frier AFB; X5 thee to
appeere D, /Y somoun the a ffor the ··· mserey E, Heere I doe
summon thee to appeare AFB; X6 E *blank*; X7 on Friday next
AFB, there a ffreyday E, [C: *beginning of f. Aviib*; D:
beginning of f. Biiib]; X8 wyll meet the and M, Mey selffe
schall met with þe ther & y may E, Ile meete thee then though
now perplext AFB; X9 ordaine thy sorow DAF, To sey they
erand be fforen E, [A: *beginning of f. B2b*]; X10 God auowe
CMD, Jake seyde y make a ffone E, boy replide I make a vow
AFB; X11 /I am as redey a thow [*sic*] E, Fryer Ile appeare as
soone as thou AFB; X12 If Friday AFB, And thow welt go to
morow E;

Frydaye cam as ye may here.

Jackes stepdame and the frere,

X15   Togyder there they mette.

Folke gadered a great pase;

To here euery mannes case

The offycyall was sette.

There was moche to do:

X20   Maters more than one or two,

Bothe with preest and clerke.

Some had testamentes for to preue,

And fayre women, by your leue,

That had strokes in the derke.

X13 as you shall hear DAFB, as you may M, But friday AFB,
[M: *beginning of f. Biiib*]; X14 Boyt Jake & hes stepdam & E,
the dancing frier AFB; X15 All iij togedyr met E, Together
they were met AFB; X16 People gathered a great peace M, And
other people a AFB, The pype cam yn to the plas E; X17
Flockt to the court to heare each case AFB, E *blank*; X19 Much
ciuill matters were to doe AFB; X20 matters mo than MD,
More libels read then one (or two AF), (orow [*sic*] B), [E:
beginning of f. 12a]; X21 Both against priest AF, [B *missing:
cropped at bottom*], & with clerke E; X22 testaments to DAFB,
Some there had AFB, [B: *beginning of p. 103*]; X23 And som
ffomen be E, Some women there through wanton loue AFB; X24
Which got stroakes AFB, Had strokys be thekys the legys yn
the darke E;

X25   Euery man put forth his case.

      Than came forth Frere Topyas

      And Jackes stepdame also.

      "Syr Offycyall," sayd he,

      "I haue brought a boye to the

X30   Whiche hath wrought me moche woo.

      "He is a grete nygromancere:

      In Orlyaunce is not his pere,

      As by my trouth I trowe."

      "He is a wytche," quod the wyfe.

X35   Than as I shall tell you blyue

      Lowde coude she blowe.

X25 Each proctor there did plead his case AFB, [M *damaged by a hole vv. 25-28*]; X26 fforet capias E, came Frier D, When forth did step Frier AFB; X27 [F: *beginning of f. B2b*]; X28 Sir Officiall aloud said AFB, The ffreyr seyde so mot y the E; X29 boye lo the M, a wicked boy AFB; X30 Which had wrought M, Hath done me mightie woe AFB, That werket mekyll woo E; X31 a witch as I do feare AFB; X32 In all orlyaunce CMD, In Orleance he can find no peare AFB; X33 By EM, trouth as I M, This of my troth I know AFB; X34 qod hes stepdame E, wytche than sayd the M, a deuill quoth the AFB; X35 you blythe C, Than her tayle bebbeythe [*sic*] E, I am wery of my lyfe M, And almost hath bereau'd my life AFB; X36 Lowd began to blow E, Her bumme than dyd she blowe M, At that her taile did blowe AFB;

Some laughed without fayle

And some sayd, "Dame, tempre thy tayle:

Ye wreste it all amysse."

X40   "Dame," quod the offycyall,

"Tell forth thy tale:

Lette not for all this."

The wyfe was ferde of a cracke;

Not one worde more she spacke:

X45   She durst not for drede.

The frere sayd, "So mote I the,

Boy, this is longe of thee,

Euill mote thou speed."

X37 So lowd th'assembly laught thereat AFB, [A: *beginning of
f. B3a*]; X38 dam stop they E, Some CD, And said her pistols
cracke was flat AFB; X39 Thow werkes all E, The charge was
all AFB, [C: *beginning of f. Aviiia*; D: *beginning of f.
Biiiia*]; X40 Dame sayde the M, the gentle officiall AFB; X41
forth on thy CD, Proceed and tell me forth AFB; X42 for this
CD, (Do thou M), (And doe AFB) not let for this MAFB; X43 was
afrayed of an other cracke CMD, wife that feard another cracke
AFB; X44 That no worde (more C), (mo MD) she spacke CMD,
Stood mute and nere a word (she AB), (more F) spake AFB; X45
not than for M, Shame put her in such dread AFB, [M: *beginning
of f. Biiija*]; X46 Ha said the frier right angerly AFB; X47
Knaue this CMD, Knaue this (is all still long A), (disgrace
is long F), (is all along sill [*sic*] B) of thee AFB; X48 mot
the spede E, That euyll CMD, euyll may thou M, Now euill
maist thou AFB;

The frere sayd, "Syr Offycyall,
X50 This boye wyll combre vs all
But yf ye may hym chaste.
Syr, he hath a pype truly
Wyll make you daunce and lepe on hye
Tyll your herte braste."

X55 The offycyal sayd, "So mote I the,
That pype wolde I fayne se,
And knowe what myrth it can make."
"Mary, God forbede," sayd the frere,
"That ye sholde the pype here
X60 Afore that I the waye hens take."

X50 The boye CD, combyres all [*sic*] E, This wicked boy will
vexe vs all AFB; X51 Vnlesse you do him chaste CMAFB, Bot he
be chastysed E; X52 hath (yet AB), (got F) a AFB, Ffor thes
boy hayt a pype/E, [E: *beginning of f. 12b*]; X53 lepe ful hye
DAFB, Well make hes dans genep [*sic*] E; X54 Tell howr hertes
brast E, And breake your harte at last AFB; X55 so may I M,
officiall replide perdie AFB; X56 pype well y se E, Such a
pipe (I faine would A), (faine would I FB) see AFB; X57 And
what AFB, myrth (that) he can (C)D, [F: *beginning of f. B3a*];
X58 forbede than sayd C, forbyd quod the M, Now God forbid
replide the AFB; X59 That he sholde pype here CD, That ere
(we AF), (I F) should that vilde pipe heare AFB; X60 that I
hens the waye take C, I a way D, Ere I my way AFB.

From line X57 on, E *differs from the other texts:*

E55   The offeciall seyde, "So mot y the,

      That pype well y se."

      He seyde, "Boy, hes het her?"

      "Ye, scer, be mey ffay:

      Anon pype vs a lay,

E60   And make vs all cher."

      The offeciall the pype hent,

      And blow tell hes brow he bent,

      But thereof cam no gle.

      The offeciall seyde, "þer ys nowth;

E65   Be God that me der b[o]wthe,

      Het ys not worthe a [fle]."

      "Be mey ffay," qod the ffreyr,

      "The boy can make het pype cler--

      I bescrow hem ffor hes mede."

E70   The offeciall bad the boy asay.

      "Nay," qod the ffreyr, "Do þat awey,

      Ffor that y fforbede."

E65 bowthe: MS bwthe; E66 fle: MS sclo;

"Pype on," qod the offeciall, "and not spar."

The ffreyr began to star.

E75 Jake hes pype hent.

As sone as Jake began to blow,

All they lepyd on a rowe

And ronde abowt they went.

The offeciall had so gret hast

E80 That boyt hes schenys brast

Apon a blokys hende.

The clerkys to dans þey hem sped,

And som all ther eynke sched,

And som ther bokes rent.

E85 And som cast ther boky[s] at þe wall,

And som ouer ther ffelowys can ffall

So weytley they lep[e].

Ther was ..... withowt let

....

E90 They stombylled on a hepe.

E85 bokys: MS boky; E86: *beginning of f. 13a*; E87 lepe: MS
lepyd; E88-89 *No gap in MS*;

        They dansed all abowthe,
        And yever the ffreyr creyd owt,
        "Mey leyffe [schall be lorne]!
        Y may no lengger dans ffor soyr:
E95   Y haffe lost halffe mey codwar
        When y dansed yn the thorne."

        Som to crey they began,
        "Mey boke is all to-toren."
        Som creyd withowt let,
E100   And som bad, "Hoo!"

        Som seyde het was a god game,
        And som seyde they were lame:
        "Y may no leynger skeppe."
        Som dansed so long
E105   Tell they helde owt þe townge
        And anethe meyt hepe.

E93 leyffe schall be lorne: MS leyffe I schall lese; E96
thorne: MS thornes; E97-100 *are doubtless experimental lines
in* E*'s source, and are meant to be cancelled;*

The offeciall began to star,

And seyde, "Hafe for they heyr.

Stent of they lay,

E110 And boldely haske of me

What thow welt hafe for þy gle.

Y schall the redey pay."

Then to stend Jake began.

The offeciall was a werey man,

E115 Mey trowet y [the pleyt].

[Som seyde] thes was a god gle,

And [som] seyde the worst þat euer they se,

Ffor het was ner neyth.

Than bespake the offeciall

E120 And leytley Gake can call--

Hes pyps he hem hent--

And gaffe hem [twenty] s[chelling]

And euer mor hes blesyng

Ffor that merey ffet.

E115 y the pleyt: MS y pleyt y the; E116 Som seyde thes:
MS Thes; E117 And som seyde: MS And seyde; E121 *begins f. 13b*;
E122 twenty schelling: MS xx s.;

E125 When Gake had that money hent
       Anon homard he went:
       Glad therof was he.
       And affter, y onderstondd,
       He waxed a wordeley marchande,
E130 A man of gret degre.

       Hes stepdame, y dar say,
       Dorst neuer after that day
       Nat wonley ones desplese.
       They lowyd togedyr all [thre],
E135 Hes ffather, hes stepdame, and he,
       After yn gret eys.

       And [whan] they ded, soyt to say,
       Tho hewyn they toke the wey
       Withowtyn eney mes.
E140 Now God that dyed ffor os all
       And dranke aysell and gall
       Bryng them all to they bles
       That beleuet on the name J[esus].

       Explicit the cheylde and hes stepdame

E134 thre: MS iij; E137 whan: MS that; E143 Jesus: MS Jhc.

From line 61 on, AFB *(ending Z) diverge from* CMD *(ending Y). Ending Y will be given first, with* C *as the copy text:*

"Pype on, Jacke," sayd the offycyall,
"I wyll here how thou canst playe."
Jacke blew vp, the sothe to saye,
And made them soone to daunce all.

Y65   The offycyall lepte ouer the deske
And daunced aboute wonderous fast
Tyll bothe his shynnes he had brast.
Hym thought it was not of the best.

Than cryed he vnto the chylde
Y70   To pype no more within that place,
But to holde him styll for Goddes grace
And for the loue of Mary milde.

Y62 here now how C; Y63 soth I say M; Y64 They daunced than both great and small M; Y66 aboute wonder fast C; Y67 he all to brest C, Tyll that he had his shynnes brast M; Y68 He thought M, not all the M; Y69 he to the M; Y70 within this place CD, more in that M; Y71 But holde M, holde styll C, [C: *beginning of f. Aviiib*; D: *beginning of f. Biiiib*]; Y72 For M;

Than sayd Jacke to them echone,
"If ye wyll graunte me with herte fre
Y75 That ye wyll do me no vylany,
But hens to departe as I come."

Therto they answered all anone
And promysed hym full ryght
In his quarell for to fyght
Y80 And defende hym from his fone.

Thus they departed in that tyde,
The offycyall and the sompnere,
His stepdame and the frere,
With grete joye and moche pryde.

Thus endeth the frere and the boye.

Y74 ye wolde me graunte with C; Y75 That he shall do C, That
they doo D; Y76 departe euen as C; Y77 [M: *beginning of*
f. Biiijb]; Y78 hym anone ryght C; Y84 With much ioy and
great pryde M.

Ending Z (A is the copy text):

"Pipe on, Jacke," said the officiall,
And let me heare thy cunning all."
Jacke blew his pipe full lowd,
That euery man start vp and dancst.
Z65   Proctors and priests and somners pranst,
And all in that great crowd.

Over the desks the officiall ran,
And hopt vpon the table, than
Straight iumpt vnto the flore.
Z70   The frier that danst as fast as he
Met him midway, and dangerously
Broake eithers face full sore.

The register leapt from his pen
And hopt into the throng of men,
Z75   His inkehorne in his hande,
Which swinging round about his head,
Some he strucke blinde, some almost dead;
Some they could hardly stand.

Z65 [A: *beginning of f. B3b*]; Z67 the deske the FB; Z68 table
that [*sic*] A; Z69 jumpt vpon the F; Z76 With swinging B;

The proctors flung their billes about;
Z80   The good wiues taile gaue many a shout,
Perfuming all the mirth;
The somners, as they had beene wood,
Leapt ore the formes and seates agood,
And wallowed on the earth.

Z85   Wenches that for their pennance came,
And other meeds of worldly shame,
Danst euery one as fast.
Each set vpon a merry pin;
Some broke their heads and some their shin,
Z90   And some their noses brast.

The officiall thus sore turmoild,
Halfe swelt with sweat and almost spoild,
Cride to the wanton childe
To pipe no more within that place
Z95   But stay the sound, euen for Gods grace
And loue of Marie milde.

Z83 [A: *from here to the end of the page, the left hand side
is pared so that the first letter of most lines is cut off*];
Z87 [F: *beginning of f. B3b*]; Z88 sett on a B; Z92 [B:
*beginning of p. 104; the top is severely pared, and this
line is missing*]; Z93 [A: *beginning of f. B4a*];

Jacke said, "As you will, it shall be,

Prouided I may hence goe free

And no man doe me wrong:

Z100 Neither this woman nor this frier

Nor any other creature heere."

He answered him anon:

"Jack, I to thee my promise plight,

In thy defence I meane to fight

Z105 And will oppose thy fone."

Jacke ceast his pipe; then all still stood,

Some laughing hard, some raging wood.

So parted at that tide

The officiall and the somner,

Z110 The stepdame and the wicked frier,

With much joy, mirth, and pride.

FINIS.

Z106 his pipes then B; Z109 Tho [*sic*] officiall A; Z111 With great joy F.

Dane Hew, Munk of Leicestre

Dane Hew, Munk of Leicestre

The Story

   Dane Hew, Munk of Leicestre is the tale of a lecherous
monk who is murdered by an outraged husband, and whose corpse
is shuffled furtively by night from the murder scene to his
abbey, from the abbey back to the murder scene, and thence to
a miller's rafters. In a final blaze of chivalric glory the
dead monk, tied on horseback, charges onto the abbey grounds,
a lance bound under his arm, and is killed for the last time.
It is probably a translation of a French fabliau, though its
ancestor is not extant: the closest French analogues are Le
Dit dou soucretain by Jean le Chapelain (Montaiglon and
Raynaud CL), Du Segretain moine (MR CXXXVI), and Du Segretain
ou du moine (MR CXXIII). The French stories extant differ in
certain minor details from the English version, and in every
case but one the French stories are more detailed, more
rationalized. In the French versions, the wife is given a
motive for her pretended acquiesence to the monk's bribery
(she and her husband have fallen into poverty). The monk's
corpse is not simply leaned against the abbey wall, but
perched "Sor le pertruis d'une privée" in the abbey. The
swapping of the corpse for a stolen side of bacon is more
plausibly accomplished in the French versions. But in Dane
Hew, the horse which carries the monk's corpse onto the
grounds of the abbey is after the abbot's mare, so that both
his movements and the abbot's terror are more understandable.
Because of this detail of the horse's pursuit of the mare,
which does not occur in any of the extant French fabliaux but
which does occur in a late fifteenth century Italian novella
by Masuccio Salernitano (the first in Il Novellino di
Masuccio Salernitano), Archer Taylor posits a common French
ancestor to the English Dane Hew and the Italian novella (in
"Dane Hew, Munk of Leicestre," Modern Philology 15 [1917-18],
221-46). Taylor argues that the later occurrences of the
tale in English are all descended from Thomas Heywood's story

of "The Faire Lady of Norwich" in his <u>History</u> <u>of</u> <u>Women</u> (1624),
and it in turn is descended from Masuccio's novella, retain-
ing features which <u>Dane</u> <u>Hew</u> does not. <u>Dane</u> <u>Hew</u> has thus no
direct descendants, but many analogues. Readers interested
in the rather complex relationships among the various ana-
logues should consult Taylor's article, and Walter Suchier,
<u>Der</u> <u>Schwank</u> <u>von</u> <u>der</u> <u>viermal</u> <u>getöten</u> <u>Leiche</u> (Halle: M.
Niemeyer, 1922).

The <u>Text</u>

     <u>Dane</u> <u>Hew</u> is article S. Seld. d. 45(6) in the Bodleian
Library, STC 13257. Its publisher, John Allde, has not dated
it; according to Arber, Allde printed books between 1560 and
1584 and so those dates can be taken as the <u>terminus</u> <u>a</u> <u>quo</u> and
<u>terminus</u> <u>ad</u> <u>quem</u> for the edition.

     <u>Dane</u> <u>Hew</u> belongs to a group of twenty-six chapbooks,
formerly bound together, from the collection of John Selden
(1584-1654). Selden left some of his books directly to
Oxford, but others (including the chapbook collection) to
his executors to dispose of. They turned over the chapbooks
with most of the rest of Selden's collection to the Bodleian
in 1659.

     To the left of the title of <u>Dane</u> <u>Hew</u> someone has written
"1602" in brown ink, and the title page also bears the number
19 in the same ink, in the upper right-hand corner, although
<u>Dane</u> <u>Hew</u> is sixth in sequence in Selden's ordering. Some of
the other chapbooks are also numbered, the lowest number
being 6 and the highest 32. Four of the books that bear
numbers--<u>The</u> <u>Proude</u> <u>wyues</u> <u>Pater</u> <u>Noster</u>, <u>The</u> <u>Mylner</u> <u>of</u>
<u>Abyngton</u>, <u>The</u> <u>Schole</u> <u>house</u> <u>of</u> <u>Women</u>, and <u>Wyl</u> <u>Bucke</u> <u>his</u>
<u>Testament</u>--also bear the name Thomas Newton, and <u>The</u> <u>Schole</u>
<u>house</u> <u>of</u> <u>Women</u> has been marked 1601. Some of the books must
originally have been owned by a Thomas Newton, perhaps the
Thomas Newton (1542?-1607) noticed in DNB and mentioned in
Wood's <u>Athenæ</u> (II, 3). He was a clergyman, physician, and
poet who attended first Oxford, then Cambridge, and then
Oxford again. He died in May 1607 at Little Ilford, Essex.

     The twenty-six books in the Bodleian collection are the
following: <u>Kynge</u> <u>Rycharde</u> <u>cuer</u> <u>du</u> <u>lyon</u> (London: W[ynkyn] de
W[orde], 1528) STC 21008; <u>Syr</u> <u>Bevis</u> <u>of</u> <u>Hampton</u> ([London]:
Thomas East [1582?]) STC 1990; <u>Syr</u> <u>Degore</u> (London: John King,

1560), STC 6472; Syr Tryamoure (London: William Copland
[1565]) STC 24303.3; Syr Eglamoure of Artoys (London: William
Copland [1548-69]) STC 7543; Dane Hew Munk of Leicestre
(London: John Allde, n.d.), numbered 19 and dated 1602 in
brown ink, STC 13257; Knight of Curtesy and the lady of
Faguell (London: Wyllyam Copland [1568?]) BR 1486; Batayll
of Egyngecourte & the great sege of Rone (London: John Skot,
n.d.) STC 198; King Edward the fourth, and a Tanner of
Tamworth (London: John Danter, 1596) STC 7503; Adam Bell,
Clim of the Clough, and William of Cloudesle (London: James
Roberts, 1605) STC 1808; A ryght pleasaunt and merye Historie,
of the Mylner of Abyngton together with the Sergeaunt that
would have learned to be a fryar [Sir Thomas More] (London:
Rycharde Jones, n.d.), numbered 10 and inscribed Tho:
Newton, STC 79 (18091); The Frier and the Boy (London: Edward
Alde [1584-9]) STC 14522.7; The smyth whych that forged hym
a new dame (London: Wyllyam Copland [1565?]) STC 22653.9;
The Wife Lapped in Morels Skyn (London: Hugh Iackson [1580?])
STC 14521, the title page missing and a manuscript one added;
Vnlucky Firmentie (parts 2-5 only), (n.p., n.d.); The Schole
house of women [Edward Gosynhill] (London: John Allde, 1572),
numbered 6, inscribed Thomas Newton, and dated 1601, STC
12107, bound together with the following item; The Defense
of Women, Edwarde More (London: John Kynge, 1560) STC 18067,
the title page missing and a manuscript one added; Jyl of
breyntfords testament, Robert Copland (London: Wyllyam
Copland [1562?]) STC 5731; XII mary Jests of the wyddow
Edyth, Walter Smith (London: Richarde Johnes, 1573) STC
22870; The Proude wyues Pater noster (London: John King
[1560]), numbered 12 and inscribed Thomas Newton, STC 25938,
last page missing and a manuscript one added; Spare your
good (London: Anthony Kytson [1555?]) STC 23014a; The teple
of glasse [John Lydgate] (London: Thomas Berthelet [1529?])
STC 17034; Robin Conscience (London: Edward Allde, n.d.)
STC 5632; Wyl Bucke his Testament, John Lacy (London: Wyllam
Copland, n.d.), numbered 16 and inscribed Tho: Newton, STC
4001; The Churle and the byrde [John Lydgate] (Cantorbury:
Johan Michel [1550?]) STC 17013; The Parlament of Byrdes
(London: Antony Kytson [c. 1565]), numbered 32, STC 19304.

The pages of Dane Hew are roughly 17 cm. by 12.5, with
a print block of 15.5 by 9.5. The book is quarto, gathered
in six, with signatures on Aii and Aiii. Catchwords appear
on all pages save the first and last. The page numbering in
the lower right-hand corners was added in 1883 and runs
consecutively through all the items of the collection, from
196 to 202 for Dane Hew.

The first page is headed "Heere beginneth a/mery Iest of Dane Hew Munk of Lei-/cestre, and how he was foure times slain/and once hanged." The rest of the page is taken up with a large woodcut (12.5 cm. by 9.5) divided into five compartments, each with a picture of one of the slayings or the hanging. The bottom picture, which represents the jousting scene, is twice as wide as the others.

The colophon reads "Imprinted at Lon/don at the long Shop adioyning onto Saint Mildreds Churche in the/Pultrie, by John Alde."

Metre

The metre of the poem is exceptionally ragged. Lines range from six syllables ("He is foorth of the town"--v. 71) to thirteen ("And when the day began to appeer in the morning"--v. 61), and no accentual or accentual-syllabic pattern is regularly discernible. The rhyming, even with allowance made for variant and dialectal forms of words, still takes a great deal of licence: a few examples are lusty/fansy (vv. 7-8), houre/door (vv. 63-4), town/noon (vv. 71-2), him/time (vv. 179-80), home/anon (vv. 235-6), her/miller (vv. 247-8).

Language and Provenience

The task of determining the dialect and date of this poem is made more difficult by the inexactness of many of the rhymes. If the poet freely allows inexact rhymes, then no rhyme that can be "corrected" by substituting a dialect form can serve as strong evidence that the poem belongs to a particular dialect. A priori, the first two lines of the poem give the best clues as to place of origin and date:

In olde time there was in Lecester town

An abbay of munks of great renown ....

These lines would place the poem well after the dissolution of the monasteries in 1539, and would suggest that the poet was writing in or near Leicester. John Allde is known to

have printed from 1560 to 1584; the latter date sets an end
limit for the time of writing of the poem. A number of words
in the poem are cited by OED as used first in the mid-
sixteenth century in the meaning implied by the poem: convey
(v. 105: 1526), straight (v. 139: 1535), lay wait (v. 9:
1535), shrewdly (v. 46: a. 1551); vow (v. 164) is even later,
1593. However, the early form thore for modern there, fixed
in rhyming position at v. 224 (rh. sore), is last cited in
OED almost a century earlier, in 1470. And OED attests boun
(which it treats as the participial adjective bound) no
later than the fifteenth century. It too is fixed in rhyming
position at v. 30 (town/bown). In addition, the rhyme night/
straight at vv. 279-80 is particularly interesting. The
diphthong in modern night comes from inflected and therefore
umlauted forms of OE neaht. A true rhyme is possible on the
descendants of the unumlauted forms: Anglian naght could
rhyme with straght (originally a form of the past participle
of stretch), or (less likely) the rare form neght could
rhyme with streght. In either event, the rhymes depend on
forms cited no later in OED than the fifteenth century. The
evidence as far as date is concerned is far from conclusive,
but in combination with the raggedness of the metre and odd-
ness of the rhyming suggests that a fifteenth-century version
of the poem may well have been modernized (ineptly) for
publication in the sixteenth. This conjecture gains support
from the fact that a similar fate befell Jack and his
Stepdame, which as The Friar and the Boy was modernized
between version D (1584-9) and version A (1617), both printed
by John Allde's son Edward.

Little reliable dialectal evidence remains in the poem.
The rhyme first/list (vv. 79-80) suggests the Southumbrian
tendency to loss of r before s (see Jordan 166), but might
imply metathesis to frist. The rhyme thrast/cast (vv. 213-4)
involves a verb (thrast) used in Southumbria, as opposed to
northern thrust. The rhyme night/straight (vv. 279-80) which
was discussed above probably depends on a non-Southern, non-
Kentish form naght. And the rhyme slo/go at vv. 193-4
depends on a form of the verb slay from northern OE or from
ON: it is apt to occur only in the north or east, areas of
the Danelaw. In other words, the language of the poem is
compatible with an origin in the East Midlands: it could be
from Leicester, it could be from London, and it could be
influenced by both areas.

Editorial Treatment

In the following text, capitalization, punctuation, and word division have been made to conform to modern usage. Abbreviations have been silently expanded. In the textual notes, John Allde's edition has been designated as J.

Dane Hew, Munk of Leicestre

In olde time there was in Lecester town
An abbay of munks of great renown,
As ye shall now after heer.
But amongst them all was one there
5   That passed all his brethern, iwis:
His name was Dane Hew, so haue I blis.
This munk was yung and lusty
And to fair women he had a fansy,
And for them he laid great wait indeed.
10   In Leicester dwelled a tayler, I reed,
Which wedded a woman fair and good.
They looued eche other, by my hood,
Seuen yeer and somewhat more.
Dane Hew looued this taylers wife sore
15 And thought alway in his minde
When he might her alone finde,
And how he might her assay,
And if she would not say him nay.
     Upon a day he said, "Fair woman free,
20 Without I haue my pleasure of thee
I am like to go from my wit."

Textual notes: <u>Dane Hew</u> *begins on f. Aib*; v. 18 not say:
J not to say;

163

    "Sir," she said, "I haue many a shrewd fit
Of my husband euery day."

    "Dame," he said, "say not nay.
25 My pleasure I must haue of thee
Whatsoeuer that it cost mee."

    She answered and said, "If it must needs be,
Come tomorow vnto me,
For then my husband rideth out of the town.
30 And then to your wil I wil be bown,
And then we may make good game.
And if ye come not, ye be to blame.
But Dane Hew, first tel thou me
What that my rewarde shal be."

35   "Dame," he said, "by my fay,
Twenty nobles of good money,
For we wil make good cheer this day."
And so they kist and went their way.

    The tayler came home at even tho,
40 Like as he was wunt to doo,
And his wife tolde him all and some
How Dane Hew in the morning would come,
And what her meed of him should be.

    "What! Dame, thou art mad, so mot I thee.
45 Wilt thou a cuckolds hood giue?
That should me shrewdly greeue."

    "Nay, sir," she said, "by sweet Saint John,
I wil keep myself a good woman
And get thee money also, iwis.

v. 33 *begins f. Aiia;*

50 For he hath made therof a promisse,

Tomorrow earely heer to be:

I know wel he will not fail me.

And I shall lock you in the chest

That ye out of the way may be mist.

55 And when Dane Hew commeth hether early,

About five of the clock truely--

For at that time his houre is set

To come hether then without any let--

Then I shall you call full lightly.

60 Look that ye come vnto me quickly."

And when the day began to appeer in the morning,

Dane Hew came thitherwarde fast renning:

He thought that he had past his houre.

Then softly he knocked at the taylers door.

65   She rose vp and bad him come neer,

And said, "Sir, welcome be ye heer."

"Good morow," he said, "gentle mistris;

Now tel me where your husband is,

That we may be sure indeed."

70   "Sir," she said, "so God me speed,

He is foorth of the town

And wil not come home til after noon."

With that Dane Hew was wel content,

And lightly in armes he did her hent

75 And thought to haue had good game.

"Sir," she said, "let be for shame.

v. 65 *begins f. Aiib;*

For I wil knowe first what I shall haue:

For when I haue it I wil it not craue.

Give me twenty nobles first,

80   And doo with me then what ye list."

        "By my preesthood," quoth he than,

"Thou shalt haue in golde and siluer anon;

Thou shalt no longer craue it of me.

Lo, my mistresse, where they be."

85   And in her lap he it threw.

        "Gramercy," she said vnto Dane Hew.

        Dane Hew thought this wife to assay.

        "Abide, sir," she said, "til I haue laid it away,"

For so she thought it should be best.

90   With that she opened then a chest.

        Then Dane Hew thought to haue had her alone,

But the tayler out of the chest anon,

And said, "Sir Munk, if thou wilt stand,

I shall giue thee a stroke with my brand

95   That thou shalt haue but little lust vnto my wife."

And lightly without any more strife

He hit Dane Hew vpon the hed

That he fel down stark dead.

        Thus was he first slain in deed.

100   "Alas," then said his wife, "with an euil speed

Haue ye slain this munk so soone?

Whither now shall we run or gone?"

        "There is no remedy," then said he,

"Without thou giue good counsail to me

v. 97 *begins f. Aiiia;*

105 To conuay this false preest out of the way,
That no man speak of it ne say
That I haue killed him or slain,
Or els we haue doon it in vain."
    "Yea, sir," she said, "let him abide
110 Til it be soon in the euentide;
Then shall we him wel conuay,
For ye shall beare him into the abbay
And set him straight vp by the wall,
And come your way foorthwithall."
115   The abbot sought him all about,
For he heard say that he was out,
And was very angry with him indeed,
And would neuer rest, so God me speed,
Until Dane Hew that he had found,
120 And bad his men to seek him round
About the place, and to him say
That he come "speak with me straightway."
    Foorth went his man til at the last,
Beeing abrode, his eye he cast
125 Aside where he Dane Hew did see,
And vnto him then straight went he.
And thinking him to be aliue
He said, "Dane Hew, so mut I thriue,
I haue sought you and meruel how
130 That I could not finde you til now."

v. 108 els we: J els that we; v. 129 *begins f. Aiiib;*

Dane Hew stood as stil as he that could not tel
What he should say. No more he did, good nor il.

With that the abbots man said with good intent,
"Sir, ye must come to my lord, or els you be shent."
135 When Dane Hew answered neuer a dele
He thought he would aske some counsail;
Then to the abbot he gan him hye.

"I pray you, my lord, come by and by
And see where Dane Hew stands straight by the wall,
140 And wil not answere, whatsoeuer I call,
And he stareth and looketh vpon one place
Like a man that is out of grace,
And one woord he wil not speak for me."

"Get me a staf," quoth the abbot, "and I shall see
145 And if he shall not vnto me answere."

Then when the abbot came there
And saw him stand vpright by the wall,
He then to him began to call
And said, "Thou false bribour, thou shalt aby.
150 Why keepest thou not thy seruice truely?
Come hether," he said, "with an euil speed."

But no woord tha[n] Dane Hew answered indeed.

"What, whoreson!" quoth the abbot. "Why spekest
                                               not thou?
Speak, or else I make God a vow
155 I wil giue thee such a stroke vpon thy head
That I shall make thee to fall down dead."
And with that he gaue him such a rap
That he fel down at that clap.

v. 152 than: J that:

   Thus was he the second time slain,

160 And yet he wroght them much more pain,

   As ye shall afterwarde heer ful wel.

    "Sir," quoth the abotts [m]an, "ye haue doon il,

   For ye haue slain Dane Hew now

   And suspended this place, I make God a vow."

165   "What remedy?" quod the abbot than.

    "Yes," quoth his man, "by sweet Saint John,

   If ye would me a good rewarde giue,

   That I may be the better while that I liue."

    "Yes," quoth the abbot, "[forty] shillings thou

            shalt haue

170 And if thou can mine honor saue."

    "My lord, I tel you, so mot I thee,

   Unto such a taylers house haunted he

   To woo his prety wife certain,

   And thither I shall him bring again,

175 And there vpright I shall him set

   That no man shall it knowe or wit.

   And then euery man wil sain

   That the tayler hath him slain,

   For he was very angry with him

180 That he came to his wife so oft-time."

    Of his counsail he was wel appaid.

   And his man took vp Dane Hew that braid

   And set him at the taylers door anon

   And ran home as fast as he might gone.

   v. 161 *begins f. Aiva*; v. 162 man: J an; v. 169 forty: J xl;

185   The tayler and his wife were in bed

        And of Dane Hew were sore afraid

        Lest that he would them bewray,

        And to his wife began to say,

        "All this night I haue dreamed of this false caitife,

190   That he came to our door," quoth he to his wife.

            "Jesus," quoth his wife, "what man be ye

        That of a dead man so sore afraid ye be?

        For me thought that you did him slo."

            With that the tayler to the door gan go,

195   And took a polax in his hand,

        And saw the munk by the door stand,

        Whereof he was sore afraid.

        And stil he stood and no woord said

        Til he spake vnto his wife:

200   "Dame, now haue I lost my life

        Without I kil him first of all."

        Foorth he took his polax or mall

        And hit Dane Hew vpon the head

        That he fel down stark dead.

205   And thus was Dane Hew three times slain,

        And yet he wrought him a train.

            "Alas," quoth the taylers wife,

        "This caitife dooth vs much strife."

            "Dame," he said, "what shall we now doo?"

210   "Sir," she said, "so mote I go,

        The munk in a corner ye shall lay

        Til tomorow before the day.

        v. 193 *begins f. Aivb*; v. 195 And took a: J And a;
        v. 210 mote I go: J mote go;

Then in a sack ye shall him thrast
And in the mildam ye shall him cast.
215   I counsail it you for the best, surely."
         So the tayler thought to doo, truely.
In the morning he took Dane Hew in a sack
And laid him lightly vpon his back.
Unto the mildam he gan him hye,
220   And there two theeues he did espye
That fro the mil came as fast as they might.
But when of the tayler they had a sight
They were abashed very sore,
For they had thought the miller had come thore,
225   For of him they were sore afraid,
That the[ir] sack there down they laid
And went a little aside, I cannot tel where.
And with that the tayler saw the sack lye there;
Then he looked therin anon
230   And he saw it was full of bacon.
Dane Hew then he laid down there
And so the bacon away did beare
Til he came home. And that was true.
         The theeues took vp the sack with Dane Hew
235   And went their way til they came home.
One of the theeues said to his wife anon,
"Dame, look what is in that sack, I thee pray,
For there is good bacon, by my fay;
Therfore make vs good cheer lightly."

v. 225 *begins f. Bia*; v. 226 their: J the;

240   The wife ran to the sack quickly,
And when she had the sack unbound
The dead munck therein she found.
Then she cryed "Out!" and said "Alas!
I see heer a meruailous case
245 That ye haue slain Dane Hew so soon.
Hanged shall ye be if it be knowen."
    "Nay, good dame," said they again to her,
"For it hath been the false miller."
    Then they took Dane Hew again
250 And brought him to the mil certain
Where they did steale the bacon before.
And there they hanged Dane Hew for store.
    Thus was he once hanged in deed.
And the theeues ran home as fast as they could speed.
255   The millers wife rose on the morning erly
And lightly made herself redy
To fetch some bacon at the last.
But when she looked vp she was agast
That she saw the munk hang there.
260 She cryed out and put them all in fere,
And said, "Heer is a chaunce for the nones,
For heer hangeth the false munk, by cocks bones,
That hath been so lecherous many a day
And with mens wiues vsed to play.
265 Now somebody hath quit his meed ful wel--
I trow it was the deuil of hell--
And our bacon is stolne away.
This I call a shrewd play.
I wot not what we shall this winter eate."
270   "What, wife," quoth the miller, "ye must all this
                          forget,

And giue me some good counsail, I pray,

How we shall this munk conuay

And priuily of him we may be quit."

　　"Sir," she said, "that shall you lightly wit.

275　Lay him in a corner til it be night

And we shall conuay him or it be daylight.

The abbot hath a close heer beside;

Therein he hath a good horse vntide.

Go and fetch him home at night

280　And bring him vnto me straight,

And we shall set him therevpon indeed,

And binde him fast, so God me speed,

And giue him a long pole in his hand

Like as he would his enmies withstand,

285　And vnder his armes we wil it thrust

Like as he would fiercely iust.

　　"For," she said, "as ye wel knowe,

The abbot hath a mare, gentle and lowe,

Which ambleth wel and trotteth in no wise.

290　But in the morning when the abbot doth rise

He commaundeth his mare to him to be brought,

For to see his workmen, if they lack ought,

And vpon the mare he rideth, as I you tel,

For to see and all things be wel.

295　And when this horse seeth this mare anon,

Unto her he wil lightly run or gone."

　　When the miller this vnderstood

He thought his wiues counsail was good,

v. 289 *begins f. Bib;*

And held him wel therwith content,
300 And ran for the horse verament.
     And when he the horse had fet at the last
     Dane Hew vpon his back he cast
     And bound him to the horse ful sure
     That he might the better indure
305 To ride as fast as they might ren.
     Now shall ye knowe how the miller did then:
     He tooke the horse by the brydle anon--
     And Dane Hew sitting theron--
     And brought him that of the mare he had a sight.
310 Then the horse ran ful right.

          The abbot looked a little him beside
     And saw that Dane Hew towarde him gan ride,
     And was almoste out of his minde for feare
     When he saw Dane Hew come so neere.
315 He cryed, "Help, for the looue of the trinite,
     For I see wel that Dane Hew auenged wil be.
     Alas! I am but a dead man."
     And with that from his mare he ran.

          The abbots men ran on Dane Hew quickly
320 And gaue him many strokes lightly
     With clubs and staues many one.
     They cast him to the earth anone;
     So they killed him once again.

          Thus was he once hanged and foure times slain,
325 And buried at the last, as it was best.
     I pray God send vs all good rest.
                         Amen.

     v. 321 *begins f. Biia.*

John the Reeve

John the Reeve

The Story

A king incognito meeting the humblest of his subjects
is a repeated motif in literature, and is particularly com-
mon in English. John the Reeve belongs to a group of king
and commoner poems of the fifteenth century. In all four
poems--John the Reeve, Rauf Coil3ear, King Edward and the
Shepherd, and The King and the Hermit--the king, taking on
an assumed name, is entertained by a poor subject; the sub-
ject is initially crusty, but warms up to his guest, and
eventually feeds him good wine and stolen venison; and in
return for his host's hospitality, the king invites the
peasant to court, where the latter realizes his guest's
identity and is rewarded, though he fears punishment for
poaching the king's deer. King Edward and the Shepherd is
incomplete, and ends before Adam the Shepherd is rewarded;
The King and the Hermit breaks off even earlier, before the
hermit friar goes to court. King Edward and the Shepherd
and The King and the Hermit are alike in that the king in
both stories has to learn a nonsensical drinking salute:
passilodion is to be answered by berafrynd in King Edward
and the Shepherd, fusty bandyas by stryke pantner in The
King and the Hermit. This feature of the story goes back to
the early thirteenth-century Speculum Ecclesiæ by Giraldus
Cambrensis, in which a Cistercian abbot entertains an incog-
nito Henry II, and abbot and monarch toast each other with
pril and wril (Opera, ed. J.S. Brewer [London: Longmans,
1873], pp. 213-15). In both Giraldus and King Edward and the
Shepherd, and also presumably in the lost ending of The King
and the Hermit, the unusual toasts are given again at court.
In Rauf Coil3ear and John the Reeve there is no such
exchange, but in these poems, too, the king is introduced to
new customs: he is scolded for lack of courtesy, a charge
brought on by Charlemagne's excessive politeness in Rauf
Coil3ear, and by Edward's speaking in Latin to his companions

in John the Reeve. The humour of the pieces derives not only
from the churlishness, suspicion, and discourtesy of the
commoners (from the point of view of those used to the
manners of the court) but also from the awkwardness of the
king introduced into a society with social rules he does not
yet know and has some trouble learning. This aspect of the
story may derive from the well-known legend of King Alfred
and the cakes, which goes back to his first biographer, the
ninth-century bishop Asser (the tale was retold in ballad
form and printed in the sixteenth and seventeenth centuries).

Other stories of a king and commoner, whether contem-
porary to these (like the fifteenth-century King and the
Barker) or later (like the sixteenth- and seventeenth-century
versions of The King and the Tanner, and the seventeenth-
century King Henry II and the Miller of Mansfield) differ in
deriving their humour entirely from the rusticity of the
peasants. For an account of the English king and commoner
poems, see F.J. Child, English and Scottish Popular Ballads,
vol. 5, pt. 1 (Boston: Houghton, Mifflin and Co., 1894),
article 273.

John the Reeve, King Edward and the Shepherd, and The
King and the Hermit were written in the north of England, and
Rauf Coilȝear in Scotland. All four pieces are set outside
the area of composition: the first two in Windsor Forest, The
King and the Hermit in Sherwood Forest, and Rauf Coilȝear
near Paris. The king involved does not seem to matter: in
John the Reeve he is Edward I; in Rauf Coilȝear, Charlemagne;
in King Edward and the Shepherd, Edward III; and in The King
and the Hermit, "god Edwerd." As the stories are distanced
in place and time from their authors and audiences, so too
are they divorced from urgent concern with the immediate
political situation. The commoners--charcoal-burner, shep-
herd, reeve, and hermit-friar--are only apparently poor: in
reality, they have ample wealth. The kings are unlimited in
their benevolence. The harsh forest laws, which gave game
from land designated as forest to the king and punished
poaching severely, end up being taken seriously by neither
side in the stories, peasant nor king. Even in King Edward
and the Shepherd, in which Adam the Shepherd complains about
the rapacity of the king's officers who plunder his goods
and abuse his family in the king's name, giving him in
exchange only a tally-stick which they have no intention of
redeeming, Adam is still well-to-do, and his problems are
over once he lets the unwitting king know what has been
going on.

King Edward and the Shepherd has been edited by W.H.
French and C.B. Hale, in Middle English Metrical Romances
(New York: Russell and Russell, 1930), pp. 949-85, and Rauf
Coil3ear by Sidney J. Herrtage, The Taill of Rauf Coilyear
... with the fragments of Roland and Vernagu, and Otuel,
EETS n.s. 39 (1982). The King and the Hermit follows after
John the Reeve in the present volume.

That John the Reeve was a popular poem, at least in
Scotland, is shown by references to it in the early years of
the sixteenth century. Gavin Douglas, in his Palice of
Honour (1501), sees "Johne the Reif" and "Raf Coil3ear" in
his magic mirror with the other great figures of world liter-
ature. Dunbar mentions "Rauf Col3ard and Johnne the Reif"
in an address to the king (c. 1510). And Sir David Lindsay
describes an archbishop as "dissagysit lyke Ihone the Raif"
in his Testament of the Papingo (1530).[1]

The Manuscript

The Percy Folio manuscript is briefly described as MS B
of Jack and his Stepdame, above. John the Reeve appears on
pp. 357-368 of the manuscript.

Metre

The poet uses a number of licences in rhyme. He rhymes
nd/ng (eg. wand/gange, vv. 346-7), d/t (eg. byte/syde,
vv. 325-6), th/f (eg. wrothe/loffe, vv. 147, 150), and wl/w
(eg. bowle/know, vv. 531, 534), and also allows the following
inexact rhymes: greeffe/office (vv. 205-6), prime/line
(vv. 559-60), abacke/rappe (vv. 727-8), and end/sent (vv.
429,432). He sometimes rhymes on syllables that are normally
unstressed (eg. bringe/likinge, vv. 3, 6). And he rhymes

---

[1] See The Poetical Works of Gavin Douglas, ed. John Small
(Edinburgh: Paterson, 1874), vol. 1, p. 65, vv. 3-4; The
Poems of William Dunbar, ed. James Kinsley (Oxford: Clarendon
Press, 1979), p. 124, vv. 31-4; The Works of Sir David
Lindsay, ed. Douglas Hamer, STS 3rd series 1 (1930), v. 506.

long close e with long or short i, as discussed under
Language and Provenience (below).

The poem is composed of six-line stanzas rhyming aabccb,
usually with the a and c lines containing four stresses and
the b lines three, but with much variation. Occasionally the
poet lengthens the stanza to aabccbdddb (eg. at vv. 211-9).

Language and Provenience

That John the Reeve is northern in its origin is plain
to be seen. The rhymes often imply retention of long a in
words with OE long a (for example, in dame/home, vv. 220-1,
with long a in home from OE hām; and in broad/made, vv. 229-
30, with long a in broad from OE brād; but rope/throate,
vv. 821-2, with long open o in rope from OE rāp rhyming on
long open o in throat from OE þrote). The rhyme Reeue/greefe
(vv. 697-8) probably implies northern devoicing of final v in
Reeue (see Jordan 217), though there is a minority form of
grief attested with a voiced final consonant. The difficult
rhyme last/wist (vv. 28-9) can only be good in the North: the
i of wist goes to e with lowering in a closed syllable
(usually a Southumbrian phenomenon, but see Kristensson, p.
74), and the æ of Old Northumbrian lætest is raised to e
before a dental, as æ sporadically is in the North (see
Kristennson, pp. 46-8).

The second stanza connects the poem with Lancashire:

As I heard tell this other yere,
A clarke came out of Lancashire;
A rolle he had reading.
A bourde written therein he ffound
That sometime ffell in England
In Edwardes dayes our king.

Within the northern dialect area, it is hard to localize
texts further because the region is homogeneous in its lan-
guage. If the poem is from northern Lancashire, however, its
use of a short e in meat (lett/meate, vv. 142-3; meate/wett,
vv. 234, 237; meate/sett, vv. 706-7) and in wheat (wheate/
gett, vv. 145-6) is not surprising, given a similar shorten-
ing of long e before final t in the language of the
Lancashire scribes of The Lady Prioress and of manuscripts P
and E of Jack and his Stepdame; the scribes probably are

indicating shortness in the vowel by doubling final t in the writing of some monosyllables with etymological long e, close or open.

More evidence as to place of origin is given by the series of rhymes [tail]/vayle/walle (vv. 654, 657, 660).   The rhyme is on long a, with long a in vail from OF valer.   Long a in walle is from OE wall, with OE short a + 1 yielding late ME /au/, late ME au + 1 yielding late ME /a:1/ in vulgar speech, according to Dobson (II, paragraphs 60 and 104). Long a in tail (from OE tæȝel) would then indicate a change from ME /ai/ to late ME /a:/, a change which occurred in Scotland and in parts of Southern Yorkshire (Jordan 132). Since the poem cannot be from the southernmost parts of Yorkshire, as it originates within the area where OE long a can be retained as long a, it probably comes either from the northern part of West Riding or over the border in northern Lancashire, if the changing of /ai/ to long a extends that far.

The reference in v. 16 to the "kinges three" with the name of Edward places the time of composition of the poem between 1377 (the year of the death of Edward III: the poem clearly places all three Edwards in the past) and 1461 (the year of the coronation of Edward IV).   Nothing about the language provides strong evidence for a date early in that period.   Herrtage is mistaken in his contention (in his introduction to Rauf Coilȝear, p. vi, fn. 1) that the construction "John daughter Reeue" (v. 364) indicates a time of composition prior to 1400.   A genitive with zero-ending is possible throughout the whole Middle English period, and the word order is attested in early modern English (see Karl Brunner, Die Englische Sprache, 2nd ed. (Tubingen: Max Niemeyer, 1962), II, 15-16.   But MED's earliest citation of the word handful as a linear measurement, as it is used in John the Reeve in vv. 326 and 608, is in 1439, in a context which clearly marks it as a new concept: "They were wonte to mete clothe by yerde and ynche, now they woll mete by yerde and handfull" (Rotuli parliamentorum 5.30b).   Moreover, at vv. 140-1 John distinguishes between ale (which he can afford) and beer (which he cannot).   The two terms were synonymous in Middle English until the introduction from Flanders of the use of hops in brewing (see MED under ale). The old-fashioned drink was then called ale, and the new drink with hops, beer.   Geoffrey Hindley places the beginning of the importation of the practice at London in the 1420s (England in the Age of Caxton [New York: St. Martin's

Press, 1979], pp. 115-6). The mid-fifteenth century, then,
seems the most probable time for the composition of the
poem.

A number of rhymes on ME /i:/ in a normally unstressed
syllable and ME /e:/ in a stressed one seem to indicate that
the poet's speech shows the effect of the vowel shift, with
unstressed /i:/ remaining the same and /e:/ in a stressed
syllable being raised to /i:/: for example, mercy/glee (vv.
1-2), thankefullye/three (vv. 246, 249), sturdye/sea (vv. 310-
1; open e in final position, as in sea, can be raised to
/e:/ in the North and East, according to Dobson, II, paragraph
125); hee/bee/meanye (vv. 348, 351, 354). But this poet
idiosyncratically rhymes ME /e:/ words with ME /i:/ words, in
yere/Lancashire (vv. 8-9), hye/thee (vv. 88-9), mee/I (vv.
175-6), greeffe/office (vv. 205-6), and greene/ffine (vv. 288,
291). He even rhymes /e:/ on short i, in Reeue/liue (vv.
196-7), kinne/queene (vv. 294, 298), and perhaps in greeffe/
office and greene/ffine if the second members of those pairs
have short i: ffine has short i earlier in the poem at v. 512
(rhyme kitchin, v. 511). Such rhymes on ME /e:/ and ME /i:/
or /I/ are true neither before nor after the vowel shift.
They cannot represent an identity in pronunciation, though
they do suggest that /e:/ was unusually tense for the poet.

Another interesting feature of the poet's language is
his consistent rhyming of dish on /s/: dish/service (vv. 393,
396), dishe/iwis (vv. 631-2), and dishe/lesse (vv. 836-7).
The poet's apparent pronunciation of dish with final /s/ is
probably related to the phenomenon of northern /š/ in an
unstressed syllable going to /s/ (see Jordan 183), but of
course dish is not normally an unstressed syllable, and is
more than usually stressed in rhyming position.

Scribal Language and Spelling

The language of the scribe of the Percy Folio Manuscript
is of course very late: mid-seventeenth century. It should
be noted that the scribe is writing conservatively, pre-
serving words and forms that are not his own: grammatical
forms such as the imperative brings at v. 707, and words such
as outcept (v. 156), pallett (v. 599), and ryke (v. 266).
Final e on words like soe and doe, mee and hee is his own, as
is the occasional spelling the for they.

Editorial Treatment

The text below closely follows the Percy Folio Manu-
script, with abbreviations expanded silently, and punctua-
tion, capitalization, and word division according to modern
usage. Emendations and other alterations, such as the
replacement of numerals with their verbal form, are indi-
cated with square brackets in the text.

John the Reeve

God, through thy might and thy mercy,
All that loueth game and glee
Their soules to heauen bringe.
Best is mirth of all solace;
5 Therefore I hope itt betokenes grace,
Of mirth who hath likinge.

As I heard tell this other yere,
A clarke came out of Lancashire;
A rolle he had reading.
10 A bourde written therein he ffound
That sometime ffell in England
In Edwardes dayes our king.

By east, west, north, and southe
All this realme well run he cowthe,
15 Castle, tower, and towne.
Of that name were kinges [three],
But Edward with the long shankes was hee,
A lord of great renowne.

Textual notes: <u>John the Reeve</u> *begins on p. 357.* Title: MS
John de Reeve; v. 16 three: MS 3;

As the king rode ahunting vpon a day
20 [Three] fawcones fflew away;
He ffollowed wonderous ffast.
The rode vpon their horsses that tyde,
They rode forth on euery side,
The country they [umbe]cast.

25 Ffrom morning vntill eueninge late
Many menn abroad they gate,
Wandring all alone.
The night came att the last;
There was no man that wist
30 What way the king was gone,

Saue a bishopp and an erle ffree
That was allwayes the king full nye.
And thus then gan they say,
"Itt is a folly, by St. John,
35 Ffor vs thus to ryde alone
Soe many a wilsome way:

v. 24 umbecast: MS out cast;

A king and an erle to ride in hast,
A bishopp ffrom his courte to be cast,
Ffor hunting, sikerlye.
40 The whether happned wonderous ill:
All night wee may ryde [in] vnskill,
Nott w[i]tting where wee bee."

Then the king began to say,
"Good Sir Bishopp, I you pray,
45 Some comfort, if you may."
As they stoode talking all about
They were ware of a carle stout.
"Gooddene, ffellow," can they say.

Then the erle was well apayd.
50 "You be welcome, good ffellow," hee sayd,
"Of ffellowshipp wee pray thee."
The carle ffull hye on horsse sate.
His legges were short and broad,
His stirroppes were of tree;

v. 41 ryde in vnskill: MS ryde vnskill; v. 42 witting:
MS wotting;

55 A payre of shooes were stiffe and store,
    On his heele a rustye spurre--
    Thus fforwardes rydeth hee.
    The bishopp rode after on his palfrey:
    "Abyde, good ffellow, I thee pray,
60 And take vs home with thee."

    The carle answered him that tyde,
    "Ffrom me thou gettest noe other guide,
    I sweare by sweete St. John."
    Then said the erle, ware and wise,
65 "Thou canst litle of gentrise.
    Say not soe ffor shame."

    The carle answered the erle vnto,
    "With gentleness I haue nothing to doe,
    I tell thee by my ffay."
70 The weather was cold and euen roughe;
    The king and the erle sate and loughe,
    The bishopp did him soe pray.

v. 61 *begins p. 358;*

The king said, "Soe mote I thee,
Hee is a carle, whosoeuer hee be:
75 I reade wee ryde him neere."
The sayd with wordes hend,
"Ryd softlye, gentle ffreind,
And bring vs to some harbor."

Then to tarry the carle was lothe,
80 But rode forth as he was wrothe,
I tell you sickerlye.
The king sayd, "By Mary bright,
I troe wee shall ryde all this night
In wast vnskillfullye."

85 "I ffeare wee shall come to no towne.
Ryde to the carle and pull him downe,
Hastilye without delay."
The bishopp said soone on hye,
"Abide, good ffellow, and take vs with thee,
90 Ffor my loue, I thee pray."

The erle said, "By God in heauen,
Oft men meete att vnsett steuen:
To quite thee well wee may."
The carle sayd, "By St. John,
95   I am affraye[d] of you eche one,
I tell you by my ffay."

The carle sayd, "By Marye bright,
I am afrayd of you this night.
I see you rowne and reason.
100 I know you not and itt were day.
I troe you thinke more then you say.
I am affrayd of treason.

"The night is merke: I may not see
What kind of men that you bee.
105 But and you will doe one thinge--
Swere to doe me not desease--
Then wold I ffaine you please,
If I cold with any thinge."

v. 95 affrayed: MS affraye;

Then sayd the erle, with wordes free,
110 "I pray you, ffellow, come hither to mee,
And to some towne vs bringe.
And after, if wee may thee kenn
Amonge lordes and gentlemen,
Wee shall requite thy dealinge."

115 "Of lordes," sayes hee, "speake no [moe]:
With them I haue nothing to doe,
Nor neuer thinke to haue.
Ffor I had rather be brought in bale
My hood or that I wold vayle
120 On them to crouch or craue."

The king sayd curteouslye,
"What manner of man are yee
Att home in your dwellinge?"
"A husbandman, fforsooth, I am
125 And the kinges bondman;
Thereof I haue good likinge."

v. 115 moe: MS more;

    "Sir, when spake you with our king?"
    "In ffaith, neuer in all my liuing;
    He knoweth not my name.
130 And I haue my capull and my crofft,
    If I speake not with the king oft
    I care not, by St. Jame."

    "What is thy name, ffellow, by thy leaue?"
    "Marry," quoth hee, "John de Reeue.
135 I care not who itt heare.
    Ffor if you come into my inne
    With [beane-]bread you shall beginn
    Soone att your soupper,

    "Salt bacon of a yere old,
140 Ale that is both sower and cold--
    I vse neither braggatt nor bere.
    I lett you witt withouten lett
    I dare eate noe other meate:
    I sell my wheate ech yeere."

v. 137 beane-bread: MS beeffe <u>and</u> bread; v. 138 *begins p.
359;*

145 "Why doe you, John, sell your wheate?"

"Ffor [I] dare not eate that I gett;

Therof I am ffull wrothe.

Ffor I loue a draught of good drinke as well

As any man that doth itt sell,

150 And alsoe a good wheat loffe.

"Ffor he that ffirst starueth John de Reeue,

I pray to God hee may neuer well cheeue,

Neither on water nor land,

Whether itt be sherriffe or king

155 That makes such statu[t]inge:

I outcept neuer a one.

"Ffor and the kings penny were layd by mine

I durst as well as hee drinke the wine

Till all my good were gone.

160 But sithence that wee are meitt so meete,

Tell me where is your receate:

You seeme good laddes eche one."

v. 146 Ffor I dare: MS Ffor dare; v. 155 statutinge: MS
statuinge; v. 161 receate: MS recreate;

The erle answered with wordes ffaire,
"In the kinges house is our repayre,
165 If wee bee out of the way."
"This night," quoth John, "you shall not spill,
Such harbour I shall bring you till:
I hett itt you today.

"Soe that yee take itt thankeffullye
170 In Godes name, and St. Jollye,
I aske noe other pay.
And if you be sturdy and stout,
I shall garr you to stand without
Ffor ought that you can say.

175 "For I haue [two] neigbors won by mee
Of the same ffr[ankp]ledge that am I:
Of o bandshipp are wee.
The Bishopp of Durham th[e tone] oweth;
The Erle of Gloster, whosoe him knoweth,
180 Lord of the other is hee.

v. 174 that you can: MS that <I> can [*Scribe adds* you *in margin*]; v. 175 two: MS 2; v. 176 frankpledge: MS freelege; v. 178 the tone oweth: MS this towne oweth;

"Wist my neighbours that I were thratt,
I vow to God, the wold not lett
Ffor to come soone to mee.
If any wrong were to mee done
185   Wee [three] durst ffight a whole afternoone,
I tell you sikerlye."

The king said, "John, tell vs not this tale:
Wee are not ordayned for battell;
Our weedes are wett and cold.
190   Heere is no man that yee shall greeue.
But helpe vs, John, by your leaue,
With a bright ffeare and bold."

"I'faith," sayd John, "that you shall want,
Ffor ffuell heere is wonderous scant,
195   As I heere haue yee told.
Thou gette[s] noe other of John de Reeue,
Ffor the kinges statutes whilest I liue
I thinke to vse and hold.

v. 185 three: MS 3; v. 196 gettes: MS getteth;

"If thou findes in my house [ffine paynmain]
200   Or in my kitchin poultry slain
Peraduenture thou wold say
That John Reeue his bond hath broken.
I wold not that such wordes weere spoken
In the kinges house another day,

205   "Ffor itt might turne me to great greeffe.
Such proud laddes that beare office
Wold danger a pore man aye.
And or I wold pray thee of mercy longe,
Yett weere I better to lett thee gange,
210   In twenty-neine devilles way."

Thus the rode to the towne.
John de Reeue lighted downe
Besides a comlye hall.
[Four] men beliue came wight;
215   They halted them ffull [right]
When they heard John call.
The served him honestly and able
And [ledd] his horsse to the stable
And lett noe tenne misfall.

v. 199 ffine paynmain: MS payment ffine; v. 214 four: MS 4;
v. 215 ffull right: MS ffull swyft; v. 218 And ledd his:
MS And his; v. 218 *begins p. 360*;

220 Some went to warne their dame
     That John had brought guestes home.
     She came to welcome them tyte,
     In a side ki[r]tle of greene.
     Her head was dight all bydeene:
225 The wiffe was of noe pryde.

     Her kerchers were all of silke,
     Her hayre as white as any milke,
     Louesome of hue and hyde.
     Shee was thicke and somedeale broad:
230 Off comlye ffashyon was shee made,
     Both belly, backe, and side.

     Then [John] called his men all,
     Sayes, "Build me a ffire in the hall,
     And giue their capulles meate.
235 Lay before them corne and hay.
     Ffor my loue rubb of the clay,
     Ffor they beene weary and wett.

v. 223 kirtle: MS kittle; v. 232 Then John calld: MS then
calld [*Scribe adds* John *in margin*];

"Lay vnder them straw to the knee,

....

240 ....

....

Ffor courtye[r]s comonly wold be jollye

And haue but litle to spend."

Then hee said, "By St. John,

245 You are welcome, euery one,

If you take it thankefullye.

Curtesye I learned neu[e]r none,

But after mee, ffellowes, I read you gone."

Till a chamber they went, all [three].

250 A charcole ffire was burning bright,

Candles on chandlours light:

Eche ffreake might other see.

"Where are your sordes?" quoth John de Reeue.

The erle said, "Sir, by your leaue,

255 Wee weare none, pardye."

vv. 239-41 *missing in MS, no gap;* v. 242 courtyers: MS
courtyes; v. 247 neuer: MS neur; v. 249 three: MS 3;

Then John rowned with the erle soe ffree:
"What long ffellow is yonder," quoth hee,
That is soe long of lim and lyre?"
The erle answered with wordes small,
260   "Yonder is Peeres Pay-ffor-all,
The queenes cheefe ffawconer."

"Ah ah," quoth John, "ffor Godes good,
Where gott hee that gay hood,
Glitering of gold itt were?
265   And I were as proud as hee is like,
There is no man in England ryke
Shold garr me keepe his gleades one yeere.

"I pray you, sir, ffor Godes werke,
Who is yond in yonder serke,
270   That rydeth Peeres so nye?"
The erle answered him againe,
"Yonder is a pore chaplaine,
Long aduanced or hee bee.

"And I myself am a sumpter man;
275   Other craft keepe I none,
      I say you withouten mis[s]."
      "You are ffresh ffellows [to your pay],
      Jolly jetters in your array,
      Proud laddes, and I trow, penyles."

280   The king said, "Soe mote I thee,
      There is not a penny amongst vs [three]
      To buy vs bread and fflesh."
      "Ah ha," quoth John, "there is small charge,
      Ffor courtye[r]s comonlye are att large,
285   If they goe neuer soe ffresh.

      "I goe girt in a russett gowne,
      My hood is of homemade browne,
      I weare neither burnett nor greene;
      And yett I troe I haue in store
290   A [thousand pounds] and somedeale more,
      Ffor all yee are prouder and ffine.

v. 275 miss: MS miste; v. 277 ffellows to your pay; MS
ffellows in your appay; v. 281 three: MS 3; v. 284 courtyers:
MS courtyes; v. 290 A thousand pounds: MS a 1000 li;

"Therfore I say, as mote I thee,
A bondman itt is good [to] bee,
And come of carles kinne.
295 Ffor and I bee in tauerne sett,
To drink as good wine I will not lett
As London Edward or his queene."

The erle sayd, "By Godes might,
John, thou art a comly knight,
300 And sturdy in euerye ffray."
"A knight!" quoth John, "Doe away ffor shame.
I am the kinges bondman.
Such wast wordes doe away.

"I know you not in your estate.
305 I am misnurtured, well I wott:
I will not therto say nay.
But if any such doe me wrong,
I will ffight with him hand to hand
When I am cladd in mine array."

v. 293 good to bee: MS good bee; v. 303 *begins p. 361*

310   The bishopp sayd, "You seeme sturdye.
      Trauelled you neuer beyond the sea?"
      Jhon sayd sharplye, "Nay.
      I know none such strange guise,
      But att home on my owne wise
315   I dare hold the hye way.

      "And that hath done John Reeue scath,
      Ffor I haue made such as you wrath
      With choppes and chances [e]re."
      "John de Reeue," sayd our king,
320   "Hast thou any armouringe,
      Or any weapon to weare?"

      "I vow, sir, to God," sayd John thoe,
      "But a pikefforke with graines [two]--
      My ffather vsed neuer other speare--
325   A rusty sword that well will byte,
      And a [thwyttel a handfull] syde
      That sharplye will share,

v. 318 ere: MS yare; v. 323 two: MS 2; v. 326 MS <u>And</u> a
handfull a thyttille syde;

"An acton and a habargyon a ffoote side;
And yett peraduenture I durst abyde
330 As well as thou, Peeres, ffor all thy painted geere."
Quoth John, "I reede wee goe to the hall,
Wee [three] ffellowes and Peeres Pay-for-all;
The proudest before shall fare."

Thither they raked anon wright.
335 A charcole ffyer [was] burning bright
With many a strang brand.
The hall was large and somedeale wyde:
There bordes were couered on euerye syde;
There mirth was [comand].

340 Then the goodwiffe sayd with a seemlye cheere,
"Your supper is readye there."
"Yett watter," quoth John, "lettes see."
By then came Johnes neighbors [two]:
Ho[dg]kin Long and Hob alsoe.
345 The ffirst ffitt here ffind wee.

v. 332 three: MS 3; v. 335 ffyer was burning: MS ffyer
burning; v. 338 were: MS werer; v. 339 comand: MS comanded;
v. 343 two: MS 2; v. 344 Hodgkin: MS Hobkin;

Second Parte

John sayd, "Ffor want of a marshall I will take the wand.
Peeres Ffawconer before shall gange:
Begin the dish shall hee.
Goe to the bench, thou proud chaplaine;
350 My wiffe shall sitt thee againe:
Thy meate-ffellow shall shee bee."
He sett the erle against the king.
They were ffaine att his bidding.
Thus John marshalled his meanye.

355 Then John sperred where his daughteres were.
"The ffairer shall sitt by the fawconere:
He is the best ffarrand man.
The other shall the sompter man haue."
The erle sayd, "Soe God me saue,
360 Of curtesye, John, thou can."

"If my selfe," quoth John, "be [bond],
Yett my daughteres beene well ffarrand,
I tell you sickerlye.
Peeres, and thou had wedded John daughter Reeue,
365 There were no man that durst thee greeue,
Neither ffor gold nor ffee."

v. 361 bond: MS bound;

"Sompter man, and thou the other had,
In good ffaith, then thou were made
Fforeuer in this cuntrye.
370 Then, Peeres, thou might beare the pri[c]e.
Yett I wold this chaplaine had a benefi[c]e,
As mote I [thriue or thee].

"In this towne a kirke there is.
And I were king itt should be his:
375 He shold haue itt of mee.
Yett will I helpe as well as I may."
The king, the erle, the bishopp can say,
"John, and wee liue wee shall quitte thee."

When his daughters were come to dease,
380 "Sitt ffarther," quoth John, withouten leaze,
"Ffor there shal be no [moe].
These strange ffellows I doe not ken:
Peraduenture they may be some gentlemen.
Therfore I and my neighbours towe

v. 370 price: MS prize; v. 371 benefice: MS benefize; v. 372
I thriue or thee: MS I tharue or three; v. 381 moe: MS more;

385 "Att [sidebord end] wee will bee
     Out of the gentles companye.
     Thinke yee not best soe?
     Ffor itt was neuer the law of England
     To sett gentles blood with [bond];
390 Therfore to supper will wee goe."

     By then came in beane-bread,
     Salt bacon, rusted and redd,
     And brewice in a blacke dish.
     Leane salt beefe of a yeere old,
395 Ale that was both sower and cold:
     This was the ffirst service.

     Eche one had of that ylke a messe.
     ....
     The king sayd, "Soe haue I blisse,
400 Such seruice [ner erst] I see."
     Quoth John, "Thou gettest noe other of mee
     Att this time but this."

v. 385 Att sidebord end wee: MS Att side end bord wee; v. 389
bond: MS bound; v. 398 *missing, no gap in MS*; v. 400 ner erst:
MS nerest;

"Yes, good ffellow," the king gan say,
"Take this seruice heer away,
405 And better bread vs bringe,
And gett vs some better drinke:
Wee shall thee requite as wee thinke,
Without any letting."

Quoth John, "Beshrew the morsell of bread
410 This night that shall come in your head,
But thou sweare me one thinge:
Swere to me by booke and bell
That thou shalt neuer John Reeue bettell
Vnto Edward our kinge."

415 Quoth the king, "To thee my truth I plight,
He shall nott witt our seruice [tonight]
No more then he doth nowe,
Neuer while wee [three] liue in land."
"Therto," quoth John, "hold vp thy hand,
420 And than I will thee troe."

v. 416 seruice tonight: MS seruice/; v. 418 three: MS 3;

"Loe," quoth the king, "my hand is heere.

"Soe is mine," quoth the erle with a merry cheere,

"Therto I giue God a vowe."

"Haue heere my hand," the bishopp sayd.

425 "Marry," quoth John, "thou may hold thee well apayd,

Ffor itt is ffor thy [prow].

"Take this away, thou Ho[dg]kin Long,

And let vs sitt out of the throng,

Att a sidebordes end.

430 These strange ffellowes think vncouthlye

This night att our cookerye,

Such as God hath vs sent."

By then came in the pay[nmayn] bread,

Wine that was both white and redd

435 In siluer cuppes cleare.

"Aha," quoth John, "our supper begines with drinke.

Tasste itt, laddes, and looke how yee thinke

Ffor my loue, and make good cheere.

v. 426 thy prow: MS thy power; v. 427 Hodgkin: MS Hobkin;
v. 433 paynmayn: MS payment;

"Of meate and drinke you shall haue good ffare,
440 And as ffor good wine, wee will not spare,
     I [garr] you to understand:
     Ffor euerye yeere, I tell thee [now],
     I will haue a tunn or towe
     Of the best that may be ffound.

445 "Yee shall see [three] churles heere
     Drinke the wine with a merry cheere.
     I pray you, doe you soe.
     And when our supper is all doone
     You and wee will dance soone:
450 Lettes see who best can doe."

     The erle sayd, "By Marry bright,
     Wheresoeuer the king lyeth this night
     He drinketh no better wine
     Then thou selfe does att this tyde."
455 "In faith," quoth John, "[I had leeuer I died]
     Then liue ay in woe and p[i]ne.

v. 441 I garr you: MS I goe you; v. 442 thee now: MS thee
thoe; v. 445 three: MS 3; v. 455 John I had leeuer I died:
MS John soe had leeuer I did; v. 456 pine: MS payne;

"If I be come of carles kinne,
Part of the good that I may winne,
Some therof shall be mine.
460 He that neuer spendeth but alway spareth,
Comonlye oft the worsse he ffareth:
Others will broake itt [syne]."

By then came in red wine and ale,
The bores head into the hall,
465 Then sheild with sauces seere,
Capons both baked and [rost],
Woodcockes, venison, without bost,
And dishmeate dight fful deere.

Swannes they had piping hott,
470 Coneys, curle[w]s, well I wott,
The crane, the hearne in ffere,
Pigeons, partridges, with spicerye,
Elkis, ffl[aun]es, with ffr[ument]ye.
John bade them make good cheere.

v. 458 *begins p. 363*; v. 462 itt syne: MS itt ffine; v. 466
rost: MS rosted; v. 470 curlews: MS curleys; v. 473 fflaunes:
MS fflomes; ffrumentye: MS ffroterye;

475 The erle sayd, "Soe mote I thee,

John, you serue vs royallye.

If yee had dwelled att London,

If King Edward where here,

He might be apayd with this supper,

480 Such ffreindshipp wee haue [ffunden]."

"Nay," sayd John, "by Godes grace,

And Edward wher in this place,

Hee shold not touch this tonne.

Hee wold be wrath with John, I hope;

485 Thereffore I beshrew the [sope]

That shall [in his mouth come]."

Theratt the king laughed and made good cheere.

The bishopp sayd, "Wee fare well heere."

The erle sayd as him thought.

490 They spake Lattine amongst them th[ree].

"In fayth," quoth John, "and yee greeue mee,

Ffull deere itt shal be bought.

v. 480 ffunden: MS ffound; v. 485 sope: MS soupe; v. 486
shall in his mouth come: MS shall come in his mouth; v. 490
three: MS there;

"Speake English, [eueryeche] one,
Or else sitt still, in the devilles name:
495 Such talke loue I naught.
Lattine spoken amongst lewd men--
Therin noe reason [doe I ken];
Ffor falshood it is wrought.

"Row[n]ing, I loue itt neither young nor old;
500 Therefore yee ought not to bee to bold,
Neither att meate nor meale.
Hee was ffalse that rowning began;
Theerfore I say to you, certaine,
I loue itt neuer a deale.

505 "That man can [nought] of curtesye
That letes att his meate rowning bee,
I say, soe haue I sele."
The erle sayd right againe,
"Att your bidding wee will be baine:
510 Wee thinke you say right weele."

v. 493 eueryeche: MS euerye eche; v. 497 reason doe I ken: MS
reason ffind I can; v. 499 Rowning: MS Rowing; v. 505 can
nought of: MS can of;

By this came vp ffrom the kitchin
Sirrupps on plates good and ffine,
Wrought in a ffayre array.
"Sirr[es]," sayth John, "sithe wee are mett
515 And as good ffellowes together sett,
Lett vs be blythe today.

"Hodgkin Long, and Hob of the Lath,
You are counted good fellows both:
Now is no time to [p]ine.
520 This wine is new come out of Ffrance--
Be God, me list well to dance;
Therfore take my hand in thine.

"Ffor wee will, ffor our guestes sake,
Hop and dance, and reuell make,
525 The truth ffor to know."
Vp he rose and drank the wine.
"Wee must haue powder of ginger therein,"
John sayd, as I troe.

v. 514 Sirres: MS Sirrah; v. 519 pine: MS thrine;

John bade them stand vp all about,
530 "And yee shall see the carles stout
Dance about the bowle.
Hob of the Lathe and Hodgkin Long,
In ffayth you dance your measures wrang:
Methinkes that I shold know.

535 "Yee dance neither [carol] nor [brawle],
Trace nor true mesure, as I trowe,
But hopp as yee were woode."
When they began of foote to ffayle,
The tumbled top ouer tayle,
540 And master and master they yode.

Fforth they stepped on stones store.
Hob of the Lathe lay on the fflore;
His brow brast out o[n] blood.
"Ah ha," quoth John, "thou makes [it tough].
545 Had thou not ffalled wee had not [lough]:
Thou gladdes vs all, by the rood."

v. 529 stand vp all: MS stand all [*Scribe adds* vp *above the
line*]; v. 535 neither carol nor brawle: MS neither gallyard
nor hawe; v. 536 *begins p. 364*; v. 543 on: MS of; v. 544
makes it tough: MS makes good game; v. 545 lough: MS laught;

John hent vp Hobb by the hand,
Sayes,"Methinkes wee dance our measures wronge,
By Him that sitteth in throne."
550 Then they began to kicke and wince.
John hitt the king ouer the shinnes
With a payre of new clowted shoone.

Sith King Edward was mad a knight
Had he neuer soe merry a night
555 As he had with John de Reeue.
To bed the busked them anon;
Their liueryes [serued them euerychone]
With a merry che[f]e.

And thus they sleeped till morning att pri[m]e
560 In ffull good sheetes of line.
A masse he garred them to haue,
And after they dight them to dine
With boyled capons good and ffine.
The duke sayd, "Soe God me saue,
565 If euer wee come to our abone,
Wee shall thee quitt our [w]arrison:
Thou shalt not need itt to craue."

v. 557 liueryes serued them eueryche one: MS liueryes were
serued them vp soone; v. 558 chefe: MS cheere; v. 559 prime:
MS prine; v. 566 warrison: MS barrison;

Third Parte

The king tooke leaue att man and [may].
John sett him in the rode way:
570   To Windsor can hee ryde.
Then all the court was ffull faine
That the king was comen againe,
And thanked Christ that tyde.

The jerfawcones were taken againe
575   In the fforest of Windsor, without laine:
The lordes did soe provyde.
They thanked God and St. Jollye.
To tell the queene of their harbor[y]
The lordes had ffull great pryde.

580   The queene sayd, "Sir, by your leaue,
I pray you send ffor that noble reeue
That I may see him with sight."
The messenger was made to wend
And bidd John Reeue goe to the king
585   Hastilye with all his might.

Heading: *In the MS, the section heading is set in beside*
vv. 571-79; v. 568 may: MS mayde; v. 578 harbory: MS harbor;

John waxed vnfaine in bone and blood,
Saith, "Dame, to me this is noe good,
My truth to you I plight."
"You must come in your best array."
590 "What too," sayd John, "sir, I thee pray?"
"Thou must be made a knight."

"A knight!" sayd John. "By Marry myl[d]e,
I know right well I am beguiled
With the guestes I herbord late.
595 To debate they will me bring.
Yett cast I mee ffor nothinge
Noe sorrow ffor to take.

"Allice, ffeitch mee downe my side acton--
My round pallett to my crowne
600 Is made of Millayne plate--
A pitchfforke and a sword."
Shee sayd shee was af[ear]d
This deede wold make debate.

v. 592 mylde: MS myle; v. 602 afeard: MS affrayd;

Allice ffeitched downe his acton syde.
605 Hee tooke itt ffor no [great] pryde,
Yett must hee itt weare.
The scaberd was rent, withouten doubt:
A large handfull the bleade hanged out.
John the Reeue sayd there,

610 "Gett leather and a [nalle, I pray]:
Lett me sow itt a chape today
Lest men scorn my geere.
Now," sayd John, "will I see
[W]hether itt will out lightlye
615 Or I meane itt to weare."

John pulled ffast at the blade.
I wold hee had kist my arse that itt made:
He cold not gett itt out.
Allice held and John draughe:
620 Either att other fast loughe,
I doe yee out of doubt.

v. 605 no great pryde: MS no litle pryde; v. 610 a nalle I
pray: MS a nayle John can say; v. 612 *begins p. 365*; v. 614
Whether: MS Hether;

John pulled at the scaberd soe hard
Againe a post he ran backward
And gave his head a rowte.
625 His wiffe did laughe when he did ffall,
And soe did his meanye all
That were there neere about.

Jhon sent after his neighbors both,
Hodgkine Long and Hobb of the Lath:
630 They were baene att his biddinge.
[Three] pottles of wine in a dishe,
They supped itt all off, [iwis],
All there att their partinge.

John sayd, "And I had my buckler,
635 There's nothing that shold me dare,
I tell you all in ffere.
Ffeitch me downe my [mittons]:
They came [vpon] my handes but once
This [two and twenty] yare.

v. 631 Three: MS 3; v. 632 off iwis: MS off as I wis; v. 637
downe my mittons: MS downe quoth he my gloues; v. 638 came
vpon my: MS came but on my; v. 639 two and twenty: MS 22;

640   "Ffeitch mee my capull," sayd hee there.
      His saddle was of a new manner,
      His stirroppes were of tree.
      "Dame," he sayd, "ffeitch me wine:
      I will drinke to thee once [syne].
645   I troe I shall neuer thee see.

      "Hodgkin Long and Hob of the Lathe,
      Tarry and drinke with me bothe,
      Ffor my cares are ffast commannde."
      They dranke [fiue] gallons verament.
650   "Ffarwell ffellowes all present,
      Ffor I am readye to gange."

      John was soe combred in his geere
      He could not gett vpon his mere
      Till Hodgkinn heaue vp [his tail].
655   "Now ffarwell, sir, by the roode."
      To neither knight nor barron good
      His hatt he wold not vayle
      Till he came to the kings gate.
      The porter wold not lett him in theratt,
660   Nor come within the walle,

v. 642 of tree: MS of a tree; v. 644 once syne: MS once
againe; v. 649 fiue: MS 5; v. 654 vp his tail: MS vp behind;

Till a knight came walking out.
They sayd, "Yonder standeth a carle stout
In a rusticall arraye."
On him they all wondred wright,

665 And said he was an vnseemelye wight,
And thus to him they gan say:

"Hayle, ffellow! Where wast thou borne?
Thee beseemeth ffull well to weare a horne.
Where had[st] thou that ffaire geere?

670 I troe a man might seeke ffull long,
One like to thee or that hee ffound,
Tho he sought all this yeere."

John bade them kis[s]e the devilles arse:
"Ffor you my geare is much the worsse.

675 You will itt not amend;
By my ffaith, that can I lead.
Vpon the head I shall you shread,
But if you hence wende.

v. 669 hadst: MS had; v. 673 kisse: MS kiste;

        "The devill him speede vpon his crowne
680 That causeth me to come to this towne,
     Whether he weare Jack or Jill.
     What shold such men as I doe heere,
     [Dwelling] att the kinges manner?
     I might haue bene att home still."

685 As John stoode fflyting ffast,
     He saw one of his guestes come at the last.
     To him he spake ffull bold,
     To him he [ffull ffast] rode;
     He vayled neither hatt nor hood
690 But sayth, "Thou hast me betold:

        "Ffull well I wott, by this light,
     That thou hast disdaind mee right,
     Ffor wrat[h] I waxe neere wood."
     The erle sayd, "By Marry bright,
695 John, thou made vs a merry night:
     Thou shalt haue nothing but good."

v. 683 Dwelling att: MS Att; v. 688 he ffull ffast rode:
MS he ffast ffull rode; v. 690 *begins p. 366*; v. 693 wrath:
MS wrat·;

The erle tooke leaue att John Reeue,
Sayd, "Thou shalt come in, without greefe.
I pray thee tarry [and wait]."

700   The erle into the hall went,
And told the king verament
That John Reeue was att the gate--
To no man list hee lout--
A long sword gird him ab[o]ut,

705   [A] long ffawchyon, I wott.

The king said, "Goe wee to meate,
And brings him when wee are sett:
Our dame shall haue a play."
"He hath [ten] arrowes in a thonge

710   (Some are short and some are long),
The sooth as I shold say,

"A rusty [p]allett vpon his crowne;
His hood is of homemade browne.
There may nothing him dare.

715   A th[w]yttill hee hath ffast in his hand
That hangeth in a p[ack]e-band,
And sharplye itt will share.

v. 699 tarry and wait: MS tarry a whle [*sic*]; v. 704 about:
MS abut; v. 705 A: MS And a; v. 709 ten: MS 10; v. 712
pallett: MS sallett; v. 715 thwyttil: MS thyttill; v. 716
packe-band: MS peake band;

"He hath a pouch hanging ffull wyde,
    A rusty buckeler on the other syde,
720 His mittons are of blacke clothe.
    ....
    Whosoe to him sayth ought but good,
    Ffull soone hee wil be wrothe."

    Then John sayd, "Porter, lett mee in.
725 Some of my goodes thou shalt win;
    I love not ffor to pray."
    The porter sayd, "Stand abacke.
    And thou come neere, I shall thee rappe,
    Thou carle, by my ffay."

730 John tooke his fforke in his h[e]nd;
    He bare his fforke on an end:
    He thought to make affray.
    His capull was wight and corneffedd;
    Vpon the porter hee him spedd
735 And him [can welnye slay].

v. 721 *missing, no gap in MS*; v. 730 hend: MS hand; v. 735
him can welnye slay: MS him had welnye slaine;

He hitt the porter vpon the crowne:
With that stroke hee fell downe,
Fforsooth, as I you tell.
And then hee rode into the hall
740 And all the dogges, both great and small,
On John ffast can the yell.

John layd about as hee were wood,
And [four] he killed as hee stood:
The rest will now beware.
745 Then came fforth a squier hend
And sayd, "John, I am thy ffreind.
I pray you, light downe [there]."

Another sayd, "Giue mee thy fforke."
And John sayd, "Nay, by St. William of Yorke;
750 Ffirst I will cracke thy crowne."
Another sayd, "Lay downe thy sword.
Sett vp thy horsse. Be not affeard.
Thy bow, good John, lay downe.

v. 743 four: MS 4; v. 747 downe there: MS downe heere;

"I shall hold your stirroppe [of wood].
755 Doe of your pallett and your hoode
     Ere the ffall, as I troe.
     Yee see not who sitteth at the meate.
     Yee are a wonder[s ffolly] ffreake,
     And also passing sloe."

760 "What devill!" sayd John. "Is yt ffor thee?
     Itt is my owne, soe mote I thee.
     Therfore I will [that it bide]."
     The queen beheld him in hast.
     "My lord," shee sayd, "ffor Godes ffast,
765 Who is yonder that doth ryde?
     Such a ffellow saw I neuer [e]re."
     Shee saith, "Hee hath the quaintest geere:
     He is but simple of pryde."

     Right soe came John as hee were wood.
770 He vayled neither hatt nor hood:
     He was a ff[oll]y ffreake.
     He tooke his fforke as hee wold just.
     Vp to the dease ffast he itt thrust.
     The queene ffor ffeare did speake,

v. 754 stirroppe of wood: MS stirroppe/; v. 758 a wonders
ffolly ffreake: MS a wonderous silly ffreake; v. 762 will
that it bide: MS will it weare; v. 766 ere: MS yore; v. 768
begins p. 367; v. 771 ffolly: MS ffaley;

775 And sayd, "Lordes, beware, ffor Godes grace,
Ffor hee will ffro[n]te some in the fface
If yee take not good heede."
They laughed, without doubt,
And soe did all that were about,
780 To see John on his steede.

Then sayd John to our queene,
"Thou mayst be proud, dame, as I weene,
To haue such a ffawconer,
Ffor he is a well ffarrand man,
785 And much good manner hee can,
I tell you sooth in ffere.

"But, lord," he sayd, "my good, it's thine,
My body alsoe ffor to pine,
Ffor thou art king with crowne.
790 But, lord, thy word is honourable:
Both stedffast sure and stable,
And alsoe great of renowne.

v. 776 ffronte: MS ffrowte;

"Therfore, haue mind what thou me hight
When thou [were] with me anight,
795   A warryson that I shold haue."
John spake to him with sturdye mood:
Hee vayled neither hatt nor hood,
But stood with him checkmate.

800   The king sayd, "Ffellow mine,
Ffor thy capons hott and good red wine
Much thankes I doe giue thee."
The queene sayd, "By Mary bright,
Award him as [is] his right:
805   Well aduanced lett him bee."

The king sayd vntill him then,
"John, I make thee a gentleman.
Thy manner place I thee giue,
And a [hundred pounds] to thee and thine,
810   And euery yeere a tunn of red wine,
Soe long as thou dost liue."

v. 794 thou were with: MS thou with; v. 804 as is his: MS as
his; v. 809 a hundred pounds = MS a 100 li;

But then John began to kneele:
"I thanke you, my lord, [so haue I sele].
Therof I am well payd."
815 Thee king tooke a coller bright
And sayd, "John, heere I make thee a knight,"
[Which] worshippe when hee sayd

Then was John euill apayd,
And amongst them all thus hee sayd,
820 "Ffull oft I haue heard tell
That after a coller comes a rope:
I shall be hanged by the throate.
Methinkes itt [goeth] not well."

"Sith thou has taken this estate,
825 That euery man may itt wott
Thou must begin the bord."
Then John therof was nothing ffaine.
I tell you truth withouten laine,
He spake neuer a word,

v. 813 lord so haue I sele: MS lord as I haue soule; v. 817
Which worshippe: MS with worshippe; v. 823 itt goeth not: MS
itt doth not;

830 But att the bords end he sate him downe,
    Ffor he had leeuer beene att home
    Then att all their Ffrankish ffare.
    Ffor there was wine, well I wott;
    Royall meates of the best sortes
835 Were sett before him there.

    A gallon of wine was put in a dishe.
    John supped itt of, both more and lesse.
    "Ffeitch," quoth the king, "such more."
    "By My Lady," quoth John, "this is good wine.
840 Let vs make merry, ffor now itt is time.
    Christs curse on him that doth itt spare."

    With that came in the porters hend
    And kneeled downe before the king.
    [One] was all berinnen with blood.
845 Then the king in hert was woe,
    Sayes, "Porter, who hath dight thee soe?
    Tell on, I wax neere wood."
    "Now in faith," sayd John, "that same was I,
    Ffor to teach him some curtesye,
850 Ffor thou hast taught him noe good.

v. 844 One was: MS Was; v. 850 *begins p. 368;*

"For when thou came to my pore place
With mee thou found soe great a grace
Noe man did bidd thee stand without.
Ffor if any man had against thee spoken
855 His head ffull soone I shold haue broken,"
John sayd, "withouten doubt.

"Therfore I warn thy porters ffree,
When any man [comes] of my countrye,
Ano[n] lett them not be sò stout.
860 If both thy porters goe walling wood,
Be God, I shall reaue their hood
Or goe on ffoote bo[u]te.
But thou, lord, hast after me sent
And I am come att thy comandement
865 Hastilye, withouten doubt."

The king sayd, "By St. Jame,
John, my porters were to blame.
You did nothing but right."
He tooke the case into his hand:
870 Then to kisse hee made them gange.
Then laughed both king and knight.
"I pray you," quoth the king, "good ffellows bee."
"Yes," quoth John, "soe mote I thee,
We were not wrathe ore night."

v. 858 man comes of: MS man out of, out *inserted above the
line*; v. 859 Anon: MS Another; v. 862 boute: MS boote;

875   Then they bishopp sayd to him thoe,
      "John, send hither thy sonnes [two]:
      To the schoole I shall them ffind;
      And soe God may ffor them werke
      That either of them haue a kirke,
880   If ffortune be their ffreind.

      "Also send hither thye daughters both.
      [Two] marryages the king will garr them haue
      And wedd them with a ringe.
      Went fforth, John, on thy way.
885   Looke thou be kinde and curteous aye:
      Of meate and drinke be neur nithing."

      Then John tooke leaue of king and queene,
      And after att all the court bydeene,
      And went fforth on his way.
890   He sent his daughters to the king,
      And they were weded with a ringe
      Vnto [two] squiers gay.

v. 876 two: MS 2; v. 882 Two: MS 2; them haue; MS them to
haue; v. 892 two: MS 2;

His sonnes both hardy and wight,
The one of them was made a knight,
895 And fresh in euery ffray,
The other a person of a kirke,
Gods seruice ffor to worke,
To [serue God] night and day.

Thus John Reeue and his wiffe
900 With mirth and jolty ledden their liffe:
To God they made laudinge.
Hodgikin Long and Hobb of the Lathe,
They were made ffreemen bothe
Through the grace of the [hend king].

905 [John] thought on the bishopps word
And euer after kept open bord
Ffor guestes that God him send,
Till death ffeitcht him away
To the blisse that lasteth aye,
910 And thus John Reeue made an end.

v. 898 To serue God night: MS to god serue night; v. 904 the
hend king: MS the king hend; v. 905 John thought: MS Then
thought.

     Thus endeth the tale of Reeue soe wight--

     God that is soe ffull of might

     To heauen their soules bring

     That haue heard this litle story--

915 That liued sometimes in the south west countrye

     In Long Edwardes dayes our king.

                    Ffinis

The King and the Hermit

The King and the Hermit

The Story

The story of The King and the Hermit and its analogues
has been discussed in the introduction to John the Reeve,
above.

The Manuscript

MS Ashmole 61 (Bodl. 6922), of the Bodleian Library,
contains two of the works in the present volume: The King and
the Hermit and Sir Corneus. It is a long narrow volume,
14 cm. by 42, with a writing block 9 by 31. The leaves are
now gathered in folio the long way, but creases across the
middle of the pages show that the paper was once folded there.
The volume is now bound in cardboard and leather, with
"Ashm. 61" stamped in gold on the spine. The book is fastened
with two clasps bearing a quartered shield.

The body of the manuscript has 162 leaves, plus an extra
leaf on which the first thirty lines of article 1 have been
rewritten; the rest of the page has been turned into a table
of contents. This extra leaf is pasted to another leaf added
at the beginning when the manuscript was bound in its present
binding. The collation of the manuscript is i, ii (with the
table of contents), A^8 (ff. 1-8), B^{10} (ff. 9-18), C^{12} (ff. 19-
30), D^{16} (ff. 30 bis-45), E^{12} (ff. 46-57), F^8 (10 - 2;
missing ix and x. Ff. 58-65), G^{12} (ff. 66-77), H^{14} (ff. 78-91),
I^{13} (12 + 1; f. 98 is single. Ff. 92-104), K^{16} (ff. 105-120),
L^{16} (ff. 121-136), M^{14} (ff. 137-150), N^5 (all singletons but
ff. 153-154. Ff. 151-155), O^6 (ff. 156-161, f. 161 now
detached), iii (marked f. 162). The manuscript is incomplete,
breaking off in the middle of The King and the Hermit. The
foliation is modern. Another foliation sequence begins on
f. 9 and runs ff. 9-91, 91[bis]-150, 160-162. There are no

quire signatures.

The whole manuscript appears to be the work of a single scribe, using "a mixed cursive hand of probably the second half [of the] ... fifteenth century, basically anglicana but containing secretary elements," according to Albinia de la Mare of the Bodleian Library. It appears to be a personal collection of romances and moral or religious pieces, probably compiled over a long time: the scribe uses three different kinds of paper, as can be seen by the watermarks (up to f. 45, an orb and cross watermark occurs; from f. 46 to f. 91, a hand and flower; and from f. 92 to the end, a unicorn). Many of the pieces end with the notation "Amen quod Rate" (and once, on f. 107a, "Amen quod Rathe"): such pieces are marked with an asterisk in the list below. Since Rate can hardly have been the author of all these pieces, he must have been the scribe. He has also decorated the manuscript repeatedly with a fish and flower design: the kind of flower varies, but often looks like a rose or roses. The device usually appears wherever Rate's name does. It is probably a visual pun, perhaps on part of his name or on the name of the place where he was living or the one where he was born. For example (though I doubt that this is the right solution of the riddle) Rosgill in Westmoreland County, which has nothing to do etymologically with either roses or fish gills, could have been his dwelling-place, though not likely his place of origin (see Language and Provenience, below).

The contents of the manuscript are as follows:

1. "Seynt Ewstas" (ff. 1a–5a; BR 211)
2. A satirical piece. ("Thus ryght wysnes do now procede." Incomplete. Ff. 5b–6a.)
*3. How a Wise Man Taught his Son ("Lordinges and ȝe wyll here." Ff. 6a–6b; BR 1985.)
*4. How the Goodwife Taught her Daughter ("Lyst and lythe a lytell space." Ff. 7a–8b; BR 1882.)
*5. "Ysombras" (ff. 9a–16b; BR 1184)
*6. The Ten Commandments from the Speculum Christiani ("Herkyns sirys þat stand abowte." Ff. 16b–17a; BR 1111.)
*7. A manual of courtesy related to Stans Puer ad Mensam ("Jhesu Cryste þat dyed vpon a tree." Ff. 17b–19b; BR 1694.)
*8. A manual of courtesy ("Who so euer wyll thryue or the." Ff. 20a–21b; BR 4127.)
9. A Latin couplet on false friendship by Tibullus (f. 21b)
10. A warning to buyers ("Who so wyll be were in purchasyng." F. 21b; BR 4148.)

11. "O asside asside dico te Romanos superare" (f. 21b)

12. A prayer ("Jhesu Lord, well of all godnes." (F. 22a; BR 2345.)

*13. A prayer ("Jhesu lord blyssed þou be." Ff. 22a-22b; BR 1720.)

14. The first eight lines of item 6 (f. 22b)

15. A prayer to the Virgin from the Speculum Christiani ("Mary moder wele þou be." Ff. 22b-23a; BR 2119.)

*16. The Debate of the Carpenter's Tools ("The shype ax seyd vnto þe wryght." Ff. 23a-26a; BR 3461.)

17. A prayer ("Welcom lord in forme of bred." Ff. 26a-26b; BR 3883.)

*18. The Knight who Forgave the Slayer of his Father, from Handlyng Synne ("By twyx two knyghtes beȝond þe se." Ff. 26b-27b.)

*19. The Earl of Toulous ("Jhesu Cryst in trinite." Ff. 27b-38b; BR 1681.)

*20. "Lybeus Desconus" (ff. 38b-59b; BR 1690)

21. Sir Corneus ("All þat wyll of solas here." Ff. 59b-62a; BR 219.)

22. A miracle of the Virgin ("Lordynges courtase and hen[d]e." Ff. 62b-68b; BR 1987.)

23. Sir Clegys ([L]ystyns lordynges and ȝe schall here." Ff. 68b-73a; BR 1890.)

24. "Festum omnium sanctorum" ("Jhesu Cryst of myȝtes most." Ff. 73a-78b; BR 1685.)

25. A translation of Bishop Grosseteste's Chasteau d'Amour ("Jhesu Cryst heuyn kynge." Ff. 78b-83a; BR 1677.)

26. The Legend of Ipotis ("All þat wyll of wysdom lere." Ff. 83a-87b; BR 220.)

27. "Passio Domini nostri" ("Lystyns lordynges I wyll ȝow tell." Ff. 87b-105b; BR 1907.)

28. "Testamentum Domini" ("Wyte[t]h wele all þat bene here." F. 106a.) Below the poem is drawn a shield quartered by a cross, a sun in each quarter, and a heart with a sun in it in the middle of the cross. The last lines of the poem read, "In wytnes of þat ych thynge,/Myne awne sele þer to I hynge."

*29. "Lamentacio beate Marie" ("In a chyrch as I gan knelle." Ff. 106a-107a; BR 1447.)

30. "The Gouernans of Man" [Lydgate's Dietary] (ff. 107a-108a; BR 824.)

*31. "Septem psalmi penitensiales" [Maydestone's version of the Penitential Psalms] (ff. 108a-111b; BR 1961)

32. Stimulus Conscientie Minor ("All myȝhty God in trinite." Ff. 12a-128a; BR 244.)

*33. "The Stasyons of Jerusalem" (ff. 128a-135b; BR 986)

*34. A prologue to The Adulterous Falmouth Squire ("All crysten men þat walke by me." Ff. 136a-138b; BR 172.)
*35. On the Resurrection ("When Jhesu was in graue leyd." Ff. 138b-144b; BR 3980.)
*36. "[Life of St.] Margaret" ("Old and ʒong þat here be." Ff. 145a-150b; BR 2673.)
 37. "Aʒens Pride" ("Wyth sherp thornys þat be kene." Ff. 150b-151a; BR 4200.)
 38. "Kyng Orfew" (ff. 151a-156a; BR 3868)
*39. "Vanyte" ("O vanyte off vanytes and all is vanite." Ff. 156b-157a; BR 2576.)
 40. The King and the Hermit ("Jhesu þat is heuyn kyng." Ff. 157a-161b. Incomplete. BR 1764.)

At the top of f. 161b, in italic hand, is written the following notation:

It to me from M austin of Hoopenor · n
on Thursday 2 couple of Rabbitts
yᵉ Thursday following 2 couple more
tuesday the 15 of August 1 couple more

The history of the manuscript is obscure. Richie Girvan has demonstrated that the scribe is not the Rate of Ratis Raving (see his introduction to Ratis Raving, STS 3rd series 2 [1939], xxxii-xxxvi). From the unknown Rate it passed somehow into the hands of the nameless beneficiary of Master Austin of Hoopenor and his rabbit-hunting; thence somehow it ended up in the collection of the famous antiquarian Elias Ashmole (1617-1692), who left his books and manuscripts to Oxford.

Metre

The stanza of The King and the Hermit is the twelve-line stanza common in romances: aabccbddbeeb. It is simply double the six-line stanza seen in other comic poems. In one instance, an apparently undamaged stanza has only nine lines (vv. 121-129). In another, the rhyme scheme is aabccbddeffe (vv. 430-441), and perhaps the same is true of vv. 396-407, where in the sequence of past participles, forgete/ete/lete/ sete the first two would normally have final n in the northern dialect in which the poem is written. However, even the rhyme sequence sene/bene/thre/be in vv. 432, 435, 438, 441 can be normalized if the first two infinitives are read without final n.

The poet is generally accurate in his rhyming. The
rhyme huntyng/tyme (vv. 208-9) is a rare exception, and as
such may be suspect. At vv. 400-1, the rhyme ȝate/þerate
depends on an artificial lengthening of the short a of at
under stress. The rhymes hale/stale/schall (vv. 468, 471,
474) probably depend on a similar lengthening in schall.

Language and Provenience

Clearly the place of origin of The King and the Hermit
is within the northern area where OE or ON long a can be
retained as long a in Middle English. The following sets of
rhymes are all on long a:

1)   skath/bothe (vv. 244-5)

ON skáðe is represented in Middle English only with
long a; bothe from ON báðar must here have northern long a.

2)   gate/late/state/hate (vv. 444, 447, 450, 453)

Hate, from OE hāte, here rhymes with gate (from ON gata,
with short a lengthened in an open syllable), late (from OE
late, again with lengthening in an open syllable), and state
(from OF estat and L status; with long a).

3)   sore/were/þer/fare (vv. 514, 517, 520, 523)

Sore, from OE sār, here rhymes with long a forms of
were and there, and with lengthened a in fare from OE faran.

4)   name/home (vv. 449-50)

Home, from OE hām, here rhymes with name with lengthened
a from OE nama.

But the rhyme stond/hunte (vv. 19-20) also shows devoic-
ing of final d after -n- in an accented syllable, a character-
istic only of the West Midlands (Jordan 200). (The rhyme
nyȝhhand/presente at vv. 421-2 probably depends on the not
uncommon form presand.)

The poem must originate in a border area, where the
Northwest Midlands meet the North.

The rhyming sequence at vv. 168, 171, 174, 177--non/
born/non/gon--shows either inaccurate rhyming, or an assimi-
lation of r̲ to following n̲ more usual in a more southerly
text (see Jordan 302 and 166).

The vocabulary of the poem, too, reflects a northerly
origin: hopys (in the sense "suppose"; vv. 412, 418), hyng
(v. 261), hend (as plural of hand, v. 415), at (for that,
v. 71), trayst (v. 88) layke (v. 367), spyre (v. 446), and
bos (v. 277).

Inflectional endings are mixed. The third person singu-
lar indicative ending in the present is -s in rhyming posi-
tion: seys (rh. deys; v. 14). But more southerly forms occur
in non-rhyming position: hath (v. 199), behouyth (v. 162).
There are repeated occurrences of such northern forms as þou
shall (e.g. vv. 343, 456), we schall (eg. vv. 228, 401, 402),
may ye (eg. v. 298), þou bou3tes (v. 224). As we haue
(v. 227) and þei ride and go (v. 513) show the northern zero
inflection of a verb coupled with its pronoun, and are con-
firmed as the poet's by being in rhyming position.

As far as dating is concerned, the evidence from the
language is slight. Final e̲ has of course disappeared. The
difficult rhyme wyldernes/wyld bestes (vv. 127-8) shows the
dropping of the unaccented vowel in the flexional ending
(with consequent reduction of the ensuing consonant cluster
/sts/ to /s:/), but that dropping of unaccented vowels took
place before the beginning of the fifteenth century in the
North (see Jordan 291). There is clear evidence of retention
of the palatal fricative: behy3ht/fortny3t is meant to con-
trast with quyte/wyte at vv. 132-5, and ily3ht/ry3ht with
whyte/tyte at vv. 291-4. But the fricative was retained in
the North and the Northwest Midlands throughout the fifteenth
century (Jordan 295).

The rhyme slepe/cope (at vv. 193-4 and vv. 283-4) seems
to imply either long a̲ or long o̲ in the noun sleep, to rhyme
with the descendant of OE cāpe. Forms with a̲ or o̲ (descended
from rare OE slāp, rather than the more usual slǣp) are
attested in OED only up to a. 1400, with Le Bone Florence of
Rome. However, the poet elsewhere rhymes long a̲ not only
with ME long open e̲ (not surprisingly, since Dobson shows
that long a̲ and long open e̲ were falling together in the
North: II, 98-115), but even with ME long close e̲: mor/suere
(vv. 376-7), dole/mele (vv. 409-10), haue/leue (vv. 488-9),
the latter three with ME open e̲, ben/non (vv. 280-1), the

former with ME close e̱; and therefore perhaps slepe/cope, the
former with ME close e̱.

A couple of words as they are used in the poem are cited
in MED no earlier than the late fourteenth century:

v. 40	hed	MED hed n(1) 1 (f)	a. 1390
v. 297	colopys	MED collop(pe (a)	a. 1376

Totted (apparently meaning "foolish") at v. 343 is not cited
at all in OED, but tot sb¹, meaning "a fool," is first cited
there in 1425. The word maze in the sense "delusion" or
"fancy" (as at v. 412, mase) is last cited in MED from works
written around 1450, but then also from The King and the
Hermit, there dated a. 1500: it is therefore unclear whether
there are occurrences of the word elsewhere in the period
after 1450 (OED's last citation is 1420). The word cope
(vv. 194, 284), in the precise sense of "a friar's garment,"
is last cited in MED from a work written c. 1465.

As the handwriting of the manuscript is of the second
half of the fifteenth century, the manuscript is not of much
help in fixing a terminus ad quem. Verse 13--"It befelle be
god Edwerd deys"--implies that the poem was not written
during the reign of an Edward. Edward III died in 1377 and
Edward IV came to the throne in 1461. The language of the
poem is consonant with a time between those dates, but does
not help to make the dating more precise.

Spelling and Scribal Language

The scribe Rate uses abbreviations frequently and
flexibly: a raised u̱ can mean ou̱, uṟ, even nouṟ, or just ṟ, a
raised a̱ can mean ra̱ or just a̱. He uses the grapheme y̱ for
both þ̱ and the vowel, sometimes distinguishing the vowel by
an accent. I have replaced his consonantal y̱ with þ̱ for
simplicity's sake.

A striking peculiarity is his repeated lack of inflec-
tional ending in the genitive in unexpected words: heuyn
kyng (v. 1), heuyn gam (v. 4), Edwerd deys (v. 13), kyng ȝate
(v. 419), flecher crafte (v. 472).

The King and the Hermit is northern in origin, and most
of the scribal forms are consistent with the North: for
example, usual final y̱d (eg. folowyd, vv. 67, 73; trowyd,

v. 104) and occasional final ys (eg. frythys, v. 21; rotys,
v. 128; arowys, v. 197), beside occasional final ed (eg.
reysed, vv. 56, 217) and occasional final es (eg. gynnes,
v. 52; hornes, v. 66, pylgrymes, v. 107). However, the
plural ending for nouns and the third person singular
present ending for verbs is most often given in abbreviation.
Spellings such as luke (v. 321), ne (v. 68), nehand (v. 414)
are northern. Lyue (v. 369) may be a northern spelling for
life, with inverse substitution of a voiced consonant for an
unvoiced one because of northern devoicing of /v/ in final
position (see Jordan 217); schych (v. 276) may be a similar
inverse spelling, with graphemes indicating /š/ substituted
for s where the northern dialect would normally have /s/ for
/š/ in an unstressed syllable (Jordan 183). The participle
brynand in -and (v. 183) is consonant with the north or
extreme west or east of the country. Not all of the northern
forms are attributable to the poet: Sir Corneus, which is
also in Ashmole 61, originates in the Southeast Midlands, and
its text is full of northern spellings (see the introduction
to Sir Corneus, below).

   Other forms suggest some southerly influence, perhaps
from an intermediate scribe: hem (v. 389) rather than
northerly them; herand (v. 251), horpyd (v. 428), and
hermyte (vv. 122, 115 etc.) with unetymological h-; go
(v. 241), ily3ht (v. 291), isalt (v. 295) as past participles;
and doth (v. 209) for the third person plural present tense.
Forms with -ond in words like hond, stond are so frequent
(eg. vv. 378, 413, 416, 419, 460) that the scribe must be
writing south of Oakden line D.

   Rate's usual spelling thoff for the descendant of ON
*þōh (vv. 159, 245, 436, 451; allthoff, v. 246) shows transi-
tion from the velar fricative /x/ in final position to /f/.
According to Jordan (294), such a transition does not take
place in Lancashire and Cumberland in Middle English.

   If Rate came from a northern area (as his spelling and
inflexional forms in the manuscript suggest), but south of
Oakden line D, and if the form thoff was not current in
Lancashire, then he most likely was from the extreme south-
west of Yorkshire.

Editorial Treatment

The many scribal abbreviations have been silently
expanded. The final marks representing -es or -ys have been
expanded as -es: both spellings are attested in the manu-
script. I have regularized word division and capitals, and
added punctuation. Initial ff in Rate's spelling stands for
F, and I have treated it as such.

The King and the Hermit

Jhesu þat is heuyn kyng,
ȝiff þem all god endyng
(If it be þi wyll)
And ȝif þem parte of heuyn gam
5   That well can call gestes same,
With mete and drinke to fylle.
When þat men be glad and blyth,
Than wer solas god to lyth,
He þat wold be stylle.
10 Off a kyng I wyll ȝou telle,
What auentour hym befelle,
He that wyll herke thertylle.

Textual notes: The King and the Hermit *begins on f. 157a.*
No title in MS.

It befelle þe god Edwerd deys--
Forsoth, so þis romans seys:
15 Herkyn[s], I wyll ȝou telle.
The kyng to Scherwod gan wend
On hys pleyng for to lend
. . . .
For to solas hym þat stond,
20 The grete hertes for to hunte
In frythys and in felle,
With ryall festes and feyr ensemble,
With all the lordes of þat contre;
With hym þer gan þei duell.

25 Tyll it befell vpon a dey
To hys fosterse he gan sey,
"Felous, wher is þe best?
In ȝour playng wher ȝe haue bene,
Wer haue ȝe most gam sene
30 Off dere in þis forest?"
They ansuerd and fell on kne,
"Ouerall, lord, is gret ple[n]te,
Both est and west.
We may schew ȝou at a syȝt
35 Two thousand dere þis same nyȝt
Or þe son go to reste."

*By vv. 14-5 in the right margin, cancelled, appear
these words: ffor soth as þe/romans seys. v. 15 Herkyns:
MS herkyng; v. 18 missing, no gap in MS; v. 31 begins
f. 157b; v. 32 plente: MS plete;*

An old foster drew hym nere.
"Lystins, lord, I saw a dere
Vnder[neath] a tre.
40 So gret a hed as he bare,
Sych one saw I neuer are:
No feyrer myht be.
He is mor than oþer two
That euer I saw on erth go."
45 Than seyd the kyng so fre,
"Thy waryson I wyll þe ȝeue
Euer mor whyll þou doyst lyue:
That dere þou late me se."

Vpon þe morne þei ryden fast
50 With hundes and with hornes blast:
To wodde þan are þei wente.
Nettes and gynnes þan leyd he.
Euery archer to hys tre,
With bowys redy bent.
55 The blew thrys, vncoupuld hundes;
They reysed þe dere vp þat stondes,
So nere þei span and sprent.
The hundes all, as þei wer wode,
They ronne þe dere [into the] wode.
60 The kyng hys hors he hent.

v. 39 Vnderneath a: MS Vnder a; v. 59 dere into the
wode: MS dere as þei wer wode;

The kyng sate onne a god courser.
Fast he rode after þe dere:
A ro chasyd h[e] ry3ht fast.
Both thorow thyke and thine
65   Thorow þe forest he gan wyn
With hundes and hornes blast.
The kyng had folowyd hym so long
Hys god sted was ne sprong:
Hys hert away was past.
70   Horn ne hunter my3t he non here.
So ranne þe hundes at þe dere
Awey was at þe last.

The kyng had folowyd hym so long,
Fro mydey to the euynsong,
75   That lykyd hym full ille.
He ne wyst wer þat he was,
Ne out of þe forest for to passe,
And þer he rode all wylle.
"Whyle I may þe deyly3ht se
80   Better is to loge vnder a tre,"
He seyd hymselue vntylle.
The kyng cast in hys wytte,
"3yff I stryke into a pytte,
Hors and man my3ht spylle.

v. 63 chasyd he ry3ht: MS chasyd hym ry3ht;

85 "I haue herd pore men call at morow
    Seynt Julyan send þem god harborow
    When þat they had nede,
    And ȝit whe[n] þat þei wer [trayst]
    And of herborow wer abayst,
90 He wold þem wysse and rede.
    Seynt Julyan, as I ame trew knyȝt,
    Send me grace þis iche nyȝht
    Of god harbour to sped.
    A ȝift I schall þe gyue
95 Euery ȝere whyll þat I lyue,
    Folke for þi sake to fede."

    As he rode whyll he had lyȝt
    At þe last he hade syȝht
    Off an hermyt[ag]e hym besyde.
100 Off that syȝht he was full feyn,
    For he wold gladly be [þer in] pleyn,
    And þeder he gan to ryde.
    [The] hermytage he fond þer;
    He trowyd a chapell þat it wer.
105 Than seyd þe kyng þat tyde,
    "Now, Seynt Julyan, a bonne [hostel],
    As pylgrymes trow full wele.
    ȝonder I wyll abyde."

    v. 88 *begins f. 158a*; when: MS whe; trayst: MS trauyst;
    v. 98 At: MS And at; v. 99 hermytage: MS hermyte;
    v. 101 be þer in pleyn: MS be in þe pleyn; v. 103 The
    hermytage: MS An hermytage; v. 106 bonne hostel: MS
    bonne vntyll;

A lytell ʒate he fond ner[by]:
110 þeron he gan to call and cry
That within myʒht here.
That herd an hermyte þer within.
Vnto þe ʒate he gan to wyn,
Bedyng his prayer.
115 And when þe hermyt saw þe kyng,
He seyd, "Sir, gode euyn[yng]."
"Wele worth þe, Sir Frere.
I pray þe I myʒt be þi gest,
For I haue ryden wyll in þis forest,
120 And nyʒht neyʒes me nere."

The hermyte seyd, "So mote I the,
For sych a lord as ʒe be,
I haue non herbour tyll.
Bot if it [wer neuer so] pore a wyʒht
125 I ne der not herbour hym a nyʒt
Bot he for faute schuld spyll.
I won here in wyldernes
With rotys and ryndes among wyld bestes
As it is my Lordes wylle."

v. 109 nerby: MS ner; v. 116 euynyng: MS euyn;
v. 124 it wer neuer so pore: MS it s·· pore;

130   The kyng seyd, "I þe beseche
       The wey to þe tounne þou wold me teche,
       And I schall þe behyȝht
       That I schall þi trauell quyte
       That þou schall me not wyte
135   Or passy[t]h þis fortnyȝt,
       And if þou wyll not, late þi knaue go
       To teche me a myle or two
       The whylys I haue deylyȝht."
       "By Seynt Mary," seyd þe frere,
140   Schorte seruys getys þou here,
       And I can rede aryȝht."

       Than seyd þe kyng, "My dere frend,
       The wey to þe towne if I schuld wynd,
       How fer may it be?"
145   "Syr," he sayd, "so mote I thryue,
       To þe towne is myles fyue
       From þis long tre.
       A wyld wey I hold it wer,
       The wey to wend (I ȝou suere),
150   Bot ȝe þe dey may se."
       Than seyd þe kyng, "Be Godes myȝht,
       Ermyte, I schall harbour with þe þis nyȝht,
       And els I wer we."

       v. 135 passyth: MS passyȝh; v. 142 *begins f. 158b;*

"Methinke," seyd þe hermyte, "þou arte a stout syre.

155 I haue ete vp all þe hyre
That euer þou gafe me.
Were I oute of my hermyte wede
Off þi fauyll I wold not dred
Thoff. þer wer sych thre.

160 Loth I wer with þe to fy3ht:
I wyll herbour þe all ny3t
And it behouyth so be.
Sych gode as þou fyndes here, take,
And aske thyn in for Godes sake."

165 "Gladly, sir," seyd he.

Hys stede into þe hous he lede:
With lytter son he gan hym bed.
Met ne was þer non:
The frere he had bot barly stro--

170 Two thake-bendesfull, without no,
For soth it was furth born.
Befor þe hors þe kyng it leyd.
"Be Seynt Mayré," þe hermyte seyd,
"Oþer thing haue we non."

175 The kyng seyd, "Garamersy, frer.
Wele at es ame I now here.
A ny3t wyll son be gon."

The kyng was neuer so seruysable:
He hew þe wode and keped þe stable.
180 God fare he gan hym dyȝht
And mad hym ryȝt well at es,
And euer þe fyre befor hys nese
Brynand feyr and bryȝt.
"Leue ermyte," seyd þe kyng,
185 "Mete, and þou haue anything,
To soper þou vs dyȝht.
For serteynly, as I þe sey,
I ne hade neuer so sory a dey
That I ne had a mery nyȝt."

190 The kyng seyd, "Be Godes are,
And I sych an hermyte were
And wonyd in þis forest,
When fosters wer gon to slepe,
Than I wold cast off my cope
195 And wake b[o]th est and weste
Wyth a bow of hue full strong
And arowys knyte in a thong:
That wold me lyke best.
The kyng of venyson hath non nede:
200 Ȝit myȝht me hape to haue a brede
To glade me and my gest."

v. 195 both: MS beth; v. 196 *begins f. 159a;*

The hermyte seyd to þe kyng,
"Leue sir, wer is þi duellyng?
I praye þou wolde me sey."
205   "Sir," he seyd, "so mote I the,
In þe kynges courte I haue be
Duellyng many a dey,
And my lord [rydys] on huntyng
As grete lordes doth many tyme
210   That ȝiff þem myche to pley.
And after a grete hert haue we redyn
And mekyll trauell we haue byden
And ȝit he scape awey.

"Todey erly in þe mornyng
215   The kyng rode on hu[n]tyng,
And all þe courte beden.
A dere we reysed in þat stondes
And gaue chase with our hundes:
A feyrer had never man sene.
220   I haue folowyd hym all þis dey
And ryden many a wylsom wey:
He dyd me trey and tene.
I pray ȝou, helpe me I wer at es.
Thou bouȝtes neuer so god serue[s]e
225   In sted þer thou hast bene."

v. 208 rydys: MS rode; v. 215 huntyng: MS hutyng;
v. 224 seruese: MS seruege;

The ermyte seyd, "So God me saue,
Thou take sych gode as we haue:
We schall not hyll [it] with þe."
Bred and chese forth he brouȝt.

230 The kyng ete [long] whyles, hym thouȝt;
Non oþer mete saw he.
Sethen thyn drynke he dreuȝe.
Theron he had sone inouȝe.
Than seyd þe kyng so fre,

235 "Hermyt, pute vp þis mete tyte,
And if I mey I schall þe quyte
Or passyd be þese monethys thre."

Than seyd þe kyng, "Be Godes grace,
Thou wonys in a mery place.

240 To schote þou schuldes lere.
When þe fosters are go to reste
Somtyme þou myȝt haue off þe best,
All of þe wylld dere.
I wold hold it for no skath

245 Thoff þou had bow and arowys bothe
Allthoff þou be a frere.
Ther is no foster in all þis fe
That wold sych herme to þe;
Ther þou may leue here."

v. 228 schall not: MS schall we not; hyll it with: MS
hyll with; v. 230 ete long whyles: MS ete whyles;

250   The armyte seyd, "So mote þou go,
     Hast þou any oþer herand þan so
     Onto my lord þe kynge?
     I schall be trew to hym, I trow,
     For to weyte my lordes prow
255   For dred of sych a thing.
     For iff I wer take with sych a dede,
     To þe courte þei wold me lede
     And to prison me bryng;
     Bot if I myȝt my raunson gete,
260   Be bond in prison and sorow grete
     And in perell to hyng."

     Then seyd þe kyng, "I wold not lete,
     When þou arte in þis forest sette,
     To stalke when men are at rest.
265   Now, as þou arte a trew man,
     Iff þou ouȝt of scheting can,
     Ne hyll it not with þi gest.
     For, be Hym that dyȝed on tre,
     Ther schall no man wyte for me,
270   Whyll my lyue wyll lest.
     Now hermyte, for þi professyon,
     Ȝiff þou haue any venison,
     Thou ȝiff me off þe best."

     v. 250 *begins f. 159b.*

The ermyte seyd, "Men of grete state,
275 Oure order þei wold make full of bate
Aboute schych mastery.
[Vs bos] be in prayer and in penans,
And arne þerine by chans
And not be archery.
280 Many dey I haue her ben
And flesche mete I ete non
Bot mylke off þe ky.
Warme þe wele and go to slepe,
And I schall lape þe with my cope,
285 Softly to ly3e."

"Thou semys a felow," seyd þe frere.
"It is long gon seth any was here
Bot þou thyselue tony3ht."
Vnto a cofyr he gan go
290 And toke forth candylles two,
And sone þei wer ily3ht.
A cloth he brou3t, and bred full whyte,
And venyson ibake tyte.
A3en he 3ede full ry3ht:
295 Venyson isalt and fressch he brou3t,
And bade hym chese wheroff hym thou3t
Colopys for to dy3t.

Below v. 275 *appears the cancelled line:* And on to
prison bryng. v. 277 Vs bos be: MS Bo be;

Well may ye wyte, inow þei had.

The kyng ete and made hym glad

300 And grete lauȝter he lowȝe:

"Nere I had spoke of archery

I myȝt haue my bred full dryȝe."

The kyng made it full towȝhe.

"Now Crystes blyssing haue sych a frere

305 That þus canne ordeyn our soper

And stalke vnder þe wode bowe.

The kyng hymselue, so mote I the,

Is not better at es þan we,

And we haue drinke inowȝe."

310 The hermyt seyd, "Be Seynt Sauyour,

I haue a pote of galons foure

Standing in a wro.

Ther is bot þou and I and my knaue:

Som solas schall we haue

315 Sethyn we are no mo."

The hermyte callyd hys knaue full ryȝt--

Wylkyn Alyn, for soth, he hyȝht--

And bad hym belyue go,

And tauȝht hym priuely to a sted

320 To feche þe hors corne and bred,

"And luke þat þou do so."

v. 304 *begins f. 160a;* v. 318 belyue go: MS be lyue <u>and</u>
go;

Vnto þe knaue seyd þe frere,
"Felow, go wyȝtly here.
Thou do as I þe sey.

325 Besyde my bed þou must goo
And take vp a slouȝte of strawe
Als softly as þou may.
A howuyd pote þ[er] stondes þer,
And Godes forbot þat we it spare

330 To drynke to it be dey.
And bryng me forth my schell,
And euery man schall haue hys dele,
And I schall kenne vs pley."

The hermyte seyd, "Now schal I se
335 Iff þou any felow be
Or off pley canst ouȝht."
The kyng seyd, "So mote I the,
Sey þou what þou wyll with me:
Thy wyll it schall be wrouȝt."

340 "When þe coppe commys into þe plas,
Canst þou sey 'Fusty bandyas'
And thinke it in þi thouȝt?
And þou schall her a totted frere
Sey 'Stryke pantner'

345 And in þe coppe leue ryȝt nouȝt."

v. 328 pote þer stondes: MS pote þat stondes;

And when þe coppe was forth brouȝt,
It was oute of þe kynges thouȝt,
That word þat he schuld sey.
The frere seyd "Fusty bandyas."
350 Than seyd þe kyng, "Alas, alas":
Hys word it was awey.
"What! Arte þou mad?" seyd þe frere,
"Canst þou not sey 'Stryke pantner?'
Wylt þou lerne all dey?
355 And if þou eft forgete it ons,
Thou getes no drinke in þese wons
Bot ȝiff þou thinke vpon þi pley."

"Fusty bandias," þe frere seyd,
And ȝafe þe coppe sych a breyd
360 That well nyȝ of i[t] ȝede.
The knaue fyllyd [it] vp and ȝede in plas.
The kyng seyd "Fusty bandyas":
Therto hym stod gret nede.
"Ffusty bandyas," seyd þe frere,
365 "How long hast þou stond here
Or þou couth do þi dede?
Fyll þis eft and late vs l[a]yke,
And betwen rost vs a st[e]yke,
Thus holy lyue to lede."

v. 358 *begins f. 160b*; v. 360 of it ȝede: MS of iȝede;
v. 361 fyllyd it vp: MS fyllyd <u>and</u> vp; v. 367 layke:
MS lyke; v. 368 steyke: MS styke;

370 The knaue fyllyd þe coppe full tyte
     And brou3t it furth with grete delyte;
     Befor hym gan it stand.
     "Ffusty bandyas" seyd þe frere;
     The kyng seyd "Stryke pantner"
375 And toke it in hys hand,
     And stroke halue and mor.
     "Thys is þe best pley, I suere,
     That euer I saw in lond.
     I hy3ht þe, hermyte, I þe 3eue,
380 I schall þe quyte, if þat I lyue,
     The gode pley þou hast vs fonnd."

     Than seyd þe ermyte, "God quyte all,
     Bot when þou commys to þe lordes haule
     Thou wyll forgete þe frere.
385 Bot wher þou commyst, ny3ht or dey,
     3it my3ht þou thinke vpon þe pley
     That þou hast sene here.
     And þou com among jentyll men
     The wyll lau3 and þou hem it ken,
390 And make full mery chere.
     And iff þou comyst here for a ny3t,
     A colype I dere þe behy3t,
     All of þe wyld dere."

     v. 374 pantner: MS pantneuer; v. 379 hermyte I þe: MS
     hermyte I schall þe;

The kyng seyd, "Be Hym þat me bouȝt,
395 Syre" (he seyd), "ne thinke it nouȝt,
That þou be þus forgete.
Tomorow sone when it is dey
I schall quyte, iff þat I may,
All þat we haue here ete.
400 And when we com to þe kynges ȝate,
We schall not long stond þerate:
In we schall be lete.
And by my feyth, I schall not blyne
Tyll þe best þat is þerine
405 Betwenn vs two be sete."

Th'ermyte seyd, "Be Hym þat me bouȝt,
Syre" (he seyd), "ne thynke it nouȝt.
I suere þe by my ley,
I haue be þer and takyn dole,
410 And haue hade many merry mele,
I dare full sauely sey.
Hopys þou I wold for a mase
Stond in þe myre þer and dase
Nehand halue a dey?
415 The charyte commys thorow sych menys hend,
He hauys full lytell þat stond[ys] hend
Or þat he go awey.

v. 415 *begins f. 161a*; v. 416 stondys: MS stond at;

"Hopys þou þat I ame so preste
For to stond at þe kyng ȝate and reste
420 There pleys for to lere?
    I haue neyȝbors her nyȝhhand:
    I send þem of my presente,
    Sydes of þe wyld dere.
    Off my presantes þei are feyn:
425 Bred and ale þei send me ageyn.
    Thusgates lyue I here."
The kyng seyd, "So mote I the,
Hermyte, me pays wele with þe:
    Thou arte a horpyd frere."

430 The kyng seyd, "Ȝit myȝt þou come sum dey
Vnto þe courte for to pley,
    Aventourys for to sene.
    Thou wote not what þe betyde may
    Or þat þou go awey:
435 The better þou may bene.
    Thoff I be here in pore clothing,
    I ame no bayschyd for to bryng
    [Ges]tys two or thre.
    Ther is no man in all þose wonys
440 That schall myssey to þe onys,
    Bot as I sey, so schall it be."

v. 423 Sydes: MS Be sydes; v. 434 go: MS gon; v. 438
Gestys: MS Ȝiftys;

"Sertes," seyd þe hermyte þan,
"I hope þou be a trew man:
I schall aventour þe gate.
445 Bot tell me fyrst, leue syre,
After what man schall I spyre,
Both erly and late?"
"Jhake Flecher, þat is my name:
All men knowys me at home.
450 I ame at ȝong man state.
And thoff I be here in pore wede
In sych a stede I can þe lede
Ther we schall be m[et] full hate."

"Aryse vp, Jake, and go with me,
455 And mor off my priuyte
Thou schall se somthyng."
Into a chambyr he hym lede:
The kyng sauȝe aboute þe hermytes bed
Brod arowys hynge.
460 The frere gaff hym a bow in hond.
"Jake," he seyd, "draw vp þe bond."
He myȝt oneth styre þe streng.
"Sir," he seyd, "so haue I blys,
Ther is non archer þat may schet in þis
465 That is with my lord þe kyng."

v. 453 met: MS made;

An arow off an elle lon[g],

In hys [b]ow he it throng,

And to þe hede he gan it hale.

Ther is no dere in þis foreste

470 And it wold onne hym feste

Bot it schuld spyll his stale.

"Jake, seth þou can of flecher crafte,

Thou may me es with a schafte."

Than seyd Jake, "I schall."

475 ....

....

....

"Jake, and I wyst þat thou wer trew,

Or and I þe better knew,

Mor þou schuldes se."

The kyng to hym grete othys swer:

480 "The couenand we made whyleare,

I wyll þat it hold be."

Tyll two trowys he gan hym lede:

Off venyson þer was many a brede.

"Jake, how thinkes þe?

485 Whyle þer is dere in þis forest,

Somtyme I may haue of þe best:

The kyng wyte sone on me.

v. 466 long: MS lond; v. 467 bow: MS low; v. 469 *begins*
f. 161b; vv. 475-7 *missing, no gap in MS*;

"Jake, and þou wyll of myn arowys haue,
Take þe off þem, and sum þou leue,
490 And go we to our pley."
And þer þei sate with "Fusty bandyas,"
And with "Stryke pantneuer" in þat plas,
Tyll it was nerehand dey.
When tyme was com þer rest to take,
495 On morn þei rose when þei gan wake.
The frere began to sey,
"Jake, I wyll with þe go
In þi felowschype a myle or two,
Tyll þou haue redy wey."

500 "Ȝe," seyd þe kyng, "mekyll thanke,
Bot when we last nyȝht togeder dranke,
Thinke what þou me behyȝht:
That þou schuld com som dey
Vnto the courte for to pley
505 Wh[at] tyme þou se þou myȝht."
"Sertes," seyd þe hermyte þan,
"I schall com, as I ame trew man,
Or tomorow at nyȝht."
Ather betauȝt oþer gode dey.
510 The kyng toke þe redy wey:
Home he rode full ryȝht.

v. 505 What tyme: MS When tyme;

Kny3tes and squyres many mo,

All þat ny3t þei ride and go,

With sy3eng and sorrowy[n]g sore.

515 They cry3ed and blew with hydoys bere,

3iff þei my3t of þer lord here,

Wher þat euer he were.

When þe kyng his bugyl blew,

Kny3tes and fosters wele it knew,

520 And lystind to hym þer.

Many man þat wer masyd and made,

The blast of þat horn made þem glad:

To þe towne þan gan þei fare.

v. 514 sorrowyng: MS sorrowyg; v. 523 *finishes the page. The following leaf is blank.*

Sir Corneus

Sir Corneus

Of the extant stories analogous to Sir Corneus, none is close enough to be a source. The poet has probably taken the object motivating his tale (the chastity-testing horn) and the setting (Arthur's court at Caerleon) from a previous story and developed his own comic version of the inevitable results. Only in this story is the horn already in Arthur's possession, and only here is he the last, rather than the first, to discover himself a cuckold.

The closest analogue is Robert Biket's Lai du cor, an Anglo-Norman poem preserved in only one manuscript, Digby 86. The manuscript is dated 1272-82, and comes from the diocese of Worcester.[1] In the lai, a young man comes to court bearing an ivory horn richly jewelled, with eerie tinkling bells on it. It is a gift to Arthur. Anyone trying to drink from the horn will spill if he is a cuckold, if he is jealous, or if his wife has entertained a foolish thought ("fol pensé," v. 236) about another man. Arthur drinks and spills, and is dissuaded from knifing Guinevere. Other men of the court try to drink and fail. Arthur laughs and forgives his wife:

> Quant voit LI ROIS ARZURS
> Sour touz est espaunduz,
> Hounk pus n'out del në ire
> Einz commença a rire,
> Graunt joie en demena.
> Ses barouns apela:

---

[1] See C.T. Erickson's introduction to his edition The Anglo-Norman Text of Le Lai du cor, Anglo-Norman Text Society 24 (1973 for 1966), p. 24.

'Seingnours, or m'enttendez.
Ne sui pas soul gabbez;
Qui cest corn me dona
Graunt doun me presenta ....'
                          (Erickson's edition, vv. 457-466)

At last Garadue, encouraged by his wife, drinks successfully
and is rewarded by the king.

A comparable episode in Malory's Tristram de Lyones (in
The Works of Sir Thomas Malory, ed. Eugène Vinaver, vol. 1,
[Oxford: Clarendon Press, 1947], pp. 429-30), taken from the
French prose Tristan, differs in these critical features: the
horn is supposed to be sent to Arthur's court, but ends up at
King Mark's, and the women, not the men, must try to drink to
establish their own loyalty.

There are extant versions of the chastity-testing horn
story in French, German, and Italian. A section of the first
of the thirteenth-century continuations to Chrétien's
Perceval le Gallois--Le Livre de Carados--is the one contain-
ing the most of the important features preserved in Sir
Corneus: the episode takes place at Arthur's court, at
Caerleon; it is the men rather than the women who attempt to
drink from the horn; and only adultery will cause the wine to
spill. An important feature that is in this poem and not the
lai--that adultery alone will cause the horn to spill its con-
tents--does not necessarily imply that the poet must have
developed his story from this and not from the lai. In all
versions, whatever the ladies and their defenders such as the
Yvain of the lai may say, the offense committed is assumed to
have been adultery.

Tom Peete Cross has argued in "Notes on the Chastity-
Testing Horn and Mantle" (Modern Philology 10 [1913], 289-99)
that the motif of the chastity-testing horn originates in
Gaelic story, but his evidence for the existence of the horn
rather than other such magic objects in medieval Gaelic story
is very slight. Motifs of chastity-testing objects are wide-
spread: see Stith Thompson H411. The next poem in this
volume, The Boy and the Mantle, uses the test of the horn in
combination with the equally well-known test of the magic
mantle. For information on the story of the chastity-testing
horn in medieval literature see especially Erickson's intro-
duction to Le Lai du cor, and F.J. Child's English and Scottish
Ballads vol. 1 (Boston: Little, Brown and Co., 1857), pp. 24-
34.

The Manuscript

Ashmole 61 is described above, in the introduction to
The King and the Hermit.

Metre

The stanza of <u>Sir Corneus</u> is the six-line, aabccb
stanza seen elsewhere in <u>John the Reeve</u> and <u>Jack and his
Stepdame</u>. The rhyming is careful, the poet allowing himself
licences in rhyming m/n (herme/wern, vv. 111, 114; and tyme/
fyne, vv. 184-5) and in rhyming stressed and unstressed
syllables (thyng/lesying, vv. 15, 18; lesyng/kyng, vv. 61-2;
kyng/dansyng, vv. 141, 144).

Language and Provenience

The overall picture the poem gives is of northern pro-
venience, in its only extant text; but many of the northern
features may be scribal. Certain of the features fixed by
rhyme might be northern or at least northerly:

1) sykerlyke/baskefysyke (vv. 115-16)

The -<u>lyke</u> ending is northerly, as opposed to southerly
-<u>liche</u>.

2) it/lette (vv. 31-2)

The raising of <u>e</u> to <u>i</u> in a closed syllable is predominantly
northerly (Jordan 34).

3) senne/amen (vv. 252, 255)

The word <u>senne</u> is predominantly a northern and Scottish word,
according to OED (see <u>sen</u>).

But other features conflict with this ascription:

1) drauȝt/craft (vv. 118-9)

Velar /x/ in medial position in <u>drauȝt</u> (from early ME <u>draht</u>)
has gone to /f/, as it did especially in the East Midlands
and Devon (Jordan 294).

2) redd/glad (vv. 121-2)

The vowel in <u>redd</u> must be <u>a</u> to rhyme with <u>a</u> in <u>glad</u> from OE
glæd: the ǣ$_2$ in OE rǣdde has shortened to <u>a</u>, thus placing
the rhyme in the area south of Brandl's boundary: the
Southeast Midlands and the South (see Jordan 49 and map p.
80).

3) yknow/saw (vv. 9, 12)

The diphthong in <u>saw</u> from OE saȝu is /aU/; OE ȝecnāwen
yielded the same diphthong in <u>ME</u> in the North (directly) and
in the West Midlands, Essex and London, and the Southwest,
by widening of /ɔU/ (see Jordan 105).

4) þerby/sey (vv. 28-9)

The past tense of <u>see</u> has many forms in Middle English, with
analogies and levellings confusing the phonological history.
M.L. Samuels' map of the southern half of England showing the
apparently fourteenth-century distribution of written forms
of "saw" ("Some Applications of Middle English Dialectology,"
<u>English Studies</u> 44 [1963], 92) shows the spelling siȝ to be
current in the London and Essex area (among others). After
silencing of the fricative, /si:/ would rhyme with <u>þerby</u>.

The place of origin of the poem seems therefore most
likely to be the area of Essex or London.

Of the past participles fixed in rhyme, <u>yknow</u> at v. 9
supports this ascription, and neither <u>do</u> at v. 104 nor <u>don</u>
at v. 100 is dialectally significant. The verbal inflexions
within lines are mostly northern (ȝe <u>schall</u>, v. 2; ȝe <u>kane</u>,
v. 3; <u>herkyns</u>, v. 2; <u>herkyn</u>, v. 12; <u>women louys</u>, v. 225).
But ȝe ... <u>se</u> (v. 159, fixed in rhyme with <u>Crystiante</u>,
v. 162) belongs to the Midlands, as does <u>cokwoldes stodyn</u>
(v. 143); the many uses of <u>hath</u> with both singular and
plural subjects (eg., vv. 100, 107, 109, 116, 168, 184;
versus northern <u>þei haue</u>, v. 118) are compatible with the
midland origin of the poem.

The date of the poem is hard to discern from the state
of the language. The manuscript is of the second half of
the fifteenth century; the poem probably is of the same
period. For the word <u>merchandabull</u> (v. 109), MED cites only
this poem, and OED gives it as the first citation, followed
by the next in 1502. On the other hand, OED cites the verb

wern (v. 114; OED warn v²) in the sense it bears in this poem for the last time c. 1475, and worthy (v. 220) in the phrase it is worthy in the sense it bears in this poem for the last time c. 1480. Sir Corneus was written no earlier than the fifteenth century, at any rate: the rhyme forth/ myrth (vv. 223-4) is probably on the vowel /U/, with /U/ in forth with influence from OE furþor, or with neutralizing of /o/ to /U/ after a labial and before r (see Jordan 35), and with /I/ in myrth velarizing to a more back sound before r (see Jordan 271). The latter change is a fifteenth-century one, shown in the Paston letters and Cely papers.

Spelling and Scribal Language

Though the poem originates in the area of London and Essex, the Ashmole 61 text is filled with northernisms (see Language and Provenience, above). Such spellings as hafe (v. 37), aboffe (v. 217), loffe (v. 218) show northern devoicing of final /v/ (see Jordan 217). While the spelling knaw (vv. 81, 150 from OE cnāwan) could be in the poet's language as well as the scribe's, the spelling awne (vv. 182, 216, 248; from OE āȝen) is northerly (see Jordan 118).

Intrusive -t appears in this scribe's writing in thruȝht (v. 105) and also in slouȝte (The King and the Hermit, v. 326).

See the introduction to The King and the Hermit for further comments on the scribe Rate and his spelling.

Editorial Treatment

The treatment of Sir Corneus is the same as that of The King and the Hermit.

Sir Corneus

All þat wyll of solas lere,

Herkyns now and ȝe schall here,

And ȝe kane vnderstond.

Off a bowrd I wyll ȝou schew

5   That ys full gode and trew,

That fell sometyme in Inglond.

Kynge Arthour was off grete honour,

Off castelles and of many a toure,

And full wyde yknow.

10 A gode ensample I wyll ȝou sey,

What chanse befell hym onne a dey:

Herkyn to my saw.

Cokwoldes he louyd, as I ȝou plyȝht:

He honouryd them both dey and nyȝht

15 In all maner of thyng.

And as I rede in [his]tory,

He was kokwold, sykerly:

For sothe, it is no lesyng.

Textual notes: <u>Sir Corneus</u> *begins on f. 59b. No title in MS.*
v. 16 history: MS story;

Herkynes, sires, what I sey:
20 Her may ȝe here solas and pley,
Iff ȝe wyll take gode hede.
Kyng Arthour had a bugyll-horn
That euermor stod hym beforn
Wherso þat euer he ȝede.

25 For when he was at þe bord sete,
Anon þe horne schuld be fette,
Theroff þat he myght drynke.
For myche crafte he couth þerby,
And oftetymes þe trewth he sey:
30 Non oþer couth he thynke.

Iff any cokwold drynke of it,
Spyll he schuld withouten lette:
Therfor þei wer not glade.
Gret dispyte þei had þerby,
35 Because it dyde þem vilony
And made þem ofttymes sade.

v. 19 Herkynes: MS Herkyngys; v. 22 *begins f. 60a;*

When þe kyng wold hafe solas,
The bugyll was fett into þe plas,
To make solas and game.
40 And þan changyd þe cokwoldes chere.
The kyng þem callyd, ferre and nere,
Lordynges, by ther name.

Than men myȝht se game inowȝe,
When euery cokwold on oþer leuȝe:
45 And ȝit þei schamyd sore.
Whereuer þe cokwoldes wer souȝht,
Befor þe kyng þei were brouȝht,
Both lesse and more.

Kyng Arthour than, verament,
50 Ordeynd throw hys awne assent
(Ssoth as I ȝow sey)
The tabull dormonte, withoute lette,
Therat þe cokwoldes wer ssette,
To haue solas and pley.

55 For at þe bord schuld be non oþer
Bot euery cokwold and hys broþer:
To tell treuth I must nedes.
And when þe cokwoldes wer sette
Garlandes of wylos schuld be fette
60 And sett vpon þer hedes.

Off þe best mete, withoute lesyng,
That stode on bord befor þe kyng,
Both ferr and nere,
To þe cockwoldes he sente anon,
65   And bad þem be glad euerychon,
For his sake make gode chere,

And seyd, "Lordynges, for ȝour lyues,
Be neuer þe wrother with ȝour wyues,
For no maner of nede.
70   Off woman com duke and kyng;
I ȝow tell without lesyng,
Of them com owre manhed."

So it befell, serteynly,
The Duke of Gloseter com in hyȝe
75   To þe courte with full gret myȝht.
He was reseyued at the kynges palys
With mych honour and grete solas,
With lordes þat were wele dyght.

With þe kyng þus dyde he duell,
80   Bot how long I can not tell:
Thereof knaw I non name.
Off Kyng Arthour a wonder case,
Frendes, herkyns how it was,
For now begynnes game.

v. 73 *begins f. 60b;*

85 Vppon a dey, withouten lette,
   The duke with þe kyng was sette
   At mete with mykell pride.
   He lukyd abowte wonder faste:
   Hys syght on euery syde he caste
90 To them þat sate besyde.

   The kyng aspyed þe erle anon
   And fast he lowȝhe þe erle vpon
   And bad he schuld be glad.
   And ȝit for all hys grete honour,
95 Cokwold was Kyng Arthour,
   Ne galle non he hade.

   So at þe last, þe duke he brayd,
   And to þe kyng þese wordes [sayd]
   (He myȝht no lenger forbere):
100 "Syr, what hath þese menn don
    That sych garlondes þei were vpon?
    That skyll wold I lere."

    The kyng seyd þe erle to,
    "Syr, non hurte þei haue do,
105 For þis was thruȝht a chans.
    Sertes, þei be fre men all.
    For non of them hath no gall,
    Therfor þis is þer penans.

v. 98 wordes sayd: MS word<u>es</u> spake;

"Ther wyues hath be merchandabull
110 And of þer ware compenabull:
     Methinke it is non herme.
     A man of lufe þat wold þem craue,
     Hastely he schuld it haue,
     For þei couth not hym wern.

115 "All þer wyues, sykerlyke,
     Hath vsyd þe baskefysyke
     Whyll þese men wer oute,
     And oft þei haue draw þat drauȝht,
     To vse wele þe lecheres craft
120 With rubyng of þer toute.

     "Syr," he seyd, "now haue I redd.
     Ete we now and make vs glad
     And euery man sle care."
     The duke seyd to hym anon,
125 "Than be þei cokwoldes euerychon?"
     The kyng seyd, "Hold þe there."

     The kyng þan after þe erlys word
     Send to þe cokwoldes bord
     (To make them mery among)
130 All maner of mynstralsy,
     To glad the cokwoldes by and by
     With herpe, fydell, and song,

v. 127 *begins f. 61a;*

And bad þem take no greffe,
"Bot all with loue and leffe,
135   Euery man with oþer."
For after mete, without distans,
The cokwoldes schuld togeþer danse,
Euery man with hys broþer.

Than he gan a nobull gamme:
140   The cokwoldes to geþer samme
Befor þe erle and þe kyng.
In skerlet kyrtells euer one
The cokwoldes stodyn euerychon
Redy vnto þe dansyng.

145   Than seyd þe kyng in hye,
"Go fyll my bugyll hastely,
And bryng it to my hond.
I wyll asey with a gyne
All þese cokwold[es] þat her [ar] in,
150   To knaw þem wyll I fonnd."

v. 134 and leffe: MS and with leffe; 149 cokwoldes: MS
cokwold; her ar in: MS her is in;

Than seyd þe erle, "For charyte,
In what skyll, tell me,
A cokwold may I know?"
To þe erle þe kyng ansuerd,
155   "Syr, be my hore berd,
Thou schall se within a throw."

The bugull was brouȝht þe kyng to hond.
Than seyd þe kyng, "I vnderstond,
Thys horne þat ȝe here se,
160   Ther is no cokwold fer ne nere
Herof to drynke hath no power,
As wyde as Crystiante,

"Bot he schall spyll on euery syde.
For any cas þat may betyde,
165   Schall non þerof avanse."
And ȝit for all hys grete honour,
Hymselfe noble Kyng Arthour
Hath forteynd syche a chans.

"Syr Erle," he seyd, "take and begyn."
170   He seyd, "Nay, be Seynt Austyn:
That wer to me vylony.
Not for all a reme to wyn
Befor ȝou I schuld begyn,
For honour off my courtassy."

175   Kyng Arthour, þer he toke þe horn
     And dyde as he was wont beforn,
     Bot þer was ȝit gon a gyle.
     He wend to haue dronke of þe best,
     Bot sone he spyllyd on hys brest,
180   Within a lytell whyle.

     The cokwoldes lokyd yche on oþer
     And thouȝt þe kyng was þer awne broþer,
     And glad þei wer of that:
     "He hath vs scornyd many a tyme
185   And now he is a cokwold fyne,
     To were a cokwoldes hate."

     The quene was þerof schamyd sore.
     Sche changyd her colour lesse and mor,
     And wold haue ben awey.
190   Therwith þe kyng gan hyr behold,
     And seyd he schuld neuer be so bold
     The soth aȝene to sey.

v. 178 He: MS Bot he; v. 184 *begins f. 61b*;

"Cokwoldes no more I wyll repreue,
For I ame one, and aske no leue,
195 For all my rentes and londys.
Lordynges all, now may ȝe know
That I may dance in þe cokwold row
And take ȝou by þe handes."

Than seyd þei all at a word
200 That cokwoldes schuld begynne þe bord
And sytt hyest in þe halle.
"Go we, lordinges, all samme,
And dance to make vs gle and gamme,
For cokwoldes haue no galle."

205 And after þat, sone anon,
The kyng causyd þe cokwoldes ychon
To wesch, withouten les.
For ought þat euer may betyde,
He sett them by hys awne syde,
210 Vp at þe hyȝe dese.

v. 206 causyd þe cokwoldes: MS causyd þe þe cokwoldes;

The kyng hymselff a garlond fette:
Vpponn hys hede he it sette,
For it myght be non oþer,
And seyd, "Lordynges, sykerly,
215   We be all off a freyry:
I ame ʒour awne broþer.

"Be Jhesu Cryst that is aboffe,
That man aught me gode loffe
That ley by my quene.
220   I[t] wer worthy hym to honour,
Both in castell and in towre,
With rede skerlyt and grene.

"For he me helpyd when I was forth,
To cher my wyfe and make her myrth,
225   For women louys wele pley.
And þerfor, sirys, haue ʒe no dowte,
Bot many schall dance in þe cokwoldes rowte,
Both by nyght and dey.

v. 220 I[t] wer: MS I wer;

"And þerfor, lordynges, take no care.
230   Make we mery: for nothing spare,
      All breþer in one rowte."
      Than þe cokwoldes wer full blythe,
      And thankyd God a [hundred] syth,
      For soth withouten doute.

235   Euery cokwold seyd to oþer,
      "Kyng Arthour is owr awne broþer:
      Therfor we may be blyth."
      The Erle of Glowsytour, vereament,
      Toke hys leue and home he went,
240   And thankyd þe kyng fele sythe.

      Kyng Arthour left at Skarlyon
      With hys cokwoldes euerychon
      And made both gamm and gle.
      A knyght þer was, withouten les,
245   That seruyd at þe kinges des:
      Syr Corneus hyȝht he.
      He made þis gest in hys gam,
      And [n]a[m]yd it after hys awne name,
      In herpyng or other gle.

v. 233 hundred: MS C; v. 238 *begins f. 62a*; v. 239 went: MS
wentet; v. 248 namyd: MS manyd.

250   And after, nobull Kyng Arthour
         Lyued and dyȝed with honour,
         As many hath don senne,
         Both cokwoldes and oþer mo.
         God gyff vs grace þat we may go
255   To heuyn.   Amen, amen.

                              End.

The Boy and the Mantle

The Boy and the Mantle

The Story

   Like the last poem The Boy and the Mantle is the tale
of a chastity test at Arthur's court, with embarrassing
results. None of the analogues of the story preserves all
of the crucial features. Most mysterious is the combination
of the chastity test using a mantle with further tests using
a horn and a knife. The best explanation is Child's tenta-
tive one that the combination stems from the appearance of a
mantel, a horn, and a knife in a Welsh list of the Thirteen
Precious Things of the Island of Britain, although these
three things do not there have the virtue of testing chastity
(Child, I, p. 266). A combination of the mantle test with
the horn test is not surprising: the stories are similar.
But the knife test is unprecedented.

   Various features of The Boy and the Mantle are found,
some in one analogue and some in another, but all in none
extant. It is probable that there was an original version of
the tale combining these features, now lost. The bearer of
the mantle in our version is a male, said to be very cour-
teous, as in the twelfth- or thirteenth-century French
fabliau Le Cort mantel or Le Mantel mautaillié (MR LV),
whereas in the German and Irish analogues she is a maiden.
In the Skikkju Rímur, a fifteenth-century Icelandic poem,
the mantle is of varying colors, as in our poem (vv. 41-6).
In Heinrich von dem Turlin's early thirteenth-century German
version, Der Mantel, the mantel looks as if it has been
slashed with scissors, as in our poem (vv. 39-40). And in a
very late manuscript (from the nineteenth-century) of an
Irish poem of indeterminable date, perhaps later than and
influenced by the present poem, but perhaps going back far-
ther than the others, the mantle curls up over the toes of an
otherwise successful aspirant because she has given a kiss,
though in the case of Caoilte, it is a kiss given to Diarmuid
before she was married to MacCriomhthain, whereas in our poem
Craddock's lady's offence was kissing Craddock. The Irish

poem is given by F.N. Robison, "A Variant of the Gaelic
'Ballad of the Mantle,'" Modern Philology 1 (1903-4), 145-57.

Readers interested in the many analogues of the tale
should consult the works suggested in the introduction to
Sir Corneus, as well as Robinson; T.P. Cross, "Notes on the
Chastity-Testing Horn and Mantle," Modern Philology 10 (1912-
13), 289-99, and "The Gaelic 'Ballad of the Mantle,'" Modern
Philology 16 (1918-19), 649-58; and Otto Warnatsch, Der
Mantel, Bruchstück eines Lanzeletromans (Breslau: W. Koebner,
1883).

The Manuscript

The Percy Folio Manuscript has been briefly described
above, as MS B of Jack and his Stepdame. On p. 284, the
first page of The Boy and the Mantle, the following appears
in the left margin:

My sweet brother sweet Couf   Edward Revell Booke
Elizabeth Revell

Upside down, in the right margin, appears the name "Llesam
Henery," in a different hand. The bearers of these names are
unknown.

Metre

The poem is in a common ballad form, with short two- or
three-stress lines in four- or six-line stanzas rhyming
abcb(db). But it is also influenced by alliterative long
line, with each of the present lines representing a half line.
The pattern is still clearly recognizable in sequences like
vv. 53-4:

```
     x  /      x  / x  x  x  / x    x   /    x   x
   She curst the weaver and the walker  that cloth that had

                                                /
                                            wrought.
```

The long line shows abb ab alliteration, and rising-falling
and rising stress patterns. However, the alliteration is
often purely decorative, not crossing the cæsura:

```
x (/)    x   x   /  x   x   /   x   /     x   x
It was ffrom the top to the toe   as sheeres had it
```

```
                                                    /
                                              shread.
```
                                                (vv. 39-40)

And in many cases there is no alliteration:

        I had rather be in a wood   vnder a green tree.
                                  (vv. 57-8)

    In a poem transcribed so long after it was written, it
is not surprising to find some remarkably inexact rhymes.
Corruption of the text may easily have occurred: omissions of
two lines are the harder to spot because of the variations
in stanza length and the more likely to occur because of the
frequency of repetition (the scribe may take the first occur-
rence of a line for the second, and a discordant rhyme in a
series of three may really belong to a separate stanza now
half missing). Then there is the usual possibility of sub-
stitutions for obsolete words.

    Two sets of rhymes are inexact in their vowels: king/
wronge (vv. 132, 134); and made/thread/speed (vv. 90, 92, 94),
the latter two with ME long close e̲, presumably raised in the
vowel shift to long i̲ by the time of the poem, the former
with ME long a̲, perhaps raised to long open e̲.

    Five sets of rhymes have consonantal differences:

    1) drawne/shame (vv. 10, 12)

The a̲u̲ diphthong of drawne has monophthongized to long a̲
before n̲ in late Middle English (see Dobson, II, 104:
"vulgar or dialectal"), for a rhyme with the long a̲ in shame.

    2) about/crowt/nought (vv. 112, 114, 116)

The undiphthongized northern /u:/ of about and crowt (from OE
abūtan and, apparently, crūdan) rhymes on /u:/ in nought
(from OE nōwiht), with ME ou before /x/ having gone to late
ME /u:/ (see Dobson II, 160 and I, p. 434). But crowt else-

where always retains the voicing in its final consonant, and
the t/d/t sequence is inexact.

3) ronge/horne/beforne (vv. 180, 182, 184)

The rhyme implies assimilation of r̲ with apico-alveolar n̲ in
horne and beforne, but n̲ rhymes inexactly with the angma.

4) greene/beseeme (vv. 42, 44)

5) dwell/nutshells (vv. 22, 24)

These rhymes are simply inexact.

Language and Provenience

The Boy and the Mantle is northern or north midland in
its origin, as is shown by the following rhymes:

knee/eye/see (vv. 186, 188, 190)

Only in the North and North Midland did OE ēa̅ʒe develop to ME
/e:/ (see Jordan 101). The rhyme sequence about/crowt/nought,
discussed under Metre, above, can also be northern; it is not
criterial, however, since a rhyme could have been arrived at
by different means in different dialect areas. Because the
poem is so short and the body of rhymes so small, its place
of origin cannot be narrowed down further.

As far as date is concerned, the rhymes certainlye/tree/
mee (vv. 118, 120, 122) point to an origin after the vowel
shift. The Boy and the Mantle is probably no earlier than
the mid-fifteenth century: the boy uses the term bitch for
Queen Guenevere, an epithet first applied to women about
1450 (see MED, bicche). The one other medieval citation for
the verb brittle (britled, v. 175) is dated before 1300, but
the verb could have been reformed from britten, which con-
tinues into the early sixteenth century. Creede (v. 82), in
the sense of a repetition of the words as an act of devotion,
is last cited in MED (crede n. [2]) c. 1475. In OED its only
post-medieval citation is in Scott's Marmion. Tout, a word
required by rhyme and context at v. 72, is cited in OED no
later than 1502; kirtle (v. 5) was a term for an ordinary
article of men's clothing up until about 1500; and potener
(v. 21) is cited no later than 1530 (OED pautener 3b²); so

the vocabulary of the poem suggests a date in the latter
half of the fifteenth century. Such a date is compatible
with the late origins of the rhyme drawne/shame (vv. 10, 12)
discussed under <u>Metre</u>, above. The rhyme madd/shread (vv. 38,
40) depends on a fifteenth-century participial form <u>shrad</u>.

Spelling and Scribal Language

     Certain features of the language, though not fixed by
rhyme, show signs of northern origin: the contracted <u>tane</u> for
<u>taken</u> (eg., in vv. 69, 133, 137); the northern and north
midland auxiliary <u>can</u>; the spelling <u>shreeuen</u> (v. 123) for
<u>shriven</u>, which suggests northern lengthening of <u>i</u> to long <u>e</u>
in an open syllable; and the spelling <u>kniue</u> (v. 173) for
<u>knife</u>, which is probably an inverse spelling showing nor-
thern devoicing of final <u>v</u>. These may be remnants of the
poet's language or that of a northern exemplar. The inflex-
ional endings on verbs (eg. <u>thou</u> <u>wast</u>, v. 106; [<u>she</u>] <u>hath</u>,
<u>maketh</u>, <u>taketh</u>, vv. 133, 136, 141) are probably late scribal
spellings.

Editorial Treatment

     The editorial treatment is the same as that of <u>John the
Reeve</u>, above.

The Boy and the Mantle

In the third day of May
To Carleile did come
A kind curteous child
That cold much of wisdome.

5 A kirtle and a mantle
This child had vppon,
With br[o]uches and ringes
Full richelye bedone.

He had a sute of silke
10 About his middle drawne.
Without he cold of curtesye
He thought itt much shame.

Textual notes: The Boy and the Mantle *begins on p. 284.*
Title: MS Boy and Mantle; v. 7 brouches: MS brauches;

"God speed thee, King Arthur,
Sitting att thy meate,
15   And the goodly Queene Gueneuer--
I canott her fforgett.

"I tell you, lordes in this hall,
I het you all he[ed]:
Excepte you be the more surer,
20   Is you for to dread."

He plucked out of his pote[n]er
(And longer wold not dwell),
He pulled forth a pretty mantle
Betweene [two] nutshells.

25   "Haue thou here, King Arthure,
Haue thou heere of mee.
Giue itt to thy comely queene
Shapen as itt [bee].

v. 18 *begins p. 285*; heed: MS heate; v. 21 potener: MS
potewer; v. 24 two: MS 2; v. 28 itt bee: MS itt is alreadye;

"Itt shall neuer become that wiffe
30 That hath once done amisse."
Then euery in the kings court
Began to care for his.

Forth came Dame Gueneuer;
To the mantle shee her b[ray]d.
35 The ladye, shee was newfangle,
But yett shee was affrayd.

When shee had taken the mantle,
Shee stode as shee had beene madd.
It was ffrom the top to the toe
40 As sheeres had it shread.

One while was itt g[o]ule,
Another while was itt greene;
Another while was itt wa[tchet]:
Ill itt did her beseeme.

v. 32 his: MS his wiffe; v. 34 brayd: MS biled; v. 38 stode: MS sttode; v. 41 goule: MS gaule; v. 43 watchet: MS wadded;

45 Another while was it blacke
  And bore the worst hue.
  "By my troth," quoth King Arthur,
  "I think thou be not true."

  Shee threw downe the mantle
50 That bright was of blee.
  Fast with a rudd redd
  To her chamber can shee flee.

  She curst the weaver and the walker
  That clothe that had wrought,
55 And bade a vengeance on his crowne
  That hither hath itt brought.

  "I had rather be in a wood
  Vnder a greene tree
  Then in King Arthurs court
60 Shamed for to bee."

  Kay called forth his ladye
  And bade her come neere,
  Saies, "Madam, and thou be guiltye,
  I pray thee hold thee there."

65 Forth came his ladye
   Shortlye and anon;
   Boldlye to the mantle
   Then is shee gone.

   When shee had tane the mantle
70 And cast it her about,
   Then was shee bare
   All aboue the [tout].

   Then euery knight
   That was in the kinges court
75 Talked, lauged, and showted
   Full oft att that sport.

   Shee threw downe the mantle
   That bright was of blee.
   Ffast with a red rudd
80 To her chamber can shee flee.

   Forth came an old knight
   Pattering ore a creede,
   And he proferred to this little boy
   [Twenty] marks to his meede,

v. 72 the tout: MS the buttockes; v. 84 twenty: MS 20;

85 And all the time of the Christmasse
    Willinglye to ffeede,
    Forwhy this mantle might
    Doe his wife some need.

    When shee had tane the mantle
90 Of cloth that was made
    Shee had no more left on her
    But a tassell and a threed.
    Then euery knight in the kings court
    Bade euill might shee speed.

95 Shee threw downe the mantle
    That bright was of blee,
    And fast with a redd rudd
    To her chamber can shee flee.

    Graddocke called forth his ladye
100 And bade her come in,
    Saith, "Winne this mantle, lady,
    With a litle dinne.

    v. 89 *begins p. 286*;

"Winne this mantle, ladye,
And it shal be thine,
105 If thou neuer did amisse
Since thou wast mine."

Forth came Craddockes ladye
Shortlye and anon,
But boldlye to the mantle
110 Then is shee gone.

When shee had tane the mantle
And cast itt her about,
Vpp att her great toe
Itt began to crinkle and crowt.
115 Shee said, "Bowe downe, mantle,
And shame me not for nought.

"Once I did amisse,
I tell you certainlye,
When I kist Craddockes mouth
120 Vnder a greene tree,
When I kist Craddockes mouth
Before he marryed mee."

When shee had her shreeuen
And her sines shee had tolde,
125 The mantle stoode about her
Right as shee wold,

Seemelye of coulour,
Glittering like gold.
Then euery knight in Arthurs court
130   Did her behold.

Then spake Dame Gueneuer
To Arthur our king:
"She hath tane yonder mantle
Not with wright but with wronge.

135   "See you not yonder woman
That maketh herselfe soe clea[n]e:
I haue seene tane out of her bedd
Of men fiueteene,

"Preistes, clarkes, and wedded men
140   From her bydeene;
Yett shee taketh the mantle
And maketh herselfe cleane."

Then spake the little boy
That kept the mantle in hold;
145   Sayes, "King, chasten thy wiffe.
Of her words shee is to bold.

v. 136 cleane: MS cleare; v. 138 fiueteene: MS fiueteeene;

"Shee is a bitch and a witch
And a whore bold.
King, in thine owne hall
150   Thou art a cuc[k]old."

[The] litle boy stoode
Looking ouer a dore,
[And there as he was looking
He was ware of a wyld bore.]

155   He was ware of a wyld bore
Wold haue werryed a man.
He pulld forth a woodkniffe:
Fast thither th[an] he ran.
He brought in the bores head
160   And quitted him like a man.

He brought in the bores head
And was wonderous bold.
He said there was neuer a cuc[k]olds kniffe
Carue itt that cold.

v. 150 cuckold: MS cuchold; v. 151 The litle: MS A litle;
vv. 153-4 *Percy's addition. No gap in MS, but evidently two
lines missing.* v. 158 than: MS that; v. 163 *begins p. 287;*
cuckolds: MS cucholds;

165 Some rubbed their kni[u]es
    Vppon a whetstone;
    Some threw them vnder the table
    And said they had none.

    King Arthur and the child
170 Stood looking them vpon:
    All their kni[u]es edges
    Turned backe [anon].

    Craddocke had a litle kniue
    Of iron and of steele:
175 He britled the bores head
    Wonderous weele,
    That euery knight in the kings court
    Had a morsell.

    The litle boy had a horne
180 Of red gold that ronge.
    He said there was noe cuckolde
    Shall drinke of my horne
    But he shold itt sheede
    Either behind or beforne.

v. 165 kniues: MS knies; v. 171 kniues: MS knies: v. 172
backe anon: MS back againe;

185 Some shedd on their shoulder,
   And some on their knee:
   He that cold not hitt his mouth
   Put it in his eye,
   And he that was a cuckold,
190 Euery man might him see.

   Craddoccke wan the horne
   And the bores head;
   His lady wan the mantle
   Vnto her meede.
195 Euerye such a louely ladye,
   God send her well to speede.

                    Ffinis.

The Friars of Berwick

The Friars of Berwick

In past ascribed to William Dunbar, The Friars of
Berwick is the most markedly literary of the poems in the
present volume. The opening lines, with their laudatory
description of the town of Berwick, show the influence of
Latin rhetorical tradition: "The rules for eulogies of cities
were developed in detail by late antique theory. The site
had first to be treated, then the other excellencies of the
city, and not least its significance in respect to the culti-
vation of the arts and sciences. In the Middle Ages this
last topos is given an ecclesiastical turn" (Ernst Curtius,
European Literature and the Latin Middle Ages, trans. Willard
R. Trask, Bollingen Series, 36 [New York: Pantheon Books,
1953], p. 157). In the poem the description of the site and
that of the city are mixed in vv. 1-23; the orders of friars
living there are proudly listed in vv. 24-7. That those
opening lines are a standard topos is made evident by the
fact that they have remarkably little to do with the rest of
the poem, "save that he wol conveyen his mateere." The
metrical form of the poem--iambic pentameter couplets--is
Chaucerian, and the heroine's name--Alesoun--points back to
the Miller's Tale as a literary influence, a generic model.

The tale has analogues in French, German, and Latin.
The one extant analogue in French fabliau is Le Povre clerc
(MR CXXXII; I do not count Jean de Condé's Clerc qui fu repus
deriere l'escrin [MR XCI] as an analogue, since its sole
point of likeness is that a hidden lover is revealed). In
Le Povre clerc, a poor scholar seeking lodging is turned away
by a woman on the grounds that her husband is not home. The
clerk notices good food and drink being prepared, however,
and then sees a priest hurry into the house. He is invited
back to the same house by the husband, returning unexpectedly
from the mill; when he enters, there is no priest in sight,
and the wife has nothing prepared for supper. The clerk then

recounts an adventure: he met a herd of pigs, and a wolf
seized one as fat as the pork the servant took from the pot a
while ago; the pig's blood was as red as the wine the boy
just brought; the scholar picked up a heavy rock, almost as
heavy as the big cake the servant has made; the wolf looked
at him just as the priest in the corncrib is looking at him
now. The story ends with the husband stripping the priest
of his robes and giving them to the clerk.

As for the German analogues, Der geaste Pfaffe by Der
Stricker (an early thirteenth-century writer) tells essen-
tially the same story with a ploughboy in place of the clerk
(see F.H. von der Hagen, ed., Gesamtabenteuer: Hundert
altdeutsche Erzählungen, vol. 3 [Stuttgart: J.G. Cotta'scher
Verlag, 1850: repr. Darmstadt: Wissenschaftliche Buchgeschell-
schaft, 1961], pp. 145-58). But a poem of the mid-fifteenth
century by Hans Rosenblüt, Von einem varnden Schüler, is
closer to The Friars of Berwick. Here the wandering scholar
seeking lodging is turned away by the woman of the house,
while the village priest sits beside her at her heavily laden
table. The scholar spies through a window, and sees the
priest and food hidden when the husband unexpectedly comes
home. The scholar enters again, and performs a spell to get
the services of the devil. He tells the husband where the
various foods may be found, and then offers to produce the
devil himself. The husband must stay still and quiet until
told to move. Then the scholar consults with the hidden
priest, and blackmails him. The priest is stripped, blackened
with ashes, and released. The scholar encourages the husband
to strike at the "devil" with a stick as he rushes away.
Then husband and scholar sit down at the table to feast all
night, and in the morning the scholar has the thanks of both
husband and wife. From this story the 1551 Fastnachtspiel by
Hans Sachs, Der fahrend Schüler mit dem Teufelbannen (in
Adelbert von Keller, ed., Hans Sachs, vol. 9 [Stuttgart, 1875;
repr. Hildesheim: Georg Olms, 1964], pp. 72-84), is probably
descended.

The earliest known instance of the tale is the Latin
version told in a collection of sermon exempla of the mid-
fourteenth century, the Scala Celi of the Dominican "Johannes
Junior," i.e. Joannes Gobius. This is a very brief version,
as befits an exemplum, and lacks many of the details found in
The Friars of Berwick. The husband is a knight, the wife a
lady, the lover a monk, and the magician a clerk. No mention
is made of such matters as how the clerk sees the assignation,
where the food is hidden, or how the lady feels about the

situation, nor of the episode in which the husband strikes at the devil. No moral is drawn by Gobius himself: the tale is simply given to be used as the preacher sees fit, and is classed under the heading "De Clerico."

A seventeenth-century French form of the tale, Le Soldat Magicien by Antoine le Métel, Sieur d'Ouville, in L'Elite des contes du Sieur d'Ouville (Rouen, 1680) is altered in some respects. For instance, the magician is a soldier, the lover a lawyer. But it is like The Friars of Berwick in having the conjurer watch the proceedings between the wife and her lover from an upper room, and in specifying that the food is hidden in an armoire. The Friars of Berwick must have had an ancestor that added these details, and that of the husband's striking at the devil (which also appears in Rosenblüt's poem) to the bare outline of the Latin exemplum. Such an ancestor need not have been a French one, as Janet M. Smith argues it is in The French Background of Middle Scots Literature (Edinburgh: Oliver and Boyd, 1934), p. 84.

For more distant analogues of the story, see Bolte-Polívka II, article 61, "Das Bürle": some versions of the Unibos tale, in which a poor man repeatedly dupes his rich neighbor or brother, incorporate the situation in which a trickster takes advantage of the presence of a hidden lover.

The Texts

The Maitland version is independently derived from the parent manuscript. The Bannatyne version and the printed text are related to one another, but the printed text is not descended from the Bannatyne version.

B

The Bannatyne MS, Advocates' 1.1.6, is a large manuscript in two volumes, held by the National Library of Scotland. It has been bound in green morocco since about 1823, and the leaves have been window-mounted in larger ones, so that the original gatherings are no longer discernible. The visible area of the remaining leaves is about 19.5 cm. by 30, with a writing block that varies, but is roughly 16 by 29. Almost all of the writing is that of one person, George

Bannatyne, an Edinburgh merchant, who wrote out the manuscript in Forfarshire in the last three months of 1568, when he was forced by the plague to abstain from his normal business.

The present foliation on the carrier leaves runs 1–192 in the first volume, 1–205 in the second. I, 1–24 is a draft manuscript, a collection of religious poems which Bannatyne afterwards used in the main manuscript. Ff. 25–7 may be part of the draft, or may be later fragments. Ff. 28–9 are a single sheet added in the eighteenth century by the manuscript's then owner, William Carmichaell. The main manuscript then begins on f. 30 and runs to the end of the second volume. On f. 30, in the poem "The wryttar to the reidaris," Bannatyne lays out the plan of the manuscript:

> Now 3e haif heir this ilk buik provydit,
> That in fyve pairtis it is dewly devydit:
> 1 The first conteynis Godis glore and oure saluation;
> 2 The next are moral, grave, and als besyd it
> [3]Grund in gud counsale; the thrid—I will nocht hyd it—
> Ar blyth and glaid maid for oure consollatioun;
> 4 The ferd of luve, and thair richt reformatioun;
> 5 The fyift ar tailis and storeis weill discydit.

The Friars of Berwick belongs to this last division, and runs from f. 180b to f. 186b of the second volume.

From Bannatyne (who died in 1606 or 1608), the manuscript passed to his daughter Janet and her husband, George Foulis. It descended through the Foulis family to their great-grandson, William Foulis, who gave it to William Carmichaell in 1712. His son John, fourth Earl of Hyndford, gave it in 1772 to the Advocates' Library, which became part of The National Library of Scotland in 1925.

For full information on the history and contents of the manuscript, see The Bannatyne Manuscript: National Library of Scotland Advocates' MS 1.1.6, with an introduction by Denton Fox and William A. Ringler (London: Scolar Press in association with The National Library of Scotland, 1980).

M

As is the Bannatyne Manuscript, the Maitland Folio Manuscript, MS Pepys 2553 of the Pepysian Library, Magdalene College, Cambridge, is an invaluable repository of late medieval and early sixteenth-century Scottish poetry. The large volume, of 183 leaves, is bound in the Pepysian leather binding. The original leaves have been window-mounted in larger ones, and so the original gatherings cannot be determined. The visible area of the original pages is 14 cm. by 28; the writing block varies from about 13 by 23 on some pages to the whole of the visible area of the original pages in others. There are several different scribes, presumably all connected with the family of Sir Richard Maitland of Lethington, in Haddington. Maitland himself went blind in 1560. W.A. Craigie argues in his edition (The Maitland Folio Manuscript, II, STS new series 20 [1927],3) that the manuscript was compiled between about 1570 and 1586, when Maitland died at the age of 92.

The carrier leaves are paginated, with The Friars of Berwick running from p. 113 to p. 129. No trace of a folio numbering in the manuscript remains, but many leaves retain original catchwords. At present, the leaves are bound in the wrong order. The biggest error is that the current p. 40 should be followed by the current p. 265, but the sequence is interrupted by pp. 41-264. Several other leaves are out of place (including the first one) or backwards, and pp. 3-18, 339-42 do not originally belong to this manuscript; pp. 67-8 too are a stray leaf. For full particulars see Craigie, vol. II, pp. 1-2.

The manuscript is rich in marginalia, particularly proper names, and would repay a great deal of close study. From the notation on p. 256, "This buke pertenis to helyne m," and from the fact that John Reidpeth, who transcribed parts of the manuscript in 1622-3, records that he borrowed it from Christopher Cockburn, it is clear that Helen Maitland, wife of John Cockburn, inherited the book on her father Richard's death and passed it down to Christopher. (Helen may have been the principal scribe of the manuscript.) It is less clear what happened to it in the intervening years before it became part of the library of Samuel Pepys. It and its sister manuscript, the Maitland Quarto, are supposed to have been given to him by John Maitland, Second Earl and First Duke of Lauderdale (b. 1616-d. 1682), for Pepys had other books from the duke's library, and the duke was Richard Maitland's great-grandson, descended from his second son, John. But it is not clear why the book should have passed from the Cockburn branch of the family to the Maitland branch, if then only to go to Samuel Pepys; nor why many proper names, neither Maitland nor Cockburn, are written in the margins, and among them the

claims "James Hunter ought this book" (p. 159) and "John
Henderson owgt this bo[ok]" (p. 167).

Whatever its history in the mid-seventeenth century, by
the late century it was in the library of Samuel Pepys, and
on his death in 1703 went to his nephew John Jackson with the
rest of his library, pending its ultimate disposition in 1724
to Magdalene College.

The contents of the manuscript are too numerous to be
listed here; it includes poems by Dunbar, Kennedy and
Henryson, as well as many by Maitland himself. All of the
poems of the manuscript are published by Craigie, The Maitland
Folio Manuscript, I, STS new series 7 (1919).

                              H

H is article 88850 in the Henry Huntington Library, San
Marino, California. Its new STC number is 7349.5; it is
listed in STC under Dunbar's name, though "The attribution to
Dunbar is dubious." Katharine F. Pantzer, editor of STC, has
written to me that the Huntington copy is still the only one
known. It is a quarto volume, unbound. The title leaf reads
THE MERRIE/HISTORIE/OF THE THRIE/FRIERS OF BER-/[WI]CKE./
Printed at Aberdene, by Edvvard/Raban, For David Melvill,
1622. I have examined it only in photocopy. The pages are
13.5 cm. by 18.5, with a print block of 9.5 cm. by 16.5,
including the signature line and running head (THE THREE
FRIERS/OF BERWICKE.). The poetry is printed thirty-six lines
to the page. The collation is A-B^4, C^2, but signatures are
visible on only A2, A4, B[1], B2, B3, and C[1]: other leaves
are too badly damaged at the bottom. Catchwords or fragments
of catchwords are still visible on most leaves. Pagination
runs from f. A2 (p. 3) to f. C2 (p. 19). F. A2a is headed
THE THREE/FRIERS OF/BERWICKE.

In his introduction to an edition of the poem in 1894
(in Anonymous Early Scottish Poems, forming a supplement to
the poems of William Dunbar, part 5 of The Poems of William
Dunbar, vol. 4 [Vienna: K. Akademie der Wissenschaften, 1894],
p. 393), J. Schipper reported that the only known extant copy
of a printed edition of the work had disappeared. It had been
in the Skene House library at the time of David Laing's
writing of the second volume to his edition of The Poems of
William Dunbar (Edinburgh: Laing and Forbes, 1832). But it
was not to be found by the time of J.P. Edmond's bibliography

The Aberdeen Printers: Edward Raban to James Nicol in 1884. A
copy surfaced in 1924 at a Sotheby's sale, which copy Henry
Huntington purchased through A.S.W. Rosenbach. It is very
likely the Skene House one, which also was printed at Aberdeen
by Edward Raban for David Melvill, 1622.

No copies are known to exist of another, earlier edition
from Edinburgh, by Robert Charteris, 1603.

Metre

The iambic pentameter couplets, markedly different from
the more popular forms seen elsewhere in this volume, are
clearly due to Chaucer's influence. The poet is careful with
both metre and rhyme, and seldom takes even such licences as
rhymes of -ame on -ane (hame/allane, vv. 37-8; name/ane,
vv. 53-4) or rhymes on normally unstressed syllables (persaving/
botkin, vv. 179-80).

Language and Provenience

That the poem is northern is, as usual with northern
texts, immediately obvious. There are several rhymes on nor-
thern long a from OE long a and long a from other sources,
eg. name/hame (vv. 239-40). The present participle ending
-and (driven to the extreme west and east of England, and the
north; MMW point K) is confirmed in rhyme at vv. 369-70
(pypand/hand). The rhyme wett/lait at vv. 93-4 depends upon a
Scottish and northern form of wet with long a from ON vatr.
The rhyme cure/flure (vv. 415-6) depends on the /u:/ in cure
from OF cure rhyming with northern /y:/ in the descendant of
OE flōr (see Jordan 54). Within the northern area, the poem
can be localized to Scotland. Fallow (English fellow) is con-
firmed in rhyme at vv. 265-6 (hallow/fallow) to have a dis-
tinctively Scottish pronunciation. The prepositions into and
intill, used in the Scottish manner where Middle English would
use in, are confirmed by scansion at vv. 7, 19, 52, etc.
Terms such as tryst (v. 121), samyn (v. 121), flawme (v. 137),
mvllis (v. 142), curch (v. 148), pleid (v. 258), quhatkin
(vv. 314, 328), glowrit (v. 342), pleiss (v. 420), effeiritlie
(v. 424), protest (in the sense "demand," v. 448), and libberla
(v. 496) are distinctively Scottish. However, the one weak
past participle ending confirmed in rhyme is the -id of forcryid

(rh. sy̲d̲, vv. 233-4), rather than the distinctively Scottish
-it̲. The poem also consistently uses the Scottish gif̲ for
if̲, and sic̲ for such̲, although such forms could be scribal.

A priori̲, the most natural place of origin for the poem
would be Berwick itself. The poem was clearly written by
someone familiar with the setting, buildings, and fortifica-
tions of the town, and with the fact that the four main orders
of friars all had foundations there. But a few linguistic
points cast doubt on this ascription. The first of these is
the frequent use of the prepositions intill̲ and into̲ for ME
in̲, a usage which belongs to the center and northeast of
Scotland, according to OED. It might be scribal, however:
Bannatyne was from Edinburgh, Maitland's family from
Haddington, and the printed text from Aberdeen, all within the
area where intill̲ and into̲ were used. Yet the two-syllable
pronouns are required by the scansion. Another point is the
use of the noun pleiss̲ at v. 420. No other medieval citation
for the noun exists, but the Scottish̲ National̲ Dictionary̲
gives modern citations of the phrase to̲ hae̲ a̲ please̲,
attributing it to northeast Scotland and Angus. But the
third and most convincing point is that the ai̲ diphthong in
stair̲ has gone to long a̲, rhyming with mair̲ ("more") at vv.
571-2. The change of ai̲ to a̲ takes place everywhere in
Scotland except̲ the southeast (see Jordan 132 and Luick 434).

This evidence that the poem originated in an area outside
of Berwickshire has implications for its date as well.
Berwick passed permanently into the hands of the English in
1482, after centuries of conquest and reconquest. If the poem
were written by a Scot elsewhere in Scotland (as opposed to a
native of Berwick who had changed his nationality but not his
language), it is inconceivable to me that he could have
written the entirely laudatory account of Berwick's defences
and other advantages after the town had passed into the hands
of the English, without at least some expression of regret or
hint of irony. If the poem was written to the north of
Berwickshire, then it must have been written between 1461 and
1482, years in which Berwick was in Scottish hands.

The evidence from the language in the poem suggests that
such a date is plausible. Both the inflexional endings -is̲
and -it̲ can be pronounced as full syllables for metrical
reasons, though neither is always so pronounced:

At Tweid̲i̲s̲ mowth thair stand(i)s a nobill toun (v. 3)

For it is wall̲i̲t̲ weill abowt with stane (v. 9)

Loss of the unaccented vowel in such syllables begins before
the fifteenth century in the North (see Jordan 291). The
older pronunciation could be retained in poetry in the six-
teenth century in the -es ending of nouns and the -ed ending
of verbs and adjectives (see Dobson II, 312 and 315), but
not in the third person singular ending of verbs (Dobson II,
313), as for example in v. 249:

    Scho stertis vp and gettis licht in hy.

As far as the vocabulary of the poem is concerned, the
picture is far from clear. There are words and meanings
attested no earlier than the sixteenth century:

v. 142	mvllis	DOST mull sb^3	1500-20 only
v. 342	glowrit	DOST glowr v	1500
v. 353	stait	OED state sb 19b	1604
v. 446	stand for	OED stand v 71b	1531
v. 448	protest	OED protest v 5	1508
v. 496	libberla	DOST libberla	c. 1500
v. 549	trap	SND trap n^2	a. 1540

But there are also words attested no later than around 1500:

v. 328	quhatkin	OED whatkin a	a. 1450
v. 444	traistis	OED traist 2b	c. 1500
v. 525	turss	OED truss v. 4b refl.	c. 1440
v. 538	presit	MED pressen 8a refl.	a. 1450 only
v. 544	fle	DOST fle v^1 2c	c. 1475 and Friars of Berwick only

No conclusions can be drawn from the evidence of the
vocabulary but that the poem is as likely to have been written
during the period 1461-82 as later.

Other evidence suggests that the 1461-82 period is
plausible. The verb beit at v. 133 became obsolete in liter-
ary English before 1500, according to OED (beet v.) though it
is cited c. 1590 in DOST (bete, beit v^1 3). The change of
angma to /n/ implied in the rhyme persaving/botkin (vv. 179-
80) took place in the North by the fourteenth century (Jordan
175). The poem was written after the vowel shift, as rhymes
like be/cumpany (vv. 269-70) show. But the rhyme þair/befoir
at vv. 377-8, probably on long open o, suggests that the date
was still in the fifteenth century, since the last citation
in OED of the form of there with o for a vowel is c. 1470.

A few odd rhymes deserve attention. The rhymes on ME
long close and long open e in freiris/ʒeiris (vv. 29-30) and
beir/heir (vv. 209-10) imply the possibility of the raising
of long open e characteristic of the northern dialect (see
Dobson II, 121), but the sequence of heir/freir rhyming on
long close e immediately followed by weir/deir rhyming on
long open e shows that open e forms could still be kept dis-
tinct (vv. 483-6).

There are two peculiar and apparently incompatible parts
of rhymes on chair: fyre/chyre at vv. 221-2 and chyre/eir at
vv. 187-8. These depend on the Scottish variants chyre and
chear, for which see DOST.

The rhyme nek/sek at vv. 545-6 is dependent on a form of
sack with e from ON sekkr.

The rhyme speid/beid at vv. 531-2, with the noun speed
from OE spēd and the verb bide from OE bīdan, is probably
attributable to shortenings in both words before a single
final consonant (see Jordan 27). Not only ME long i, but
also ME long close e tended to shorten to short i (see
Dobson II, 132n).

A further historical point may have some bearing on the
provenience of the poem. The poet is clearly confused on the
colors pertaining to the different orders of friars. Allane
and Robert are Jacobins. The Jacobins are not White Friars,
as the poem suggests ("The Jacobein freiris of þe quhyt hew,"
v. 24), but Black Friars. The Carmelites were known as the
White Friars (from their white habit), the Minors or
Franciscans as the Gray Friars (from their gray habit). Most
likely, Friar Johne was a Franciscan, members of his order
being traditionally foes of the Jacobins. But he is called a
Black Friar or dressed in black (at vv. BH126, B485, B516),

though "Black Friar" was the usual name for the Jacobins themselves, from their black cloaks worn over white habits. In M and H, he is called a Gray Friar or dressed in gray at vv. M126, MH485, MH516. Either the poet made one mistake or two. He might have believed the Jacobins to be White Friars, and have correctly called Johne a Gray Friar, in which case the scribes of M and (inconsistently) of H made Johne a Black Friar to enhance his demonic appearance (see vv. 471-85 and ff.). Or he might have believed the Jacobins to be White Friars, and though intending Johne to belong to another order, have called him a Black Friar, in which case the scribes or ancestors of M and inconsistently of H have corrected the poem, changing him to a Gray Friar. The latter case is the more likely, since two independent corrections are more probable than two independent and mistaken alterations. In either event, the poet was confused. Perhaps he had seen the Jacobins wearing their white habits, without their black cloaks over them, and thought they were the White Friars. Certainly his confusion implies that he was not familiar with the orders. Two explanations are possible. First, that he was writing in Berwick after 1539 (the date of the dissolution of major religious foundations in England). But this explanation is implausible for the linguistic reasons given above. Second, that he lived in an area of Scotland other than Berwick (the most important center for friars in all of Scotland), one to which the Jacobins had no frequent access. This second explanation seems preferable.

Spelling and Scribal Language

All three texts are firmly localized: B in Edinburgh in 1568, M in Lethington, Haddington in 1570-86, H in Aberdeen in 1622.

Both B and M show their Scottish origin in spellings: quh- for Middle English wh-, the use of ch to represent palatal and velar fricatives, and a differentiation of but ("without," eg. vv. B96, B112, M229) and bot ("but," eg. v. 49). The form of ȝ used by both scribes is similar to a z. Sic and gif are Scottish forms for "such" and "if" used consistently in both manuscripts, though they could be carried over from the poet's language. The use of ane before consonants as well as vowels is Scottish. The term þir ("these") is northern and Scottish, as are the form scho ("she") and the spelling sal(l) ("shall"). The consistent

spelling -it of the past tense and past participle ending of
weak verbs is Scottish. Spellings such as gaip ("gape,"
v. 346) and wait ("wot," v. 61) are inverse spellings, show-
ing that the ai diphthong has gone to long a, as in most of
Scotland. Here -i- has become simply a conventional sign of
length, as it is in both manuscripts with -e- (eg. weill,
v. 9) and with -o- (eg. befoir, v. 107), and in M with -u-
(eg. tuik, v. M251). Both manuscripts show signs of late
raising of ME/a:/ to a very open /æ:/, close to long open e
(see Jordan 276): for example, both B and M sometimes have
the spelling deme for dame (vv. B72, M267). Both also show
northern lengthening of i to long e in an open syllable (eg.
rever, v. 2) and devoicing of final v (eg. aboif, vv. M185,
B186). Both (through inverse spelling) show northern dis-
placement of w by v (eg. ewin, v. M76, serwand, v. B452).

H, being later and a printed text, shows a great deal
of modernization, and conforms much more in its spelling and
vocabulary to the English of England: the quhilk is consis-
tently replaced by which (eg. v. 7), thir by these (eg. v.
32), ane by a (eg. v. 28), and intill by some rephrasing
(eg. v. 28). The gudman becomes southern English mine
husband (v. 83), and the old genitive allthair best is con-
verted to most well (v. 20).

Editorial Treatment

B is the copytext. Emendations to B are not indicated
in the text of the poem: only a careful examination of the
textual notes will show whether the reading of a given line
is actually in B itself, is in M or H, or is conjectural.
The treatment of variants in the textual notes is handled in
the same way as for Jack and his Stepdame, above.

The spelling of the text is that of B; the spelling of
the notes is that of the first manuscript or text listed
after the variant. Punctuation is not given in the notes,
and upper case letters are retained only when they correspond
with modern usage. In the text itself, punctuation, word
division, and capitalization are editorial. Expanded con-
tractions are underlined in the notes, but not in the text.
Systematic substitutions of which for þe quhilk and these for
thir in H are not noted.

The Friars of Berwick

As it befell and happinnit into deid,
Vpoun a rever the quhilk is callit Tweid--
At Tweidis mowth thair standis a nobill toun,
Quhair mony lordis hes bene of grit renovne,
5   And mony a wourthy lady fair of face,
And mony ane fresche lusty galland wass--
Into þis toun, the quhilk is callit Berwik
(Vpoun the sey thair standis nane it lyk,
For it is wallit weill abowt with stane,
10   And dowbill stankis castin mony ane,
And syne the castell is so strang and wicht,
With staitlie towris and turattis he on hicht,
With carnallis closit craftely withall,
The portcules most subtelly to fall

Textual notes: Title: not in MSS, The Three Friers of
Berwicke H; Heading: Heir begynnis *etc.* B *only*; 1 hapnit
(vpon M), (in H) deid MH, [B: *begins on f. 348a*; M: *begins on
p. 113*; H: *begins on f. A2a*]; 3-4 B *reverses the order of
vv. 3-4*; 3 Tweedes faire mouth H; 5 mony wourthy ladeis fair
M, Quhair mony a lady bene fair of face B; 6 Quhair mony
fresche 3oung galand M; 7 towne which called is Berwicke H;
8 se it is na vther lyk M; 9 For it well walled is about H;
10 stankes are casten H; 11 castell it is M, And then the H;
12 With strait towris B, turrets on the hight H; 13 The car-
walles closed H, closit most craftelie of all M, The wallis
wrocht craftely B;

15 Quhen þat thame list to draw þame vpoun hicht,
    That it may be into na mannis micht
    To win þat houss be craft or subteltie;
    Quhairfoir it is maist fair all-utirly,
    Into my tyme, quhairevir I haif bene,
20 Moist fair, most gudly, and allthair best besene:
    The tovne, þe wall, the castell, and þe land,
    The vallayis grein vpoun þe vther hand,
    The grit Croce Kirk, and eik the masonedew,
    The Jacobein freiris of the quhyt hew,
25 The Carmeleitis, Austins, and Minouris eik--
    The four ordouris of freiris wer nocht to seik,
    And all into þis wourthy toun dwelling),
    So appinit it intill ane fair May morning
    That twa of þir quhyt Jacobyne freiris
30 (As thay wer wont and vsit mony ʒeiris

15 That quhen thay list to draw it vpon M, that they please
to H, [M: *beginning of p. 114*; H: *beginning of f. A2b*]; 16 it
micht be of na maner of micht B, so that no folkes by anie
kinde of might H; 17 Could winne the same by H; 18 maist gud
allutirly B, Thairto is it most M, And there-within is fayre
artillerie H; 19 Vn to my sicht quhair euir M, In all my
dayes where ever H; 20 gudly most plesand to be sene B, and
most well beseene H; 21 toun the castell M, towne the water
the castell H; 22 The he wallis vpoun þe vpper hand B; 24 The
freiris of Jacobinis quhyt of hew M, The Jacobines they friers
are of whyte hew H; 25 carmeleitis and þe monkis eik B,
carmelitis augustinianis and als the m[i]nouris eik M, The
Carmelites and the Minouries eeke H; 26 ordouris wer not for
to B; 27 wourthy place duelling M, They wer all in þis toun
dwelling B, These friers were in Berwicks town once dwelling
H; 28 appinit in a may B; fair morowing M, Where-as it hapned
in a H; 29 of þe Jacobyne B, of the Jacobine milke-white
friers H; 30 wonit of vsage ʒeir by ʒeiris M;

To pass amang þair brethir vponland),

Thir sillie freiris thus walk thay furth on hand.

Freir Allane was ane, Freir Robert þe vder.

Thir silly freiris with wyffis weill cowld gluder.

35 Rycht wonder weill plesit þai all wyffis

And tauld þame tailis of haly sanctis lyffis.

Quhill on a tyme thay purposit to pass hame,

Bot verry tyrit and wett wes Freir Allane,

For he wes awld and micht nocht wele dure travell,

40 And als he had ane littill spyce of gravell.

Freir Robert wes ȝoung and verry hett of blude,

And be þe way he bure both clouk and hude

And all þair geir, ffor he wes strong and wicht.

Be þat it drew neir towart þe nicht,

45 And thay wer cumand to þe tovne full neir,

Freir Allane said, "Robert, gud bruder deir,

31 brethir vpaland B, To walke amongst H; 32 Thir halie
freiris M, These sillie friers passed foorth from hand H, Wer
send of þame best practisit and cunnand B; 33 allane and
frier B, Ffreir robert the ane freyr allane hecht þe toþir M,
[B: *beginning of f. 349a*]; 34 weill can gluddyr M, As friers
fashion is, with wyves could well gloother H; 35 Right won-
derous well they pleased the wyves H, And tell þame talis and
halie mennis lyveis M; 36 them fayre tales H, Richt wounder
weill þai plesit all the wyffis M; 37 Till on M, Till night
was at hand and they should goe home H; 38 But right tyred H,
Richt weirie was and tyrit freyr M; 39 wele travell BH, not
dure the travell M; 40 littill spyte of B, ane grit spyce of
the gravell M, Because hee had some spyce of the gravell H;
41 and wounder hait M, young could byde raine and winde H;
42 both clothis and B, Hee bare both their gownes yet bode
not behinde H; 43 geir he bure for M, Yea bore all their
geare for hee was full wight H; 44 drew weill towart M, neare
towardes the H; 45 As thay wer cumand towart þe B, war cumin
to the toun weill neyr M; 46 said than gud B;

It is so lait, I dreid þe ȝet be closit,

And we ar tyrit, and wonder evill disposit

To luge owt of þe toun bot gif þat we

50   In sume gud houss this nycht mot herbryt be."

      Swa wynnit þair ane woundir gude hostillar

Without þe toun intill a fair manar,

And Symon Lawrear he wes callit be name.

Ane fair blyth wyf he had of ony ane,

55   Bot scho wes sumthing dynk and dengerous.

Thir silly freiris come then to þat mannis houss

And hailsit hir richt furth full courteslye.

To thame scho anserit agane in hye.

Ffreir Robert sperit eftir the gudman,

60   And scho to thame richt softlie anserit than:

"He went fra hame, God wait, on Weddinsday,

In þe cuntre to seik for corne and hay,

47 þe ȝettis be M, I feare the H; 48 and verry evill B, And I
am tyrit M, wondrous ill disposed H; 49 towne except that H,
To lig without the M, [M: *beginning of p. 115*]; 50 hous þat
we micht harberit M, H *damaged and partly illegible*; 51 So
there did dwell a wondrous H, So wuniit þair ane wounder gay
of cheir M, [H: *beginning of f. A3a*]; 52 Without Berwicke
into a H; 53 Lawrear wes his name B,/Simon Lawrell hee called
was by name H; 54 had and comelie dame H; 55 and dengtious B,
something duike [*sic*] and H; 56 come to M, These sillie H,
The silly freiris quhen thay come to þe houss B; 57 richt
bayth full M, With fair hailsing and bobbing courteslye B,
Saluting her and becked courteouslie H; 58 And sche rewardit
þame agane in hy M, And shee to them did answere perfectlie
H; 59 Frier Robert then inquirde for the goodman H; 60 scho
agane anserit thame than B, And in this wyse shee quicklie
answered than H; 61 wait weddinsday B, God wots on H; 62
cuntre for to seik corne B, In to the cuntre to se for M;

And vþir thingis quhairof we haif neid."

    Freir Allane said, "I pray grit God him speid

65 And sauf him sound intill his leill travale."

    Freir Robert said, "Dame, fill ane stoup of aill

That we may drink, for I am wonder dry."

With þat þe gudwyfe walkit furth in hy

And fillit þe stowp and brocht in breid and cheiss.

70 Thay eit and drank and satt at þair awin eiss.

    Freir Allane said to þe gudwyf in hye,

"Cum hiddir, deme, and sett ȝow doun me bye;

And fill the stoup agane, dame, I ȝow pray,

For or we pairt full weill we sall ȝow pay."

75   The freiris wer blyth, and mirry tailis cowld tell.

And even with þat thay hard þe prayer bell

Off thair abbay, and than thay wer agast

Becauss thay knew the ȝettis wer closit fast,

63 vther sindrie thingis as we haue neid M, wee stand in
neede H; 64 Freir Robert said BM, pray to god M; 65 Him haill
and sound in to his travell B, And keepe him safe and sound
in his travaile H; M *here has vv. 64-5 repeated and cancelled*;
66 stoupe with aile H, And hir desyrit the stowp to fill of
aill B; 67 wonderous dry H, am verray dry M; 68 þe wyfe went
furth richt schurtly B, good-wyfe went full speedilye H;
69 brought them bread H, Sche fild ane stoip and brocht in
cheis and breid M; 70 drank and levit all þair pleid M; 72
Cum heir fayr dame and sit ws doun heirby M; 73 fill this
stoip M, fill once againe the stoupe I H, the cop agane anis
to me B; 74 Before wee goe full well wee will you pay H,
Freir Robert said full weill payit sall ȝe be B; 75 freiris
wox blyth M; 76 ewin so thay M, But even H, heard their owne
prayer- H; 77 thair awin abbay B, Off þat abbay M, Within the
abbie and were sore agast H; 78 thai wist þe M, war lokkit
fast M, For then they H, [B: *beginning of f. 349b*];

That thay micht nocht fra thensfurth gett entre.

80 The gudwyfe than thay prayit for cheritie

To grant thame herberye for that ane nicht.

Bot scho to þame gaif anser with grit hicht:

"The gudman is fra hame, as I ȝow tald;

And God it wait, gif I durst be so bald

85 To herbry freiris into this houss with me,

Quhat wald Symon say? Ha, benedicite!

I trew I durst never luik him in the face.

Our Lord Jesus me sauf fra sic ane cace

And keip me owt of perell and fra schame."

90   Than sillie Freir Allane said, "Na, fair dame,

For Godis saik heir me quhat I sall say.

Put ȝe ws owt, we will be deid or day.

The way is evill, and I am tyrit and wett.

And as ȝe knaw it is so verry lait

95 The ȝettis ar closit we may nocht gett in:

79 fra thyn git M, thay on na wayiss micht gett entre B; 80
thai pray for M, Than the gudwyfe thay B; 81 herbrye that B,
herberie þair fore þat nicht M, them lodging onelie for one
H, [M: *beginning of p. 116*]; 82 And scho to þame anone
ansuerit on hicht M, them did aunswere high on hight H; 83
as ȝow [*sic*] M, Mine husband is H; 84 god wait gif I dar be
M, And I God knowes dare no wayes bee H; 85 freiris in this B,
harber friers within the house H; 86 say aye benedicite M,
would my Simon say benedicitie H; 87 looke intill his face H,
Bot in his absence I abusit his place B, [H: *beginning of f.
A3b*]; 88 Our deir lady mary keip (mee) fra sic (a) cace B(H);
89 and of schame B; 90 said fayr MH, Than auld freir B; 91 I
soone shall H, godis luif ȝe heir quhat I wald say M; 92 wee
shall bee H, In gud faith we will both be B; 93 is ill and
wee are tyrde H; 94 Our ȝettis ar closit that we may nocht in
gett B; 95 closde that we can not H, And to our abbay we can
nocht win in B;

Till our abbay on na wayiss may we win.

Thairfoir it behuvis ws byd her still,

And put ws halelie, dame, into ȝour will."

　　The gudwyf lukit vnto þe freiris tway

100　And at the last to thame this could scho say:

"ȝe byd nocht heir, be Him þat hes ws coft,

Bot gif ȝe list to lig vp in ȝone loft

Quhilk is weill wrocht into þe hallis end;

ȝe sall fynd stray, and clathis I sall ȝow send;

105　Quhair, and ȝe list, pass on baith on feir,

For on no wayiss will I repair haif heir."

　　Hir madin than scho send hir on befoir

And bade thame follow baith withowttin moir.

　　Thay war full blyth, and did as scho thame kend,

110　And vp thay went into þe hallis end,

Intill a loft, wes maid for corne and hay.

Scho maid thair bed and syne went doun her way.

96 Unto our abbay in no case wee may win H, To causs ws
perreiss but help ȝe haif grit syn B; 97 it doeth behoove us
to byde still H, Thairfore behuvis ws to byd M, Thairfoir of
verry neid we mon byd still B; 98 dame intill ȝour M, And ws
submit alhaill into B; 99 luikit to the M, looked on those H;
100 þame can scho M, last unto them did shee H; 101 þat ws all
coft B, hes me coft M; 102 Except yee H; 103 is wrocht in to
ȝon hallis M, wrought even into H; 105 And gif ȝe leist to
pas bayth on in feyr M, If yee list not then passe your wayes
in feire H; 106 Ffor I will haue no langar repayr heir M,
None other wayes will I repaire you heere H; 107 sendeth up
before H, Than hir madin scho sendis þame befoir M; 108 And
hir thay followit baith B, þame wend withouttin wourdis more
M, both and stay no more H; 109 blyth to do as scho þame kend
M; 110 wend richt in the M, went to lodge at the H; 111 loft
the mayde with H; 112 bed syne past doun but delay B, doun
away M, Did make their bedde and then shee went her way H;

Scho closit þe trap and thay remanit still

Into þe loft, and had not all thair will.

115   Freir Allane lay doun as he best micht.

Freir Robert said, "I hecht to walk this nicht.

Quha wait?   Perchance sum sport I ma espy."

Thuss in þe loft I latt the freiris ly,

And of the gudwyf now will I speik mair.

120   Scho wes richt blyth that thay wer closit thair,

Ffor scho had maid ane tryst that samyn nicht

Freir Johne hir luvis supper for to dicht.

And scho wald haif none vder cumpany

Becauss Freir Johine that nicht with hir sowld ly,

125   Quha dwelland wes into þat samyne toun,

And ane gray freir he wes of grit renown.

He guvirnit alhaill the abbacy.

Silwer and gold he had aboundantly.

He had a prevy posterne of his awin

130   That he micht ische, quhen þat him list, vnknawin.

113 Closit B, Closing the H; 114 loft thay wantit of thair B, Into that loft they had H; 115 allane liggis doun M; 116 I vowde to H, [M: *beginning of p. 117*]; 117 some sportes I H, may asey M; 118 loft latt I thir freiris B; 119 now I will speik B, of this fayr wyff I wyll ȝow tellyne mair M; 120 right glad the friers were H, was full blyth þat thay war chosin þair M; 121 that selfe-same night H; 122 her love his supper H; 123 Thairfoir sche desyrit nane M, [B: *beginning of f. 350a*; H: *beginning of f. A4a*]; 124 Johne all nicht with hir wald ly M; 125 that self-same towne H, was within that nobill toun M; 126 ane blak freir BH, Ane M; 127 gouernit all the haly abasy M; 130 Quhair he B, þat he list B, quhen him M, ishe and passe away unknowne H;

Now this into þe toun I leif him still,
Bydand his tyme, and turne agane I will
To thiss fair wyfe, how scho þe fyre cowld beit,
And thringis on fatt caponis to þe speit,
135   And fatt cunyngis to the fyre cowld lay,
And bad hir madin in all þe haist scho may
To flawme and turne and rost thame tenderly;
Syn to hir chalmer scho is went in hy.
Scho pullit hir cunt and gaif hit buffetis tway
140   Vpoun þe cheik, and till it can scho say,
"3e sowld be blyth and glaid at my requeist:
Thir mvllis of 3ouris ar callit till ane feist."
Scho said till it, and soft þerat scho leuch,
"He did not ill þat fand 3ow half aneuche.
145   And or I sleip I think 3e sal be pleisit:
3our appetyt and myn sall both be easit."

Scho cleithis hir in a kirtill of fyne reid;
Ane fair quhyt curch scho casts vpoun hir heid;

131 Thus in the town I will him levin still M, But thus in
Berwickes Towne I H; 133 wyfe now she H; 134 And thristit on
B, Scho thringis M, capounis on the M, And throng the fattest
capons on the H; 135 fatt cunyng to fyre did scho lay B, And
eeke fatte conies to the fyre shee lay H; 136 all haste H,
Syne bad the madin B, haist thow may B; 137 To flame and MH;
138 And to hir chalmer so scho went B, Then to her chamber is
shee gone in H; 139 her makin gave H; 140 þe cheikis syne till
it cowd scho B; 141 Thou shouldst be H; 142 Thay mullis M,
These mulles of thine are H; 143-146 *appear in* M *only*; 143 and
softlie at scho leucht M; 147 Sche castis on ane kirtill M,
Shee putteth on a kirtle fyne of red H; 148 scho puttis vpoun
B, Ane quhyt curchey sche cast vpon M, shee bindes about her
H;

Hir kirtill-belt wes silk and silwer fyne,
150 With ane proud purse and keyis gingling syne.
On every finȝer scho werrit ringis two:
Scho was als prowd as ony papingo.
And of ane burde of silk, richt costlie grein,
Hir tusche wes with silwer weill besene.
155 Than but scho come into the hall anone,
And syn sche went to se gif ony come.
And ewin so Freir Johne knokit at þe ȝett.
His knok scho knew and in scho cowld him lett.
Scho welcomit him vpon ane fayr maneir.
160 He thankit hir and said, "My awin luve deir,
Haif thair ane pair of bossis gud and fyne--
Thay hald ane gallone full of Gascone wyne--
And als ane pair of pertrikis, richt new slane,
And eik ane creill full of breid of mane.

149 Hir kirtill wes of silk B, Her belt was wrought of silke
H; 150 Embrodred purse her keyes hung clincking syne H, Hir
vþer garmentis as the reid gold did schyne B; 151 scho werris
ringis B, On ilkane fingar M, shee put on ringes H, [M:
beginning of p. 118]; 152 And was H; 153 The burde scho
cuverit with clath of costly greyne B, Shee layde on a board-
cloath of costlie greene H; 154 Hir napry aboif wes wounder
weill B, Of silver-worke shee was full well fore-seene H;
155 And but M, Then foorth shee H, scho went to se gif ony
come B; 156 And askt her mayde if shee heard anie one H,
Scho thocht full lang to meit hir lufe frier Johine B; 157
With that Frier John was knocking at H, Syne schortly did
this freir knok at B; 158 scho kend and did so him in lett
B, Whose knocke shee knew and quicklie him in let H; 159 him
in all hir best maneir B, vpon a good manniere H; 160 my
sweit luif M; 161 Thair is ane M, of bottles good H; 163
pertrikis new M, And eeke a paire of partrich even new H,
[H: *beginning of f. A4b*]; 164 And als þat creill is full M,
Also a maund full bread of fynest maine H;

165 This haif I brocht to ȝow, my awin luve deir;

     Thairfor, I pray ȝow, be blyth and mak gud cheir.

     Sen it is so þat Semon is fra hame,

     I will talk þe hameliar now, gud dame."

     Scho sayis, "ȝe ar full hertly welcome heir

170 At ony tyme quhen þat ȝe list appeir."

     With that scho smylit wounder lustely;

     He thristis hir hand againe richt prevely.

     Thus at þair sport I will þame levin still,

     Bydand þair tyme, and turne againe I will

175 And tell ȝow of thir silly freiris two

     Wer lokit in þe loft amang þe stro.

     Ffreir Allane still into þe loft can ly;

     Freir Robert had ane littell ielosy,

     For in his hairt he had ane persaving,

180 And throw þe burdis he maid with his botkin

165 This I haif brocht B, Thus haue M, my sweit luif deyr M,
mine onelie deare H; 166 Thairfoir I reid now þat we mak M,
That you and I there-with might make good cheare H; 167 so
son symon M, Since it H; 168 hameliar heir now dame M, talke
right homelie with you madame H, I wil be hamely now with
ȝow gud B; 169 ar weill mayr wylcum M; 170 In such a wyse
when that you will appeare H, Than symon is or sal be all
this ȝeir M; 171 wounder suttellie M, wondrous lovesomlie H;
172 He thristit hir B, agane full preuilie M, Againe hee
thrust her hand right H; 173 them yet leave still H, Than in
hett luve thay talkit vderis till B, [B: *beginning of f.
350b*]; 174 Till other tyme H, Thus at þair sport now will I
leif þame still B; 175 To tell M; 176 That liggit in M; 177
allane in þe loft still can B, Frier Allane on his couch
full still did lye H; 179 had great perceiving H; 180 the
wall he M, made with some sharpe thing H;

        A litill hoill. On sic a wyiss maid he

        That all thay did thair doun he micht weill se,

        And every word he herd þat thay did say:

        Quhen scho wes prowd, richt woundir fresche and gay,

185   And quhat scho war vpon hir heid aboif.

        Scho callit him baith hert, lemmane, and luve.

        So prelatlyk he sat into þe chyre,

        Scho rownis than ane pistill in his eir.

        Thuss sport þai thame and makis melodie.

190   And quhen scho saw þe supper wes reddy,

        Scho gois belyfe and cuveris þe burd annon,

        And syne the pair of bossis hes scho tone,

        And sett þame doun vpoun þe burde him by.

            And evin with þat thay hard the gudman cry.

195   He knokit at þe ȝett and callit fast.

        Quhen thay him hard they wer than both agast,

181 wyse got hee H, hole richt prevelie maid M; 182 All þat
thay B, all þair deid þair M, did below hee could well H;
183 Yea everie H, heard which they H, And he micht heir all
þat ever thay culd say M; 184 proude and wondrous H; 185 Scho
callit him baith hert le<u>mm</u>ane <u>and</u> luve B; 186 both lemman
heart and H, And how sche clippit him bayt<u>h</u> hart and luif M,
Lord god gif than his curage wes aboif B; <u>1</u>87 prelatlyk sat
he into B, Full prelate-lyke H, sat intill his chyre M, [M:
beginning of p. 119]; 188 pistill intill <h> eyre M, And shee
did round epistles in H; 189 Thuss sportand thame and makand
melody B, make great melodie H; 190 Quhen M; 191 Shee quicklie
went and deckt the board H; 192 syn ane pair M, And then the
pair of bottles hath H; 193 burde hir by BH, *H has a hole
through the first two letters of* <u>downe</u>; 194 ewin so than hard
M; 195 And knokand at þe ȝett he <u>cryit</u> fast B, Who knocked at
H, and shouted fast H; 196 heard then were they all agast H,
Fra thay him knew þai war all sayr agast M;

And als Freir Johine wes sumthing in effray:

He stertit vp and wald haif bene away.

Bot all for nocht: he micht no way win owt.

200   The gudwyfe spak than with a visage stowt:

"3one is Symone that makis this deray

That I micht now haue tholit weill away.

I sall him quyt, and I leif half a 3eir,

That merrit hes ws this in sic maneir;

205   Becauss of him we may nocht byd togidder.

I me repent as now that 3e come hidder,

For we wer weill gif þat he wer away."

    "Quhat sall I do? Allace," the freir can say.

"Into this case, Lord, how sall I me beir?

210   Ffor I am schent and Symone fynd me heir.

I dreid me sair, and he cum in this innis

And find me heir, þat I los both my quhynnis."

    The gudwyf said, "I hald it for the best

That I 3ou hide quhill he be brocht to rest

197 wes in a fellone fray B, And good frier H; 198 He stert vp
fast and B, Full soone start up H, And stertis vp M; 199 noway
get out M, [H: *beginning of f. Blb*]; 200 gud wyf speiris w<u>ith</u>
M; 201 mak<u>is</u> all this fray B, Yonde is H, makes all this H;
202 micht <u>th</u>olit full weill had bene away B, Whom I might
thole had bidden yet away H; 203 Ile quit him this if I H, and
I may leif ane 3eir M; 204 That cu<u>mm</u>ert hes B, Him þat hes
meroit ws on this maneir M, For tr<u>ou</u>bling us when wee should
make good cheare H; 205 Becauss for him B; 206 I doe repent at
this tyme yee H, I sair repent and wo is 3e B; 207 weill and
he had bene away M, Wee were so well if hee had bidden away H,
þat 3e wer B; 208 alace frier John can H; 209-12 *are in* M *only*;
213 Hyd 3ow scho said quhill he be brocht to rest B, I mon 3ow
hyd till he be brocht till rest M; 214 hyde till hee H, in to
3one troich I think it for þe best B, Perchance scho sayis all
cu<u>mm</u>is for the best M;

215   Into ȝone troich that lyis into ȝone nwke,"
      Wald hald a boll of meill quhen þat scho buke.
      Than vndir it scho gart him creip in hy
      Quhair he had rowme aneuche þat he micht ly.
           Scho closit him and syne went on hir way,
220   And till hir madin smertlie can scho say,
      "Away all þis and slokkin out þe fyre.
      Go cloiss the burde and tak away þe chyre,
      And lok vp all into ȝone almery,
      Baith meit and drink, and ga belyf in hy."
225   Baith cunnyngis, caponis, and wyld fewlis fyne,
      The mayne breid als, þe bossis with þe wyne--
      Sche hid vp all, and strowit the hous so clene
      That na liknes of feist micht thair be sene.
      And syne withowttin ony mair delay
230   Scho castis of allhaill hir fresch array,

215 trogh which standeth in the nooke H, It lyis mekle and
huge in all ȝone B, Ane kneddin troche þat lay in till ane nuk
M; 216 of flour quhen M, hold sixe bowles of H, It held a B,
þat we buke B; 217 And vnder M, There-under then shee causde
him H; 218 enough at ease to lye H, And bad him lurk thair
verry quyetly B; 219 and then went H; 219a Quhat sall I do
allace the freir can say B only; 220 And to her mayden softlie
can H, Syne to hir madin spedyly scho spak B; 220b Go to the
fyre and the meitis fra it tak B only, [B: beginning of f.
351a]; 221 Take way this geare and H, Be bissy als and B; 222
away yonde chayre H, cloiss ȝone burd B; 223 lok in all in
ȝon M, Soone locke up all with-in the panterie H, [M: beginning
of p. 120]; 224 drinke ha done full speedilie H, drink with
wyne and ail put by B; 225 The conies H, and the wylde H, B
blank; 226 breid þe M, maine-shot bread the bottels with H,
als thow hyd it with B; 227 Shee lockt up all and dight the H,
That being done thow sowp þe houss clene syne B; 228 feist
meit micht be M, na apperance of feist be heir sene B; 228a
Bot sobirly our selffis dois sustene B only; 229 syn but ony
langer delay M, The good-wyfe then with-out longer delay H;
230 of haill B, all hir M, Did quicklie put off all her H;

And bownit hir into hir bed anone

And tholit him to knok his fill, Symone.

    Quhen he wes tyrit, forknokit and forcryid,

Abowt he went vnto þe vder syd,

235   Till ane windo wes at hir beddis heid,

And cryit, "Alesoun, awak, for Goddis deid!"

And on Alesone fast cold he cry.

    And at þe last scho anserit crabitly:

"Ach, quha be this that knawis sa weill my name?

240   Go henss," scho sayis, "for Symon is fra hame,

And I will herbry no gaistis heir, perfay.

Thairfoir I pray ȝow, wendis on ȝour way,

For at this tyme ȝe may nocht lugit be."

    Than Symone said, "Fair dame, ken ȝe nocht me?

245   I am ȝour Symone, and husband of this place."

    "Ar ȝe my spous Symone?" she sayis; "Allace,

Throw misknawlege I had almaist misgane.

Quha wenit that ȝe sa lait wald haif cum hame?"

231 hir till hir M, Than went scho to hir B, And then shee
went in-to H; 232 And let him knok þarout his M, And let her
husband knocke with-out alone H; 233 he for knoking tyrit wes
and cryid B, hee with knocking tyred was h[e]e cryde H; 234
And went about H; 235 Unto a window stoode at H, B *blank*; 236
Saying Alison awake for Christes dead H, B *blank*; 237 And an
on Alesoun fast he could cry M, When Allison had tholde him
long to crye H; 238 As halfe a-sleepe shee answearde
crabbedlye H; 239 Say quha be þat sa weill knawis my M, Now
who is that that H, [H: *beginning of f. B1b*]; 240 hence quod
shee mine husband is H; 241 will haue no M, will harber heere
no guestes perfay H; 242 ȝow to wend on B, you wende on wende
on your H; 243 And at M, nocht harbreit be M; 244 dame knaw
ȝe M, Then Simon spake deare wyfe ken H; 245 Simon good-man of
H; 246 scho sayd allace M, yee that Simon? my spouse shee H;
247 Be misknawlege B, misknawlege almaist I had gane wrang M,
almost miss-done H; 248 haue cuming [*sic*] hame M, Who would
have thought yee should so late come home H;

Scho stertis vp and gettis licht in hy
250   And oppinit than the ʒet full haistely.
Scho tuk fra him his geir, as was þe gyse,
Syne welcomit him on the maist hairtly wyiss.

He bad þe madin kindill on þe fyre,
"Syne get me meit, and tak þe all thy hyre."
255   The gudwyf said richt schortly, "ʒe me trow,
Heir is no meit þat ganand is for ʒow."

"How sa, fair deme? Ga gait me cheiss and breid
And fill þe stowp. Hald me no mair in pleid,
For I am verry tyrit, wett, and cauld."

260   Than vp scho raiss and durst nocht mair be bauld,
Bot coverit ane burde and set on breid in hy,
And syn cauld meit scho brocht delyuerlie,
(Ane sowsit nolt fute and ane scheipis heid full swyth)
And fillit þe stowp and feniʒet to be blyth.

---

250 And openeth then H, full speedilye H, And leit hym in and
þat delyuerlye M; 251 him þe geir M, geir at all devyiss B,
Shee let him in on the most heartlie wyse H; 252 on maist B,
And leit him in vpon ane haistie wyse M, And tooke from him
the geare as was the guyse H; 253 <Sche tuik fra him> he had
the M, on ane fyre M; 254 Syne graith me B, And get MH, and
tax all my hyre M, get him meate and shee should have good
hyre H; 255 said shortly B, saide sweet Simon yee may trow H;
256 meate this night that gaines for H; 257 dame gar get M,
At least good dame goe fetch mee H; 258 Ga fill BH, me with
na pleid M, stoupe and holde it to mine head H; 259 am werie
tyrit and bayth cauld and wet M, am hungrie wearie wette and
colde H, [M: *beginning of p. 121*]; 260 and maid na mair debait
M, rose as reason bade shee should H; 261 Cuverit þe burde
þairon sett meit in hy B, Covered the boarde and set on bread
of rye H; 262 Ane sowsit nolt fute and scheipheid haistely B,
A sowst neats foote a sheepes-head set shee by H; 263 soust
fute M, (And sum B), (Even such H) cauld meit scho brocht to
him belyve BH; 264 fillit ane cop and M, stowp the gudman than
wes blyth B, stoupe then Simon waxed blythe H; *In the right
margin of M, from v. 265 to v. 280, appear copies of fragments
of lines from this page, in two different hands.*

265   He sittis doun and sweiris, "Be all hallow,

      I fair richt weill and I had ane gud fallow.

    Dame, eit with me and drink, gif þat ȝe may."

       The gudwyf said meiklie, "Hop I nay;

    It wer mair meit into ȝour bed to be

270 Than now to sit desyrand cumpany."

       Freir Robert said, "Allace, gud bruder deir,

    I wald þe gudman wist þat we wer heir.

    Quha wait? Perchance sum bettir wald he fair,

    For sickerly my hairt will ay be sair

275 Gif ȝone scheipheid with Symon birneist be

    And thair so gud meit in ȝon almeire."

    And with þat word he gaif ane hoist annone.

      The gudman hard and speirit, "Quha is ȝone?"

265 Than satt he doun and swoir be B, Hee ate and dranke and
sayde by H; 266 weill had I ane M, well had I but one H; 267
Dame drinke with mee and eate I doe you pray H; 268 sayde the
devill-a-bitte I may H, Said þe gudwyf devill in the tim <I>
may I B; 269 mair tyme in to M, meete now in your H, [B:
beginning of f. 351b]; 270 Than heere to H; 270a-b:
    The freiris twa þat in the loft can ly
    Than hard him weill desyrand cumpany
M *only*; 271 said allane gud M, sayde unto his brother H; 272
Alace I H, good-man kende us heere H; 273 better might hee H,
perchance the better we may fair M; 274 will euir be M, For
sure it is mine H; 275 scheipis heid M, If yonde course meate
with H, [H: *beginning of f. B2a*]; 276 Sa mekill gud cheir
being in þe almeire B, While daintie cheare standes in the
panterie H; 277 hee coached lowde anone H; 278 Till Simon
heard and asked who H; 278a-b:
    Me think þair is men in to ȝon loft
    The gudwyf ansuerit with wourdis soft
M *only*;

The gudwyf said, "ȝone ar ȝour awin freiris tway."

280   Symone said, "Tell me quhat freiris be thay?"

"ȝone is Freir Robert and silly Freir Allane,

That all this day hes travellit with grit pane.

Be thay come heir it wes so verey lait

Houris wes rung and closit wes þair ȝait,

285 And in ȝond loft I gaif þame harberye."

The gudman said, "Sa God haif part of me,

Tha freiris twa ar hairtly welcome hidder.

Gar call þame doun þat we ma drink togidder."

The gudwyf said, "I reid ȝow lat þame be;

290 Thay had levir sleip nor sit in cumpanye."

The gudman said vnto þe madin sone,

"Go pray þame baith to cum withouttin hune."

279 ar freiris B, sayde yonde are your friers H, /ȝon ar ȝour
awin freyris brether tuay M; 280 Quoth Simon then tell H, I
pray the dame tell M, freiris ar thay MH; 281 Shee sayde Frier
Robert and sillie olde Allane H; 282 Who all this day have
walked in great H, hes gane with meikill pane M; 283 thay war
heir M, When they H; 284 Curfiw wes B, was the ȝet M, Prayer
bell was H, ȝait *added in different hand* B; 285 harbrye B,
There-fore above I H; 286 parte on mee H; 287 The selfe-same
friers are H; 288 Ga call BH; 289 þame ly M; 290 Ffor thay M,
nor be in baudery M, had rather sleip H; 290a-d:

        To drink and with [*sic*] it ganis nocht for thame
        Lat be fair dame thay wourdis ar in vane
        I will þame haue be goddis dignite
        Mak no delay bot bring þame doun to me

M *only*; [M290a: *beginning of p. 122*]; 291 þe maid thone B,
vnto his madin M, Unto the mayden spake the good-man than H;
292 cum till me annone B, come to mee frae hand H, bayth cum
M;

And sone þe trap the madin oppinit than,

And bad thame baith cum doun to þe gudman.

295   Freir Robert said, "Now be sweit Sanct Jame,

The gudman is verry welcome hame.

And for his weilfair dalie do we pray.

And we sall cum annone, ȝe may him say."

And with þat word thay start vp baith anone,

300   And doun þe trap delyverly thay come

And salust Symone also sone as thay him se;

And he agane thame welcomit hairtfullie.

He said, "Cum ben, myne awin bredir deir,

And sett ȝow doun, ȝe bayth, besyd me heir,

305   Ffor I am now allane, as ȝe may se.

Thairfoir sitt doun, and beir me cumpanye,

And tak ȝow part of sic gud as we haif."

Freir Allane said, "Ser, I pray God ȝow saif,

293 þe trop the B, And vp the M, The mayden soone did open the trappe doore H; 294 And sayde yee friers come downe vpon the floore H; 295 said fayr dame be sanct M, Frier Robert sware and sayde by sweete Sainct John H; 296 is even right well-come H, is dewlie wylcum M; 297 And we sall cum anone ȝe may him say M, Alace hee had ill travelling this day H; 298 We sall annone cum doun to him ȝe say B, come vnto him yee may say H, Him for to pleis in all þat euer we may M; 299 Than with B, baith attone B, Then suddenlie they H; 300 trappe with right good speede they H, the leddyr delyuerly ar gone M; 301 Halsit symone B, Saluted Simon H; 302 againe did halsse them courteouslie H; 303 And said cum heir myne awin BH, owne poore brethren H; 304 doun sone besyd B, downe even besyde H; 305 am heir allane M; 306 Where-fore I pray you beare H; 307 tak ȝour parte M, take a parte of such cheare as I have H; 308 said I MH, pray to god M, you to save H;

Heir is annuch, forsuth, of Godis gud."

310   Than Symon swere thame, "Be the haly rud,
3it wald I gif ane croun of gold, for me,
For sum gud meit and drink amangis ws thre."

    Freir Robert said, "Quhat meitis wald 3e haif,
Or quhatkin drink desyre 3e for to craif?

315   For I haif mony sindry practikis seir
Be3ond þe sey in Pareiss did I leir
That I will preve, ser, glaidly for your saik,
And for our demys, that harbry cowd ws maik.
I tak on hand, and 3e will counsale keip,

320   That I sall gar 3ow haue or that 3e sleip
Of the best meit that is in þis cuntre,
And Gascone wyne, gif ony in it be,
Or be þair ocht within ane hundreth myle,
It sal be heir within a littill quhyle."

309 For heir is now annuch of B, For heere is enough of Gods
graces goode H; 310 symon anserit now be the rud BH; 311 gold
fra me M, [H: *beginning of f. B2b*]; 312 drink amang ws M; M
here has v. 316, cancelled; 313 meate now would H, quhat
drinkis wald 3e <haif> craif B; 314 Or else what drinke H, Or
quhat meitis desyre 3e for to haif B; 315 have sundrie prac-
tickes well discearnde H, [B: *beginning of f. 352a*]; 316 paris
cuth I M, the seas in Paris which I learnde H; 317 That I wald
preve glaidly B, The which I gladlie proove will for H; 318
for 3our demys B, our dame that M, dames who did us lodging
make H; 319 Ile take in hand if yee H; 320 3ow se or ever <y>
I sleip B, To cause you see even heere before yee H; 321 best
þat M, [M: *beginning of p. 123*]; 322 Off gascone B, wyne and
ony M, anie that there bee H; 323 þair ony within B, Or if it
bee with-in H; 324 bony quhyle BH;

325 The gudman had grit marvell of the taill
And said, "My brodir, my hairt will neir be haill
Bot gif 3e preve that practik or we parte,
Be quhatkin science, nigromansy, or airt."
    Frier Robert said, "Of this 3e haif no dreid,
330 For I can do fer mair and þair be neid."
    Than Symon said, "Freir Robert, I 3ow pray,
For my saik that science 3e wald assay
To mak ws sport."
                    And than the frier vprais:
He tuk his buk and to þe flure he gais.
335 He turnis it our and reidis a littill space
And to þe eist direct he turnis his face;
Syne to þe west he turnit and lowtit doun,
And tuk his buk and said an orisoun.
And ay his eyne wer on þe almery
340 And on þe troch quhair þat Freir Johine did ly.

325 marvell at this tale H, gudman marvallis meikill of þat
taill M; 326 sayde deare brother H, said my hairt neir B;
327 or 3e parte B, Except yee trye your skill before wee
parte H; 328 Through your science H, B *blank*; 329-332 M *only*;
333 mak ane sport B, freir vpstart B; 334 þe freir he B, And
tuk M, Taking his booke unto the H; 335 reidis it a B, And
turnis our and reidis on ane space M, turnes the leaves and
H; 336 east hee turnes about his H, And in the eist he turnit
ewin his face M; 336a-b:
        And maid ane croce and than the freyr cuth lout
        And in the west he turnit him ewin about
M *only*; 337 and lukit doun B, Than in the north he M, Than to
the west he turneth looking downe H; 338 and red ane B, And
closde the booke H; 339 his e was on M, But still his H, the
panterye H; 340 trogh where-in Frier H, þat the freyr cuth ly
M;

Than sat he doun and kest abak his hude:

He granit, he glowrit, he gaipit as he wer woid,

And quhylis still he sat in studeing,

And vþir quhylis vpoun his buk reding.

345   And quhylis with baith his handis he wald clap,

And vþir quhylis he wald baith glour and gaip,

And on this wyse he ʒeid the hous abowt

Weill thryiss and mair, and ay the freir cowd lowt

Quhen that he come ocht neir the almery.

350   Thairat our dame had woundir grit invy,

For in hir hairt scho had ane persaving

That he had wit of all hir govirning.

Scho saw him gif þe almery sic stait,

Vnto hirself scho said, "Full weill I wait

355   I am bot schent: he knawis full weill my thocht.

Quhat sall I do? Allace þat I wes wrocht!

341 He set him doun M, his heid M; 342 granit and he glowrit
as B, He girnit he M, wer weid M, Moste fearfullie gaping as
H; 343 And quhylum he sat still in ane studeying M, Whiles
sate hee still his handes abroade fast spreading H; 344 And
quhylum on his buik he wes reyding M, booke was reading H;
345 And with B, And quhylum with M, with handes and heeles
full lowde would H; 346 quhylis wald he glour B; 347 Thus did
Frier Robert reade the H, Syne in þe sowth he turnit him
abowt B; 348 Weill twys or thrys and M, mair than lawly cowd
he lowt B, Five or six times so lowlie could hee stoupe H;
349 come neir B, came neare hand the panterye H; 350 Where-at
our H; 351 in hart M, had some perceiving H, [H: *beginning of
f. B3a*]; 352 had knawin all B, That Frier Robert knew well
her H; 353 sic ane stait M, sic a straik B, the panterie such
H; 354 On till hir self M, Untill her-selfe H, [M: *beginning
of p. 124*]; 355 shent the frier knowes all my H, He knawis
full weill þat I haue in my M; 356 alace what have I wrought
H;

Get Symon wit, it wil be deir doing."

Be þat þe freir had left his studeing

And on his feit he startis vp, full sture,

360   And come again and said, "Alhaill my cure

Now is it done, and ȝe sall haif playntie

Of breid and wyne, þe best in this cuntre.

Thairfoir, fair dame, get vp deliuverlie

And ga belyfe vnto ȝone almerie

365   And oppin it, and se ȝe bring ws syne

Ane pair of boissis full of Gascone wyne.

Thay hald a galloun and mair, that wait I weill.

And bring ws als the mayne breid in the creill,

Ane pair of cunyngis fat and het pypand,

370   The caponis als ȝe sall ws bring fra hand,

Twa pair of pertrikis--I wait thair is no ma--

And eik of pluveris se þat ȝe bring ws twa."

357 wit it war my vndoing M, If Simon know it will bee a
deare doing H; 358 freyr hes left M; 359 Moste furiouslie
hee stampeth on the floore H; 360 Then came H, and seyit all
his cure B; 361 Is done anone and M; 362 this cietie M, Bread
meat and wyne H; 363 Quhairfoir fair M, up full speedilie H;
364 And gang belyff vnto ȝour almerie M, And goe your wayes
into yonde panterie H; 365 And appinit it B, and sone ȝe M,
Soone open it H, [B: *beginning of f. 352b*]; 366 of bottles
full H; 367 Thay had ane B, mair I wait it weill M, Which
holde more than a gallon I warrand H; 368 ws all the B, in a
creill B, us eeke the H, in the maund H; 369 Thair is ane pair
of capounis pypand het M, Two roasted conies fatte and hote
with-all H; 370 capons eeke to us dame bring yee shall H, And
als ane pair of cunyngis weill I wait M; 371 na mair M, Foure
partriches I know there is no lesse H; 372 eik the plovaris
and se ȝe bring ws þair M, Of ploovers dame see that yee
bring a messe H;

The gudwyf wist it wes no variance.

Scho knew the freir had sene hir govirnance.

375   Scho saw it wes no bute for to deny.

And than scho went vnto the almery

And oppinit it, and than scho fand richt þair

All þat þe freir had spokin of befoir.

    Scho stert abak as scho wer in afray

380   And sanit hir, and smyland cowd scho say,

"Ha, banadicitie! Quhat may this bene?

Quhaevir afoir hes sic a fairly sene,

Sa grit a marvell as now hes apinit heir?

Quhat sall I say? He is ane haly freir.

385   He said full swth of all þat he did say."

    Scho brocht all furth, and on þe burd cowd lay

Baith breid and wyne, and vþir thingis moir:

Cunyngis, caponis, as ȝe haif hard befoir.

373 good-wyfe saw Rob made no H; 374 knew that he had H; 375
Sche wist it M, And thought it H; 376 With that scho B, scho
ȝeid on to M, But quicklie went un-to the panterye H; 377
fand thair B, Then shee brought foorth together with her
mayde H; 378 frier before un-to her sayde H; 379 Starting
abacke H; 380 Then crost her-selfe and smyling can shee H,
And sanis hir and to symon can say M; 381 Haly benedicite M,
this mene M, benedicitie who hath heere beene H; 382 Quha
hard euir of sic M, Or who hath ever such lyke marvels seene
H; 383 ane farlie as now is hapnit M, a wonder is now hapned
H; 385 ȝe said M, that ȝe culd say M, I find it sooth of all
that hee did say H; 386 Mayde take all foorth and on the
boarde it lay H; 387 wyne withouttin moir M, other good
thinges H, [H: *beginning of f. B3b*]; 388 Cunyngis and caponis
B, The capounis cunyngis as M;

Pertrikis, pluveris befoir thame hes scho brocht.

390 The freir knew weill and saw thair wantit nocht,

Bot all wes furth brocht evin at his devyiss.

Fra Symone saw it appinnit on this wyiss,

He had grit wondir, and sweris be þe mone,

"Freir Robert hes richt weill his devoir done.

395 He may be callit ane man of grit science

Sa suddanly þat all this purviance

Hes brocht ws heir, throw his grit subteltie,

And throw his airt and his filosophie.

In ane gud tyme it wes that he come hidder.

400 Now fill þe cop þat we ma drink togidder

And mak gud cheir eftir this langsum day,

Ffor I haif riddin ane woundir wilsome way.

Now God be lovit, heir is suffisance

Vnto ws all, throw зour gud govirnance."

389 Pertrikis and pluveris B, þame as sche M, plovers to the
board shee H, [M: *beginning of p. 125*]; 390 knew and M, Frier
Rob knew all and H; 391 was sooth she brought at H, was
brocht as him list devyse M; 392 And Symone B, When Simon H,
it ferd vpon this M; 393 had much wonder and sware by H; 394
That Freir Robert weill his dett had done B, That Frier
Robert full well his deede had doone H; 395 зe may M, Thou
art quod hee a H; 396 suddanly maid all B, That hast so soone
made thus great purveyance H; 397 heir all throw his subtilte
M, Thou bringest heere through thy great H; 398 throw his
knawlege in filosophie B, And by thine arte and great philo-
sophie H; 399 wes quhen he B, In full good time it was that
thou came H, It was in gude tyme þat M; 400 Now powre out
wyne and let us drinke H; 401 mak ws murrie efter this ewill
day M; 403 be praysde heere H, On till ws all throw his wyse
gouernance M; 404 To serve us all through H, And god be lovit
heir is aneuche sufficiance M;

405   And than annone thay drank all round abowt
        Off þe gud wyne, and ay thay playit cop owt.
        Thay sportit thame and maid richt mirrey cheir
        With sangis lowd, baith Symone and the freir.
        And on this wyiss the lang nicht our thay draif.
410   Nothing thay wantit that thay desyrd to haif.
            Than Symon said to þe gudwyf in hy,
        "Cum heir, fair dame, and sett ȝow doun me by
        And tak parte of sic gude as we haif heir,
        And hairtly I ȝow pray to thank this frier
415   Off his bening grit besines and cure
        That he hes done to ws vpoun this flure;
        He brocht ws meit and drink haboundantlie,
        Quhairfoir of richt we aucht mirry to be."
            Bot all þair sport, quhen thay wer maist at eiss,
420   Vnto our deme it wes bot littill pleiss,

405 drank evin round B, And w<u>ith</u> that wourd thay drank round
M; 406 Of gascone wine the frei<u>ri</u>s playit (still) cop owt
B(H); 407 and makis mirry B, made full merrie H, Thay eit and
drank and M; 408 W<u>ith</u> loud sang bayth M, And eeke full lowde
sang Simon H; *Here* M̄ *has the lines* <Quhill at the last þai
waxit bly<u>th</u> ilkane/Than symon> *cancelled*; 409 Quhill on M,
nicht thay ourdraif B, Even an this wyse the darksome night
ore-drave H; 410 thay want that B, Thay wantit nothing þ<u>at</u>
thay desyr to craif M, Wanting no-thing that they could w̄ish
to have H; 411–418 M *blank*; 411 The good-man sayde H, [B:
beginning of f. 353a]; 412 Come hither dame H; 413 take a
parte of such as H; 414 But first of all I pray yow thanke
the frier H; 415 For his benigne businesse and great cure H;
416 Which hee H, upon the flore H; 417 And brocht B, brought
fyne meate and wyne aboundantlie H; 418 There-fore forsooth
let us right merry be H; 419 All þair sport þocht þai war
weill at eis M, But sing or say or use what sporte they
please H; 420 On till our dame it micht hir nothing pleis M,
little ease H;

For vþer thing wes more into hir thocht.

Scho wes so red hir hairt wes ay on flocht

That throw the freir scho sowld discoverit be.

To him scho lukit ofttymes effeiritlie,

425 And ay disparit in hart was scho, by chance

That he had witt of all hir purveance.

This satt scho still, and wist no vdir wane:

Quhatevir thay say scho lute thame all allane.

Bot scho drank with þame into cumpany

430 With fenȝeit cheir, and hert full wo and hevy.

Bot thay wer blyth annwche, God watt, and sang,

For ay the wyne was rakand thame amang,

Quhill at the last thay woix richt blyth ilkone.

Than Symone said vnto þe freir annone,

435 "I marvell mikell how that this may be,

Intill schort tyme that ȝe sa suddanlye

421 Vther M, more in till hir M, thing thair wes in to B,
An-other thing shee had into H; 422 Sche had sic dreid hir
hart wes all on M, How shee might scape and not to shame bee
brought H; 423 Throw M, On Frier Robert shee looked grievous-
lie, [H: *beginning of f. B4a*]; 424 A syd to him sche caist
ane fremmit e M, And thought through him shee should dis-
covered bee H; 425 scho/B, And in her heart shee did despare
lyke-wyse H, M *blank;* 426 purveance to B, That they did eate
her dainties in that guyse H, M *blank;* 427-428 *are added in
the right margin of* M; 427 Still scho sat and lait þame all
allane M, Yet still shee sate and durst not make her moane H;
428 lute him all B, they did shee let them aye alone H,
Quhatevir scho thocht sche wist no vdir wane M; 429-430 M
blank; 430 heart sad and heavie H; 431-432 *are added in the
right margin of* M, *directly following 427-428;* 432 The wyne
was walkand evir þame amange M; 433 thay waxit blyth ilkon M,
Till at the last that thay were drunke each one H; 435
Forsooth I marvell much how this can bee H; 436 In to schort
M, In so short H;

Hes brocht to ws sa mony denteis deir."

"Thairof haif ȝe no farlie," quoth the freir,

"I haif ane pege full prevy of my awin,

440   Quhenevir I list will cum to me vnknawin

And bring to me sic thing as I wald haif.

Quhatevir I list, it neidis me nocht to craif.

Thairfoir be blyth, and tak in pacience,

And traistis weill I sall do diligence:

445   Gif þat ȝow list or lykis to haif moir,

It sal be had, and I sall stand þairfoir.

Incontinent that samyn sall ȝe se.

Bot I protest þat ȝe keip it previe.

Latt no man wit that I can do sic thing."

450   Than Symone swoir and said, "Be Hevynnis King,

It sal be kepit prevy as for me.

Bot bruder deir, ȝour serwand wald I se,

437 brocht ws heir sa mony denteis seyr M, us such store of
daintie cheare H; 438 ȝe nocht farlie said the M, no marvell
quoth BH; 440 When ere I please will H, Will cum to me quhen
þat I list vnknawin M; 441 as I will haif B, such thinges as
H; [M: *beginning of p. 126*]; 442 Quhat I so list me neidis
nocht to M, Looke what I please I need it not H; 443 Quhair-
foir be M, and live in H; 444 And trest ȝe weill B, And trust
mee sir Ile doe my diligence H; 445 þat ȝe list or thinkis
to B, that yee please at this time to H; 446 He sall it bring
and þat I sall stand fore M, You shall it have my life shall
H; 447 Incontinent richt heir þat ȝe may se M, that same
heere shall H; 448 keip this previe M, If yee protest yee
will keepe secresie H; 449 man know that H; 450 The good-man
sware H, Than Symon said I sweyr be M; 451 kept full secret
as H, kepit counsale as M;

Gif it ȝow pleiss, that we may drynk togidder,

For I wait nocht gif ȝe ma ay cum hidder,

455 Quhen that ws list or lykis, sic as this."

The freir said, "Nay, so haif I hevynis bliss,

Ȝow to haif the sicht of my serwand--

It cannocht be, ȝe sall weill vndirstand,

That ȝe may se him graithly in his kynd,

460 Bot ȝe annone sowld go owt of ȝour mynd,

He is so fowll and vgly for to se.

I dare nocht awnter for to tak on me

To bring him hidder, heir into our sicht,

And namely now, so lait into þe nicht,

465 Bot gif it wer on sic a maner wyiss:

Him to translait or ellis dissagyiss

Fra his awin kynd into ane vder stait."

Than Symone said, "I mak no moir debait.

453 Gif ȝe pleis M, we might drinke H; 455 Quhen we list M,
that we want our nedis sic B, To haue your friendship in such
case as H; 456 so mot I haif hevynis B, said sir as I would
faine have blisse H, Than symon sayis swa haue I joy or blis
M; 457-461 M *blank*; 457 Although yee should him see I you
warrand H, [B: *beginning of f. 353b*]; 459 his awin kynd B,
That graithlie yee may see him in H, [H: *beginning of f. B4b*];
460 yee alace would runne out H; 462 not venture for H, nocht
vndertak it vpone me M; 462a Ffor dyuers causis now apperand-
lie M *only*; 463 him hither even in-to your sight H, him heir
so lait vpon the nycht M; 464 late with-in the H, now in till
freyr Allanis sicht M; 465 war vpon this wyse M, Except it
bee in such a sorte of wyse H; 466 to transforme or else to
dis-a-guyse H, To translait him in ane vþer gyse M; 467 owne
shape in-to some other H, kynd in till ane M; 468 said let us
have no debate H, symon sayis ȝe mak M;

       As pleisis ʒow, so likis it to me,
470   As evir ʒe list, bot fane wald I him se."
           Freir Robert said, "Sen that ʒour will is so,
       Tell vnto me withouttin wourdis mo
       Intill quhat kynd ʒe list þat he appeir."
           Than Symone said, "In liknes of a freir,
475   In habite quhyt sic as ʒourself can weir,
       For quhyt cullour will do nabody deir,
       And ewill spreitis quhyt cullour euer will fle."
           Freir Robert said that swa it cowld nocht be;
       "That he appeir into our habeit quhyt;
480   Vntill our ordour it wer a grit dispyte
       That ony sic vnworthy wicht as he
       Intill our habeit ony man sowld se.
       Bot sen it pleissis ʒow þat now ar heir,
       ʒe sall him se in liknes of a freir,

469 you that lyke-wyse pleaseth me H, How euer ʒe will it
lykis weill to me M; 470 Bee as hee will yet faine I would
him H, Bot brother deir ʒour seruand wald I se M; 471-472
M *only*; 473 kynd sall I him gar appeir B, In-to what shape
would yee hee should appeare H, In to quhat stait ʒe M; 474
The good-man sayde H; 475 In quhyt habite sic M, In quhyt
cullour richt as ʒour self it war B, whyte lyke as your
selves are aye H; 476 will na body B, Ffor colour quhyt it
will to no man deir M, H *blank*; 477 For the whyte sprites
doe no man harme they say H, B *blank*; 478 said I say it may
nocht M, sayde that wayes it may not bee H; 478a For sic
caussis as he may weill foirse B *only*, That dare I not graunt
un-to you truelie H, M *blank*; 479 he compeir in to B, appeir
in till our M; 480 For till M, It were un-to our order great
H; 481 sic ane vnwourthy M, [M: *beginning of p. 127*]; 482
habeit men sowld behald or se B, In our habeit þat ony M,
In-to our H; 483 þat ar B, plesis to ʒow þat now is heir M,
Yet since it pleaseth you hee shall appeare H;

485 In habeit gray as is his kynd to weir,

Into sic wyiss þat he sall no man deir,

So that ȝe do as I sall ȝow deviss,

To hald ȝow cloiss and reule ȝow on this wyiss:

Quhatevir it be ȝe owdir se or heir,

490 ȝe speik no word, nor mak no kynd of steir,

Bot hald ȝow cloiss quhill I haif done my cure."

Than said he, "Semon, ȝe mone be on þe flure

Neirhand besyd, with staff into ȝour hand.

Haif ȝe no dreid: I sall ȝow ay warrand."

495   Than Symon said, "I assent þat it be swa."

And vp he start and gat a libberla

Into his hand, and on þe flure he stert,

Sumthing effrayit, thoch stalwart was his hart.

    Than to þe freir said Symone verry sone,

500 "Now tell me, maister, quhat ȝe will haif done."

485 In gray habite as M, gray which hee usde for to weare H,
habeit blak it was his B; 486 In such a wyse H, ȝe sall him
se in liknes of a freir B; 487 ȝif ȝe so do <u>and</u> rewill ȝow
at all wyiss B, If you please this then doe as I advyse H;
488 and still at my deviss B, Holde you full close and still
in anie wyse H; 489 Quhat sua it be b̲at outher ȝe se M; 490
Speake yee no H, ȝe speik nothing nor ȝit ȝe mak no steir M;
491 you still till I H; 492 Than he said symon M, And yee
good-man must stand upon H; 493 Neir besyd I sall be ȝour
warrand M, With hardie heart a good staffe in your H; 494
dreid bot still by me ȝe stand M; 495 assent it H; 496 Than
vp he start and tuik ane M, [libber]loe *partly illegible in*
H; 497 Intill his M, [H: *beginning of f. Cla*]; 499 Than
symon said till freyr robert sone M, Un-to the freir then
spake the good-man soone H; 500 Tell M, yee would have H;

"Nothing," he said, "bot hald ʒow cloiss and still.

Quhatevir I do, tak ʒe gud tent þairtill,

And neir þe dur ʒe hyd ʒow prevely.

And quhen I bid ʒow stryk, strek hardely:

505   Into þe nek se þat ʒe hit him richt."

"I warrand þat," quoth he, "with all my micht."

Thuss on þe flure I leif him standand still,

Bydand his tyme, and turne agane I will

Till Freir Robert, þat tuk his buke in hy

510   And turnit our þe levis full besely

Ane full lang space, and quhen he had done swa,

Towart þe troch withowttin wordis ma

He goiss belyfe, and on this wyiss sayis he:

"How, Hurlbasie, anone I coniure the

515   That thow vp ryss and sone to me appeir,

In habeit gray, in liknis of a freir.

Owt of the troch quhair þat thow dois ly

Thow rax the sone and mak no dyn nor cry.

---

501 No-thing quod hee but H; 502 good heede there-till H, And
quhat I do ʒe tak gud M; 503 ʒe hald ʒow M, Neare hand the
doore goe hyde you H; 504 When I bid you stryke then lay on
hardilie H; 505 Up-on the necke bee sure to hit H, [B:
beginning of f. 354a]; 506 Ile warrand H, That sall I warrand
quoth B; 508 Hyding him-selfe and H; 509 Robert who tooke H,
How þat þe freir did tak his B, 510 And our B, levis bissaly
M; 511-512 M *blank*; 512 withowttin B, Towardes the south with-
out speaking wordes more H; 513 Hee went apace and on this
wyse spake hee H, Syn ʒeid to the trouche and on this wys
said he M; 514 Ha how Hurlybass now I B, Hay hoe Hurls-baigs
ryse I now conjure H; 515 That vp þow ryse and syn to appeir
M, Stand up foule fiende and H; 516 habeit blak in B, In gray
habite (in M), (and H) lyknes MH; 517 of this troch B, Out
fra the M, thow can ly M, From out the trogh where thou
a-long doest ly H; 518 mak ws no tary M, Stretch foorth thy
limbes cast off the stone in hye H;

Thow tumbill our þe troch þat we may se,

520 And vnto ws thow schaw the oppinlie,

And in this place se þat thow no man greif,

Bot draw thy handis boith into thy sleif,

And pull thy cowll doun owttoure thy face.

Thow may thank God thow gettis sic a grace.

525 Thairfoir thow turss the to thyne awin ressett.

Se this be done, and mak no moir debait.

In thy departing, mak thow no deray

Vnto no wicht, bot frely pass thy way.

And in this place se þat thow cum no moir

530 Bot I command the, or ellis the charge befoir.

And our þe stair se that thow ga gud speid;

Gif thow dois nocht, on thy awin perrell beid."

     With þat þe freir that vnder þe troch lay,

No wounder thocht his hart wes in effray.

519 Thow turne our M, Now tumble H, [M: *beginning of p. 128*];
520 And syn till ws M, Thy forme and shape before us openlie
H; 521 se na man þat thow greif M, With-in this H, man
grieves H; 522 draw thine handes farre in within thy slieves
H; 523 coull lenche attour thy M, cowle low downe up-on thy
H; 524 god that thow B, And thanke thy God thou gettest so
good grace H, Ffor þow sall byd no langar in this plais M;
525-532 *missing in* M; 525 With speede goe packe thee H; 526
Let this H; 527 departing se thow mak no B, And as thou
passest see thou make no fray H; 528 With anie wight but
swiftlie passe away H; 529 But I commaund and charge thee
heere before H; 530 That in this place thou come not anie
more H; 531 Now over H, thou get good H; 532 For if thou ···
······ e will moe perils breede H, *damaged*; 533 freyr vnder
the trouche þat lay M, that Frier John who under H, [H:
beginning of f. C1b]; 534 Raxit him sone bot he wes B,
Stretched him soone but was in great effray H;

535 And vp he raiss and wist na bettir wayn,

  Bot of the troch he tumlit, our þe stane.

  Syne fra þe samyn queirn--he thocht it lang--

  Vnto þe dur he preisit him to gang,

  With hevy cheir and drery countenance,

540 Ffor nevir befoir him hapnit sic a chance.

     And quhen Freir Robert saw him gangand by,

  Vnto þe gudman lowdly cowd he cry,

  "Stryke herdelie! For now is tyme to the."

     With that Symone a felloun flap lait fle:

545 With his burdoun he hit him on þe nek.

  He wes sa ferce, he fell outtour þe sek

  And brak his heid vpoun ane mustard stone.

  Be this Freir Johine attour the stair is gane

  In sic a wyiss that mist he hes the trap

550 And in ane myr he fell, sic wes his hap,

535 bettir wayy B, Yet up he rose it might no better bee H,
M *blank*; 536 And off the trogh the stone soone tumbled hee H,
Than of the trouche he tumblit sone anone M; 537 samyn
quhairin he thocht him lang B, All what Frier Rob had sayde
hee did ere long H, M *blank*; 538 Towardes the doore hee
bowned for to gang H, And to the dure he schapis him to gone
M; 539 With ewill cheir M; 540 before had hapned him such
chance H; 541 Bot quhen freyr robert him saw gangand M, him
passing by H; 542 gudman full lowdly B, good-man full lowde
can hee H, Than on symon he cryis hastelye M; 543 Stryk stryk
herdely B, Stryke Simon stryke for now is tyme for thee H;
544 that Simon full fellon flappes let H; 545 his buddoun he
M, him in the M; 546 fell attour ane sek M, fell quyte ore a
secke H; 547 vpon the mustard M; 548 Be þat the freyr attour
the stair was gone M, With that Frier John cleane over the
H; 549 sic wyiss B, wys he missit hes M, wyse for-sooth hee
mist the H; 550 a ditch hee H, He fell in ane meikle myre as
wes M;

Wes fourty fute on breid vnder the stair;

ȝeit gat he vp with clething nothing fair.

Full drerelie vpoun his feit he stude,

And throw þe myre full smertly than he ȝude,

555 And our þe wall he clam richt haistely

Quhilk round abowt wes laid with stanis dry.

And off his schape in hairt he wes full fane.

I trow he sal be laith to cum agane.

With that Freir Robert start abak and saw

560 Quhair þat the gudman lay sa woundir law

Vpoun þe flure, and bleidand wes his heid.

He stert to him and went he had bene deid

And clawcht him vp withowttin wordis moir

And to the dure delyverly him bure;

565 And fra þe wind wes blawin twyiss in his face,

Than he ourcom within a lytill space.

551 Well fourtie foote of depth under H, fourty futis of breid B, [B: *beginning of f. 354b*]; 552 Yet hee got out with H, And thus his pairt was nathing wounder fayr M; 553 In to þat tyme consideniring how it stude M; 554 Out of the myre full smertlie at he woide M, That myrie hole had done him little good H; 555 And on the M, clame full haisteley M, Yet over the H, he climbed hastilie H; 556 Was made all round about with stones full hie H, Was maid about and all with stanis dry M; 557 of þat schape M, he wex full M, Off his eschaping in B; 558 Now he M, I thinke hee should bee H; 559 At last Frier H, start about and M; 560 Quhair þe BH, goodman was lying wondrous low H; 562 stert till him M, Hee caught him up thinking hee H; 563 Frier Robert then thought good to stay no more H; 564 But presentlie tooke Simon to the dore H, [M: *beginning of p. 129*]; 565 And for the wynd was blawand in M, And when the winde had well blowne in H; 566 He sone ourcome in till ane M, Hee did revive within H;

And than Freir Robert franyt at him fast

Quhat ailit him to be so sair agast.

   He said, "3one feynd hes maid me in effray."

570   "Lat be," quoth he, "the werst is all away;

Mak mirry, man, and se 3e morne na mair.

3e haif him strikin quyt owttour þe stair.

I saw him slip, gif I þe suth can tell:

Doun our þe stair intill a myr he fell.

575   Bot lat him go--he wes a graceles gaist--

And boun 3ow to 3our bed, for it is best."

   Thuss Symonis heid vpoun þe stane wes brokin,

And als Freir Johine into the myre hes loppin

And hurt his heid and weit him wounder ill,

580   And Alesone, scho gat nocht all hir will.

And thus my taill I end heir of the freir:

No moir thair is, bot Chryst ws help most deir.

Ffinis.

567 Robert asked o ··· H, *damaged*, And syn the freir hes
franit M; 568 sore ··· H, *damaged*; 569 feynd had maid M,
3one freir hes maid me thussgait say B, [H: *beginning of f.
C2a*]; 570 quod Rob H, is now away H; 571 Bee merrie H, And
mak mirrey and M; 572 For yee have stricken him quyte over
the H; 573 sooth may tell H, him skip gif M; 574 At our the
bak in till M, Under the stair in-to a H; 575 Tush let H,
Lat him now go he is ane gaineles gaist M; 576 bowne yee to
your bedde I holde it best H, And to 3our bed 3e bowne to
tak 3ow rest M; 577 the wall was M; 578 Johne auttour the
stair was loppin M, And eeke Frier H, myre is loppen H, And
our þe stair the freir in myre B; 579 wounder ewill M, Hee
wette his head and drest his cloathes full ill H, And tap
our taill he fyld wes woundir ill B; 580 alesone on na
wayiss gat hir B, And the good-wyfe could not get halfe her
H; 581 This is the story that hapnit of that frier B, This
is a feate which happened of a frier H; 582 /Chryst send ws
peice and lat ws nevir haue weyr M, The Lorde helpe us and
Christ his sonne so deare H.

Explanatory Notes

Explanatory Notes

The Lady Prioress

v. 1 glad in all thys gesttyng: "make this tale joyous for
everyone"? This use of the verb glad is not
attested elsewhere.

v. 3: "I would hate (more literally, it would be
unpleasant for me) to be reproached by those who
are not expert [in poetry]."

v. 4 many maner of men: "many kinds of men."

v. 11 ther terme ys soen tought: "their limits are soon
seen."

v. 15 all and som: "one and all."

v. 25: "Many men love her extravagantly."

v. 37 narrow torned and went: literally, "turned this way
and that in tight circles" (from the phrase turn
and wind, with confusion from the verb wend).

vv. 38-
41: The wooers are clearly differentiated from each
other, down to the presents they bring: the
knight brings game, the parson rosaries, candles,
and wine, and the merchant presumably brings
money. In The Long Wapper they are not distin-
guished at all; in Les Trois galants au cimetière
there is no systematic distinction; in the
Decameron and the Farce de trois amoureux de la
croix the lovers are distinguished only by name,
and in Schimpf und Ernst only by status (a stu-
dent, a nobleman, and a burgess's son who belongs
to a regiment).

The Lady Prioress cont'd.

v. 52   Jues: Saracens were more usual adversaries, since
                 they held the Holy Land throughout most of the
                 medieval period. Cf. Les Trois galants au
                 cimetière, in which the young woman says to the
                 first lover "... vous me prometés tant de bien et
                 dictes que vous ferés tant de choses pour moy,
                 mesmes pour aller en Jerusalem..." (pp. 33-4).
                 The last abortive crusade began and ended in 1464
                 when its leader, Pope Pius II, died before his
                 ship left port at Ancona.

v. 56   so that: "provided that."

vv. 71-2:   "If anyone says 'no,' whoever says 'no,' here is
            my glove as a gage of my willingness to fight."

v. 78   vpryght: i.e., flat on his back.

v. 86:   "It is so well known [anyway]."

vv. 89-
     90:   Refusing burial to a corpse because of debt was
           a literary theme, not a historical reality. See
           the introduction to The Lady Prioress, The
           Story, for an instance of the theme in contempo-
           rary romance.

v. 104   He: i.e., the knight.

v. 108:   "That his sweetheart had become 'my love' [to
          him]."

v. 121:   The devil's garment here is made of rags, as
          implied in v. 154. In contemporary art the devil
          was usually portrayed as bestial, with shaggy fur,
          and costumes in contemporary plays undoubtedly
          tried for the same effect. In 1393 Charles VI of
          France and five of his lords were acting as hommes
          sauvages in a ludus at court, and imitated the
          fur also associated with the wild man by coating
          themselves with pitch and, stuck in that, frayed
          linen. The results were tragic: the Duke of
          Orleans brought a torch too close to one, trying
          to guess who he was, and a fire spread among
          them, killing four of the courtiers. Probably a

The Lady Prioress cont'd.

costume made of real fur was more usual (and
safer). The Lucifer in Les Actes des apôtres
(played at Bourges in 1536) "estoit vestu d'une
peau d'ours, ou à chaucun poil pendait une
papillotte" (cited by Gustave Cohen, Histoire de
la mise en scène dans le théâtre religieux fran-
çais du moyen age 2nd ed. [Paris: Librarie Honoré
Champion, 1951], p. 95). But perhaps the mer-
chant's rags formed a cloak meant loosely to
suggest rough fur. His counterpart in Les Trois
galants au cimetière has a much more impressive
costume, "car il n'y avoit pas plaint l'argent à
ce faire ainsi acoustrer pour coucher avec la
belle fille": "... voicy venir celluy qui faisoit
le diable, acoustré d'une teste de diable mer-
veilleuse et espoventable, et tout le demorent de
l'abit estoit de mesme. Et gettoit feu et flambe
par la bouche et par les naseaulx, et avoit une
chaine de fer au tour de luy, donc il faisoit
grant bruyt, et n'y avoit joincte dessus son
corps que en cheminant ou ployant bras ou jambes
il ne rendist feu et flambe, tant estoit sub-
tillement abillé" (p. 39, p. 38).

v. 130:   Cownsell is used as a collective noun: hence the
pronoun they.

v. 138:   "Running, roaring, with his chains, as was appro-
priate for devils." The merchant carries chains,
a symbol of the bonds of hell, as do the pretended
devils in The Long Wapper of Antwerp and the
Farce de trois amoureux de la croix. In the
account book of expenses for the playing of the
mystery of the Passion at Mons in 1501, a major
expense is for the devil's chains: "Item pour iii
kaisnes de fer, pesant ensemble cxx livres, ser-
vant pour le deable Lucifer d'Enfer en hault, à
iii s. la livre, xviii l." (ed. Gustave Cohen, Le
Livre de conduite du régisseur, Publications de
la Faculté des Lettres de l'Université de
Strasbourg 23 [1925], p. 507.

v. 147:   "I must have been cursed from birth; I might have
found a better place to lodge."

The <u>Lady</u> <u>Prioress</u> cont'd.

v. 184:   Feeling the bull's horns, the priest assumes he
               is being carried off to hell on a devil's back,
               as Vices traditionally were in morality plays.

v. 189:   A bell was a sanctified object, and its ringing
               had power against demons.

v. 200   Nether on other wyst: "Not one of them knew about
               the others."

v. 202   hys merthys wer but lewed: "his entertainment was
               poor."

v. 208   what mysschyffe heron geth: "what evil follows from
               this."

v. 213:   "Thus the two of them came to an agreement"?   The
               phrase <u>to</u> <u>make</u> <u>boast</u> usually means "to brag."

v. 221:   "For a hundred years," i.e. forever.

vv. 229-
     30:       "There was no hedge high enough, nor water broad
               enough, to keep me from you and the fulfilment of
               my desire."

v. 236:   A mark was a large unit of money, worth half a
               pound; it would buy a cow.

vv. 238-9:   "He endowed the convent, by means of legal deeds
               of conveyance, with possession [of property] in
               perpetuity."

The <u>Feast</u> <u>of</u> <u>Tottenham</u>

vv. 19-
     20:       Cf. burlesque A, v. 39: "Ther was pestells in
               porres, and laduls in lorres."

v. 22:   Cf. burlesque A, v. 36: "Sowters in serropes,
               and sadduleres in sew": and burlesque P, v. 33:
               "Soutteries in sorrope, sadelers in scowe."

The Feast of Tottenham cont'd.

v. 23:   Cf. P, v. 46: "Then ther com masfattus in mortros
            alle soow."

v. 27:   "For people of all ranks, high and low."

v. 28:   Cf. A, v. 38: "Gryndulstons in grwell ...."

v. 29:   Cf. A, v. 37: "Mylnestons in mortrews ..." and P,
            v. 35: "Ther wer mylstonnis in molde...."

v. 40   horstordis: MS blobsterdis is emended to horstordis.
            MED's derivation of blobsterd (cited only from
            this text) is unsatisfactory: "? Blend of lopster
            and blober." The poem nowhere else makes use of
            such a combination; it is consistent in listing
            markedly inedible things combined with or substi-
            tuted for edible ones. Burlesques are often
            scatological.

v. 49   comfyt: MS cambys as a plural of comb, with meaning
            unknown, is unsatisfactory, particularly with
            northern a. Comfyt/cullis is admittedly the
            weakest rhyme in the poem, but there are other
            examples of rhymes on the unstressed syllable
            (eg. maistry/cucry, vv. 10-11), and one of
            inexact rhyme (larke/cart, vv. 52-3). Because
            the rhyme is so weak, it would have invited
            scribal emendation.

v. 51   blandament: This word is troubling as the only
            abstraction in the poem, and because blandiment,
            a by-form of blandishment, is not cited before
            1510 (see OED). C.H. Hartshorne (in Ancient
            Metrical Tales [London: William Pickering, 1829]
            reads blandamete, and Thomas Wright (Early English
            Poetry: The Turnament of Totenham and the Feest
            [London: William Pickering, 1836]) reads
            blandamets, but the mark of abbreviation that
            curls back over the et more likely indicates an
            n than an s or an e.
                 Cf. P, v. 35: "... with cart whyllus in
            durryde."

The Feast of Tottenham cont'd.

vv. 55–
60:      Cf. P, vv. 36–7: "Ther wer stedis of Spayn welle
         poudyrt in past,/They wer fasside with charkolle,
         for that was noo wast."

v. 65:   Cf. P, v. 35: "... with cart whyllus in durryde."

v. 75:   "That could be sliced."

v. 91:   "Tybbe became embarrassed" (literally, "grew shy
         of heart"). The emendation of meaningless MS
         tharre to charry depends upon the assumption that
         chary could have been used as early as the
         writing of this poem with this meaning. OED's
         first citation of chary in the sense "fastidious,
         shy, particular" (chary, a. 4b) is 1567.

v.96 3ole: According to OED, "Yule" is "used as an exclama-
         tion of joy or revelry at the Christmas festivi-
         ties." The earliest citation in this sense is
         1546.

v. 102:   "Without their bodies bursting."

The Tale of the Basin

v. 1 many man tellys: The adjective many was often used
              distributively with a singular noun, without an
              article.

v. 7:   i.e., supposing it were true.

v. 9:   "And [they] loved each other well."

v. 16:   The term husbandry has a double meaning here: he
           is a poor manager and a feeble spouse.

v. 21 Seint Tyve: There were two Saint Ives, the first
              (1253–1303) born in Brittany, the patron saint
              of lawyers, and the second (c. 1040–1116) an
              important canonist and Bishop of Chartres.

The Tale of the Basin cont'd.

vv. 21-2:   The "olde seid saw" is first cited in the
              Oxford Dictionary of Proverbs from c. 1470:
              "Fore he that cast hym for to thryve, he must
              ask offe his wiffe leve." It is also cited by
              Whiting (Proverbs ... before 1500) under heading
              M155 ("A Man may not wive and thrive all in a
              year"), which does not seem to me to be the same
              proverb.

v. 29:   i.e., its income served to pamper the priest.

v. 30:   The sole citation for Whiting C106: "To teach one
              how the Cat sneezes (i.e., put in one's place,
              bully)."

v. 60:   "The game is being misplayed." Under draught 3e,
              drauen a draught, MED gives the meaning "to play
              a trick, or engage in a deceitful or sinful
              activity." The metaphor is from the game of
              checkers.

v. 76 Saynt Albon: Alban, the first British martyr, is said
              to have been born and eventually killed, probably
              during the third century, at Verulamium, which
              later became St. Albans, in Hertfordshire.

v. 77 Sir John: "Sir" was a conventional courtesty-title
              for a priest; "John" was an equally conventional
              name for one.

v. 79 he berys þe bell: i.e., like a bellwether among sheep,
              he is a leader among good fellows.

v. 82 castys þe ston: i.e., he is a shot-putter.

v. 126 as stille as any ston: The phrase can mean both "as
              motionless as a stone" and, as it does here, "as
              quietly as a stone." See Whiting S772 for many
              other examples of the phrase.

v. 155:   "It was a bizarre group for a person to have met."

v. 182 Foule mot yow falle: "May evil befall you," a common
              imprecation.

The Tale of the Basin cont'd.

v. 183:   A verb of motion is understood.

v. 191   folys of þe fayr: i.e., performing fools, a normal
              part of the entertainment at fairs. Cf. OED fair
              sb.[1] 1. citation 1764 "Has he not ... made him-
              self the fool of the fair?" Samuel Foote, Mayor
              of Garret.

v. 202   with a sory chaunce: A frequently occurring phrase
              of ill-defined meaning. Roughly, "with bad
              luck."

v. 208   Be cockys swete wounde: a weakened oath by God's
              (i.e., Christ's) wounds.

v. 220:   The five joys of Mary are traditionally the
              Annunciation, Nativity, Resurrection, Ascension,
              and Assumption.

Jack and his Stepdame

v. 2   eysell and gall: The drink offered to Christ on the
              cross was believed to have been mingled vinegar
              and bile ("Et dedèrunt ei vinum bibere cum felle
              mistum." Matt 27:34, Vulgate).

v. 8   wyves thre: Only two are mentioned in the poem, the
              boy's mother and the cruel stepdame. But things
              go by threes in stories like this, eg. the three
              gifts granted below.

v. 41:   A verb of motion is understood.

v. 50:   "He cared for nobody's opinion."

v. 76   full good to pleise: "very easy to please."

v. 90:   "You will hit the target."

v. 148   He: i.e., the father.

v. 157   dame hurte: Dame is a genitive.

Jack and his Stepdame cont'd.

vv. 166-8: "Jack said, 'I want you to notice, this ammuni-
tion was well fired, as if it had been a cannon-
ball.'"

v. 180: "Your backside isn't pawned," i.e., you don't
have to leave anything behind as a pledge?

vv. 195-6 byche, wycche: Both terms could normally be
applied to males at this time: see MED bicche 2b,
OED witch sb[1].

v. 199 I will wete: "I will find out [if he is a witch]."

v. 246: "But he could nowhere [get] out."

v. 269 I can non oþer se: "I can see no alternative."

v. 285 both tame and talle: Talle seems to have the mean-
ing of tame, including meek or humble. OED lists
no such definition, but examples under +1 (Quick,
prompt, ready, active) are susceptible to such a
reading and OED says the sense in both quotations
is doubtful: c. 1374 Chaucer, Compl. Mars 38 Sche
[Venus] made him [Mars] at hir lust so humble &
talle. 1542 Udall Erasm. Apoph. 51 For lesse
money ... myght I bye a bondeman, that should
dooe me tall & hable service.

v. 309 þou haddist be: "you would have been."

v. 335 Owt: Out was a conventional cry of alarm.

v. 367 The goodman was in dispeyre: The experience of being
subject to the pipe is apparently unpleasant
while it lasts (cf. vv. 241-261), and its sound
is pleasant only in retrospect (vv. 311-12, 412-
14, 419-20).

vv. 370-1: Stoke ("stock") and bloke ("block") are both
simply pieces of wood. Cf. the proverbial asso-
ciation of straw and block in Whiting S823, To
stumble at a Straw, "Stomblynge atte a straawe
and lepynge over a blocke," 1495; perhaps the
pairing of stock (rather than straw) and block
here is influenced by such phonologically similar

Jack and his Stepdame cont'd.

	forms as those in Chaucer's Reeve's Prologue, A 3919-20: "He kan wel in myn eye seen a stalke,/ But in his owene he can nat seen a balke."
v. 394:	They are so eager that they leap over the bottom half of a divided door.
v. 399:	i.e., everybody.
v. P5-6:	This is the earliest cited use of the proverb in English, Whiting L569.
v. RQ7	norysshyd forth: continued to bring up.
vv. X6ff:	The court to which Jack is summoned is an ecclesiastical one, as is clear from the facts that there are priests and clerks in it (v. X21), and that it deals with the proving of wills (v. X22) and with matters of sexual licentiousness (vv. X23-4). Jack is to be charged with being a necromancer (v. X31) or black magician; a charge of sorcery could still have been tried in a church court in the fifteenth century. Theoretically, though in medieval England rarely actually, the punishment for a convicted sorcerer was burning. The official of v. X6 would have been an archdeacon, presiding over a low-ranking ecclesiastical court.
v. X23:	"And [there were] fair women...."
v. X26:	Frere Topyas obviously takes his name from Chaucer's Sir Thopas (topias, like topace, was a variant form of topaz) as an oblique indication that the author of this continuation recognizes the indebtedness of the poem to Chaucer's comic pieces in the Canterbury Tales.
v. X32:	Orleans is represented in Chaucer's Franklin's Tale as a center for the study of magical arts. See The Canterbury Tales, V, 1116ff.
v. E121	he: i.e., Jack.
v. Z88	set vpon a mery pin: "was in a merry frame of mind." See OED pin sb[1] 15 and Whiting P215, To hang on a jolly Pin.

<u>Dane</u> <u>Hew</u>

Title Dane: <u>Dan</u> (ultimately from Latin <u>dominus</u>) was a
       title given to monks.

v. 2 An abbay of munks: Historically, it was an abbey of
      Augustinian canons (living under a Rule, like
      monks, but in Holy Orders, as priests). They
      were attached to the church of St. Mary of the
      Fields (Sancte Marie de Pratis) in Leicester.
      It was an extraordinarily wealthy establishment,
      valued at over 960 pounds at the time of the dis-
      solution in 1539. Records of the bishop's visi-
      tation to St. Mary's in 1440 survive (see A.H.
      Thompson, ed., <u>Visitations</u> <u>of</u> <u>Religious</u> <u>Houses</u> <u>in</u>
      <u>the</u> <u>Diocese</u> <u>of</u> <u>Lincoln</u>, Canterbury and York
      Series, Vol. 24 [London: Canterbury and York
      Society, 1919], II, 206-17). At many abbeys
      there were grievous complaints of sexual licen-
      tiousness among the monks or canons, but St.
      Mary's was not among them, at least in 1440.

v. 21: "I am likely to go out of my mind."

v. 41 all and some: "the whole story."

v. 45 cuckolds hood: Hoods and hats were readily visible
       signs of status and occupation (physicians'
       hoods, cardinals' hats). The cuckold's hood (or
       as in <u>Sir</u> <u>Corneus</u>, v. 186, his hat) is an invis-
       ible badge like the horns.

v. 92: A verb of motion is understood.

v. 150: "Why are you not performing your canonical duties
         properly?"

v. 164 suspended this place: The abbot has profaned the
        abbey and made it unfit for worship by the
        "murder."

v. 165 What remedy?: i.e., there is no remedy, a statement
        which the abbot's man contradicts.

v. 188: "[The tailor] began to say." Such switches of
         subject are common in Middle English.

v. 252: The thieves hang Dane Hew where the bacon had
         been stored as food for the winter.

John the Reeve

Title: The manuscript has John de Reeve, and the poem
            throughout refers to the central character as
            either John de Reeue or John Reeue, as if Reeve
            were only his surname, rather than indicating his
            station as well. I have changed the title since
            contemporary references are to John the Reeve
            (Douglas, Dunbar, and Lindsay: see the introduc-
            tion to the poem), but left the name unaltered
            elsewhere: it seems to me likely that the poem
            was originally inconsistent on this point.

            John is a reeve in the sense that he is a
            minor official appointed by his fellow villagers
            as chief representative of his vill. Being
            appointed reeve was one of the hazards of not
            being a free man: at v. 125 John identifies him-
            self as a bondman belonging to the king. As
            reeve he would have been overseer to his fellow
            bondmen and would probably have kept the farm
            accounts for the king's manor to which he
            belonged.

v. 6:   "If a person likes mirth."

v. 17   Edward with the long shankes: Edward I (reigned 1272-
            1307).

v. 31   Save a bishopp and an erle ffree: This is the only
            one of the poems of this group in which the king
            has companions on his adventure.

v. 62   no other guide: i.e., no guide at all.

v. 92:   A proverb, Whiting M210: "Men may meet at unset
            steven."

v. 125:   For a serf, the best owner was the king. The
            king's bondmen were subject to fewer taxes and
            restrictions.

v. 137:   John doesn't dare keep his wheat and barley for
            fine bread and good ale or beer, but it is not
            clear from the context exactly why. As a bond-
            man, he would have been required to mill his wheat
            at a manorial mill and perhaps to brew at a

John the Reeve cont'd.

> manorial brewing-house, and to pay for the privi-
> lege; perhaps he doesn't dare to eat wheat bread
> because he ostensibly cannot afford to have his
> meal ground at the mill and will not risk being
> caught with a handmill.
>   An alternative explanation is that John has
> run afoul of regulations fixing the prices of
> both bread and beer, if he has been selling them
> (see verses 148-9), and the fines incurred have
> persuaded him to have nothing to do with brewing
> or baking.

v. 165:   "If we are not visiting people."

v. 170 St. Jollye: Saint Julian, patron saint of hospital-
        ity.

v. 176 frankpledge: John and his two neighbors belong to
        the same tithing or frankpledge, a group of ten
        or twelve householders responsible for ensuring
        each other's submission to the law. Most males
        over twelve years of age in the vill had to be a
        member of a tithing. The system of frankpledge
        does not seem to have existed in the north of
        England (see Sir Frederick Pollock and Frederic
        Maitland, The History of English Law Before the
        Time of Edward I, 2nd ed. [Cambridge: University
        Press, 1898], I, 569). The language of the poem
        and the fact that one of the bondmen's masters is
        the Bishop of Durham point to the north of
        England as the locale of the poem, but the custom
        of frankpledge agrees with the places named in
        setting the events of the poem in the south.

vv. 178-9: There are apparently three major landholders in
        this one vill: the king, the bishop, and the earl.

v. 179 The Erle of Gloster: The title shows the poet's
        knowledge of history, since the last Earl of
        Gloucester died in 1347. The more modern title
        duke is used at v. 564: the first Duke of
        Gloucester was created in 1385. The same fluc-
        tuation in titles--Earl or Duke of Gloucester--
        is evident in Sir Corneus, below.

John the Reeve cont'd.

vv. 193-8:   John is denying that he has been cutting fuel.
              He apparently lives in Windsor Forest, an area
              under Forest Law: penalties both for poaching
              deer and cutting wood in areas designated as the
              king's forest were severe.

vv. 199-
    200:      Here John is apparently worried that he will be
              found to be too wealthy, and suspected of skim-
              ming off the profits of the king's estate, as
              Chaucer's Reeve did to his lord's.

v. 205:   "For it might result in great trouble for me."

v. 210   twenty-neine devilles way: The usual phrase is "in
              twenty devils' way." John's phrase is a humorous
              intensification of the expletive.

v. 224:   Apparently John's wife is adjusting her head-
              dress as she comes to meet them.

vv. 263-4:   "Where did he get that hood, so gay that it is
              glittering with gold?"

v. 273:   "It will be a long time before he is promoted."

v. 283   there is small charge: "that matters very little."

v. 307   any such: i.e., a knight.

v. 342:   Bringing water in for washing the hands was a
              regular ceremony before courtly meals, but not
              to be expected in a serf's house.

v. 364   John daughter Reeue: "John Reeue's daughter."

v. 370   beare the price: "surpass all others."

v. 412   by booke and bell: The phrase was a common assevera-
              tion in Middle English. The bell and book were
              those used in the mass.

vv. 464-
    73:       Of the foods listed, the boar and venison would
              have been poached illegally from the forest; the

John the Reeve cont'd.

                wildfowl were not protected by Forest Law but
                would have been poached from some lord's warren.

v. 499   neither young nor old: i.e., not at all.

v. 540   master and master: i.e., first one on top, and then
           the other.

v. 544   thou makes it tough: "you make it look hard."

v. 600:   Milan was famous for its steel and armor.

v. 601:   As a bondman, John is not entitled to carry a
           sword.

v. 637   my mittons: The mittens are heavy cloth ones, used
           to protect a workman's hands from thorns and
           brush when he is hedging and the like.

v. 668   to weare a horne: i.e., like a devil, but also like
           a forester. The men of the court, seeing John's
           mittens, his bow and arrows, and his gear, take
           him for a forester, responsible for both trees
           and game in the king's forest. John responds, at
           v. 677, by offering to prune them. Legally, John
           was not allowed to carry bow and arrows in an
           area under forest law.

v. 749   St. William of York: William Fitzherbert, Archbishop
           of York, consecrated archbishop in 1143, deposed
           in 1147, restored in 1153, and dead within weeks,
           perhaps poisoned. The party opposed to him
           accused him of simony. Miracles occurred at his
           tomb, and he was canonized in 1227.

vv. 781ff: Characteristically, John's first reaction to the
           discovery of his guest's identity is irony. His
           second (vv. 793-5) is to stand on his rights.
           Only after the king shows generosity to him does
           he finally kneel.

v. 821   After a coller comes a rope: This is an earlier use
           of the proverb than those cited in the proverb
           dictionaries. The saying implies that those
           raised to knighthood (with the collar signifying

<u>John the Reeve</u> cont'd.

their rank) are then in danger of a halter taking
the place of the collar because of their emi-
nence: obscurity is safer.

vv. 830-5:   The rhymes in this stanza (downe/home and wott/
sortes) are poor and suggest corruption of the
text.

<u>The King and the Hermit</u>

v. 1   heuen kyng: This scribe often uses genitives with no
inflectional ending.

vv. 8-9,
v. 12:   An oblique and polite way of asking his audience
to be quiet and listen.

v. 13   be god Edwerd deys: Edward III?

v. 43   more than oþer two: "bigger than any two others."

v. 52   he: i.e., the old forester.

v. 53:   A verb of motion is understood.

v. 69:   Probably "the horse's spirit was broken," but
could be "the hart had escaped."

v. 77:   "Nor [how] to get out of the forest."

v. 86:   Saint Julian was the patron saint of hospitality.

v. 106   Seynt Julyan, a bonne hostel: Compare Chaucer's
<u>House of Fame</u>, 1022 ("Seynt Julyan, loo, bon
hostel") and <u>Sir Gawain and the Green Knight</u>,
776 ("'Now bone hostel,' coþe þe burne, 'I beseche
you ȝette.'") The phrase is a prayer to be
lodged well in the refuge the traveller has found.

v. 111   That within: "that [anyone] within."

The King and the Hermit cont'd.

v. 117   frere: The hermit is apparently a friar of either
the Carmelite or Augustinian order. Both orders
had their origin in eremiticism; but both, soon
after their arrival in England, moved towards
communal life in larger towns. Nevertheless,
the early foundations were in isolated areas,
the hermit's life was the ideal underlying both
orders, and it was possible to have a small
priory in an outlying area with only a single
friar. For information on both orders, see Dom
David Knowles, The Religious Orders in England,
2 vols. (Cambridge: Cambridge University Press,
1956, 1955), I, 194-204, II, 144-151.

vv. 122-3: The construction changes in mid-sentence: there
are two prepositions, for and tyll, with the same
function. "I have no lodging fit for such a
lord as you are."

v. 159   sych thre: "three such as you."

vv. 155-6: i.e., you have never been my master.

v. 230: It seemed to the king a long time that he was
eating the dry food.

v. 232   he: i.e., the hermit.

v. 233   he: i.e., the king.

v. 248: "That wishes you the harm that you imagine."

v. 249: "In that case, you can supply yourself with food
here."

v. 251: i.e., do you have any errand other than
entrapping me?

vv. 256ff: The syntax is very loose here: "For if I were
taken in such a deed, they would lead me to
court and bring me to prison, [and] unless I
could get my ransom, [I would] be bound in
prison and [suffer] great sorrow and [be] in
danger of hanging."

The King and the Hermit cont'd.

v. 262   I wold not: i.e., if I were you.

v. 303   made it full tow3he: "joked persistently about it."

v. 319:   "And showed him secretly to a place."

v. 326   slou3te: The word slou3te is unattested in OED. It
         probably represents slough sb2 (with intrusive
         -t) in the sense "a ... covering layer," a sense
         which is not attested there until 1610.

v. 328   howuyd: The word is unattested in OED or MED;
         Hazlitt reads hownyd, a form for honeyed. I take
         howuyd as meaning "lidded," related to houve, a
         substantive meaning "cap" or "headcovering."

v. 331   schell: Apparently in the North and Scotland sea-
         shells were used as drinking-vessels. See OED
         under shell.

vv. 341,
    344:    Fusty bandyas and stryke pantner or pantneuer
            appear to be nonsense syllables, but they can be
            resolved into the following components:

            fusty: smelling of the cask
            ban: bon, or good
            dias, dyas: medicines

            stryke: skim
            pant: gasp
            ner: never

            "This is a good fusty medicine." "Drink it at
            one gulp."

vv. 358ff: In his disgust, the hermit jerks the cup from
            the king and nearly knocks it on the ground.
            When the servant refills it, the king gives the
            toast, but does not move fast enough: the hermit
            takes the cup, toasts, and drains it. Not
            until v. 376 does the king finally get a drink.

The King and the Hermit cont'd.

vv. 379-81: "I assure you, hermit, I grant you in recompense
            that I shall pay you back if I live for the good
            game you have invented for us."

v. 415:   "Of the charity [that] comes."

v. 428 me pays wele with þe: "You please me well."

v. 471:   A deer will often empty its bladder when wounded
            or killed.

v. 487:   "Let the king watch me carefully."

v. 505:   "When you saw you could."

v. 516:   "[To see] if they might."

Sir Corneus

v. 24 Wherso þat euer: "wheresoever."

v. 28:   "For he could [do] much cunning by means of it."

vv. 31-2:   The verbs are both subjunctive, and the tenses
            mixed. Modern "agreement of tenses" would put
            "drynke" in the past.

v. 52:   A seat at a table dormant or fixed table (as
            opposed to the removable ones on trestles) would
            be a position of honor in the king's hall.

v. 59:   The lovelorn were said to wear willow garlands.
            The first citation in OED of willow as a symbol
            of mourning for the loss or death of a beloved is
            1584.

v. 81:   i.e., "I cannot name the length of time he stayed."

v. 101 were vpon: This is an adverbial use of upon. Compare
            the Wife of Bath's Prologue, v. 559: "[I] wered
            upon my gaye scarlet gytes."

Sir Corneus cont'd.

v. 112:   "If a man asked them for love, he would quickly
            have it, for they could not refuse him."

v. 116 baskefysyke: from bask or baisk, "bitter," and
                fisike or modern physic, "medicine." In the
                sole other citation for this word in MED (under
                bask-fisik), the bitter treatment implied there
                too may be sexual intercourse: "Do alle youre
                men be war of the furst frutes and wyne, the
                whiche be right lustye atte the begynning and
                hynderyng to mennes hele; and so is a thyng
                called basfysike" (Travel Instructions, 282: see
                C. Horstmann, "Rathschläge für eine Orientreise,"
                Englische Studien 8 [1885], 277-84).

v. 119 lecheres craft: this may be a pun on lecher and
                leecher (a physician).

v. 126 Hold þe there: i.e., "hold your tongue." The duke
                has used the disparaging word "cokwold."

v. 127 erlys: The Duke of Gloucester is referred to as
                "duke" and "erle" interchangeably throughout the
                rest of the poem. See the note to John the Reeve,
                v. 179.

v. 165:   "No cuckold shall benefit from it."

v. 170 Seynt Austyn: perhaps the Bishop of Hippo (354-430),
                but more likely the local St. Augustine (d. 604)
                who founded the Christian church in southern
                England, and was the first Archbishop of Canter-
                bury.

v. 171:   "That would disgrace me."

v. 177:   "But yet there happened a trick." Arthur usually
                drinks from the horn without difficulty (vv. 27,
                176); the situation has changed.

v. 186:   See the note to Dane Hew, v. 45.

v. 188 lesse and mor: this is a tag useful in rhyming posi-
                tion, here seeming to mean that the queen's
                blushes came and went.

Sir Corneus cont'd.

v. 192:   "To speak against [i.e., deny] the truth."

v. 194   aske no leue: i.e., "don't need to ask permission
          to be one"?

v. 199   at a word: "at once."

v. 213:   "For there could be no other way about it."

v. 241   Skarlyon: Caerleon-upon-Usk, one of the traditional
          locations of Arthur's court, and the place of
          his crowning in Malory.

v. 246   Syr Corneus: i.e., the horned one, a cuckold himself.
          The name is also used in Malory, but without such
          implications, for the father of Lucas the Butler.

v. 249:   i.e., "to bear that name whenever the gest is per-
          formed, to a harp or other instrument."

The Boy and the Mantle

v. 1   the third day of May: The third day of May was an
        unlucky day in Chaucer: the day on which Pandarus
        began his wooing of Criseyde for Troilus (Troilus
        and Criseyde II, 56), the day on which the two
        lovers Arcite and Palamon fought in the woods
        outside Athens (Knight's Tale I, 1462-3), the day
        on which lusty Chauntecleer fell prey to the fox
        in the Nun's Priest's Tale (VII, 3187-95). The
        Boy and the Mantle may be simply following
        Chaucer in making May 3 a dangerous date for the
        servants of Venus, or may be following directly
        whatever tradition Chaucer himself followed
        (assuming that Chaucer's use of the date was not
        a merely personal reference, a wedding anniver-
        sary or the like). An article by Alfred Kellogg
        and Robert C. Cox, "Chaucer's May 3 and Its Con-
        texts" (in Kellogg's Chaucer, Langland, Arthur:
        Essays in Middle English Literature [New
        Brunswick, N.J.: Rutgers University Press, 1972],
        pp. 155-98) supplements Robinson's editorial note
        to Canterbury Tales I, 1462, reporting the various

The Boy and the Mantle cont'd.

> reasons which have been suggested for Chaucer's
> choice of that particular date for three such
> occasions. Among the most useful of the explana-
> tions suggested is D.W. Robertson's, that May 3
> is the date of St. Helena's Invention of the
> Cross and consequent casting down of the idol of
> Venus ("Chaucerian Tragedy," ELH 19 [1952], 19).
>   In the analogues in which a time is specified
> it is Pentecost (Le Lai du cor, Le Livre de
> Carados, Le Mantel mautaillié and Ulrich von
> Zatzikhoven's Lanzelet). That feast day, above
> all others, was one on which Arthur convention-
> ally would not eat until some great adventure
> had befallen.

v. 2   Carleile: Carlisle is one of the usual places for
       Arthur's court in alliterative poetry (for
       instance, in The Awntyrs off Arthure).
          The analogues are set in Caerleon (Le Lai du
       cor and Le Livre de Carados) and in Cardigan
       (Lanzelet).

v. 3:   The child is kind and curteous in the sense that
          he is well-born and courtly; this does not pre-
          vent him from using strong language at vv. 147-50
          below.

v. 6   vppon: This is an adverbial use of upon. See Sir
          Corneus, v. 101 and note.

v. 9   sute: Here the term suit seems to mean a garment of a
          pattern or color matching the other clothes,
          though that meaning is not attested in OED. Pre-
          sumably what he has drawn about his middle is a
          belt, over the kirtle and under the mantle.

vv. 11-12: "He would have thought it shameful not to be con-
            versant with courtesy."

v. 20:   "[It] is appropriate for you to dread."

v. 24:   In the analogues, the mantle usually emerges from
           a magically small container.

v. 28 as it bee: i.e., "however it may come to be fashioned."

The Boy and the Mantle cont'd.

vv. 43-4:   Light blue or watchet was unbefitting because
             blue was the color of chastity and loyalty.

v. 86:   "Willingly to feed [him]."

v. 88:   "Supply his wife with something she needed."

v. 100 bade her come in: In some of the analogues (the
             French fabliau, and Ulrich von Zatzikhoven's
             Lanzelet) the successful lady is not present
             while the others are trying the mantle.

v. 102:   "Without any fuss."

v. 136:   "Who pretends to be so virtuous."

v. 152 ouer a dore: It is apparently a half-door.

v. 172:   The cutting edge of the knife curled back and
             became blunted.

v. 180:   Red is a conventional epithet of gold.

vv. 181-4:   Such mixtures of direct and indirect quotation
             were common in Middle English writing.

The Friars of Berwick

v. 4 mony lordis hes bene: The form hes was used for the
             plural of have from the fifteenth century in
             Scotland.

vv. 13-14:   "Skilfully enclosed with battlements as well;
             the portcullises [designed] to fall most ingeni-
             ously when they have decided to raise them, so
             that it may be in no one's power to capture that
             building by guile or ingenuity." The town is
             walled, and double-ditched; the castle has towers
             and turrets and battlements; the portcullises are
             designed so that if an attacking party slips in
             as far as the opening to the castle, the first
             attackers will be caught within the gate tower,
             between the lowered portcullises and an inner
             gate. Portcules in v. 14 is a plural form; hence
             the þame in v. 15.

The <u>Friars</u> <u>of</u> <u>Berwick</u> cont'd.

vv. 24-7:   The four orders of friars were, as the poem
              implies, the Jacobins or Dominicans, the
              Carmelites, The Hermit Friars of St. Augustine,
              and the Franciscans or Friars Minor. Berwick
              was the only town in Scotland to have all four
              orders, and the fact is a testimony to the
              importance of the place in the later Middle Ages.
              See the Introduction to <u>The</u> <u>Friars</u> <u>of</u> <u>Berwick</u>
              under <u>Language</u> <u>and</u> <u>Provenience</u> for a discussion
              of why the poet calls the Jacobins white.

v. 28:   May mornings are the conventional settings for
              romance, lyric, and allegory alike.

v. 32   sillie freiris: <u>Silly</u> is used as a recurring epithet,
              carrying more or less ironic connotations of
              "holy" from the older form <u>sely</u>, and also meaning
              "pitiable" or "harmless."

v. 44   Be þat: "By the time that."

v. 48   wonder evill disposit: "very ill prepared."

v. 54:   "A fair, merry wife he had, [fairest and
              merriest] of anyone."

v. 56:   <u>Come</u> is the past tense.

v. 77   abbay: Friars did not live in abbeys; their dwellings
              were called cloisters, or simply houses, and
              later, convents. The poet here shows his lack of
              familiarity with the mendicant orders.

v. 92   Put ʒe ws owt: "If you put us out."

v. 95:   "The gates are closed [so that] we may not get
              in."

v. 116   to walk this nicht: "To walk like a ghost"? More
              likely, the <u>l</u> of <u>walk</u> simply indicates long <u>a</u>,
              and the verb is <u>wake</u> in a Scottish spelling.

v. 127:   "He governed the whole estate of the abbot."
              Again the terminology is wrong: friars were not
              governed by abbots.

The Friars of Berwick cont'd.

v. 153:   The term burde has caused confusion in B and H,
            where it is taken to refer to a table Alesoun is
            covering in the bedroom. But later (v. 191) she
            covers one in the hall. Here the burde is prob-
            ably an embroidered ornamental strip of cloth;
            see MED bord(e and DOST burd(e n2.

vv. 175-6: "And tell you of these two innocent friars [who]
            were locked in the loft amongst the straw."

v. 181 On sic a wyiss maid he: "He made [it] in such a
            manner."

v. 188:   Cf. Chaucer's Wife of Bath's Tale, v. 1021 ("Tho
            rowned she a pistel in his ere"). But in WBT
            the term pistel has only the sense "narration";
            here, in the context of v. 187, it also carries
            suggestions of the epistle as part of the divine
            service, with Alesoun as reader and Johne as
            prelate.

v. 189 makis melodie: Cf. the sexual implications of the
            term melodie in Chaucer's Miller's Tale, v. 3652
            and v. 3306.

v. 191:   The burd here is the table. It would be a
            trestle table: the maid is ordered to take it
            down at v. 222.

v. 202:   "Whom I would not have minded well away from
            here now."

v. 206:   "I regret that you have come here at this parti-
            cular time."

v. 212 quhynnis: Obviously the meaning is "testicles." The
            term is probably whin, a name for a kind of stone.

vv. 215-
    16:     Mixtures of direct and indirect quotation of this
            kind are frequent in Middle English.

v. 233:   The prefix for- in forknokit and forcryid means
            "exhausted by the action of the verb": "exhausted
            by knocking and shouting," "all knocked and
            shouted out."

The Friars of Berwick cont'd.

v. 239:   The original reading was probably "quha bes this,"
             "bes" being the northern form of the third singu-
             lar indicative.

v. 254   and tak þe all thy hyre: "and receive a good recom-
             pense"?

vv. 275-6:   "If that sheep's head over there is polished
             clean by Simon when there is such good food in
             the cupboard."

v. 279   ȝour awin freiris: Symon has apparently given money
             to the Jacobins and been enrolled as a lay-
             brother.

v. 283   Be thay come: "By the time that they came."

v. 286   Sa God haif part of me: "As I hope for God to have
             an interest in me."

v. 288   Gar call þame doun: "Have them called down."

v. 300:   Trap here means "ladder" (see DOST trap, n^2)
             rather than "trapdoor," as it does above.

v. 305:   He is "allane" in the sense that his wife has
             refused to sit and eat with him.

v. 319:   "I undertake, if you will keep it confidential."

v. 334   to þe flure: The term floor is used oddly in this
             poem, as if it were a location within the room
             rather than underlying the entire area (see
             vv. 416, 492, 497, and 507). Probably there is
             a raised wooden floor at one end of the room,
             the dais on which the table would be set. The
             term floor seems to apply only to the dais.

v. 353:   "She saw him treat the ambry with such ceremony."

v. 357   Get Symon wit: "If Symon gets knowledge," "if Symon
             finds out." deir doing: The general sense is
             clear enough, though it is not clear whether
             deir represents the poetic adjective from OE dēor,
             meaning "severe, grievous," or whether it

The Friars of Berwick cont'd.

>   represents the ordinary objective <u>dear</u> from OE
>   d<u>ēo</u>re, in some ironic sense.

v. 406 cop owt: The phrase <u>to</u> <u>play</u> <u>cop</u> <u>out</u>, meaning "to
>   drink the cup empty," is attested by DOST from
>   Dunbar's poems (c. 1500) to Robert Sempill's
>   (1583).

v. 408 freir: Presumably <u>freir</u> is singular for the sake of
>   the rhyme.

v. 420 pleiss: See the Introduction to the poem, under
>   <u>Language</u> <u>and</u> <u>Provenience</u>, for the rarity of the
>   noun <u>please</u>.

v. 442 it neidis me nocht: "it is not necessary for me."

v. 443 tak in pacience: The verb in this phrase is usually
>   transitive, as in Chaucer's Knight's Tale, vv.
>   1084-5: "taak al in pacience/ Oure prisoun."
>   Here it is used absolutely.

v. 446 and I sall stand þairfoir: "and I shall insist on
>   it."

v. 454-5:   "For I do not know if you will always be able to
>   come here, whenever we want, in this way."

v. 462:   "I do not dare venture to take the responsi-
>   bility."

v. 485:   The fiend naturally wears gray rather than the
>   white of harmless spirits because a gray habit
>   shows his evil nature: a vigorous dig at the
>   Franciscans or Gray Friars.

vv. 488-
>   91:   The raising of demons was thought to be perilous.
>   If the conjurer stepped out of his charmed circle,
>   or said the wrong thing, he could be seized.
>   Symon is to remain still and silent until ordered
>   to move.

The Friars of Berwick cont'd.

v. 514:   Hurlbasie (B Hurlybas, H Hurls-baigs) is the
               demon's name. The only other citation in DOST is
               from Dunbar, as "a fanciful term of endearment."
               Hurl- is probably from the verb, with the meaning
               "hurtle"; -basie probably represents bausy, adjec-
               tive, likely meaning "large and clumsy"; the com-
               pound Bausy Broun was used by Dunbar as a fiend's
               name.

v. 536:   "But he tumbled the trough off, over the [mill]
               stone." The stone to a handmill or quern is
               apparently lying beside the kneading trough.

v. 537:   "Then from that quern--it seemed far away to him--
               he hurried to go to the door."

v. 543 now is tyme to thee: "now is your time."

vv. 546-7:   "[Symon] was so fierce, he fell over the sack and
               cracked open his head on the mustard stone." As
               elsewhere in the poem, domestic objects are men-
               tioned as if assumed: the stone or quern beside
               the trough, the sack (of grain waiting to be
               ground?), and the mustard stone, which may be the
               same as the stone mentioned above, or may be a
               smaller one, since mustard would be ground in much
               smaller quantitites than grain.

v. 549:   Johne goes down the (upper) stairs and misses the
               movable steps, the trap, below them, falling over
               into a broad mire. Removable stairs would be a
               useful means of discouraging small raiding parties
               from taking a lonely dwelling on the outskirts of
               one of the most hotly contested places on the
               Scots border; the drywall around the house (vv.
               555-6) is an outer ring of defence, with the mire
               serving as a primitive moat.

Glossary

Glossary

Some entries in the glossary are simply equivalencies (e.g. ermyte = hermit KH 152), meant to help readers who might not recognize the familiar word hermit in the unfamiliar spelling ermyte in The King and the Hermit, v. 152. A typical definition entry will include one or more spellings of the word as it appears in the text, then label the part of speech, give a definition, and identify the first place in the poems the word occurs with that definition and perhaps one or more additional places. There may then be further definitions; if the word occurs with a variety of meanings, usually only those that are not normal modern meanings will be given. Closely related parts of speech (e.g. adjective and adverb) may be treated within the same entry. Some entries will be followed by an additional entry form in square brackets. This is to give readers a point of departure for research when a modern form of the word is not obvious or does not exist. These entry forms are usually from OED, but with words from The Friars of Berwick, DOST entry forms are also given where they differ from OED.

The alphabetical order of the glossary is far from simple. The symbol þ is equivalent to modern th and is treated as such. The symbol ȝ is more difficult: at the beginning of words it is equivalent to modern y and in the middle of words is the ancestor of modern (now silent) gh. The symbol i may represent modern j, y may represent modern i, u and v are interchangeable, and w may take the place of modern u. Initial ff was used by some scribes where modern spelling would have only f. Words with these symbols are alphabetized roughly as if they had their modern spelling--roughly because, given the many variant spellings, it is often necessary to compromise between where a word theoretically ought to be and where a reader might be looking for it. Of necessity, there are many cross references.

It would be useful for readers unfamiliar with fifteenth-century English to remember some other common late medieval spellings and grammatical forms. Final e in some of these texts is virtually random: it appears where it should not and does not where it should. Consonants may be unexpectedly doubled after usually long vowels and single after short ones. The symbols ei and ey often appear where modern spelling has ai or ay. Scottish and northern texts may have the following grammatical forms: final and for the ending of the present participle (e.g. cumand = coming); final it (or yt) for the weak past tense and past participle (e.g. cryit = cried); final is (or ys) for the plural ending of nouns or the third singular present tense ending of verbs (e.g. dedis = deeds, thynkys = thinks). In the Scottish Friars of Berwick initial quh would have the spelling wh in more modern texts, and final cht would be ght.

Abbreviations Used in Glossary

adj = adjective
adv = adverb, adverbial
art = article
BM = The Boy and the Mantle
comp = comparative
conj = conjunction, conjunctive
dem = demonstrative
DH = Dane Hew
DOST = Dictionary of the Older Scottish Tongue
FB = The Friars of Berwick
FT = The Feast of Tottenham
imp = imperative
impers = impersonal
indef = indefinite
int = interjection
irreg = irregular
JR = John the Reeve
JS = Jack and his Stepdame
KH = The King and the Hermit
LP = The Lady Prioress
MED = Middle English Dictionary
n. = note

OED = Oxford English Dictionary
pa = past
pers = person
phr = phrase
pl = plural
ppl = participial
pple = participle
prep = preposition
pres = present
prob = probably
pron = pronoun
q.v. = quem vide, which see
refl = reflexive
rel = relative
sb = substantive
Sc = Scottish
SC = Sir Corneus
sing = singular
t = tense
TB = The Tale of the Basin
usu = usually
v = verb
vbl = verbal

abak, abacke _adv_: back, off, away JR 727, FB 341

abayst _pa_ _pple_: unconfident KH 89 [abash]

abbacy _sb_: the estate of an abbot FB 127

abyde _v_: await defiantly JR 329; abod _pa_ _t_: endured LP 226

able, abyl _adj_: suitable, appropriate FT 75; used as _adv_: ably JR 217

abod _v_: pa _t_ abide, _q.v._

abone _quasi-sb_: (our) abone, a position above our current one JR 565 [_a northern form of the adverb_ above]

abowthe = about JS E91

abrode _adv_: abroad, outdoors DH 124

aby(e) _v_: atone, make restitution JS 218, DH 149

acton _sb_: stuffed jacket or jerkin worn under armor JR 328

adrad _pa_ _pple_: frightened LP 76

aferd, afeard, affeard, _pa_ _pple_: afraid LP 141, JR 602 [afear]

af[f]ray, effray _sb_: alarm, fright LP 224, FB 197; an attack JR 732

afoir _adv_: before FB 382; afore that _conj_: before JS X60 [afore]

after _prep_: according to the instructions of LP 120

againe, aȝen _adv_: in response JR 508, FB 172; back KH 294

againe, ageyn _prep_: opposite to JR 350; against JS 371

against _prep_: opposite to JR 352

aglood _v_: glided up or away LP 227 [aglide _pa_ _t_]

agon _pa_ _ppl_: departed JS 165 [ago]

agood _adv_: vigorously, heartily JS Z83

airt = art   FB 328

ayther = either LP 162

all(e) adj: every TB 125; sb: everything FT 25; adv:
    altogether JS 373

allane = alone FB 305

al(l)hail(l) adv: entirely FB 230; adj: entire FB 127 [OED
    all-whole, DOST alhale, alhail]

allthair adj: of all FB 20 [see OED all, DOST alther, all-
    thair]

allthoff = although KH 246

all-utirly adv: completely, absolutely FB 18 [all-utterly]

almery, almeire sb: cupboard FB 223, 276 [OED ambry, DOST
    almery]

als adv = as FT 38; = also FB 40

also sone adv phr: immediately, as soon as could be TB 52
    [as soon]

amerveylid pa pple: surprised, astonished JS 416 [amarvel]

amang = among FB 31

among adv: from time to time TB 30, JS 253, SC 129; at the
    same time JS 260

and sb = hand LP 196

and conj: if LP 65; even if JR 100

-and: the northern, and particularly Scottish, ending of
    the present participle, e.g. cumand(= coming) FB 45

ane indef art, adj: a, an, one FB 6, 28; a one FB 10

anethe = vnneth, q.v.

aneuche = enough FB 144

angerly adv: angrily JS 169

anhungrid ppl adj: hungry JS 67 [anhungered]

anight adv: at night, by night   JR 794

annuch, annwche = enough FB 431

anon adv: at once JS 57; anon as conj phr: as soon as
    TB 179

apayd(e), appaid ppl adj: satisfied JS 426, DH 181;
    pleased JR 49 [apaid]

ap(p)init = happened FB 28, 383

apon = vpo(u)n, upon, q.v.

araye sb: attire, dress JS 291; state of things JS 297 [array]

are sb: grace KH 190 [ore]

are adv = ere, before KH 41

aspyed v: espied SC 91 [aspy pa t]

assay, asey v: venture TB 192; woo DH 17; test SC 148

assent sb: sanction SC 50

assent v = assented JS 44

astere v: restrain JS 101, 125 [a- + steer; unattested]

at conj: that KH 71

ather = either KH 509

attour prep: over FB 548 [atour]

aught, aucht = pa t owe, q.v.

avanse v: benefit SC 165

aventour, awnter v: (ad)venture KH 444, FB 462

aventour, aventure, awnter sb: adventure LP 225, KH 432,
    FB 462 [see DOST aunter]

avownce = advance FT 81

awen, awne, awin = own LP 67, SC 182, FB 129

awld = old FB 39

awnter = aventour, q.v.

aȝen = againe, q.v.

bad = pa t bid LP 75

baine, baene adj: ready, willing JR 509, JR 630

bayschyd pa pple: abashed, dismayed KH 437

baith adj = both FB 108; (of three things) FB 186 [DOST
    bathe, baith]

bald = bold FB 84

bale sb: suffering, pain JS 3

baly = belly TB 39

baly-naked adj: entirely naked TB 162

bandshipp sb: bondship, serfdom JR 177

bare = bore TB 100

baskefysyke: see SC 116 n.

bate sb: contention, strife KH 275

bauld = bold, q.v.

be prep = by, q.v.

beawte = beauty LP 22

bebled pa pple: covered with blood JS 279

become pa pple: gone JS 419

becrached pa pple: thoroughly scratched JS 278 [be +
    cratch]

beddys sb: beads LP 40

beden(e), bydeene <u>adv</u>: together BM 140; in a little while JR 224; as a group KH 216

bedyng <u>pres</u> <u>pple</u>: praying KH 114 [bid]

bedone <u>pa</u> <u>pple</u>: adorned BM 8 [bedo]

beforn, befoir = before SC 23, FB 378

beggyd <u>pa</u> <u>pple</u>: located LP 147 [big]

begylyd = beguiled LP 199

begin <u>v</u>: sit at the head of JR 826

begynne, begyen = begin LP 27, TB 137

beglued <u>pa</u> <u>pple</u>: deluded LP 199 [beglue]

behy3ht <u>v</u>: promise KH 132; <u>pa</u> <u>t</u> KH 502

behynde <u>adv</u>: in arrears TB 72

behouyth <u>v</u>: [it] is proper KH 162

beid = bide FB 532

beir = bear FB 209

beit <u>v</u>: make a fire FB 133 [OED beet, bete, DOST bete, beit]

belasshe <u>v</u>: thoroughly lash JS 203 [be + lash]

beleuet = believe JS E143

beliue, belyfe, blyff, blive <u>adv</u>: at once, immediately, quickly LP 231, TB 44, JS 85

ben <u>adv</u>: into the main room of the house FB 303

bendfull <u>sb</u>: a bandfull, a bundle KH 170

bene = be FB 381

benedicite, banadicitie <u>interj</u>: <u>expressing</u> <u>astonishment</u>, Bless us! JS 301, FB 381

bening <u>adj</u> = benign FB 415 [DOST bening]

bere <u>sb</u> = bier LP 124

bere <u>sb</u>: clamor KH 515

berinnen <u>pa</u> <u>ppl</u>: overrun with JR 844 [berun]

bescrow <u>v</u> = beshrew, <u>q.v.</u>

beseeme <u>v</u>: befit, suit JR 668, BM 44

besene <u>pa</u> <u>pple</u>: in appearance FB 20; provided FB 154 [OED
    besee <u>pa</u> <u>pple</u>, DOST besene]

beshet <u>v</u>: shut in JS 142 [beshut]

beshrew, bescrow <u>v</u>: curse JS E69; beshrewyd <u>pa</u> <u>pple</u>:
    treated bad<del>l</del>y, abused LP 200

besyd <u>adv</u>: close, near FB 493

besides <u>prep</u>: beside JR 213

besines <u>sb</u>: diligence FB 415 [OED business, DOST
    bes<del>i</del>nes]

bespake <u>v</u>: spoke up JS 349 [bespeak <u>pa</u> <u>t</u>]

bestrood <u>v</u>: strode across LP 228 [bestride <u>pa</u> <u>t</u>]

betauȝt <u>v</u>: bid KH 509 [beteach <u>pa</u> <u>t</u>]

bet(t)ell <u>v</u>: calumniate JR 413; betold <u>pa</u> <u>pple</u>:
    derid<del>e</del>d, deceived JR 690

bethought <u>v</u> <u>refl</u>: considered LP 45; resolved LP 46;
    <u>pa</u> <u>pple</u>: LP 13 [bethink <u>pa</u> <u>t</u>]

bet(te) <u>adj</u>: better TB 154

betold: <u>pa</u> <u>pple</u> betell, <u>q.v.</u>

betwen <u>adv</u>: in the intervals KH 368 [between]

bewray <u>v</u>: expose DH 187

byd = bide FB 97

bydand = biding FB 174

bydeene <u>adv</u> = bedene, <u>q.v.</u>

byden <u>pa</u> <u>pple</u>: endured KH 212 [bide]

bill <u>sb</u>: written plea in a legal case JS Z79

byn = are LP 3

birneist = burnished. See FB 275n.

blandament <u>sb</u>: blandishment FT 51 [blandiment]

blawen = blown FB 565

blawndisare <u>sb</u>: blaundsore, a chicken dish FT 34

bleade = blade JR 608

blee <u>sb</u>: complexion, face BM 50

bleidand = bleeding FB 561

blew vp <u>v</u> <u>phr</u>: sounded a blast JS Y63

blyff, blive <u>adv</u> = beliue, <u>q.v.</u>

blyn(n)e <u>v</u>: cease, desist JS 312, KH 403 [blin]

bliss <u>sb</u>: gladness, joy JS P11; soo haue I blisse: as I hope
    for [the] happiness [of heaven] TB 61

blyth = blithe FB 54

blithe <u>adv</u>: cheerfully TB 102

blive <u>adv</u> = beliue, <u>q.v.</u>

bloke = block JS 371

blowen <u>pa</u> <u>pple</u>: spread around, proclaimed LP 86 [blow]

blude = blood FB 41

bod <u>v</u>: endured LP 145 [bide <u>pa</u> <u>t</u>]

boiss = boss, <u>q.v.</u>

boyt = both JS E80

bok(k)e sb: buck, male deer LP 38, 139

bold(e), bauld adj: strong, fierce JR 192; audacious
     FB 260; to be bold: to take the liberty LP 115, JR 500
     [DOST bald]

boll sb: a six-bushel measure FB 216

boll = bull LP 182

bolt sb: arrow JS 85

bond sb: string KH 461; obligation JR 202

bond adj: in a state of serfdom JR 361

bond pa pple = bound, shackled KH 260; pa t = bound JS 344

bondman sb: serf JR 125

bord(e) sb: a table FT 79

borowe: See JS 180n.

borrow sb: town LP 30 [borough]

bos v impers: [it] is necessary for KH 277 [contracted form
     of behoves]

boss, boiss sb: a leather wine bottle FB 161 [DOST bos]

bost sb: clamor LP 213; without bost: without exaggeration
     JR 467 [boast]

bot; bot (3)if, bot gif: see but; but (3)if, but gif

botkin sb: bodkin, dagger FB 180 [DOST boitkin, botkin]

bought pa pple: atoned for JS E65, JR 492 [buy]

bou3tes v: second pers pa t buy KH 224

boun v refl: get ready FB 576; bownit pa t FB 231

bourde, bowrd sb: an idle tale, a joke JR 10, SC 4

boushe = bush LP 69

boute <u>adv</u>:   outside   JR 862

bown <u>pa</u> <u>pple</u>:   under obligation   DH 30 [bind]

bowrd <u>sb</u> = bourde, <u>q.v.</u>

bowthe = bought, <u>q.v.</u>

braggat <u>sb</u>:   a drink made of honey and ale   JR 141 [bragget]

braid, brayde, breyd <u>sb</u>:   a moment   DH 182; a sudden
     movement, jerk T͞B 184, KH 359

braid, brayd <u>v</u>:   rushed BM 34; broke into speech SC 97;
     brayed v͞p <u>v</u> <u>phr</u>: burst into action LP 139 [braid <u>pa</u> <u>t</u>]

brake, brak = broke LP 143, FB 547

brand <u>sb</u>:   a sword   DH 94; a burning piece of wood   JR 336

brast(e) <u>v</u>:   break   JS X54; <u>pa</u> <u>t</u> JR 543; <u>pa</u> <u>pple</u>   FT 102
     [bur͞st]

brawle <u>sb</u>:   a French dance   JR 535

brede <u>sb</u>: (piece of) roast meat   KH 200

bredir = breþir, <u>q.v.</u>

breid = breadth FB 551

breyd <u>sb</u> = braid, <u>q.v.</u>

breke <u>sb</u> = shorts   LP 166   [breek]

breke <u>v</u> = broke   LP 196

bremblis = brambles JS 247

brere <u>sb</u> = briar   JS 229

breþer, brethir, bredir <u>sb</u> = brothers   SC 231, FB 31

brewice <u>sb</u>:   broth, or bread soaked in broth   JR 393 [brewis]

bribour <u>sb</u>:   vagabond   DH 149   [briber]

bright <u>adj</u>:   beautiful   JR 82

brynand = burning KH 183

bring v: escort, accompany DH 174; forth brought v phr:
    expressed, brough to light LP 12

britled v: cut to pieces BM 175 [brittle pa t]

broake v: enjoy the use of JR 462 [brook]

broch sb: a taper LP 40 [broach]

brocht = brought FB 214

brode adv: broadly, extensively LP 86 [broad]

brouch = brooch BM 7

browne sb: a brown fabric JR 287

bruder = brother FB 46

brunt sb: an assault, charge LP 145

brute sb: a meat or poultry soup FT 56 [browet]

buckler sb: a small round shield JR 634

buffet sb: slap, pat FB 139

bugyll sb = bugyll-horn, q.v.

bugyll-horn, bugyll sb: the horn of a bugle or wild ox KH
    518; used as a drinking vessel SC 22, 38

buk = book FB 334

buke = baked FB 216

burd = board FB 180

burde sb: See FB 153n.

burdoun sb: a stout staff FB 545 [OED bourdon, DOST
    burdoun]

bure = bore FB 564

burnett sb: high quality wool cloth JR 288

busked <u>v</u>: took (oneself) JR 556

but, bot <u>conj</u>: unless LP 49, FB 530; <u>adv</u>: only, just JR 323, 812; neither more nor less than LP 140, FB 355; see FT 102n. [DOST bot]

but (3)if, but gif, bot (3)if, bot gif <u>conj</u>: unless TB 26, JS X51

but <u>adv</u>: out FB 155

bute <u>sb</u>: use, avail FB 375 [OED boot, DOST bute]

by, be <u>prep</u>: in the course of TB 174, KH 13; before TB 180; because of KH 279; alongside of JS 383

by and by <u>adv</u> <u>phr</u>: immediately DH 138

caitife <u>sb</u>: wretch, villain DH 189

call <u>v</u>: ask, invite KH 5

calltrape <u>sb</u>: a foot trap or snare LP 196 [caltrop]

can, con <u>v</u>¹: have knowledge of FT 97, JR 360; couth, cowth, cold, <u>pa</u> <u>t</u>: knew TB 16, SC 28, BM 4; could KH 366, SC 30

can, con <u>v</u>²: began to, proceeded to, did TB 36, JR 48; cowld <u>irreg</u> <u>pa</u> <u>t</u>: did FB 100

capul <u>sb</u>: horse FT 50, JR 130 [caple]

care <u>sb</u>: suffering LP 176, TB 223; attention LP 174

care <u>v</u>: be uneasy, anxious BM 32

carle <u>sb</u>: bondman JR 47

carnall <u>sb</u>: battlement FB 13 [OED carnel; <u>not</u> <u>in</u> DOST]

carol <u>sb</u>: a ring-dance with song JR 535

cas(e) <u>sb</u>: an occurrence LP 14, DH 244

cast <u>v</u>: intend JR 596; <u>pa</u> <u>t</u>: considered KH 82; caste <u>pa</u> <u>pple</u>: intended TB 167; castin <u>pa</u> <u>pple</u>: dug FB 10 cauld adj = cold   FB 259

certain(e) adv: certainly   DH 173, JR 503

certes, sertes adv: certainly   FT 46, JS 294

chalmer = chamber   FB 138

chance, chaunce sb: a mischance   TB 165, DH 261, JR 318;
     fortune FT 12

chandlour sb: a candlestick   JR 251   [chandler]

chape sb: a scabbard   JR 611

chapelery sb: scapular, a short cloak   JS 251

chapmon sb: a peddler   TB 143   [chapman]

charcoll = charcoal   FT 59

charge v: order   FB 530

charlett sb: a custard containing pork   FT 43   [charlet]

charry: see FT 91n.

chaste v: train, correct by discipline   JS 30

chaunce sb = chance, q.v.

checkmate sb: an equal in a contest   JR 799

cheere, chere, chier sb: fun DH 37, KH 390; food DH 239;
     facial expression JS 369; with a good chere phr:
     cheerfully, with a good will   JS 411

cheeue v: succeed   JR 152   [cheve]

chefe sb: fortune   JR 558

cheke = choke   JS 116

chese = choose   TB 210, KH 296

chese crust sb: cheese rind   FT 43

chyre = chair FB 187

chop <u>sb</u>: a cutting blow JR 318

churl <u>sb</u>: serf JR 445

clam = climbed FB 555 [DOST clim <u>pa</u> <u>t</u>]

clathis <u>sb</u>: bedclothes FB 104 [DOST clath]

clawcht <u>v</u>: snatched up FB 563 [OED cleek, DOST cleke <u>pa</u> <u>t</u>]

cleare <u>adj</u>: bright, shining JR 435

cleith <u>v</u>: clothe FB 147 [OED clead, DOST cleth(e, cleith]

clen <u>adv</u>: entirely, absolutely LP 154 [clean]

clepe <u>v</u>: call TB 157

clething <u>sb</u>: clothing FB 552 [OED cleading, DOST clething]

cloiss <u>adv</u>: close, secretly FB 488 [DOST clos, clois]

cloiss <u>v</u>: close, fold up FB 222 [DOST close, clois]

close <u>sb</u>: a farmyard JS 141; a cloister DH 277

closit <u>pa</u> <u>pple</u>: enclosed FB 120 [close]

clowte <u>sb</u>: clout, heavy blow TB 198; a rag JS 274

clowted <u>pa</u> <u>pple</u>: patched JR 552

cocks, cockys <u>sb</u>: God´s [a weakened form] TB 208, DH 262

codwar <u>sb</u>: scrotum JS E95 [codware]

cofyr <u>sb</u>: coffer, chest KH 289

coft <u>pa</u> <u>pple</u>: redeemed FB 101 [OED coff; DOST copen]

cokwold = cuckold SC 14

cold = <u>pa</u> <u>t</u> can <u>v</u>1, q.v.

coller <u>sb</u>: the chain which forms part of the insignia of knighthood JR 815 colop sb: a slice of fried meat KH 297   [collop]

com = came LP 33

comand pa pple = commanded JR 339

combre v: destroy JS X50; combred pa pple hampered JR
    65$\overline{2}$ [cumber]

comen = come JR 572

comfyt sb: a sugar glaze FT 49

comly adv: seemly JR 299 [comely]

commannde pres ppl = coming JR 648

compenabull adj: companionable SC 110 [companable]

con = can, q.v.

coney, cunyng sb: rabbit JR 470, FB 135 [OED cony, DOST
    cuning]

connyng adj: expert LP 3 [cunning]

consayet sb: notion LP 12 [conceit]

cons(s)ell, councell sb: private purpose LP 85; secret
    TB 172; kepe consell phr: observe secrecy LP 95
    [counsell]

conuay v: remove secretly DH 105 [convey]

cookerye sb: food JR 431

cop = cup FB 400

cope sb: a long cloak, esp. a friar´s KH 194

corse sb: body LP 112, 214

costrell sb: a vessel for holding liquid FT 49 [costrel]

councell sb = consell, q.v.

counted pa pple: accounted JR 518

cowld, cowd v: did FB 100; was able JS 312 [can v²irreg
    pa t]

cowle, cowll sb: a garment with a hood worn by religious
    LP 57, FB 523

couth, cowth v: knew TB 16, SC 28; could JR 14, KH 366,
    SC 30 [can v¹ pa t]

crabitly adv: crossly FB 238 [OED crabbedly, DOST
    crabitly]

cracched v: scratched JS 247 [cratch]

cracke sb: breaking of wind JS X43

craif v = crave, q.v.

crake v: make a cracking noise JS 378

crave, craif v: demand by right LP 91; ask for DH 78, FB
    314; beg JR 120

creator = creature LP 17

creede sb: a repetition of the Apostles' Creed BM 82

creill sb: creel, wicker basket FB 164 [DOST crele,
    creill]

crepe = creep JS 266

croce = cross FB 23

cry on v phr: call in supplication on FB 237

Crystiante sb: the Christian part of the world SC 162

crofft sb: enclosed land for farming JR 130

crouch v: cringe submissively JR 120

croun sb: a coin, the French ecu FB 311 [OED crown, DOST
    croun(e]

crowt v: push BM 114 [crowd: unattested sense]

cucry sb: cookery FT 11

cullys sb: a strong broth FT 50 [cullis sb¹]

cumand pres pple = coming FB 45

cunyng sb = coney, q.v.

curch sb: a kerchief FB 148

cure sb: charge (laid upon one) FB 360; care FB 415

curteous, curtesse adj: having courtly manners TB 80, BM 3

cur(r)y sb: cookery FT 35

dame, deme sb: mother LP 147; lady JS 32

danger v: damage, harm JR 207

dare v: hurt JR 635 [dere]

dase v: be stupefied, bewildered KH 413 [daze]

deal(e), dele sb: bit; neuer a dele: not a bit JS 14, DH
     135, JR 504

dealinge sb: conduct JR 114

dease, dese sb: dais, high table JR 379, SC 210

debate sb: physical fight, strife JR 595

ded = did LP 227, = died JS E137

deere adv: in excellent manner JR 468 [dear]

deggyd = dug LP 146

degre sb: manner, way JS P9

deid adj = dead FB 92 [DOST dede, deid]

deid sb = death FB 236 [DOST dede, deid]

deid sb = deed FB 1 [DOST dede, deid]

deir sb: harm FB 476 [OED dere, DOST dere, deir]

deir v: harm FB 486 [OED dere, DOST dere, deir(e]

dele sb = deal, q.v.

delyuerlie, delyverly adv: quickly FB 262, 564
    [deliverly]

demyd v: considered LP 140 [deem pa t]

dengerous adj: haughty FB 55 [dangerous]

denteis sb: delicacies FB 437 [OED dainty, DOST daynté,
    pl]

der(e) = dare KH 125, 392

deray sb: harmful disturbance FB 527; noisy disturbance
    FB 201

dese = dease, q.v.

desease sb: harm JR 106 [disease]

desyrand pres pple: asking for FB 270 [desire]

desire v: ask for JS 108

deuer sb = devoir, q.v.

devyiss sb: plan FB 391 [OED device, DOST devis(e]

deviss v: direct FB 487 [devise]

devoir, deuer sb: duty, appointed task LP 100, FB 394

dicht v = dight, q.v.

dy3ed = died KH 268

dight, dicht, di3t, dy3ht v: prepare KH 180, FB 122; pa t:
    dressed LP 136; got ready, prepared FT 13, JR 562; pa
    pple: dressed JR 224, handled JR 846

diligence sb: endeavor; do (one's) diligence: exert self
    FB 444

dynk adj: finely dressed FB 55

direct adv: straight, directly FB 336

dyscuryd pa pple: made known LP 130 [discover]

disdaind pa pple: treated with contempt JR 692

dyses = decease LP 237

disese sb: uneasiness TB 27

dishmeate sb: food cooked in a dish, like a pie JR 468

disparit pa pple: despairing FB 425

dispyte sb: indignation SC 34; outrage FB 480 [despite]

dissagyiss = disguise FB 466 [DOST disagyse]

distans sb: discord SC 136

dyuers adj: different JS 384

do(e) of v phr: take off JR 755

do(e) away v phr: stop JR 301; abandon JR 303

done = do JS 321

dongestek sb: steak made of dung? FT 58

doo sb = doe LP 38

doralle sb: custard pie of meat or fruit FT 58 [dariole]

dorge = dirge LP 93

dowbill = double FB 10

downce = dance FT 84

dowte, doute = doubt JS 99, SC 234

dowter = daughter LP 19

draif v: passed, spent (time) FB 409 [drive pa t]

drad adj: afraid JS 287 [dread]

draughe = drew JR 619

drau3ht, draw3t sb: a drink SC 118; move in a game TB 60
    (see n.)

drawen pa pple: withdrawn, removed FT 79

dred adj: afraid LP 203 [dread]

drede sb = dread TB 177

dresse v: make (oneself) ready FT 84

dreu3e = drew KH 232

dronken = drank TB 127

dry3e = dry KH 302

dure v: endure FB 39

durst v = dare JR 158, dared TB 34

dwell v: delay BM 22

dwelland = dwelling FB 125

echon(e) = each one JS 213

effeiritlie adv: fearfully FB 424 [OED effeiredly, DOST
    efferitly]

effray sb = affray, q.v.

effrayit pa pple: frightened FB 498 [effray]

eft adv: again KH 355

eftir = after FB 401 [DOST efter]

egged pa pple: provoked LP 145 [egg]

eik adv: also FB 23 [OED eke, DOST eke, eik]

eyne = eyes FB 339

eynke = ink JS E83

eyre = heir TB 10

eysell sb: vinegar JS 2 [eisell]

eit = ate FB 70, = eat FB 267

elk sb: member of the deer family JR 473

ell adv = ill LP 159

elle sb: forty-five inches KH 466

ellis adv: otherwise TB 2 [else]

empere sb: supreme command JS RQ12 [empire]

endewed v: invested with property LP 238 [endue pa t]

ensample sb: an example SC 10

ensemble sb: an assembling KH 22 [MED ensemble]

er(e) adv: formerly JR 318; before JR 766; conj: before
     TB 161

ermyte = hermit KH 152

erst adv: earlier; ner erst: never before JR 400

ersward adv: backward FT 88 [arseward]

es v: help KH 473 [ease]

es(e) sb: comfort, advantage TB 29, KH 176 [ease]

estate sb: status, rank JR 824

ete(n) = ate FT 36, TB 127, JS 77

even, evin, ewin adv: exactly FB 391; at the same time FB
     76, 194; ewin so: just then FB 157 [OED euen, DOST
     evin, ewin]

euen sb: evening DH 39, JR 70

euentide sb: evening DH 110

euer adv: constantly, perpetually JS 259

euermoo adv: emphatic form of ever TB 80

euery quasi-pron: everybody BM 31

eueryeche = every JR 493

euerchon(e) = every one JS 142

evill, ewill adj: bad, rough FB 93; adv: badly FB 48,
    ill JR 818

euin, ewin = even, q.v.

euynsong sb: canonical service for sunset KH 74 [evensong]

ewin = even, q.v.

except(e) conj: unless BM 19

eyne = eyes FB 339 [DOST ey, eye]

fabyll sb: deceptive fiction, falsehood LP 47

fayer adv: directly, straight LP 111 [fair]

ffayle v: miss (a step) JR 538 [fail]

fayle sb: failure FT 87 [fail]

fain, ffaine, fayne, feyn, fane adj: glad JR 353, glad
    under the circumstances JS 281; adv: gladly JR 107

fair v = fare, q.v.

fairly, farlie sb: wonder FB 382, 438 [OED ferly, DOST
    farly]

fall(e) v: come to pass, occur; foule mot yow falle: may
    evil befall you TB 182

fallow = fellow, q.v.

fand v: provided FB 144 [find pa t]

fane = fain, q.v.

fansy sb: an inclination DH 8 [fancy]

ffare, fare sb: doings LP 216; mode of proceeding TB 146;
    food JR 439; comfort KH 180

fare, fair v: do TB 57; go TB 98; faris <u>impers third sing</u>:
   happens TB 72; ferd <u>pa t</u>: did, got <u>on</u> TB 55

farforth <u>adv</u>:   far   LP 100

farlie = fairly, <u>q.v.</u>

ffarrand <u>adj</u>:   handsome   JR 357

fast(e), ffast <u>adv</u>:   readily   LP 47; strongly, vigorously
   JR 616; earnestly SC 88; firmly, fixedly TB 139; <u>adj</u>:
   firmly attached TB 154

faute, fawt <u>sb</u>: fault LP 6; want of food KH 126

fauyll <u>sb</u>:   cunning, duplicity   KH 158   [favel]

ffawchyon <u>sb</u>:   a sword; also a pruning knife JR 705
   [falchion]

fawcon = falcon JR 20

ffawconer <u>sb</u>: keeper and trainer of hawks JR 261 [falconer]

fay(e) <u>sb</u>:   faith   JS 179; in gode fay: in truth   TB 148

febull = feeble   TB 19

fe, fee <u>sb</u>:   an estate in land   KH 247; money   LP 242, JR
   366; in fee: by heritable right LP 239

ffeeare = fire   JR 192

feir = fere, <u>q.v.</u>

fele <u>adj</u>:   many   JS 224, SC 240

fele <u>v</u>:   feel out, discover   LP 6

feliship = fellowship   TB 207

fell(e) <u>sb</u>:   a moorland ridge   KH 21

felloun <u>adj</u>:   fierce, terrible   FB 544   [OED felon, DOST
   felloun]

fellow, ffelow, felaw, fallow sb: an agreeable companion
TB 78, FB 266; title of address for a servant KH 323 [OED
fellow, DOST fallow]

fend = fiend LP 126

feni3et, fen3eit = feigned FB 264, 430

ferd = pa t fare, q.v.

ferde pa pple: frightened, afraid JS X43

ffere, fere, feir sb: company; in fere, on feir: together
FT 83, JR 471

feste v: take hold of KH 470 [fast]

fest sb: a gathering for pleasure or sports KH 22 [feast]

fet(te) v: pa t: fetched TB 54, DH 301, SC 26; pa pple:
SC 211 [fet]

fett = feet LP 106

feturlok sb: (horse´s) fetlock FT 63 [fetterlock]

fewl = fowl FB 225

fylde = field JS 193

filosophie sb: magic FB 398 [philosophy]

ffind v: maintain; ffind to schoole: maintain while at
school JR 877

fyne adj: consummate, supreme SC 185

fyrred = furred LP 165

fit sb: sexual intercourse DH 22

ffitt, fytte sb: a section of a poem JR 345; a stave of
music JS 354

flap sb: a blow FB 544

fflaun sb: custard or cheesecake JR 473

flawme v: baste FB 137 [flamb]

fle v: fly; lait fle: struck FB 544 [OED fly, DOST fle]

flecher sb: arrowmaker KH 472 [fletcher]

fflyting pres pple: chiding, wrangling JR 685

flocht sb: flutter FB 422

flure sb: see FB 334n.

folly adj: foolish JR 758

fond = found KH 103

fone = foes JS Y80, Z105

fonnd v: attempt, try SC 150 [fand]

foorth of, forth of prep phr: out of DH 71

foorthwithall adv: immediately DH 114

for- prefix: exhaust oneself by doing the action of the
    verb to which it is prefixed; forknokit, forcryid
    pa pples: tired of knocking and crying, "all knocked and
    shouted out" FB 233

for conj: because SC 107; so far as concerns (a person or
    thing) JS 263; prep phr = for God: as God knows, by
    God JS 332

forbode = forbidden LP 90

forbot sb: prohibition; Godes forbot: God forbid KH 329

foretope sb: the crown of the head LP 197

forlore pa pple: lost LP 220 [forlese]

forme sb: backless bench JS 364

forsed pa pple: stuffed FT 59 [farce]

forsoth, forsooth, forsuth adv: truly LP 10, JS 20

forteyned pa pple: happened SC 168 [fortune]

forth adv: not at home SC 223

forwhy conj: because BM 87

fosterse sb: foresters, huntsmen KH 26

fowle adv: badly LP 144 [foul]

fra prep: from FB 61; conj: from the time that FB 392
    [OED fro, DOST fra]

franyt v: asked, made inquiries FB 568 [OED frayne, DOST
    frain(e), pa t]

Ffrankish adj: French; Ffrankish fare: over-polite
    behavior JR 832

ffrankpledge sb: tithing or group of ten householders
    responsible for each other's good behavior JR 176

freake = freke, q.v.

free, fre adj: noble, of gentle birth DH 19; (of an
    offer) readily given JR 109; adv: nobly, honorably
    LP 240

freir = friar FB 24

freyry sb: a brotherhood SC 215 [frary]

freke, ffreake sb: man JS 37, JR 252

frere = friar JS 182

fresh, fresche, fresse adj: healthy looking or youthful
    LP 28; full of vigor JR 895; gaily attired JR 277

fryth sb: a wood KH 21

ffronte v: strike JR 776

ffrumentye sb: a dish of hulled wheat boiled in milk
    JR 473

fruture = fritter FT 61

full adv: very TB 20, KH 292

ffunden = found   JR 480

ffurth = forth LP 136

fute = foot   FB 263

ga = go FB 224

gadered = gathered JS X16

gaff, gaif v: gave FB 82; ne gaff: did not care JS 50
    [give pa t]

gaip = gape FB 346

gaipit = gaped FB 342

gais = goes FB 334

gaist = guest FB 575 [DOST gaist]

gait = get FB 257

gall(e) sb: spirit to resent injury SC 96

galland sb: a fine gentleman FB 6 [OED gallant, DOST
    galland]

gam(e), gamme sb: fun TB 5, JS 163; jest SC 247; amorous
    play DH 31; delight KH 4

gan v: began (to) LP 21, JR 403 [gin pa t]

ganand ppl adj: appropriate FB 256 [OED gainand, DOST
    ganand]

gang(e) v: go JR 209, FB 538

gangand pres pple: going FB 541 [gang]

gape sb: a breach in a hedge or thicket LP 177 [gap]

gar(r) v: cause (one) to (do) something JR 173, gart
    pa t FB 217; cause something to be done FB 288

garamersy = gramercy, q.v.

gate = got JR 26

gate sb: journey KH 444

gent adj: noble, high-born LP 73

gentle sb: one of gentle birth JR 386

gentleness sb: good breeding JR 68

gentrise sb: kindness, courtesy JR 65 [gentrice]

gest sb: a story in verse FT 47, SC 247

gest = guest KH 5

gesttyng vbl sb: tale-telling, recitation LP 1 [gest v]

geth = goeth, goes LP 208

geþer = gather SC 140

gett v: earn JR 146 [get]

geve = give JS 69

geue pa pple = given JS 79

gyde = guide, q.v.

gif conj = if TB 149, FB 84 [n. and Sc. form]

gyf(fe), gif v = give LP 2, JS 80

gyle sb: trick, wile SC 177 [guile]

gyn(n)e sb: trick TB 85, SC 148; pl traps KH 52 [gin]

gingling = jingling FB 150 [OED jingle, DOST gingle]

gird, girt pa pple: fastened JR 704; clothed JR 286 [gird]

gytryn v: play on the gittern, an instrument like a guitar
    TB 81 [gittern]

glad(e) v: make glad JR 546; become or be glad, rejoice TB
    120; LP 1, see note.

gle sb: fun, entertainment TB 5; musical entertainment JS
    314, SC 249 [glee]

gleade <u>sb</u>: bird of prey, <u>usually</u>, a kite JR 267 [glede]

glent <u>v</u>: moved aside quickly LP 177 [glent <u>pa</u> <u>t</u>]

glour <u>v</u>: stare with eyes wide open FB 346; glowrit <u>pa</u> <u>t</u> FB
    34̄2 [OED glower, DOST glowr]

gluder <u>v</u>: flatter FB 34 [OED glother, DOST gluther,
    glūder]

god(e) = good, <u>q.v.</u>

godeman = goodman, <u>q.v.</u>

godewyf(e) = goodwife, <u>q.v.</u>

gois(s) = goes FB 191, 513

gonne <u>sb</u>: a missile JS 167 [gun]

go(o) <u>v</u>: be in a specified condition TB 181, 182; walk JS
    4̄06

good, gode <u>sb</u>: money LP 91; goods KH 163; <u>adj</u>: easy JS 76

gooddeene = good evening JR 48

goodman, godeman, gudman <u>sb</u>: male head of a household TB
    36; host of an inn FB̄ 83 [DOST gud(e)man]

goodwife, godewyf(e), gudwyf(e) <u>sb</u>: female head of a
    household TB 152, FB 68 [DOST̄ gud(e)wife]

gone = go TB 128, DH 102

goule <u>adj</u>: red BM 41 [gules]

gouernaunce, govirnance <u>sb</u>: behavior JS 417; deed(s) FB
    374 [governance]

govirning <u>sb</u>: conduct FB 352

grace <u>sb</u>: fortune JS 381; a favor FB 524

graceles <u>adj</u>: wicked FB 575

grain <u>sb</u>: prong of a fork JR 323

graithly adv: properly, really FB 459 [gradely] [OED
     gradely, DOST graithly]

gramercy, garamersy int: thanks JS 78, KH 175

granit = groaned FB 342

graunt v: agree, consent LP 134 [grant]

gravell sb: kidney stones FB 40

gravy sb: a sauce based on broth, almond milk, and often
     wine or ale FT 28

greeffe, greffe sb: harm JR 205; offense, displeasure SC
     133 [grief]

green(e), grein, grene, gryne sb: green clothing or cloth
     JR 288, SC 222; tree or plant LP 157

greeue, greif v: trouble DH 46, JR 190 [grieve]

greffe = greeffe, q.v.

grein, grene = green, q.v.

grett(e) = great LP 53, 54

grett sb: gravel LP 157 [grit]

grimly adj: grim-looking LP 227

gryndulstone sb: grindstone FT 28 [grindlestone]

gryne = green, q.v.

gryse v: shudder, tremble with horror LP 151; grose pa t
     LP 206 [grise]

grit = great FB 4

grose = grise pa t, q.v.

gud = good FB 46, gudly = goodly FB 20

gudman = goodman, q.v.

gudwyf = goodwife, q.v.

guise, gyse sb: custom, habit TB 171, JR 313, FB 251 [DOST
     gys(e]

habargyon sb: a sleeveless coat of mail JR 328 [habergeon]

haboundantlie = abundantly FB 417

hacche sb: a half-door JS 394 [hatch]

hafe, haif = haue, q.v.

haill adj: well FB 326 [hale]

hailsit v: greeted, saluted FB 57 [hailse pa t]

hairtfullie adv: heartily FB 302 [OED heartfully, DOST
     hartfully, hairt-]

hairtly adj: affectionate FB 252 [OED heartly, DOST
     hartly, hairtly]

hale v: pull KH 468

halelie = wholly FB 98

haly = holy FB 310

hall(e) sb: large public room in a substantial house FT
     26, JS 144

hallow sb: saint(s) FB 265

hame = home FB 61

hand sb: on hand: shortly, in due course FB 32; fra hand:
     at once FB 370

handfull sb: a measure of four inches in length JR 326

hap sb: luck FB 550

happy adj: lucky JS 12

harbor, harber, harborow sb: shelter, lodging JR 78, KH 86
     [harbour]

harbory, herbry, herberye sb: shelter, lodging JR 578, FB
     81 [OED harboury, DOST herbery]

hardely adv: boldly FB 504 [OED hardily, DOST hardely]

harnes(se) sb: genitals TB 209, JS 276 [harness]

haske = ask JS E110

hate adv: eagerly KH 453 [hot]

hate = hat SC 186

haul = hall KH 383

haunt v: resort habitually to DH 172

haue, hafe, haif v = have; imperative absolute: take this
    JS E108, BM 25, 26

he = high FB 12

hearne = heron JR 471

hecht = hight, q.v.

hed sb: the antlers of a deer KH 40 [head]

hede sb: heed, carefull attention TB 176

heder = hither JS 324

heyr = hyre, q.v.

hem = them FT 98; hemself = themselves JS 101

hend adj: courteous, gracious JR 76, 745

hend sb = hands, northern form JR 730, KH 415

hend adv: near KH 416

hende = end JS E81

hengett = hung TB 201

hent v: take DH 74; pa t: took, mounted KH 60; pa pple:
    seized LP 178

hepe = heap JS 360

hepe v: hop, limp JS E106 [hip]

her = their JS 371

herand = errand KH 251

herberye, herbry = harbory, q.v.

herbry v: lodge FB 85; herbryt pa t FB 50 [OED harbry, DOST
    herbry

herke = hark JS 325

hert sb: courage KH 69 [heart]

hertly adv: heartily, cordially FB 169 [OED heartly, DOST
    hertly]

hes = have, Sc. pl FB 4

hes = is JS E57

het = it JS X57

hether = hither DH 55

hett adj: hot FB 41 [het]

hett v = hight, q.v.

hew v: chopped [hew pa t]

hewyn = heaven JS E138

hevy adj: doleful JS 369 [heavy]

hey = high LP 229

hicht sb: height FB 12; haughtiness FB 82 [OED height,
    DOST hicht]

hidder, hider = hither TB 91, FB 399 [DOST hidder]

hyde sb: (human) skin JR 228

hydoys = hideous KH 515

hye = high JS 255

hye v: hasten, go quickly TB 92, JS 267

hye, hy3e sb: haste JR 88, SC 74

hight, hy3(h)t, hecht, hett v: promise, vow JR 168, KH 379; order LP 64; hy3t, hy3ht pa t: promised JS 105; was called KH 317

hyld = held JS 398

hyll v: hide KH 228

him = himself DH 206

hyne sb: lad, boy JS 12 [hind]

hyng(e) = hang KH 261, 459

hyre, heyr sb: wages, reward JS E108, FB 254

history sb: story SC 16

hit = it TB 21

ho = who LP 71

hoist sb: a cough FB 277 [host]

hold sb: keeping, possession BM 144

hold v: observe, abide by JR 198; consider JS 426

holde = held TB 14

holt sb: a wood, copse LP 157

homard = homeward JS E126

honestly adv: honorably, respectably JR 217

hop(e) v: suppose, think JR 484, FB 268; hopys 2nd sing KH 412

hore adj: grey with age SC 155 [hoar]

horpyd adj: bold KH 429 [orped]

horstord = horseturd FT 40

hostel sb: lodging, entertainment KH 106

hostillar sb: an innkeeper FB 51 [OED hosteler, DOST
     hostilar]

houris sb: the time for set prayers said at one of the
     seven hours of the day prescribed FB 284

how int: hey! FB 514

howuyd: See KH 328n.

hue = yew KH 196

hund = hound KH 50

hune sb: delay FB 292 [hone]

hurled v: dashed, moved violently JS 360

husbande sb: manager of a household TB 12; married man
     TB 19

husbandman sb: a farmer JR 124

husbandry sb: management of a household TB 16

ibake pa pple = baked KH 293

ibore pa pple = born LP 218

iche adj: same KH 92

yche = each SC 181; ychon = each one SC 206

yee = eye JS 258

i´faith = in faith JR 193

yknow pa pple = known SC 9

ily3ht pa pple = lighted KH 291

ylke adj: same (thing) JR 397; each TT 83 [ilk]

ilke a adj: each, every FT 4 [ilka]

ilkone pron: each one FB 433 [DOST ilkan(e]

imette pa pple = met TB 155

in sb = in(ne), q.v.

incontinent adv: at once FB 447

indorde pa pple: glazed with egg, saffron etc. FT 51
     [endore]

inkehorne sb: container for ink JS Z25

in(ne) sb: dwelling-place JR 136; lodging KH 164; innis
     pl in sing sense inn FB 211

inowgh, inouȝe, inow, inowȝe = enough JS 51, KH 233, 298,
     309

insame adv: together JS RQ1

intill prep: in FB 52, 65; on FB 28

into prep: into the possession of (by will) LP 238; in
     FB 1, 7

invy sb: hostility FB 350 [envy]

ys adj = his LP 196

isalt pa pple = salted KH 295

ische v: issue FB 130 [OED ish, DOST isch(e]

iwysse, ywis adv: certainly TB 59 [iwis]

ielosy sb: suspicion FB 178 [OED jealousy, DOST jelousy,
     jelosy]

jerfawcon sb: a large falcon JR 574 [gerfalcon]

jetter sb: swaggering fellow JR 278

jolly adj: showy, flashy JR 278

jolty = jollity JR 900

iordan sb: a chamber-pot FT 37

jorney sb: a day's business JS 284 [journey]

iowell = jewel LP 193

iussall sb: mince FT 37 [jussell]

iust v: joust DH 286

ken(ne) v: know (a person) JR 382; see JR 112; recognize
        JR 479; teach KH 333; kend pa t gave instructions FB 109

kepe, keep v: practise JR 275; guard, preserve JS RQ10;
        keepest 2nd sing: observe with due formality DH 150

kercher sb: kerchief JR 226

kest v: threw off FB 341 [cast, pa t]

kind, kynd(e) sb: form FB 473; nature TB 73; natural state
        FB 459; adj: well born BM 3

kirk(e) sb: church JR 373

kirtle, kirtill, kyrtell sb: a man´s tunic JS 251, SC 142;
        a woman´s gown JR 223

knaue sb: a male servant KH 313

knaw = know SC 150

knytt, knyte pa pple: joined, bound FT 86, KH 197

knyth = knight LP 172

ky = cows KH 282

lad sb: serving-man JR 206

ladde = led TB 41

layke v: play KH 367 [lake]

laine sb: concealment; without laine: to tell the truth
        JR 575

laith = loath FB 558 [DOST lathe, laith]

lang = long FB 409

langsum adj: long FB 401 [OED longsome, DOST langsum]

last **adj**: the end; at the last: finally DH 257

late = let FT 92, KH 48

late **adv**: recently JR 594

lath **sb**: a barn JR 517 [lathe]

laudinge **vbl sb**: praising JR 901

laund **sb**: an open space, untilled ground LP 181

law = low FB 560

lay **sb**: strain, tune JS RQ4

lay to **v phr**: See TB 29n.

lead **v**: adduce (testimony) JR 676

leaze, les **sb**: falsehood; withouten leaze: to tell the
     truth JR 380, SC 207 [lease]

ledden = led JR 900

leef, leffe, leue **adj**: beloved, dear JS 298, KH 184; **adv**:
     gladly, willingly SC 134 [lief]

leest **adj**: lowest in position FT 24 [least]

leeuer = leuer, **q.v.**

leffe = leef, **q.v.**

left **v**: remained SC 241

leggyd **adj**: having legs (of a particular kind) LP 148

leif = live FB 203

leyffe = life JS E93

leill **adj**: loyal, faithful FB 65 [OED leal, DOST lel(e,
     leil(l]

leir = lere, **q.v.**

leytley = lightly, **q.v.**

lemmane sb: lover FB 186

lend v: tarry, remain KH 17

lenger = longer JS 219

lepe = leapt JS 254

lere, leir v: learn KH 240, FB 316

les = leaze, q.v.

lese v^1:   slice FT 75 [leach]

lese v^2:   lose TB 209; lesyst 2nd sing LP 133 [leese]

les(s)yng sb: a lie LP 48, SC 18 [leasing]

lesse quasi-sb: those of lower rank FT 27

lest = last KH 270

lett(e), lete v^1:   desist, forbear TB 152, JS X42 [let v^1]

lett(e), lete v^2:   refrain FT 31; delay JS 396, JR 182;
     hinder TB 56 [let v^2]

lett(e), let sb: hindrance; without(en) lett: without
     hesitation, without pause DH 58,   JR 142, SC 32

letting pres pple: delay JS 327

leuch, leuȝe v = laughed FB 143, SC 44   [DOST lauch]

leue v: supply oneself with food KH 249 [live]

leue adj and adv = leef, q.v.

leuer, levir, leeuer comp adj: rather LP 161, FB 290; adv:
     rather TB 141 [OED liever, DOST levar, levir]

leuyd v: abandoned, forsook (a practice) TB 218 [leave pa
     t]

leuyd v: lived TB 221 [live pa t]

levin = leave, inf FB 173

lewd, lewed adj: bad, worthless LP 202; secular JR 496

lewh = laughed JS 253

lewtnesse sb: wickedness TB 218 [lewdness]

ley sb: faith KH 408 [lay]

libberla sb: staff, cudgel FB 496 [OED libberla, DOST libber-lay]

lig = lie FB 102

lyght adv: quickly LP 167

ly3te = lite, q.v.

lightly, lyghtly(e), leytley, ly3tly adv: quickly JS 240, DH 59, JR 614

lyke impers v: pleases FB 455; lykyd pa t: pleased, suited JS RQ4

like adj: likely DH 21; is like: has the appearance of being JR 265

likinge vbl sb: pleasure JR 126

line sb: linen JR 560

lyre sb: the face JR 258 [leer]

lyst v: listen LP 30

list, lystyth impers v: [It] pleases JR 521; [it] pleased TB 128; ye list, list hee (used personally): you please, he pleased DH 80, JR 703

lyst(e) sb: desire, longing LP 36 [list]

lite, lyte, ly3te sb: little, not much TB 53; adj: small JS 95

lyth v: listen to KH 8 [lithe]

lytter sb: straw KH 167

lyue sb = life KH 369; on lyve: alive TB 19

liueryes <u>sb</u>: lodgings JR 557 [livery]

ly3e = lie KH 285

loffe <u>sb</u>: sweetheart LP 108 [love]

loge = lodge KH 80

loke = look, <u>q.v.</u>

londe <u>sb</u>: the countryside JS 211 [land]

long <u>adj</u>[1]: tall JR 257

longe <u>adj</u>[2]: attributable to JS X47

look(e), loke, luke, luik <u>v</u>: take care, make sure TB 47,
     JS X7; consider JR 43$\overline{7}$

loppin <u>pa</u> <u>pple</u> = leaped FB 578 [DOST lepe]

lord(e) <u>sb</u>: male head of a household FT 54

lordyng <u>sb</u>: gentleman SC 42

lorne <u>pa</u> <u>pple</u>: lost JS 308 [leese]

lorra <u>sb</u>: a dish like custard FT 20 [lorey]

lost(e) <u>pa</u> <u>pple</u>: wasted JS 21; destroyed JS 379

loth <u>adj</u>: unpleasant; me were loth: it would be
     unpleasant for me LP 3 [loath]

lough(e), lowgh = laughed JS 93

lovshe <u>v</u>: rush, dash LP 168 [lush]

lout <u>v</u>: bow JR 703; lowtit <u>pa</u> <u>t</u> FB 337

louesome <u>adj</u>: lovely, beautiful JR 228

louff = love LP 34

lovit <u>pa</u> <u>pple</u>: praised FB 403 [love]

lowe <u>adj</u>: humble, meek DH 288

lowyd = loved JS E134

low3he v: .smiled SC 92 [laugh pa t]

lowyth v = love 3rd pl LP 25

lowtit = pa t lout, q.v.

luge = lodge FB 49; lugit = lodged FB 243 [DOST luge]

luke, luik = look, q.v.

lust sb: desire, appetite JS 56

lustely adv: pleasantly FB 171

lusty adj: vigorous, valiant FB 6

lute = let pa t FB 428

ma v = may FB 117

ma = mo, q.v.

made pa pple: endowed with prosperity JR 368 [make]

madin sb: maid servant FB 107 [OED maiden, DOST maidin, madin]

mair = more FB 119

maist = most FB 18

maistre, maistry = mastery, q.v.

maistrys = mistress TB 162

mall sb: a mace, a club with spiked head DH 202

manar, manner sb: a country residence JR 683, FB 52 [OED manor, DOST maner, -ar]

mane, mayne sb: bread of mane = pain-demaine, the finest kind of bread FB 174 [maine]

manhed sb: manhood SC 72 [manhead]

manly adv: generously TB 73

mark sb¹: target JS 90

marke sb²: a money of account, equal to eight ounces of silver LP 236

marshall sb: officer in charge of the arrangement of ceremonies, esp. the seating plan JR 346

marshalled v: arranged in order at a feast JR 354

mase sb: a delusive fancy KH 412 [maze]

mashefat sb: a mashing-vat FT 23 [mash-fat]

masyd pa pple: dazed, out of one´s wits KH 521 [maze]

masonedew sb: hospital or poor house FB 23 [OED measondue, DOST maison, maso(u)n-dew]

master sb: one who overcomes another JR 540

mastery, maistre, maistry sb: feat(s) FT 17, KH 276; masterpieces FT 10

matins sb: canonical office for daybreak TB 174 [matin]

mattake sb: a kind of pickaxe LP 104 [mattock]

mawmany sb: a sweet, spiced dish made with fowl FT 29 [malmeny]

may sb: a maiden JR 568

may, ma v: have power JS 130, JR 93; can TB 149, JR 45, mowe 2nd pl may TB 6

me = my LP 71

meanye sb: a company of persons JR 354 [meinie]

measure, mesure sb: dance JR 533; melody, tune JS 98

meate, meit, meyt, mete, mett sb: food FT 13, JR 234

meate-ffellow sb: table companion JR 351

meddyll = meddle LP 4

medyl = middle LP 178

meed, mede sb: wage, reward JS E69, DH 265; to meede: as a reward BM 84

meete, mete, meit adv: in a fit or proper manner JS 87, JR 160; adj: appropriate FB 269

meill = meal FB 216

meit, meyt sb = meate, q.v.

meitt = met JR 160

mekyll adj: much KH 212 [mickle]

mell v: copulate LP 46

mene refl v : behave or conduct oneself LP 43

merchandabull adj: saleable SC 109 [merchantable]

mere = mare JR 653

merke adj: dark JR 103 [murk]

merrit pa pple: hampered, interrupted FB 204 [OED mar; DOST mer]

merth = myrth, q.v.

meruailous = marvellous DH 244

mervelously adv: to a marvelous degree LP 46

mery adv: merrily LP 110

mes = miss, q.v. JS E139

messe sb: a serving of food JR 397

mesure = measure, q.v.

mete adv = meete, q.v.

mete sb: meat, q.v.

methe sb: an alcoholic drink made of fermented honey and
    water LP 210 [mead]

mett = meet LP 156

meve = move, q.v.

myche = much KH 210

micht sb = might FB 16

mycull = mikell, q.v.

myddes sb: middle JS 405 [mids]

mydey = mid-day KH 74

mydyll erd sb: middle earth, the world LP 161 [middle-erd]

midward sb: the middle JS 345

mikell, mycull adv: greatly FB 435; adj: much TB 51; sb: a
    great quantity, much TB 29 [OED mickle, DOST mikil(1)]

mildam sb: the dammed up water above a mill DH 214
    [milldam]

myld(e) adj: kind, considerate, gentle JS P8, RQ8

mylne post sb: post supporting a windmill FT 32 [millpost]

mynstralsy sb: a body of minstrels SC 130 [minstrelsy]

myr(e) sb: a piece of swampy ground LP 186, FB 550

myrth, merth sb: enjoyment SC 224; musical entertainment
    JS 419; pl entertainments, diversions LP 202

misfall v: happen unfortunately JR 219

misgane pa pple: gone wrong FB 247 [OED misgo, DOST
    (misga)]

misknawlege sb: failure to recognize FB 247 [OED
    misknowlege, DOST misknawlage]

misnurtured pa pple: ill-bred JR 305

miss, mes, without(en) <u>phr</u>: without fail JS E139, JR 276

myssefelisshyppe <u>sb</u>: perverse company TB 155 [<u>unattested</u>; mis- + fello<u>w</u>ship]

myssey <u>v</u>: say something slanderous or evil KH 440 [m<u>i</u>s-say]

mitton: a protective hand covering for a hedger or the like JR 637 [mitten]

moe, ma <u>sb</u>: more JR 115; more (in number) FB 371; more per<u>so</u>ns JR 381 [OED mo, DOST ma]

moir = more FB 108

moist = most FB 20

mone <u>v</u>: must FB 492 [OED mone, DOST mon]

mone = moon LP 35, = money TB 64

mood <u>sb</u>: spirit, pride JR 796

more <u>quasi-sb</u>: those of higher rank and power FT 27

morne <u>v</u>: mourn FB 571

mor(r)ow <u>sb</u>: morning LP 68, TB 174

mortrewys <u>sb</u>: a kind of soup FT 23 [mortress]

moste = must TB 113

mot(e), mut <u>v</u>: may TB 182, DH 128; must TB 114 [mote]

move, meve <u>v</u>: proceed from LP 9; mention LP 13

mowe = may <u>2nd</u> <u>pl</u> TB 6

muk cart <u>sb</u>; a dung cart FT 53

mvllis <u>sb</u>: the lips of an animal; applied to the lips of th<u>e</u> vulva FB 142 [mull]

mut = mot, <u>q.v.</u>

na = no FB 16, 90

nalle sb: awl JR 610 [an awl > a nawle]

namely adv: especially FB 464

nane = none FB 8

narrow adv: closely, straitly LP 37

naught adv: not at all JR 495

ne conj: nor FT 9, KH 77, SC 96; adv¹: not TB 64

ne adv²: nearly KH 68 [nigh]

neder, nedur adj: lower FT 52, TB 40 [nether]

nedis adv: necessarily TB 131 [needs]

nedur = neder, q.v.

neer = never LP 232

neere prep: nearer, closer JR 75 [near]

nehand = ny3hhand, q.v.

ney3e v: come near to KH 120 [nigh]

neirhand = nerehand, q.v.

neyth = night JS E118

neke = neck JS 389

ner, neir = ne'er, never JR 400, FB 326

nere = were [it] not KH 301 [ne + were]

nerehand, neirhand adv: close at hand FB 493; nearly
      KH 493 [OED near hand, DOST nere hand]

nese sb: the nose KH 182

nete sb: cattle JS 38 [neat]

nether adj: none (of three) LP 200 [neither]

neuen v: name FT 17 [neven]

neur = never JR 886

new adv: newly JR 520

newfangle adj: fond of novelty BM 35

nyce adj: foolish, stupid TB 146

ny(e) adv: near JR 32; nearly JS 171 [nigh]

night sb: at nightfall, in the evening DH 279

ny3hhand, nehand, ny hand, adv: nearby KH 421; nearly JS
    342 [nigh hand]

nygromancere sb: wizard, conjurer JS X31 [necromancer]

nigromansy sb: magic FB 328 [OED necromancy, DOST nigra-,
    nigromansy]

nithing sb: a miser JR 886

no adv: not KH 437 [no adv¹]

no, without adv phr: certainly KH 170 [no adv³]

noble sb: gold coin, worth ten shillings in the late
    fifteenth century DH 36

nobull adj: splendid FT 35 [noble]

nocht, no3t sb: nothing TB 16, FB 390; adv: not TB 92, FB
    26 [OED nought, DOST nocht]

nolt sb: cattle FB 263 [DOST nowt]

nons, for þe phr: "on this occasion," but usually, as
    here, a mere tag with little or no meaning JS 188, DH
    261 [nonce]

nooen = none LP 32

noone = nun LP 16

nor conj: than FB 290

norysshyd v: brought up, nurtured JS RQ7 [nourish pa t]

noþer, nouþer adv: neither LP 157, TB 38 [nouther]

nothyng, noþyng adv: not at all LP 76, JS RQ4

nought, nou3t, nowght, nowth sb: nothing LP 10, JS 329;
    adv: not at all KH 395

nouþ adj: good for nothing TB 33 [nought]

nowght, nowth sb = nought, q.v.

nwke sb: a corner in a room FB 215 [OED nook; DOST nuk(e]

o adj: one JR 177

ocht sb = ought, q.v.

ocht adv: at all FB 349 [OED aught, DOST ocht]

of prep: some of JS 353

of = off LP 166, JS 382, JR 236

off = of FT 15, TB 1

office sb: a place in the public service JR 206

offycyal sb: presiding officer of an ecclesiastical court
    JS X6

oft-time, oftetymes adv: often DH 180, SC 29

olde adv: of old TB 21

on = one LP 200

one adj: the same SC 142

oneth = vnneth, q.v.

ons, onys = once TB 34

ony = any FB 54

or conj: before DH 276, JR 119

ordeyne, ordayn v: assign, allot JS X9; ordayned pa pple: prepared JR 188 [ordain]

ordinaunce sb: appointed course JS 135 [ordinance]

ore = over JR 874

orisoun sb: a prayer FB 338 [OED orison, DOST oris(u)n]

oste sb: lodging JS 283 [host]

other sb: another one LP 200

ober conj: or JS 18

ought, ocht, ou3t sb: anything JR 174, KH 266, SC 208

our = over FB 335

ourcom v: came to, recovered FB 566 [OED overcome, DOST overcum pa t]

owt, out interj: an exclamation of lamentation JS 335

out of prep: beyond LP 25

outcept v: except JR 156

owdir adv: either FB 489 [OED other adv 2, DOST owther, owder]

owe v: own JR 178; aught, aucht pa t: bore (good will) SC 218; with pres t meaning: are bound FB 418

ower = our LP 58

owttoure, outtour prep: over FB 523, 546 [OED out-over, DOST out-our]

packe-band sb: packthread [unattested: pack + band]

payd pa pple: satisfied, pleased JR 814

payment = pavement FT 65

paynmain sb: white bread [pain-demaine]

pairt = part FB 74

palfrey, palfray sb: small saddlehorse FT 57, JR 58

pallett sb: armor for the head JR 599

papingo sb: popinjay, parrot FB 152 [OED popinjay, DOST
    papīngo]

pardye, perdy int: by God, certainly TB 68, JR 255

paryche = parish LP 29

part sb: share.   See FB 286n.

pase sb = pace JS X16

pass v: go on, proceed FB 37

passing ppl adv: very JR 759

paste sb: dough FT 57

pattering pres pple: reciting, mumbling BM 82

pay sb: satisfaction JR 277

pege = page FB 439

pelet sb: a stone projectile, cannon-ball JS 173 [pellet]

peraduenture adv: perhaps JR 201

perdy = pardye, q.v.

pere = peer JS X32

pere sb: a pear tree LP 111 [perry]

perfay int: truly FB 241 [OED perfay, DOST parfay]

persaving vbl sb: perception FB 179 [OED perceiving, DOST
    persavīng]

person = parson LP 29, TB 6

pertrik = partridge FB 163 [DOST partrik]

pese v: be quiet [peace]

pet(t) = pytt, q.v.

pewer = pure LP 20

pikefforke sb: pitchfork JR 323 [pickfork]

pine sb: suffering caused by hunger JR 456

pine v: become wasted or feeble JR 519; torment JR 788

pypand = piping FB 369

pyre = peer LP 29

pistill sb: a spoken story; also, an extract from an
    apostolic letter FB 188 [OED pistle, DOST pistil(1)]

pytt, pet sb: hell LP 185; a grave LP 105 [pit]

place, plase sb: a convent, religious house LP 18, DH 121

play, pley sb: a crafty proceeding DH 268; a diversion JR
    708; a source of delight SC 20

plase = place, q.v.

plate sb: a sweet, flat cake JR 512

playntie = plenty FB 361

pley = play, q.v.

pleid sb: discussion, talk FB 258 [OED plead, DOST plede,
    pleid]

pleyn, in adv phr: plainly KH 101 [plain]

pleyne v: complain JS 270 [plain]

pleyng sb: sport KH 17 [playing]

pleynte sb: complaint JS 185 [plaint]

pleiss sb: pleasure FB 420 [OED please, DOST (plese),
    pleis]

plight, ply3t, pleyt v: promise JS 109; pledge JS 262

pluver = plover FB 372

polax sb: a battle-ax DH 195 [pole-ax]

porra sb: a vegetable or fish soup FT 19 [porray, porrey]

posterne adj: private, side or back (entrance) TB 126

potage sb: thick vegetable soup FT 21 [pottage]

potener sb: a small bag BM 21 [pautener]

pottle sb: a two quart measure JR 631

practik sb: artful contrivance FB 315 [practic]

precedent sb: head LP 58 [president]

precyous adj: of moral or spiritual worth LP 20

preisit v: hastened, pushed forward FB 538 [press pa t]

prelet = prelate LP 29

present = presented LP 39

prest(e) adj: willing KH 418; prest to: ready for JS 48

preue = prove, q.v.

prevely = privily, q.v.

prevy = privy, q.v.

price, prise sb: first place, place of honor FT 48, JR 370

pride, pryde sb: magnificent ornamentation JR 605;
    satisfaction, elation JS Z111; pomp, magnificence SC
    87

prime sb: the first hour of the day JR 559

prise = price, q.v.

privily, priuely, prevely adv: stealthily, secretly TB 91,
    DH 273

priuyte sb: a thing kept secret KH 455

privy, priue, prevy adv: secret, clandestine TB 101, FB
     129

proctor sb: attorney, legal representative JS Z65

professyon sb: the vow made by one entering a religious
     order KH 271

propre adj: excellent JS 11

protest v: demand as a right FB 448

proud adj: splendid FB 150

prove, preue v: establish validity (of a will) JS X22;
     test FB 317; provyd pa pple: found by experience LP 20

provyde v: to see to something beforehand JR 576

prow sb: advantage, profit JR 426, KH 254

purveance, purviance sb: supply of food FB 396, FB 427
     [purveyance]

quaint adj: strange JR 767

queirn sb: pair of stones for grinding meal FB 537 [quern]

quell v: kill LP 49

quha = who FB 117

quhaevir = whoever FB 382

quhair = where FB 4

quhairevir = wherever FB 19

quhairfoir = wherefore: because of which FB 418

quhairof = whereof

quhat = what FB 86

quhatkin adj: of what kind FB 314; whatever FB 328
     [whatkin]

quhen = when FB 15

quhilis adv: sometimes FB 343 [whiles]

quhilk = which FB 2, 7

quhill conj: till, until FB 37, 214

quhynnis sb: see FB 212n.

quhyt = white FB 24

quyer sb: the chancel of a church LP 125 [choir]

quyt = quite LP 171

quit(te), quyte, white v: repay TB 49, JR 93; quit pa pple
      paid DH 265; pa t quitted: behaved BM 160

raft pa pple: taken TB 142 [reave]

ragys = rags LP 154

raiss = rose FB 260

rakand pres pple: going quickly FB 432 [rake]

raked v: moved, went quickly JR 334

rakyl sb: chain, fetter LP 138

rappe sb: breaking of wind JS 119

raste v: rushed TB 166 [rase pa t]

raunson = ransom KH 259

rax v: stretch FB 518

read(e) = rede, q.v.

reason v: discuss, argue JR 99

reaue v: tear, split JR 861

receate, ressett sb: accommodation JR 161, FB 525
      [receipt]

rech v: care, want to do something TB 48 [reck]

red adj: frightened FB 422 [rad]

red(e), read(e), reed v: advise, counsel FT 83, JR 75; read DH 10; redd pa pple: expounded the significance SC 121

rede sb: a scheme, plan JS 340

redey adv: readily JS E112 [ready]

redy adj: straight, direct KH 499 [ready]

reed v = rede, q.v.

reeue sb: a bailiff, overseer JR

register = registrar JS Z73

reid sb: red cloth FB 147 [red]

relese sb: conveyance LP 238 [release]

reme = realm SC 172

ren = run DH 305

renning = running DH 62

rent sb: revenue, income LP 40; property yielding income SC 195

rentt v: break LP 173 [rend]

repair, repayre sb: usual dwelling place JR 164; concourse of people to a place FB 106

repreue v: express disapproval about SC 193 [reprove]

reseyued = received SC 76

reson sb: narrative LP 5 [reason]

ressett = receate, q.v.

ryall = royal JS 256, KH 22

richt = ryght, q.v.

ryen = run LP 153

ryght, wright sb: justifiable claim LP 113; to þe right:
     in a proper manner FT 14

ryght, wright, ry3t, richt adv: straight, direct JS 134,
     DH 310; in a proper manner JR 215; altogether, quite
     JR 664; just JR 334; richt furth adv phr: straightway,
     at once FB 57; adj: direct JS 401

ryke sb: a kingdom JR 266 [riche]

rynd sb: bark KH 128

rynge v: make resound JS 120

rynnyng = running LP 138

rise = rice FT 45

ryve adv: promptly, speedily TB 20, JS 210 [rife]

ro sb: a small deer KH 63 [roe]

rode = rood, q.v.

rolle sb: a roll of parchment, a scroll JR 9

ronge = rang BM 180

ronne = ran KH 59

rood, rode, rud sb: Christ's cross JS 16, JR 546, FB 310

rost = roasted JR 466

rot = root KH 128

round adv: on all sides DH 120

rovte, rowte sb: a disorderly crowd TB 197, JS 404; a
     group SC 227 [rout]

row sb: a circle TB 190

rowne v: whisper JR 99, FB 188; pa t rowned JR 256 [round] rowsshe = rush LP 170

rowte sb¹ = rovte, q.v.

rowte sb²: a blow JR 624 [rout]

ruban = ribbon FT 45

rud = rood, q.v.

rudd sb: complexion BM 51 [rud]

russall sb: a reddish thing FT 38 [russel]

russett sb: coarse woolen cloth JR 286

rusted pa pple: rust colored JR 392 [rust; influenced by
    reested: rancid?]

sa = so FB 257

saif = save FB 308

sain, sayn = say JS 32, DH 177

sair = sore q.v.

sall = shall FB 74

salust v: saluted FB 301 [salus pa t]

salvyd v: healed LP 243 [salve pa t]

samyn = sammen, q.v.

samme, same adv: together TB 9, KH 5 [sam]

sammen, samyn adv: together FT 86; adj: same FB 121
    [samen]

sanct = saint FB 36

sande sb: ordinance TB 13

sang = song FB 408

sanit v: crossed FB 380 [sain pa t]

sauf = save FB 65

sauȝe = saw KH 458

sauour sb: a taste or smell FT 62

saw sb: a proverb TB 21; a story SC 12; speech TB 191

scape, scapyd v: escaped LP 207, KH 213; scapyd pa pple:
    LP 162 [scape pa t]

scath, skath sb: harm JR 316, KH 244 [scathe]

schamyd v: felt shame SC 45 [shame pa t]

schape sb: escape FB 557 [scape]

schaw = show FB 520

sched = pa t sheede, q.v.

schell sb: a sea-shell used as a drinking vessel KH 331

schenys = shins JS E80

schent = shent, q.v.

schet = shoot KH 464

scheting = shooting KH 266

schew = show KH 34, SC 4

schych = such KH 276

scho = she FB 55

schorte adj: inadequate in quantity KH 140 [short]

schote = shoot KH 240

scornyd pa pple: mocked SC 184

se, see, sey v: saw LP 150, JR 400, KH 505, SC 29 [see pa
    t]

seemlye adj: suitable to the occasion JR 340

seere, seir adj: various JR 465, FB 315 [sere]

sey v = se, q.v.

sey sb = sea FB 8, 316

seid = said TB 21

seik = seek FB 26

seir = seere, q.v.

sek = sack FB 546

sekyrly = sikerly, q.v.

sele sb: happiness JR 507

seme v: appears JS 290; semyd pa t impers: it was
   suitable for (someone) LP 138 [seem]

sen conj: considering (that) FB 167

send v: grant BM 196

senne adv: from that time onwards SC 252 [sin]

serke sb: surplice JR 269 [sark]

sertes = certes, q.v.

serued v: sufficed JR 557

service, seruese, seruys sb: performance of a servant's
   duties KH 140; payment for such performance KH 224; a
   religious office LP 98; the hours of the breviary DH
   150; a course of food JR 396

serwand = servant FB 452

seth = sith, q.v.

sethen adv: then KH 232 [sithen]

sethen conj: since KH 315 [sithen]

sett vp v phr: put up in a stable JR 752 [set]

sette pa pple: situated KH 263 [set]

sewyn = seven JS 414

sewryd pa pple: assured LP 129 [sure]

sew sb: soup or broth FT 15

shapen pa pple: fashioned BM 28 [shape]

share v: cut JR 327 [shear]

sharpely adv: quickly JS 375

sheede v: spill BM 183; shedd, sched pa t JS E83, BM 185
    [shed]

sheild sb: meat cooked in boar skin JR 465 [shield]

shent, schent pa pple: ruined, disgraced DH 134, FB 210,
    355 [shend]

sherd sb: a gap in a hedge or bank LP 160 [shard]

sherwly = shrewdly, q.v.

shet = shut JS 153

shete = shoot JS 84

shett = [winding-]sheet LP 66

sheuell = shovel TB 189

shew = show LP 233

shewed = shown LP 201

shoone = shoes JR 552

shope v: created LP 210 [shape pa t]

show(e), shew, schaw v: perform openly JS 353; shewed
    pa pple displayed LP 201

showyll = shovel LP 103

shread v: prune JR 677; pa pple cut to shreds BM 40
[shred]

shreeuen pa pple: confessed BM 123 [shrive]

shrewd(e), shrewed adj: bad, vile JS 28, 290; vigorous
DH 22

shrewdly, sherwly adv: severely DH 46; grievously LP 145

shrowe = shrew JS 114

sic adj: such FB 88, 181

sich, sych = such FT 8, KH 122

side, syde adj: long JR 223, 326

sidebord sb: a table at the side of a hall JR 385

sy3eng = sighing KH 514

sikerly, sykerlyke, sekyrly adv: certainly, without doubt
JS 392, JR 39, SC 115

sillie adj: See FB 32n.

silwer = silver FB 128

sympyll, simple adj: deficient in mental powers LP 12;
free from pride JR 768

syn conj: considering (that) FT 82 [sin]

sindry adj: various FB 315 [sundry]

syn(e) adv: thereupon JR 644; afterwards JR 462; then FB 11

sire, syer sb: a person of importance FT 5, LP 187

sirres sb: gentlemen JR 514 [sir pl]

sith(e), syth(e), seth conj: since LP 74, JR 514; adv:
then, afterwards LP 134

sythe sb: times SC 240

sithence that conj phr: considering that JR 160 [sithence]

skath = scath, q.v.

skeppe = skip JS E103

skerlyt sb: rich cloth SC 222; as adj: SC 142 [scarlet]

skyen = skin LP 170

skyll sb: cause, reason SC 102; knowledge SC 152

slakyd pa pple: abated, decreased TB 164 [slake]

sle = slay LP 54

slech v: assuage TB 46 [sletch]

slo = slay DH 193

slokkin v: extinguish FB 221 [slocken]

slou3te sb: an enclosing layer KH 326 [slough]

smache sb: a slight suggestion TB 25 [smatch]

smyland = smiling FB 380

smytte pa pple: discharged JS 167 [smite]

snarre = snare LP 180

soft adv: softly FB 143

soyr sb: bodily pain or suffering JS E94 [sore]

soyt = sooth q.v.

solace, solas sb: entertainment JR 4, SC 1

solas v: entertain KH 19 [solace]

somedeale, somedele adv: somewhat JS RQ6, JR 229

somner, sompnere sb: a petty officer who summons people to
    court JS Y82 [summoner]

soon(e), sone, son adv: early DH 110, KH 397; without delay JS
    324; quickly DH 101

sooper = supper JS 145

sooth, soth, soyt adj: true TB 7; sb: truth JS 52

sope sb: a small drink JR 485

sord = sword JR 253

sore, sair adv: intensely, painfully LP 192, JS 67;
    severely, grievously JS Z91; violently JS Z72

sore, sair adj: bitter KH 514

sorre sb: a spiced, colored dish of chopped eels or other
    fish FT 40

sorrow sb: harm, damage JR 597

sory adj: painful TB 165 [sorry]

soth = sooth, q.v.

souȝht pa pple: discovered SC 46 [seek]

sowend = sound LP 48

sower = sour JR 140

sowyd = sewed LP 66

sowld = should FB 124

sowne = sound JS 140

sowsit pa pple: pickled FB 263 [souse]

space sb: time FB 335

spake, spacke = spoke JS 147

span v: ran quickly KH 57 [spin pa t]

spare v: avoid effort TB 99; sparyd pa t avoided LP 157

speciall sb: sweetheart, mistress TB 197 [special]

sped, spede, speed v: succeed TB 64; sped of: succeed in
    getting KH 93; cause one to succeed JS 64, 131; spedd
    pa t; refl: rushed JS E82, JR 734 [speed]

speed s̲b̲: fortune DH 100

speirit, sperit, sperred v̲: asked JR 355, FB 59, 278 [speer
    p̲a̲ t̲]

speit = spit FB 134

spell s̲b̲: tale TB 4

sperit, sperred = speirit, q̲.̲v̲.̲

spyce s̲b̲: a slight touch of a malady FB 40

spicery s̲b̲: spices FT 42

spill(e) v̲: perish, be destroyed JR 166, KH 84

spyre v̲: ask KH 446 [speer]

spoild p̲a̲ p̲p̲l̲e̲: injured JS Z92 [spoil]

sport s̲b̲: entertainment FB 333; amorous dalliance FB 173

sport v̲: amuse (oneself) FB 189; sportit p̲a̲ t̲ FB 407

spreit s̲b̲: spirit FB 477 [sprite]

sprent v̲: sprang KH 57 [sprent p̲a̲ t̲]

sprynge s̲b̲: a lively dance tune JS 330

spryttuall = spiritual LP 21

sprong p̲a̲ p̲p̲l̲e̲: foundered KH 68 [spring]

stair s̲b̲: flight of steps FB 531

stait = state, q̲.̲v̲.̲

stale s̲b̲: urine KH 471

stalke v̲: walk stealthily LP 122

stand v̲: strive FB 446

standand = standing FB 507

stane = stone FB 9

stank sb: a moat FB 10

star v: glare madly JS E74 [stare]

start, sterte, stertit v: leapt, jumped LP 169, JS 368, FB
    198 [start pa t]

state, stait sb: rank KH 274; ceremony FB 353

statutinge vbl sb: ordinance, decree JR 155

sted(e) sb: place KH 225 [stead]

sted(e) sb: a large horse FT 55, KH 68 [steed]

stedffast adv: bindingly JR 791

steyke = steak KH 368

steir = stir FB 490

stent(e), stend v: restrain JS 356; stop JS 174 [stint]

stere v¹: restrain JS 359 [steer]

stere v² = styre, q.v.

sterte = start, q.v.

steuen sb: appointed time; att vnsett steuen: by chance
    JR 92

stid = stead FT 68

stiffe adj: strong, stoutly built JR 55

styll = stile LP 160

styll(e) adv: quietly, silently LP 122, TB 175

stylle adj: silent JS 261

styre, stere v: begin to move LP 123, 188; bestir
    (oneself) LP 112 [stir]

stodyn = stood SC 143

stoke sb: log JS 370

stond = stound, q.v.

stond = stood KH 365

stone sb: a stone missile JS 168

store, sture adj: massive JR 541; coarse JR 55; stern FB
     359 [stour]

store sb: reserve JS 68, JR 289; food collected for future
     use DH 252

stound(e), stond sb: a time, a while TB 206, KH 19

stoup sb: a cup, tankard FB 66

stout, stowt adj: proud, arrogant KH 154; formidable,
     menacing JR 47, FB 200

straight, streyte adv: upright DH 139; immediately JS 368

strang adj: massive, stout JR 336 [strong]

stray = straw FB 104

streyte = straight, q.v.

strek = strike FB 504

streng = string KH 462

strenger = stronger JS 35

strife, stryff sb: trouble, pain DH 208; contention DH 96;
     without stryff: without demur JS 303

stryk = strike FB 504

stryk(e), strek v: go KH 83; hit FB 504; stroke pa t:
     skimmed KH 376 [strike]

strikin = struck FB 572

stro = straw KH 169, FB 176

stroke = stryke pa t, q.v.

strowit = strewed (with rushes) FB 227

studeing vbl sb: studying, meditating FB 343

sturdy adj: stern, rough JR 172, 796; impetuously brave JR 300

sture = store adj, q.v.

subtelly adv: ingeniously FB 14 [subtly]

subteltie sb: cunning FB 397; a trick FB 17

such adj: such and such DH 172

suffisance sb: sufficient supply FB 403 [sufficience]

sum adv: a little, somewhat FB 273 [some]

sum indef pron: someone, somebody TB 115 [some]

sumdel sb: some part TB 46 [somedeal]

sumpter sb as adj: driver of a packhorse JR 274

sumthing adv: somewhat FB 55

supped v: drank JR 837 [sup pa t]

sure adj: safe, secure DH 69; surer comp: more secure BM 19

suspended pa pple: profaned DH 164

sute sb: See BM 9n.

swa = so FB 51

swelt pa pple: overpowered with heat JS Z92 [swelt]

sware, swere = swore LP 35, FB 310

swete v: work hard TB 38 [sweat]

swetyng sb: sweetheart TB 112 [sweeting]

swett sb: sweetheart LP 67 [sweet]

swynke v: toil TB 38 [swink]

swyth(e) <u>adv</u>: TB 106,   quickly FB 263 [swith]

swth <u>sb</u>:   truth FB 385 [sooth]

tach <u>sb</u>:   fault, bad habit TB 24 [tache]

tail, tayle <u>sb</u>:   backside FT go, JR 539

tald = told FB 83

talle = tall; see JS 285n.

tane = taken BM 69

tassell <u>sb</u>:   clasp BM 92

tell = till LP 131

tend <u>v</u>:   listen JS 6

tene, tenne <u>sb</u>:   pains taken LP 42; something annoying JR
     219 [teen]

tenid <u>pa pple</u>:   annoyed JS 158 [teen]

tent <u>sb</u>:   attention FB 502

term(e) <u>sb</u>:   limit LP 11; expression JS P4

tha = tho <u>dem pron</u>, <u>q.v.</u>

þair = their FB 31

þairtill = thereto FB 502

thake-bendfull <u>sb</u>: amount that could be held by the band of
     twisted straw normally used to hold a bundle of straw
     for thatching KH 170 [thack + bend + full]

tham(e), thaym = them TB 128, FB 15

than = then LP 84

thare <u>v</u>:   dare LP 51 [tharf]

thay = they FB 30

the <u>pron</u> = they JR 22, KH 55

theder = thither LP 116

thee, the v: thrive, prosper TB 58, JS 313

then = than LP 161

ther adv: in that case, then KH 249

theron adv: immediately after that KH 233

thertylle adv: thereto KH 12

þertoo adv: besides TB 81

þerwith adv: thereupon JS 62

they = the JR 875, = thy LP 219

thider = thither TB 175

thyke adv: thickly JS 388 [thick]

thynke v1 impers: (it) seems (to) JS 291; pa t tho3t,
     thou3t: (it) seemed (to) TB 196, KH 230

think(e) v2: intend JR 198; have an opinion JR 430; pa t
     thou3th JS 184

þir, thir adj: these FB 29, 32

this adv: in this way, thus FB 131, 427

tho, þo, tha dem pron: those FT 36, JS 391; dem adj: those
     FB 287

tho = to JS E138

tho(e), thoo adv: after that, thereupon LP 63, DH 39

tho(o) = though LP 191, JR 672

thoch, thocht = though FB 498, 534

thoff = though KH 245

tho3t = pa t thynke, q.v.

tho3t sb = thought TB 15

tholit v: allowed FB 232; endured without complaint FB 202
     [thole pa t]

thoo = tho adv, q.v.

þore = there FT 30, DH 224

þoro, thorow prep: through JS 139; by means of LP 42, TB 13
     [thorough]

thou3t, thou3th = pa t thynke, q.v.

thrast v: push violently DH 213 [threst]

thratt pa pple: threatened JR 181 [threat]

thryiss = thrice   FB 348

thring v: thrust FB 134; throng pa t KH 467

thrist v: squeeze FB 172 [thrust]

throng v: thrust KH 467 [thring pa t]

throw sb: brief while, moment SC 156

throw = through FB 423

thru3ht prep: because of SC 105 [through]

thusgates adv: thus KH 426

thwyttel sb: a knife JR 326 [thwittle]

tyde sb: time LP 60, JS 265, JR 22

tyll, till prep: to LP 234, JR 249; for KH

tyred pa pple: dressed LP 127 [tire]

tyte adv: quickly, soon JR 222

to prep: for JR 599; till KH 330

togyder = together JS X15

toke = tooke, q.v.

tome sb: opportunity JS 395 [toom]

tone = taken FB 192

ton(e), the = the (first) one TB 10, JR 178

tooke, toke v: gave JS 73; tooke ... for: considered JR 605

toppor sb: head [unattested; prob. from top]

toraged pa pple: very ragged JS 272 [to- + rag]

torente pa pple: torn in pieces JS 171, 272 [to- + rend]

totoren pa pple: torn in pieces JS E98 [to- + torn]

tober = other (of two) TB 11

totted adj: foolish KH 343 [unattested]

toure = tower SC 8

toute, towte sb: buttocks TB 199, SC 120

towe = two JR 384

tow3he = tough KH 303

towoke v: awoke completely LP 96 [to- + wake]

trace sb: a series of steps in dancing JR 536

train sb: a trick DH 206

trayst adj: trustful KH 88

traist v: trust FB 444

translait v: transform, alter FB 466 [translate]

trap sb: a ladder or movable flight of stairs FB 300

travale sb: labor FB 65 [travail]

trauell sb: labor, trouble KH 133; moving from place to place FB 39 [travel] tree sb: wood JR 54

trey sb: trouble, vexation KH 222 [tray]

tremeld = trembled TB 140

trew = trow, q.v.

tried pa pple: sifted FT 66

trifull sb: false or idle tale TB 1 [trifle]

tryst sb: a date FB 121

troblylyd v: disturbed, disquieted LP 42 [trouble pa t]

troch = trough FB 340

troe = trow, q.v.

troich = trough FB 215

trow(e), trew, troe v = believe, think LP 147, FT 2, TB 189

trow sb: trough KH 482

trowth, trowet sb: faith JS 107, E115 [troth]

truth sb: solemn promise JR 415

tumbill v: throw FB 519

tumlit = tumbled FB 536

tunn sb: large wine cask JR 443 [tun]

turatt = turret FB 12

turss v: be off FB 525 [truss]

tusche sb: rich cloth FB 154 [tissue]

twa = two FB 29

tway adj: two FB 99

twayen sb: pair, couple LP 159 [twain]

twyn v: separate, disjoin TB 136

vder = other FB 33

umbecast v: went round JR 24 [umbecast pa t]

vncoupuld v: released (dogs) from being fastened in couples KH 55 [uncouple pa t]

vncouthlye adv: in a strange manner JR 430

vndernom pa pple: reproved, rebuked LP 3 [undernim]

vnfaine adj: reluctant JR 586

vnneth, oneth, anethe adv: hardly, scarcely LP 207, TB 193, JS E106 [uneath]

vnskill sb: folly JR 41

vnskillfullye adv: foolishly, ignorantly JR 84

vntill prep: to JR 806

vnto prep: until LP 68

vphent v: raised TB 108 [uphend pa t]

vpo(u)n, apon prep = upon; apon a boke: from a book LP 98, FB 344

vponland adv: in the country FB 31

vprais v: rose to (one's) feet FB 333 [uprise pa t]

vprise sb: rising from bed TB 172

vpstert v: jumped up TB 152 [upstart pa t]

vse v: observe or comply with (a law) JR 198; vsyd, vsit pa pple: accustomed LP 11, FB 30

vayle v: take off (a hat) JR 657 [vail]

variance sb: divergence from the truth FB 373

vent = went JS 208

venter = venture LP 55

verament adv: really, truly TB 110, JS 43

vilany, vyllanye, vylony sb: disgrace SC 35; wicked
     conduct, vile deed JS Y75; wicked language FT 95
     [villainy]

voyede v: go away LP 132 [void]

vow sb: a solemn affirmation DH 164

wayn = wane, q.v.

wait sb: attendance; laid ... wait: lurked in ambush DH 9

wait v: pres t wit, q.v.

wake v: work all night KH 195

wald = wold, q.v.

walker sb: a fuller BM 53

walling pres pple: boiling; walling wood: raging mad JR
     860

wan = won BM 191

wand sb: a staff carried as a sign of office JR 346

wane, wayn sb: expedient FB 427, 535 [wone]

wantit v: was lacking FB 390; lacked FB 410 [want pa t]

wanton adj: naughty, unruly JS Z93

ware adj: aware JR 47; prudent TB 219, JR 64

ware sb: commodities SC 110

warne v: inform JR 220

warrand v: protect FB 494; undertake, pledge oneself FB 506
     [warrant]

warrison, waryson sb: a reward JR 566, KH 46

wast <u>sb</u>: uninhabitated and uncultivated country JR 84

wast <u>adj</u>: idle, vain JR 303

watchet <u>sb</u>: light blue BM 43

watt = <u>pres</u> <u>t</u> wit, q.v.

wayiss = ways FB 96

we <u>adj</u>: wretched, miserable KH 153 [woe]

weare = were JR 681

wedd <u>v</u>: give (a woman) in marriage JR 883 [wed]

wede, weed(e), weed(es) <u>sb</u>: clothing, garments JS 252, JR 189, KH 451

weend = wend, q.v.

weele, weill = well BM 176

weit <u>v</u> = wet FB 579

weleaweye <u>int</u>: alas JS 300 [wellaway]

weyte <u>v</u>: look out for, watch for KH 254

weytley = wightly, q.v.

wele = well KH 107

wench(e) <u>sb</u>: female servant TB 158; wanton woman JS Z85

wend(e), weend, went, wynd <u>v</u>: go LP 172, KH 143; go off, depart TB 44; wendis <u>pl</u> <u>imp</u>: go FB 242; went <u>sing</u> <u>imp</u>: JR 884; went(e) <u>pa</u> <u>pple</u>: gone FB 138

wend, went <u>v</u> = <u>pa</u> <u>t</u> wene, q.v.

wene <u>v</u>: think, believe FT 71; went <u>pa</u> <u>t</u> JS 209; wend(e) <u>pa</u> <u>t</u>: intended SC 178 [ween]

wer = where KH 29

werke = work JR 268

wern v: refuse a request, deny something SC 114 [warn]

werryed pa pple: made war upon BM 156 [warray]

werrit = pa t wear FB 151

wesch = wash SC 207

wete = wit, q.v.

wex(e), woix v: grew, became FT 91, TB 12, 56, FB 433 [wax
    pa t]

whas = was LP 108

where = were JR 478

while, quhill conj: till FB 433

whyle sb: time; long whyles: for a long time KH 230; the
    whylys: while KH 138

whyleare adv: a while before KH 480 [whilere]

white = quit, q.v.   wycche sb: male witch JS 197

wicht adj: = wight, q.v.

wicht sb: person FB 528 [wight]

wyde adj: with a wide opening JR 718

wyde adv: far abroad SC 162

wife sb: woman TB 145; pl wyffis FB 34

wight, wicht adj: strong, stout FB 11; quick JR 733;
    adv: quickly JR 214

wy3ht, wicht sb: person JR 655, FB 528

wightly, wy3tly, weytley adv: swiftly, rapidly JS 390

wyll sb: carnal desire LP 96; wish TB 17

wyll v: wish to (do something) LP 65

wyll(e) adv: astray KH 78, KH 119 [will]

wyiss = wise, q.v.

wilsome, wylsom adj: lonely, wild, dreary FB 402; leading astray KH 221

win, winne, wynne v: make one's way KH 65; capture FB 17; get JR 458; steal or fetch TB 86

wince v: kick JR 550

wynd(e) v: wrap about (something) JS 275; writhe, wiggle JS 374

wynd = wend KH 143

wynke v: sleep TB 39

winne, wynne = win, q.v.

wynnit v: dwelt, resided FB 51 [win v^2 pa t]

wise, wyiss sb: manner DH 289, FB 181

wysse v: guide KH 90 [wis]

wyst = pa t wit, q.v.

wit(t), wyte, wete v inf: know TB 61; find out JS 199, KH 269; wott, wot(e), wait, watt pres t: know LP 83, JS 341, FB 84; wyst pa t: knew LP 27, KH 76; wist subj: knew JR 181

wit sb: knowledge FB 352

wyte v^1: blame JS 58, KH 134

wyte v^2: look on KH 487

wyte v = wit v, q.v. KH 269

with prep: by JR 594, FB 275; from KH 228

withall adv: likewise, as well JS 256

within adv: indoors TB 23

without(en) conj: unless DH 20; prep: outside of FB 52

withowte adv: outdoors TB 23

witt = wit, q.v.

witting pres pple: knowing JR 42

wo(e) adj: grieved, miserable JR 845, FB 430 [woe]

wode = wood q.v.

wodman sb: madman JS 242 [woodman]

woid = wood, q.v.

woix = wex, q.v.

wold v: want JR 203; wish JS 29; wolde pa t: wanted to LP
    156

wol(l) = wyll, q.v.

won v: dwell, stay JS 187, JR 175

wonder adj: wonderful SC 82

wonder, woundir adv: very JS 255, FB 51

wonders adv: wonderfully JR 758

wone sb^1: habit, custom JS P1

won(e) sb^2: dwelling JS P11; wons pl form, sing meaning
    KH 356

wonley = only JS E133

wons = pl wone sb^2, q.v.

wonte, wunt pa pple: accustomed TB 127, DH 40 [wont]

woo = woe JS P3

wo(o)d(e), woid adj: insane JS 282, FB 342

woodkniffe sb: dagger for cutting up game BM 157

worde = world TB 135

wordeley = worthy JS E129

worshype sb: honor JR 817; good name LP 92

worth v: befall KH 117

worthy adj: appropriate SC 220

wot(e) v: pres t wit, q.v.

wrang = wrong JR 533

wrath adj: very angry JR 484 [wroth]

wrech sb: miser TB 45 [wretch]

wreste v: utter   JS X39   [wrest]

wright = ryght, q.v.

wro sb: a nook or corner KH 312

wrocht, wro3t = wrought, q.v.

wronge v: clasped and twisted (the hands) JS 254 [wring pa
    t]

wrought, wrocht pa pple: done TB 89, made FB 103 [work]

wrought, wro3t v: did, performed TB 17; made DH 206 [work
    pa t]

ws = us FB 92

wunt = wonte, q.v.

3afe = gave KH 359

3ate, 3att, 3et, 3ait = gate TB 126, JS 208, FB 47

ye, 3e adv: yes JS 151, KH 500 [yea]

yee = eye JS 258

3ede, 3eid = yode, q.v.

yef = if JS 122

yeft = gift JS 104

ȝeir, ȝere = year KH 95, FB 30

ȝet sb = ȝate, q.v.

ȝet, yett, ȝit, ȝeit adv: again TB 63; in addition, also JR
    342; at length KH 88 (yet]

ȝeue, ȝiff v = give KH 2, 46; make over in discharge of an
    obligation KH 379; devote (oneself) KH 210

yeuer = ever JS E92

ȝyff, ȝif = if TB 160, KH 83

ȝift = gift KH 94

ȝit adv = ȝet q.v.

yode, yede, ȝede, ȝeid, ȝude v: went TB 63, JR 540, FB 347
    [go pa t]

ȝole int: exclamation of revelry at Christmas FT 96 [Yule]

ȝone = yon FB 215

ȝong man sb: yeoman KH 450 [young man]

yore adv: for a long time LP 217

ys = yes JS 334

ȝude = yode, q.v.

Index of Proper Names

Index of Proper Names

Proper names are listed with a reference to the first time they appear in each poem, and the first time of each major variation in spelling (eg., Jak, Jake, Jacke, Gake) or form (eg., Peeres-Pay-ffor-all, Peeres, Peeres Ffawconer). Familiar proper names such as God, Jhesu, Crist, Mary, London, Kent, England, Scotland, France, and Spain are not listed here.

Albon, Saynt: TB 76n.

Alesoun   FB 236, Alesone   FB 237

Allane   FB 33, Freir Allane FB 64

Allice   JR 598

Almayne: Germany FT 56

Arthour, Kynge SC 7, King Arthur BM 13

Austins = Augustinian Friars FB 25

Austyn, Seynt: SC 170n.

Berwik = Berwick-upon-Tweed, now in northeast England, once in southeast Scotland FB 7

Carleile = Carlisle, in northern England BM 2

Carmeleitis = Carmelite Friars FB 25

Corneus, Syr   SC 246

Craddocke   BM 99

Croce Kirk = Church of the Cross FB 23

Durham, Bishop of   JR 178

Edward [I] JR 12, London Edward   JR 297, Edward with the
        long shankes JR 17, King Edward JR 478, Long
        Edward JR 916.

Edwerd [III?], god KH 13

Ffrankish = French JR 832

Gascone = Gascon, from Gascony in France FB 162

Gloster, Erle of JR 179

Glowsytour, Erle of KH 238, Duke of Gloseter KH 76

Gueneuer, Queene BM 15, Dame Gueneuer BM 33

Hew, Dane   DH 6

Hob   JR 344, Hob of the Lath   JR 517

Hodgkin Long   JR 344, Hodgikin Long   JR 902

Hurlbasie   FB 514

Jack or Jill: Tom, Dick, or Harriet   JR 681

Jacobein, Jacobyne = Jacobin (Friars), Dominicans FB 24, FB 29

Jak   JS 148, Jake JS E75,   Jacke JS Y61, Gake JS E125

Jhake Flecher   KH 448, Jake KH 454

Jame, Saynt   JS 112, JR 132, FB 295: either one of the
        apostles James, more likely St. James the
        Greater.

John, Syr   LP 82, TB 77: the conventional lecherous priest

Johne   FB 122, Freir Johine FB 124

Jhon, Seynt   JS 191, Saint John DH 47, St. John JR 35: the
        most likely St. John intended is the author of
        the book of Revelations.

John de Reeue   JR 134, John Reeue JR 202, John the Reeue
        JR 609, Jhon JR 312

Jollye, St. JR 170, Seynt Julyan KH 86 = Saint Julian, patron
        saint of hospitality

Kay BM 61

Lecester = Leicester, in the central Midlands DH 1

Millayne = Milan JR 600

Minouris = Friars Minor, the Franciscans FB 25

Orlyaunce = Orleans in France, noted as a center for the
        study of magic JS X32

Pareiss = Paris FB 316

Peeres Pay-ffor-all JR 260, Peeres JR 270, Peeres Ffawconer
        JR 347

Perkyn FT 80

Robert FB 33, Ffreir Robert FB 59

Sauyour, Seynt = the holy Savior KH 310

Scherwood = Sherwood, the forest in the north central
        Midlands KH 16

Symon Lawrear FB 53, Symon FB 86, Semon FB 167

Skarlyon = Caerleon-upon-Usk, in southern Wales SC 241

Tybbe FT 91

Topyas, Frere JS X26

Tweid = Tweed, the river beside which Berwick lies FB 2

Wylkyn Alyn KH 317

Williame, St., of Yorke: JR 749n.

Windsor: the location of a royal court, west of London
        JR 570; the fforest of Windsor JR 575

Bibliography

Bibliography

The bibliography is divided into three sections. The first, a list of previous editions of the works presented in this volume, is ordered poem by poem, and each entry is numbered to avoid repeating much information: later citations of collections of poems such as Hazlitt's Remains of the Early Popular Poetry of England, for example, refer back to the first citation and give only such additional information as differs from the particulars applicable to the earlier listed poem only. The second section lists lexical and proverb dictionaries, under their titles (by which most of them are best known) rather than their editors. The third section is a select list of other works cited in the text, select in the sense that the long catalogues of works appearing in the manuscripts or bound in chapbook collections with the poems of this edition are not represented.

Previous Editions

The Lady Prioress

(1) Halliwell, J.O., ed. Early English Poetry, Ballads, and Popular Literature of the Middle Ages. Vol. 2. London: Percy Society, 1840. Pp. 107-17.

(2) Jamieson, Robert, ed. Popular Ballads and Songs. Vol. 1. Edinburgh: Constable, 1806. Pp. 249-65.

(3) Prinz, Johannes, ed. A Tale of a Prioress and her Three Wooers. Berlin: E. Felber, 1911.

The Feast of Tottenham

(4) Downing, Janay Young, ed. A Critical Edition of
    Cambridge University Library MS Ff. 5. 48. Ann
    Arbor, Mich.: University Microfilms, 1969. Pp.
    295-9.

(5) Hartshorne, Charles Henry, ed. Ancient Metrical
    Tales. London: W. Pickering, 1829. Pp. 145-50.

(6) Hazlitt, W. Carew, ed. Remains of the Early Popular
    Poetry of England. Vol. 3. London: John Russell
    Smith, 1866. Pp. 93-7.

(7) Wright, Thomas, ed. Early English Poetry: The
    Turnament of Totenham and the Feest. London:
    W. Pickering, 1836.

The Tale of the Basin

(8) Downing. Item 4. Pp. 166-75.

(9) Hartshorne. Item 5. Pp. 198-208.

(10) Hazlitt. Item 6. Pp. 42-53.

(11) Jamieson. Item 2. Pp. 272-82.

(12) Neumeister, Rudolph, ed. Der verzauberte Topf: ein
     mittelenglisches Gedict. Erlangen dissertation,
     1906.

(13) Wright, Thomas, ed. Early English Poetry: The Tale
     of the Basyn and the Frere and the Boy. London:
     W. Pickering, 1836.

Jack and his Stepdame

(14) Dyboski, Roman, ed. Songs, Carols, and other
     Miscellaneous Pieces from the Balliol MS. 354,
     Richard Hill's Commonplacebook. EETS 101 (1907):
     120-27.

(15) Flügel, Ewald, ed. "Liedersammlungen des XVI. Jahrhunderts, besonders aus der Zeit Heinrichs VIII." Pt. 3. Anglia 26 (1903): 104-132.

(16) Furnivall, Frederick J., ed. Bishop Percy's Folio Manuscript. Vol. 4. Loose and Humorous Songs. London: published by the editor, 1868. Pp. 9-28.

(17) Halliwell, J.O., ed. Early English Miscellanies, in Prose and Verse. London: Warton Club, 1855. Pp. 46-62.

(18) Hazlitt. Item 6. Pp. 55-81.

(19) Jenkinson, Francis, ed. The Frere and the Boye. Cambridge: Cambridge University Press, 1907.

(20) Ritson, Joseph, ed. Pieces of Ancient Popular Poetry. London: T. and J. Egerton, 1791. Pp. 35ff.

(21) Wright. Item 13.

(22) Zupitza, Julius, ed. "Jak and his Stepdame." Archiv für das Studium der neuren Sprachen und Literaturen 90 (1893): 57-82.

Dane Hew

(23) H[aslewood], J[oseph], ed. In The British Bibliographer. Ed. Sir Egerton Brydges and Joseph Haslewood. Vol. 2. London: R. Triphook, 1812. Pp. 593-601.

(24) Hartshorne. Item 5. Pp. 316-29.

(26) Hazlitt. Item 6. Pp. 130-46.

John the Reeve

(26) Hales, John W. and Frederick J. Furnivall, eds. Bishop Percy's Folio Manuscript: Ballads and Romances. Vol. 2. London: N. Trübner, 1868. Pp. 550-94.

(27) Hazlitt, W. Carew, ed. <u>Early</u> <u>Popular</u> <u>Poetry</u> <u>of</u>
     <u>Scotland</u> <u>and</u> <u>the</u> <u>Northern</u> <u>Border</u>, Edited by David
     Laing, LL.D., in 1822 and 1826. Vol. 1. London:
     Reeves and Turner, 1895. Pp. 250-83.

(28) Small, John, ed. <u>Select</u> <u>Remains</u> <u>of</u> <u>the</u> <u>Ancient</u>
     <u>Popular</u> <u>and</u> <u>Romance</u> <u>Poetry</u> <u>of</u> <u>Scotland</u>. Edinburgh
     and London: W. Blackwood and Sons, 1885. Pp. 42-
     79.

The <u>King</u> <u>and</u> <u>the</u> <u>Hermit</u>

(29) C[onybeare], [J.J.] ed. In <u>The</u> <u>British</u> <u>Bibliographer</u>.
     Edited by Sir Egerton Brydges and Joseph Haslewood.
     Vol. 4. London: R. Triphook, 1814. Pp. 81-95.

(30) Hartshorne. Item 5. Pp. 293-315.

(31) Hazlitt. Item 6. Vol. 1. 1864. Pp. 11-34.

(32) Kurz, Albert, ed. <u>König</u> <u>Eduard</u> <u>und</u> <u>der</u> <u>Einsiedler</u>,
     <u>eine</u> <u>mittelenglische</u> <u>Ballade</u>. Erlangen disserta-
     tion, 1905.

Sir <u>Corneus</u>

(33) Child, F.J., ed. <u>English</u> <u>and</u> <u>Scottish</u> <u>Ballads</u>.
     Vol. 1. Boston: Little, Brown and Co., 1857. Pp.
     24-34.

(34) Hartshorne. Item 5. Pp. 209-221.

(35) Hazlitt. Item 6. Vol. 1. 1864. Pp. 35-49.

(36) Hedenus, Hermann. <u>Syre</u> <u>Corneus</u>: <u>ein</u> <u>mittelenglisches</u>
     <u>Gedicht</u>. Erlangen dissertation, 1904.

(36A) Michel, ed. <u>Sir</u> <u>Corneus</u>. Roxburghe Club. Unidenti-
      fied: a ghost? Cited in BR.

(37) Wright, Thomas, ed. In Frühlingsgabe für Freunde
     älterer Literatur, edited by Theodor Georg von
     Karajan. Vienna: Ritter von Mösle's Witwe and
     Braumüller, 1839. Reissued in Karajan's Der
     Schatzgräber. Beiträge für altere deutsche
     Literatur. Leipzig, 1842.

The Boy and the Mantle

(38) Child, F.J., ed. The English and Scottish Popular
     Ballads. Vol. 1, pt. 2. Boston: Houghton,
     Mifflin and Co., 1884. Pp. 257-74.

(39) Hales and Furnivall. Item 26. Pp. 301-311.

(40) Percy, Thomas, ed. Reliques of Ancient English
     Poetry. Vol. 3. London: J. Dodsley, 1765. Pp.
     38ff.

(41) Wheatley, Henry B., ed. Re-edition of item 40.
     Vol. 3. London: Bickers and Son, 1877. Pp. 3-12.

The Friars of Berwick

(42) Baildon, H. Bellyse, ed. The Poems of William
     Dunbar. Cambridge: Cambridge University Press,
     1907. Pp. 211-24.

(43) Browne, William Hand, ed. Selections from the Early
     Scottish Poets. Baltimore: Johns Hopkins University
     Press, 1896. Pp. 135-53.

(44) Craigie, W.A., ed. The Maitland Folio Manuscript
     Text: Vol. 1. STS 2nd series 7 (1919): 133-148.
     Notes: Vol. 2. STS n.s. 20 (1927): 1-35 and 94.

(45) Fox, Denton and William A. Ringler, Intro. The
     Bannatyne Manuscript: National Library of Scotland
     Advocates' MS 1.1.6. London: Scolar Press, 1980.

(46) Laing, David, ed. The Poems of William Dunbar.
     Vol. 2. London: Laing and Forbes, 1834. Pp. 3-32.

(47) MacKenzie, W. Mackay, ed. The Poems of William
     Dunbar. Edinburgh: Porpoise Press, 1932. 2nd ed.
     London: Faber and Faber, 1955. Pp. 182-95.

(48) Pinkerton, John. Ancient Scotish Poems. Vol. 1.
     London: C. Dilly, 1786. Pp. 65-85.

(49) Ritchie, W. Tod, ed. The Bannatyne Manuscript. STS
     2nd series. 26 (1930): 261-77.

(50) Schipper, Jakob, ed. The Poems of William Dunbar.
     Vol. 5. Anonymous Early Scottish Poems. Denk-
     schriften der Kaiserlichen Akademie der Wissen-
     schaften, no. 43. Vienna: K. Akademie der
     Wissenschaften, 1894. Pp. 1-44.

(51) Select Poems of William Dunbar. Perth: Morison,
     1788.

(52) Sibbald, J., ed. Chronicle of Scottish Poetry.
     Vol. 2. Edinburgh: J. Sibbald, 1802. Pp. 372-90.

(53) Small, John, ed. The Poems of William Dunbar. Text:
     Vol. 2. STS 1st series 4 (1893): 285-304. Annota-
     tions: Walter Gregor. Vol. 5. STS 1st series 29
     (1893): 372-4. Introduction Æneas G. Mackay.
     Vol. 3. STS 1st series 16 (1889): lxxxiv-lxxxvi.

Lexical and Proverb Dictionaries

Dictionary of the Older Scottish Tongue from the Twelfth
     Century to the End of the Seventeenth. Edited by Sir
     William A. Craigie, A.J. Aitken, James A.C. Stevenson,
     Janet M. Templeton. 5 vols. to date (A-Pn). Chicago:
     University of Chicago Press, 1937-.

Middle English Dictionary. Edited by Hans Kurath, Sherman
     M. Kuhn, et al. 11+ vols. to date (A-Red). Ann Arbor:
     University of Michigan, 1956-.

Oxford Dictionary of English Proverbs. Revised by F.P.
Wilson. Originally edited by W.G. Smith (Oxford:
Clarendon Press, 1935). 2nd ed. revised by Sir Paul
Harvey (1948). 3rd ed. Oxford: Clarendon Press, 1970.

Oxford English Dictionary, The. Edited by J.A.H. Murray,
Henry Bradley, W.A. Craigie, C.T. Onions. 12 vols. plus
Supplement. Oxford: Clarendon Press, 1933. A revised
version of A New English Dictionary on Historical
Principles. Oxford: Clarendon Press, 1884-1928.

Proverbs, Sentences, and Proverbial Phrases from English
Writings Mainly before 1500. B.J. Whiting and Helen L.
Whiting. Cambridge, Mass.: The Belknap Press of
Harvard University Press, 1968.

Scottish National Dictionary, The. Edited by William Grant
and David Murchison. 10 vols. Edinburgh: Scottish
National Dictionary, 1929-.

Other Works Cited

Arber, Edward, ed. A Transcript of the Registers of the
Company of Stationers of London 1554-1640 A.D. 5 vols.
Birmingham: privately printed, 1875-94. Reprint. New
York: P. Smith, 1950.

Austin, Thomas, ed. Two Fifteenth-Century Cookery Books.
EETS 91 (1888).

Avowynge of King Arthur, The. In Sir Amadace and The Avowing
of Arthur: Two Romances from the Ireland MS., edited by
Christopher Brookhouse. Copenhagen: Rosenkilde and
Bagger, 1968.

Awntyrs off Arthure at the Terne Wathelyn, The. Edited by
Ralph Hanna. III. Manchester: Manchester University
Press, 1974.

Bedwell, William. The Survey and Antiquity of the Towns of
    Stamford in the County of Lincoln and Tottenham-High-
    Cross in Middlesex, together with the Turnament of
    Tottenham: Or, the Wooing, Winning, and Wedding of Tibbe
    the Reeu's Daughter there. London: J. Norton, 1631.

Biket, Robert. The Anglo-Norman Text of Le Lai du cor.
    Edited by C.T. Erickson. Anglo-Norman Text Society,
    no. 24. London: Blackwell for the Society, 1973.

Bliss, A.J. "Three Etymological Notes: II. Boy and Toy."
    English and Germanic Studies 4 (1951-2): 22-9.

Boccaccio, Giovanni. The Decameron. Translated by J.M. Rigg.
    2 vols. London: Dent, and New York: Dutton, 1968
    (vol. 1), 1955 (vol. 2).

Bolte, Johannes and Georg Polívka. Anmerkungen zu den
    Kinder- unde Hausmärchen der Brüder Grimm. 2nd ed.
    5 vols. Leipzig: Dieterich'sche, 1913-32. Reprint.
    Hildesheim: Georg Olms, 1963.

British Museum. Catalogue of the Harleian Manuscripts in the
    British Museum. London: British Museum, 1808.

Brown, Carleton and Rossell Hope Robbins. The Index of Middle
    English Verse. New York: Columbia University Press,
    1943.

Brunner, Karl. Die englische Sprache. 2nd ed. 2 vols.
    Tübingen: Max Niemeyer, 1960-62.

Chaucer, Geoffrey. The Works of Geoffrey Chaucer. Edited by
    F.N. Robinson. 2nd ed. Boston: Houghton Mifflin, 1957.

Child, F.J., ed. The English and Scottish Popular Ballads.
    5 vols. in 10. Boston: Houghton, Mifflin and Co.,
    1882-98.

Cohen, Gustave, ed. Histoire de la mise en scène dans le
    théâtre religieux français du moyen age. 2nd ed.
    Paris: Librairie Honoré Champion, 1951.

_____, ed. Le Livre du conduite du régisseur. Publica-
    tions de la Faculté des Lettres de l'Université de
    Strasbourg, no. 23. Strasbourg: University of Strasbourg,
    1925.

Craigie, W.A., ed. The Maitland Folio Manuscript. Vol. 1
    STS 2nd series 7 (1919), Vol. 2 STS 2nd series 20 (1927).

Cross, T.P. "The Gaelic 'Ballad of the Mantle.'" Modern
    Philology 16 (1918-19): 649-58.

_____. "Notes on the Chastity-Testing Horn and Mantle."
    Modern Philology 10 (1912-13): 289-99.

Curtius, Ernst. European Literature and the Latin Middle
    Ages. Translated by Willard R. Trask. Bollingen
    Series, no. 36. New York: Pantheon Books, 1953. Origi-
    nally published as Europäische Literature un lateinisches
    Mittelalter. Bern: A. Francke AG Verlag, 1948.

Davis, Norman, ed. Paston Letters and Papers of the Fifteenth
    Century. 2 vols. Oxford: Clarendon Press, 1971-76.

Dictionary of National Biography. Ed. Sir Leslie Stephen and
    Sidney Lee. 63 vols. London: Smith, Elder, and Co.,
    1885-1900.

Dietz, Klaus. "Mittelenglisch oi in heimischen Ortsnamen und
    Personennamen: II. Das Namenelement Boi(e) und die
    Etymologie von boy." Beiträge zur Namenforschung 16
    (1981): 361-405.

Dobson, E.J. English Pronunciation 1500-1700. 2nd ed.
    2 vols. Oxford: Clarendon Press, 1968.

_____. "The Etymology and Meaning of Boy." Medium
    Ævum 9 (1940): 121-54.

_____. "Middle English and Middle Dutch Boye." Medium
    Ævum 12 (1943): 71-76.

Donaldson, E. Talbot. "The Psychology of Editors of Middle
    English Texts." In his Speaking of Chaucer. London:
    Athlone Press, 1970. First published in English Studies
    Today 4 (1966): 45-62.

Douglas, Gavin. The Poetical Works of Gavin Douglas.
    Edited by John Small. Edinburgh: Paterson, 1874.

Downing, J.Y., ed. A Critical Edition of Cambridge University
    Library MS Ff. 5. 48. Ann Arbor, Mich.: University
    Microfilms, 1969.

Dunbar, William. The Poems of William Dunbar. Edited by
    James Kinsley. Oxford: Clarendon Press, 1979.

Edmond, J.P. The Aberdeen Printers: Edward Raban to James
    Nicol. 1620-1736. 4 vols. Aberdeen: J. and J.P.
    Edmond and Spark, 1884-86.

Emden, A.B. A Biographical Register of the University of
    Oxford to A.D. 1500. 3 vols. Oxford, Clarendon,
    1957.

Farce de trois amoureux de la croix. In Recueil de farces
    françaises inédites du quinzième siècle, edited by
    Gustave Cohen. Cambridge, Mass.: Mediæval Academy of
    America, 1949. Pp. 57-67.

Furnivall, F.J., ed. The Babees Boke [etc.] (Manners and
    Meals in Olden Time). EETS 32 (1868).

_____, ed. Bishop Percy's Folio Manuscript. Vol. 4.
    Loose and Humorous Songs. London: published by the
    editor, 1868. Reprint. Detroit: Singing Tree Press,
    1968.

Giraldus Cambrensis. Opera. Edited by J.S. Brewer.
    London: Longmans, 1873.

Girvan, Richie, ed. Ratis Raving. STS 3rd series 2 (1939).

Gobius, Joannes. Scala Celi. Ulme: Johannes Zainer, 1480.
    Copy made by Luella Carter, University of Chicago 1928.
    Ff. 37a-37b; Carter pp. 146-7.

Görlach, Manfred. The Textual Tradition of the South
    English Legendary. Leeds Texts and Monographs New
    Series, no. 6. Leeds: University of Leeds, 1974.

Griffiths, J.J. "A Re-examination of Oxford, Bodleian
     Library, MS Rawlinson C. 86." Archiv für das Studium
     der neueren Sprachen und Literaturen 219 (1982):
     381-8.

Hales, J.W. and F.J. Furnivall, eds. Bishop Percy's Folio
     Manuscript: Ballads and Romances. 3 vols. London:
     Trübner and Co., 1868. Reprint. Detroit: Singing Tree
     Press, 1968.

Heinrich von dem Türlin. Diu Crône. Edited by Gottlob
     Heinrich Freidrich Scholl. Bibliothek des litterarischen
     Vereins in Stuttgart, no. 27. Stuttgart: Litterarischen
     Vereins, 1852.

_____. Der Mantel: Bruchstück eines Lanzeletromans.
     Edited by Otto Warnatsch. Breslau: W. Köbner, 1883.
     Pp. 8-54.

Heywood, Thomas. Γυναικεῖον: or nine bookes of various
     history, concerninge women. [London]: Adam Islip, 1624.

Hills, W.P. "Richard Hill of Hillend." Notes and Queries.
     177 (1939): 452-6.

Hindley, Geoffrey. England in the Age of Caxton. New York:
     St. Martin's Press, 1979.

History of Jack Horner, The. Newcastle, 1760.

Hodnett, Edward. English Woodcuts 1480-1535. 2nd ed.
     Oxford: Oxford University Press, 1973.

Horstmann, C. "Rathschläge für eine Orientreise."
     Englische Studien 8 (1885): 277-84.

Jordan, Richard. Handbook of Middle English Grammar. Trans-
     lated and revised by Eugene Joseph Crook. Janua
     Linguarum Serie Practica, no. 218. The Hague: Mouton,
     1974. Originally published as Handbuch der mittel-
     englischen Grammatik, 1925; revised by H. Ch. Matthes,
     1934; 3rd ed. with updated bibliography by Klaus Dietz
     (Heidelberg: Carl Winter Universitätsverlag, 1968).

Kane, George. "Editorial Resources and Methods." In his
    edition, Piers Plowman: The A Version. Will's Visions of
    Piers Plowman and Do-Well. London: Athlone Press, 1960.
    Pp. 115-165.

Kellogg, Alfred L. and Robert C. Cox. "Chaucer's May 3
    and Its Contexts." In Chaucer, Langland, Arthur:
    Essays in Middle English Literature, edited by Alfred
    L. Kellogg. New Brunswick, N.J.: Rutgers University
    Press, 1972.

King Edward and the Shepherd. In Middle English Metrical
    Romances. Edited by W.H. French and C.B. Hale. New
    York: Russell and Russell, 1930. Pp. 949-85.

Knowles, Dom David. The Religious Orders in England. 2
    vols. Cambridge: Cambridge University Press, 1955
    (vol. 2), 1956 (vol. 1).

Kökeritz, Helge. Shakespeare's Pronunciation. New Haven:
    Yale University Press, 1953.

Kristensson, Gillis. A Survey of Middle English Dialects
    1290-1350: The Six Northern Counties and Lincolnshire.
    Lund Studies in English, no. 35. Lund: C.W.K. Gleerup,
    1967.

Kurvinen, Auvo. "MS. Porkington 10, Description with
    Abstracts." Neuphilologische Mitteilungen 54 (1953):
    33-67.

Laing, David, ed. The Poems of William Dunbar. Vol. 1.
    Edinburgh: Laing and Forbes, 1832.

Lancashire Cuckold, The. London: J. Blare, 1690.

le Métel, Antoine, Le Soldat Magicien. In L'Elite des contes
    du Sieur d'Ouville. Originally published Rouen, 1680.
    Facsimile edition by Gustave Brunet. Paris: Librairie
    des bibliophiles, 1883. Pp. 150-60.

Lindsay, Sir David. The Works of Sir David Lindsay. Edited
    by Douglas Hamer. STS 3rd series 1 (1930).

Livre de Carados, Le. In The Continuations of the Old
    French Perceval of Chrétien de Troyes, edited by
    W.J. Roach and R. Ivy. Vol. 1. Philadelphia: American
    Philosophical Society, 1949. Pp. 231-8. Vol. 2. 1950.
    Pp. 370-7. Vol. 3, part 1. 1952. Pp. 194-204.

"Long Wapper of Antwerp, The." In Northern Mythology, com-
    piled by Benjamin Thorpe. Vol. 3. North German and
    Netherlandish Popular Traditions and Superstitions.
    London: Edward Lumley, 1852. Pp. 217-8.

Luick, Karl. Historische Grammatik der englischen Sprache.
    1 vol. in 2. Leipzig: C.H. Tauchnitz, 1921-40. Reprint.
    Oxford: Basil Blackwell, 1964.

Luneten Mantel, Der. In Fastnachtspiele aus dem fünfzehnten
    jahrhundert. Edited by Adelbert von Keller. Vol. 2.
    Bibliothek des literarischen Vereins, no. 29. Stuttgart:
    Anton Hiersemann, 1853. Reprint. Darmstadt: Wissen-
    schaftliche Buchgesellschaft, 1965. Pp. 664-78.

Madden, Sir Frederic, ed. Syr Gawayne: A Collection of
    Ancient Romance Poems. London: Bannatyne Club, 1839.

Malory, Thomas. The Works of Sir Thomas Malory. Edited by
    Eugène Vinaver. 3 vols. 2nd ed. Oxford: Clarendon
    Press, 1967.

Masuccio Salernitano. Novellino. [Venice: Johannes and
    Gregorius de Gregoriis, 1492].

McIntosh, Angus. "The Analysis of Written Middle English."
    Transactions of the Philological Society of London.
    (1956): 26-55.

McKitterick, D.J. The Library of Sir Thomas Knyvett of
    Ashwellthorpe, c. 1539-1618. Cambridge: Cambridge
    University Press, 1978.

Montaiglon, Anatole de and Gaston Raynaud, eds. Recueil
    général et complet des fabliaux des xiiie et xive
    siècles. 6 vols. Paris: Librairie des Bibliophiles,
    1872-90.

Moore, Samuel, Sanford Brown Meech, and Harold Whitehall.
    "Middle English Dialect Characteristics and Dialect
    Boundaries." In Essays and Studies in English and

Comparative Literature by Members of the English Department of the University of Michigan. University of Michigan Publications in Language and Literature, no. 13. Ann Arbor: University of Michigan Press, 1935. Pp. 1-60.

Mossé, Fernand. A Handbook of Middle English. Translated by James A. Walker. Baltimore: The Johns Hopkins Press, 1952.

Mynors, R.A.B. Catalogue of the Manuscripts of Balliol College Oxford, Oxford: Clarendon Press, 1963.

Nicolas de Troyes. "Les Trois galants au cimetière. Le Grand Parangon des nouvelles." Originally published in 1536. Edited by Krystyna Kasprzyk. Paris: M. Didier, 1970. Pp. 33-40.

Oakden, J.P. Alliterative Poetry in Middle English. 2 vols. Manchester: Manchester University Press, 1930-35. Reprint (2 vols. in 1). Hamden, Conn.: Archon Books, 1968.

Pauli, Johannes. Schimpf und Ernst. Originally published in 1522. Edited by Johannes Bolte. Berlin: Stubenrauch, 1924.

Pollard, A.W. and G.R. Redgrave. A Short Title Catalogue of Books Printed in England, Scotland, and Ireland and of English Books Printed Abroad 1475-1640. London: The Bibliographical Society, 1926. I-Z. Vol. 2. 2nd ed. Revised by W.A. Jackson, F.S. Ferguson, Katharine F. Pantzer. London: The Bibliographical Society, 1976.

Pollock, Sir Frederick and Frederic Maitland. The History of English Law Before the Time of Edward I. 2 vols. 2nd ed. Cambridge: Cambridge University Press, 1898. Reprint. Cambridge: Cambridge University Press, 1968.

Queste del saint Graal. Edited by Albert Pauphilet. Paris: Champion, 1923.

Rauf Coilȝear. Edited by Sidney J. Herrtage. The Taill of Rauf Coilyear ... with the fragments of Roland and Vernagu, and Otuel. EETS new series 39 (1882).

Robbins, Rossell Hope and John L. Cutler. Supplement to the Index of Middle English Verse. Lexington: University of Kentucky Press, 1965.

Robinson, F.N. "A Variant of the Gaelic 'Ballad of the Mantle.'" Modern Philology 1 (1903-04): 145-47.

Robertson, D.W., Jr. "Chaucerian Tragedy." ELH 19 (1952): 1-37.

Rosenblüt, Hans. Von einem varnden Schüler. In Fastnachtspiele aus den fünfzehnten Jahrhundert, edited by Adelbert von Keller. Vol. 3. Bibliothek des literarischen Vereins, no. 30. Stuttgart: Anton Hiersemann, 1853. Reprint. Darmstadt: Wissenschaftliche Buchgesellschaft, 1965. Pp. 1172-76.

Sachs, Hans. Hans Sachs. Edited by Adelbert von Keller. Vols. 9 and 20. Bibliothek des literarischen Vereins, nos. 125 and 193. Stuttgart: Anton Hiersemann, 1875 and 1892. Reprint. Hildesheim: Georg Olms, 1964.

Samuels, M.L. "Some Applications of Middle English Dialectology." English Studies 44 (1963): 81-94.

Serjeantson, M.S. "The Vocabulary of Cooking in the Fifteenth Century." English Association Essays and Studies 23 (1937): 25-37.

Sir Amadace and The Avowing of Arthur: Two Romances from the Ireland MS. Edited by Christopher Brookhouse. Copenhagen: Rosenkilde and Bagger, 1968.

Sir Gawain and the Green Knight. Edited by J.R.R. Tolkien and E.V. Gordon. 2nd ed. Revised by Norman Davis. Oxford: Clarendon Press, 1967.

Skikkju Rímur. In Versions nordiques du fabliau français, Le Mantel mautaillié, edited by Gustaf Cederschiöld and F.-A. Wulff. Lund: C.W.K. Gleerup, 1877.

Smith, Janet M. The French Background of Middle Scots Literature. Edinburgh: Oliver and Boyd, 1934.

Smithers, G.V., ed. Kyng Alisaunder. Vol. 2. EETS 237 (1957 for 1953).

Stricker, Der. Der geaste Pfaffe. In Gesamtabenteuer: Hundert altdeutsche Erzählungen, edited by F.H. von der Hagen. Vol. 3. Stuttgart: J.G. Cotta'scher Verlag, 1850. Reprint. Darmstadt: Wissenschaftliche Buchgesellschaft, 1961. Pp. 145-58.

Suchier, Walter. Der Schwank von der viermal getöten Leiche.
    Halle: M. Niemeyer, 1922.

Taylor, Archer. "Dane Hew, Munk of Leicestre." Modern
    Philology 15 (1917-18): 221-46.

Thompson, A.H., ed. Visitations of Religious Houses in the
    Diocese of Lincoln. Vol. 2. Canterbury and York Series,
    vol. 24. London: Canterbury and York Society, 1919.

Thompson, Stith. Motif-Index of Folk-literature: A Classifi-
    cation of Narrative Elements in Folk-tales, Ballads,
    Myths, Fables, Mediæval Romances, Exempla, Fabliaux,
    Jest-Books, and Local Legends. 6 vols. Indiana Univer-
    sity Studies, v. 19, nos. 96 and 97, v. 20, no. 100,
    v. 20, no. 101, v. 21, nos. 105 and 106, v. 22, nos. 108,
    109, and 110, v. 23, nos. 111 and 112. Bloomington, Ind.:
    Indiana University, 1932-6.

Tournament of Tottenham, The. In Middle English Metrical
    Romances, edited by W.H. French and C.B. Hale. New
    York: Prentice-Hall, 1930. Pp. 987-98.

Towneley Secunda Pastorum, The. In The Wakefield Pageants
    in the Towneley Cycle, edited by A.C. Cawley.
    Manchester: Manchester University Press, 1958. Pp. 43-
    63.

Ulrich von Zatzikhoven. Lanzelet: eine Erzählung. Edited by
    K.A. Kahn. Frankfurt am Main: H.L. Brönner, 1845.
    Reprint. Berlin: De Gruyter, 1965.

Vanden Jongen geheeten Jacke: die sijns Vaders beesten
    wachte int velt ende vanden brueder dye daer quam on
    Jacke te castien. Antwerp: Michael Hillien, 1528.

Watson, Andrew G. The Library of Sir Simonds D'Ewes.
    London: The Trustees of the British Museum, 1966.

Wright, Thomas and J.O. Halliwell, eds. Reliquiæ Antiquæ.
    Vol. 1. London: W. Pickering, 1841.